The Fisher Body
Craftsman's Guild

The Fisher Body Craftsman's Guild

An Illustrated History

JOHN L. JACOBUS

McFarland & Company, Inc., Publishers

Jefferson, North Carolina, and London

The present work is a reprint of the illustrated case bound edition of The Fisher Body Craftsman's Guild : An Illustrated History, *first published in 2005 by McFarland.*

LIBRARY OF CONGRESS CATALOGUING-IN-PUBLICATION DATA

Jacobus, John (John L.)
The Fisher Body Craftsman's Guild :
an illustrated history / John L. Jacobus
p.   cm.
Includes bibliographical references and index.

ISBN 978-0-7864-7161-4

softcover : acid free papers ∞

1. Fisher Body Craftsman's Guild — History.
2. General Motors automobiles — Models — Societies, etc.
3. General Motors automobiles — Models — Design and construction — History.
4. General Motors automobiles — Models — Pictorial works.   I. Title.
TL237.J34 2013   629.22'12 — dc22   2005003504

BRITISH LIBRARY CATALOGUING DATA ARE AVAILABLE

Cover photograph: Entries in the 1966 national Guild
competition in Warren, Michigan. The author's model
is the red sport coupe in the center foreground.

Manufactured in the United States of America

*McFarland & Company, Inc., Publishers
Box 611, Jefferson, North Carolina 28640
www.mcfarlandpub.com*

To Charles M. Jordan, Guildsman, MIT engineer,
automobile designer, auto industry executive,
automobile hall of fame inductee
and friend of Guildsmen everywhere;

to the memory of Carlyle W. "Mac" McClellan, patriot,
Fisher Body executive and Guild administrator (1957–1968)
who loved Guildsmen as his own; and

to the memory of my father, Dwight, who loved the Guild.

Table of Contents

CHAPTER III. MODEL CAR COMPETITION (1937–1968)

Between pages 124 and 125 are 16 color plates containing 41 photographs

CHAPTER IV. THE SEARCH FOR GUILDSMEN

APPENDICES

Preface

This book is about the people of General Motors' Fisher Body Craftsman's Guild, an auto design competition sponsored by the Fisher Body Division of General Motors for teenagers to compete for college scholarships by designing scale model "dream cars." Held during the 1930s, '40s, '50s and '60s, it helped identify and nurture a whole generation of top auto designer and design executive talent which followed in the footsteps of the industrial design pioneers like Walter Dorwin Teague, Henry Dreyfuss, Raymond Loewy and Norman Bel Geddes. The design competition sorted out and separated the much sought after innovators of auto design from the run-of-the-mill emulators of auto design. Detroit has always coveted the innovators of design, the ones with "gasoline in their veins," the designers at heart who looked beyond what they see to tomorrow. These people loved cars. After formal training, many of the Guild people returned to the auto industry and dedicated their careers to the creative process of designing the cars we see and drive every day.

A synopsis of the *Fisher Body Craftsman's Guild* written by Roger B. White, Transportation Specialist, Transportation Collections, National Museum of American History, Behring Center, Smithsonian Institution, printed on a foamcore placard and placed in the Guild exhibit case at the Smithsonian, read as follows:

Fisher Body Craftsman's Guild (1930–1968)

From 1930 to 1968 millions of boys fascinated by cars joined the Fisher Body Craftsman's Guild. About 600,000 members enrolled each year in the 1950's making the Guild second in size only to the Boy Scouts of America for young men.

Sponsored by the Fisher Body Division of General Motors Corporation, the Guild promoted the ideals of William A. Fisher, the division President. Fisher believed that hands-on, high precision skills were essential to personal success in what he called "this machine civilization."

The Guild first asked members to build scale models of a Napoleonic Coach, the Fisher Body Division's trademark. In 1937, the challenge expanded to include automobile designs. Models were judged for craftsmanship, advanced styling and originality. Contestants competed in 2 age groups and winners/finalists received scholarships and cash prizes. [Many] of the prize-winning models foretold the style trends that appeared in new cars.

The annual Guild competitions were a major public relations program for General Motors Corporation and [many] winners went on to prominent design careers in the automotive industry.[1]

William L. (Bill) Porter, a noted top General Motors automobile stylist and designer, and auto design teacher at Detroit's College for Creative Studies, recently stated,

One of the great things that the Craftsman's Guild did for American design was that it identified talent at an early age so that these youngsters could proceed to get professional educations. In many fields requiring trained talent, the process of early identification is well established. Can you imagine a concert violinist who was not receiving training by the time they were 10 years old? Same with sports like swimming or ice hockey. Not so with design. Many designers do not learn of the field until they are in college, thus missing out on the valuable skill-acquiring years as a teen when learning comes easiest.[2]

Regarding the Guild's search for auto styling talent, Roy Boyer, a General Motors official and former supervisor of the Craftsman's Guild, was quoted in the *New York Times*, April 2, 1967, as saying,

The talented person in this field is always difficult to find. ... We are always looking for creative people, and this is one way of encouraging a continuing source of talent, not only GM, but for the entire industry. ... Many of the winners eventually have gone to work for such companies as American Motors, Ford, Chrysler in addition to GM, where nearly half of the creative designers are said to be ex–Guild members. ... Chuck Jordan, in-charge of GM's automotive design was a top winner in 1947.

Here was a take-home, industrial arts aptitude test that identified teenagers with innate artistic ability, creativity, imagination, spatial relationship acuity (form, function, balance, proportion, and shape), manual dexterity, an aesthetic eye, good taste, a propensity for perfection, and high intellect, all the qualities sought after by the automobile industry. Through this highly competitive model-making competition held in Detroit each year, the design innovators, the crème de la crème, some as young as 12 years old, were pampered, courted and wooed by top GM executives. So sought after were they, and so rare a talent, that top GM design executives corresponded with the top winners through their college years to ensure they were on GM's payroll when they graduated.

This book is about how some of America's top auto designers got started and found their place in the auto design world, including designers such as Virgil M. Exner, Jr., Charles M. Jordan, Elia "Russ" Russinoff, Galen Wickersham, Edward F. Taylor, Ronald C. Hill, Charles W. Pelly, Terry R. Henline, Paul Tatseos, Bill Molzon, Stuart Shuster, Ronald J. Will, David P. Onopa, and John M. Mellberg, among others. They provide autobiographic accounts of how their love of cars and the Guild influenced their career selection and ultimately their lives. Their essays reveal Craftsman's Guild, automotive and automotive design history.

In addition to auto designers, the Craftsman's Guild helped identify and nurture a whole new generation of product designers who have touched practically every product we see and use every day in our homes, offices and communities. In the 1950s, some of these industrial designers became part of some of the first corporate design offices in America. They have changed our aesthetic world and made it a better place.

This book is also about how many of America's top product designers got started and found their place in the design world; designers such as Stanley C. Waechter, Gale P. Morris, James Lee Garner, Gary Graham, Charles A. Gibilterra, William A. Moore, E. Arthur Russell, Allen T. Weideman, Robert E. Davids, Theodore A. Becker, Richard Pietruska, Michael Pietruska, Ronald Pietruska, Kenneth J. Dowd, and Harry E. Schoepf, among others. Architectural designers such as John B. Di Ilio, Robert F. McDonnell and

Leo C. Peiffer are also included in this group. They have provided autobiographic accounts of the Guild experience, how it influenced their lives, and how their love and passion for cars got them started. Again, their essays reveal Craftsman's Guild, automotive and automotive design history.

The book describes aspects of building a miniature model Napoleonic Coach and some of the scholarship winners who participated in the coach competition from 1930 to 1948. Making the scale model Napoleonic Coach from scratch was how the Guild got started. Great ingenuity, intellect, engineering aptitude and technical skill were required to follow and interpret the complex blueprint plans. Who were some of the participants? What was it like to compete? When did they participate and where were they from? How did they ever devote the one thousand or more hours of labor needed to build a competitive coach? After winning a scholarship, what career choices did they make?

Autobiographic and biographic essays about the coach builders are presented that describe their hopes and dreams. These were remarkably talented, creative and intelligent people who were attracted to the Craftsman's Guild as teenagers.

The book describes aspects of the scale model dream car competition and many of the scholarship winners who emerged from that competition from 1937 to 1968. Who were some of the participants? What was it like to build a winning model car? When did they participate and where did they hail from? Whatever happened to those clean-cut young men who won thousands in university scholarships, and what career choices did they make?

Recently acquired autobiographic and biographic essays by the former model dream-car designers are presented, which share aspects of their lives and their accomplishments. The Craftsman's Guild, for many, was the singular turning point of their lives once a scholarship had been awarded (e.g., their talent potential formally recognized by GM design executives) through the competitive design process.

Whether coach builders or model car makers, there were some basic truths about the Craftsman's Guild participants: they were dreaming about their futures and where they might fit into the world. They knew how to have fun even though most people called it hard work. Although Guild rules required the independent work of the contestant, family support was a necessary, if not essential, ingredient to be successful. Contestants learned something about several essential human qualities like perseverance, resourcefulness, ingenuity, and good old American know-how. Associated with that was the fundamental work ethic of finishing what one starts and the knowledge that our labor is valued and rewarded. The lessons learned in the Guild prepared many of the participants for the future as human beings and as professionals.

The Guild was essentially about people, and this book celebrates the famous auto executives, designers, product designers and other people whose lives were entwined, to various degrees, with the Guild, such as William A. Fisher, Charles F. Kettering, Harley J. Earl, William L. Mitchell, Charles M. Jordan, Virgil M. Exner, Jr., Virgil M. Exner, Sr., Richard A. Teague, William S. (Bill) Knudsen, Semon E. (Bunkie) Knudsen, Edward Cole, Robert W. Henderson, Strother MacMinn, Robert A. Cadaret, Richard Arbib, Charles W. Pelly, Jerry Hirshberg, Thomas H. Semple, and Terry R. Henline, among many others.

One of the great tragedies in auto design history was when the Craftsman's Guild was discontinued by GM executives in 1968 because the benefits, in their view, did not exceed the costs. This book focuses on the Craftsman's Guild program that GM and

Fisher Body Division sponsored continuously for some 34 years (minus World War II) and describes its history, people, benefits, accomplishments and achievements. Knowing what we know today, would it be canceled? The inescapable conclusion is that Craftsman's Guild–type youth programs need to be reinstituted in our schools, or sponsored again by industry, in order to identify top, innovate design talent that can be nurtured and guided into the professional ranks of industrial design, product design and automotive design.

As a tribute to the legacy of the Fisher Body Craftsman's Guild, *Automobile Quarterly* magazine sponsored three automobile styling contests (rendering and drawing contests), in the late '80s, for aspiring student and adult auto designers with the results being judged by leading industry design executives (e.g., Chuck Jordan, Jerry Hirshberg, Strother MacMinn, and Richard A. Teague). In inaugurating their first design competition, in which there were 500 entries, *Automobile Quarterly* stated the following:

> From 1930 to 1968, the Fisher Body Craftsman's Guild sought to harness and nurture the visions of American youth. Among its goals, of course, was corporate visibility, but the Guild also produced generations of designers, many of whom by dint of persistent creativity, rose to the top ranks of industrial design and today shape products for that more perfect world. We honor their energy and enthusiasm with a design contest that encourages the visionaries of today to share their dreams of tomorrow [*Automobile Quarterly*, 1987, vol. 25, no. 2].

Fisher Body Craftsman's Guild Friends and Associates was formed to write this book about the history, the memorabilia and people of the Fisher Body Craftsman's Guild as well as to inform and educate the community about the accomplishments of this long forgotten high school industrial arts program from the 1950s. This is a nonprofit, educational endeavor, designed to preserve the history of the Craftsman's Guild. Since the vast majority of the book's contributors graduated from the Art Center College of Design, a portion of the proceeds from the sale of the book (after the manuscript expenses are deducted) will be donated to that famous Pasadena, California, institution to help young people studying to be auto designers or product designers. Former Guildsmen have generously donated their time and effort to this project to help give young people a chance to follow their dreams just as the Guild program did for them 40 or 50 years ago.

FBCG Friends and Associates

The Fisher Body Craftsman's Guild Friends and Associates is a non-chartered, non-profit cyber-network, designed to provide a database to register the names and addresses of former Guild participants and their relatives, support and aid in the identification of two- and three-dimensional Guild memorabilia, educate the public with periodic newsletters, sponsor reunions for former Guild participants and their families, support scholarships for aspiring auto and product designers and preserve the Guild's history. FBCG Friends and Associates does not accept monetary donations, but does accept memorabilia particularly from former Guildsmen who do not have the room to keep it or whose heirs do not want it. If you have memorabilia you would like to donate, or have questions, please contact the author at www.fisherguild.com, or in care of the publisher, McFarland & Company, Inc., Box 611, Jefferson, North Carolina 28640.

Caveats and Conditions

Even though the author worked with current GM Media Archives and GM Design Center personnel, as well as many former and retired General Motors designers, chief designers, design directors and design executives in order to create this book, it was written without the imprimatur of General Motors Corporation. They do not endorse this product in any way.

The analysis and interpretation of the Fisher Body Craftsman's Guild are solely those of the author.

What I have written is true to my work experience as a writer (for which I am truly grateful) and the genes of both sides of my family, both Lindsey and Jacobus, a combination of writer, artist and engineer. This has resulted in a non-fiction book with historical facts, autobiographies and biographies, and the presentation of judgments and opinions. I hope to explain the meaning of an otherwise esoteric and arcane subject, the Fisher Body Craftsman's Guild.

Detective work, sweat and tears were required to piece the Guild story together. Guild facts were extracted from many disparate resources (phone calls and phone interviews, letters and correspondence, eBay.com memorabilia, email, various local and national library searches and several national automotive history collection searches, to name just a few) over a long period of time. This was my hobby for many years. A hundred or more friends, neighbors and associates of the Guild (including many former Guildsmen) came forward to answer my questions, share their knowledge, and resolve many of the puzzles and enigmas surrounding the Craftsman's Guild. As far as I know, this is the only technical book about the Fisher Body Craftsman's Guild.

Memorabilia Collection

The Fisher Body Craftsman's Guild was discontinued in 1968 and does not exist anymore except in the hearts and minds of the many Guild enthusiasts who contributed generously to this book. The Fisher Body Division, GMC, ceased to exist in 1984. Please direct your inquiries online to www.fisherguild.com to communicate with the author. Please see the Web site *Fisher Body OnLine* (http://www.geocities.com/sponcomr26/index.html) to learn more about the history and memorabilia of the Fisher Body Division (GMC) and the public relations and advertising program it conducted from 1930 to 1968 called the Fisher Body Craftsman's Guild. This is also a good Web site to learn more about Skip Geear's FBCG Foundation and Mini-Museum. If you are interested in collecting related memorabilia for your own collections, a good place to start is www.ebay.com.

I

Introduction

Background

In his prepared notes for an *Automobile Quarterly* article about the Guild, Virgil M. Exner, Jr., described the values and virtues of the Fisher Body Craftsman's Guild, saying that it

> inspired study and taught patience in the struggle for creativity and understanding of the basic design process. It made one learn automotive design terminology, mechanical technology, manual dexterity and to become familiar with past automotive history, existing design endeavors and future possibilities. It was demanding, educational and fun. It promoted and channeled young talent. It was greatly appealing to youth. Whether one completed a model or not, won or not, or chose to even pursue design or crafts in any way — it gave youth incentive and opportunity to experience trying a worthwhile and interesting vocation.[1]

This book describes the history of General Motors' Fisher Body Craftsman's Guild, a creative model-making competition for teenagers and young men which consisted initially of constructing 1/18 scale Napoleonic Coaches (the same coach image as the Fisher Body Division trademark accompanied by the words "Body by Fisher") and then 1/12 scale model futuristic dream cars. The young model makers competed for university scholarship trust funds worth as much as $5,000 to the top junior and senior division winners. Contestants, called Guildsmen once they entered the competition, ultimately had their eye on a big dream, and that was a university or college education. The program appealed to 12 to 15 year olds (junior division) and college bound 16 to 19 year olds (senior division) for both the coach building and model car making competitions.

The miniature model Napoleonic Coaches were built from blueprint plans initially, then a how-to book, to precise and exacting specifications. They could be scratch-built or constructed from a kit consisting of blocks of wood, rough cast pieces of aluminum, pieces of cloth and thread, and cans of paint. The coaches were highly complex and required 1,000 to 1,500 hours to construct. The coaches largely tested technical model-making skills such as precision, accuracy and the artistic interpretation of blueprint plans. The young people who made them were creative, resourceful and ingenious. The mind and hands had to work together, and great intelligence and resourcefulness was needed to succeed. The Napoleonic Coach competition was held from 1930 to 1948 when it was supplanted by the futuristic model car making competition. This was done for two primary reasons: (1) there were few schools where youngsters could learn automobile design, and thus, feed industry's voracious demand for innovative designers, and (2) interest in Fisher's coach building competition had waned significantly after World War II.[2]

Privately, Fisher Body and GM management knew the model coaches were too complex and time consuming, but they also knew the Craftsman's Guild concept had captured the imagination of the public and youth across America. The Fisher brothers' idea of allowing kids to compete for university scholarships using their minds and hands was endorsed by top educators and educational institutions across the country (e.g., MIT, University of Michigan, Notre Dame, Tulane, Caltech, Georgia Tech, Purdue, Penn State, Carnegie Tech, Brooklyn Poly and the National Science Foundation). Even a Nobel Prize winner from MIT endorsed the tenets, values and virtues of the Craftsman's Guild. The program had proven it could generate a tremendous amount of public good will and had captured the public's attention in newspaper articles and radio broadcast announcements of the national scholarship winners. Scholarship winners attended top universities and studied engineering, architecture, industrial design, fine arts, music, business, law and medicine.

The most promising and talented design-oriented scholarship winners were recruited after college to work at Fisher Body Central Engineering or GM Styling. A 1956 survey estimated 206 former Guildsmen working at Fisher Body Central Engineering and another 35 working at GM Styling. An internal Fisher Body Division study done in 1956 concluded that the Craftsman's Guild was the primary source of GM's styling talent. In 1957 it was estimated that about 35 percent of GM's stylists were Guild graduates.[3] A July 22, 1960, head count showed about 47 Guildsmen being employed by GM Styling with an average age of 30.[4] By 1985, 25 former Guildsman would still be working at GM Design Staff (the new name of GM Styling), and today, only a few remain. One of the last Guildsmen still on campus is Stuart Shuster, working as a contractor in the area of educational relations and creative resources. Translated, this means he's involved in the everyday process of recruiting, hiring and training of promising, young, innovative auto designers.

The model cars, on the other hand, were completely scratch-built and solely created from the builders' imagination, carved from a few scraps of sugar pine, adorned with a few ordinary household items for bright work, and painted using a few spray cans of auto lacquer from Pep Boys auto supply. The cost of materials in the end was minimal. GM provided only general specifications to the model car builders, but beginning in 1954, provided hard rubber wheels molded to scale at no cost to contestants. The model cars had more to do with the automobile design process (e.g., creativity, sculpting, artistic ability and the aesthetic eye) than had the coaches. The labor required to complete a model car was one-fourth to one-half that needed to build a miniature coach. The model car competition was initiated in 1937, and, it is believed, operated through 1940, then, after being interrupted by World War II, continued successfully from 1946 until 1968.

In August 1927 the Fisher brothers attended a dinner at the Book-Cadillac Hotel in Detroit honoring a young man, Colonel Charles A. Lindbergh, who only a few months earlier (May 1927), flying solo, had piloted a single engine monoplane across the Atlantic from New York to Paris. In 1928, the Fisher brothers were awarded top honors by the Detroit AIA Section for the marble tower of their Fisher Building, which dominated the Detroit skyline, and basked in the glory of the so-called Eighth Wonder of the World — the GM Building.[5] In 1929, Raymond Loewy opened his industrial design business (Raymond Loewy International) by remodeling an ugly duplicating machine into a handsome piece of office equipment.[6] Stewart-Warner offered an auto accessory for sale that year called the Neon Tube Stop Light, a safety device and forerunner of the modern-day center high-mounted stoplight (CHMSL), which sat inside the rear window sill at eye level and served as an instant signal to the driver behind.[7]

Because they loved craftsmanship, the hallmark of their business, and they wanted to advertise their Fisher bodies, the Fisher brothers conceived the idea of a foundation for boys called the Fisher Body Craftsman's Guild, designed to teach the practical meaning of being a craftsman. The Fishers were convinced that more highly skilled and competent craftsmen were needed for an age increasingly focused on machines. Despite the stock market crash of November 1929, the Fisher brothers announced the Fisher Body Craftsman's Guild in the *Detroit Times* on August 26, 1930, with the headline, "$50,000 Spurs Boy Workers, Fisher Body President Launches Nation-Wide Guild to Develop Craftsmen."[8] The initial program, configured around building a miniature model Napoleonic Coach, would be pursued during the Great Depression. Although funded by the corporation over the long run, this initial scholarship program was one of many Fisher family charitable activities created as a foundation.

Despite the fact that by 1932 automobile sales, and hence Fisher Body sales, had plummeted by 70–75 percent and 25 percent of the male heads of household were out of work, life continued as usual for many middle class Americans. The American imagination and spirit was captivated by heroines and heroes. In 1932, Amelia Earhart became the first female pilot to fly solo across the Atlantic, and in March 1933, with the inauguration of President Franklin D. Roosevelt, the New Deal arrived, which would benefit all Americans.[9] In October 1933, the Washington Nationals lost the World Series to the New York Giants with FDR in attendance.

The auto world did not stand still either, as automotive technologies continued optimistically with the No Draft Ventilation System, door button locks, pull-to front door armrests, interchangeable car parts, larger window openings for better visibility, 50 mph rollover tests, door safety locks, and shatterproof, safety plate glass. Cadillac, Marmon and Peerless marquees introduced cutting edge technology in the form of the V-16 engine, raising the stakes in the luxury automobile game. The streamlined Chrysler and DeSoto Airflows were introduced (1934), Fisher Body innovated the steel Turret Top (1935), and competing lightweight, stainless steel trains that could reach 120 mph crossed the western continental U.S. from Chicago to Los Angeles. Fisher Body introduced the Unisteel body (1936), and by 1937, the European race car champion Rudolf Caracciola had driven a Mercedes-Benz race car (designated M-B W125) with a top speed of 197.51 mph to four wins.

Despite the economic conditions, Americans were optimistic and in motion. Attended by millions of Americans, the Chicago World's Fairs, first and second seasons, were held in 1933 and 1934. Millions viewed the miniature model Napoleonic Coaches made for the Fisher Body Craftsman's Guild and displayed in GM's Hall of Progress. In 1935 Admiral Byrd's second expedition to Antarctica was initiated. By 1936, industrial designer and visionary Walter Dorwin Teague had designed Texaco's familiar green and white porcelain enamel gas stations, highlighted with red stars easily identified by motorists. In that same year, Gordon M. Buehrig's Cord 810 was introduced, which featured concealed headlights, rounded, flowing body lines, sleek style and sex appeal. In a match race held November 1, 1938 (called a 100-grander after the $100,000 purse), Seabiscuit beat War Admiral by 4 lengths (in 1:56 and 3/5 of a second time) at Baltimore's Pimlico Race Track before a crowd of 78,000, the second largest number of spectators ever assembled for one sporting event. In 1939, the New York World's Fair captured the imagination of Americans with an attendance of 21 million and an estimated 5–10 million alone viewing the GM Futurama exhibit, with the miniature model Napoleonic Coaches demonstrating exemplary craftsmanship and made for the Fisher Body Craftsman's Guild competition. In 1939, David O. Selznick's sound and Technicolor Civil War epic, *Gone with the Wind*, starring Clark Gable and Vivien Leigh, grossed $120 million for a production cost of only $4.5 million. By this time Fisher Body Division, General Motors Corporation, and the auto industry as a whole girded for war and the production of war materiel.

Despite the apparent affluence of some, things weren't quite as rosy for many families, and the chances of a college education dimmed for many eligible youths. The Fisher Body Craftsman's Guild offered this hope and opportunity. The *Detroit Times* promoted the program, for example in an October 24, 1930, article, by showing pictures of William A. Fisher with young contestants examining one of Walter C. Leuschner's master models and completed parts of a miniature Napoleonic Coach. Or, alternatively, they showed William A. Fisher standing with the top scholarship winners and their Napoleonic Coaches in August after the scholarship winners were announced. Thirty-two major metropolitan area newspapers actively sponsored Guild chapters across America in the 1930s and published week-by-week steps and instructions. Walter C. Leuschner and Frank C. Riess, creators of the Napoleonic Coach plans and master models, toured the country selling the Guild program and meeting boys and their parents.

As a side benefit, this industrial arts education program evolved into a successful talent search and recruiting tool for GM management. The kids who won scholarships were recruited by GM, Fisher Body, and other Detroit car makers after they graduated from college. The Craftsman's Guild started as an educational foundation, or educational movement for boys, and became an international coeducational automotive design competition. GM subsidiaries in the United Kingdom (Vauxhall), Switzerland (GM Suisse), West Germany (Opel) and Australia (Holden) sponsored Craftsman's Guild programs. Opel and Vauxhall Craftsman's Guilds were coeducational. In the 1960's, 81 percent of the U.S. participants who won cash awards were either in college prep high school programs or already attending college. Millions of dollars in scholarships and cash incentives were awarded to creative young people.

In addition to the above, the Guild was a prototype for modern-day public relations and advertising. The Craftsman's Guild became a common household word for participants. The Guild came to teenagers via GM auto dealerships, their industrial arts instructors, YMCA leaders, Scout leaders, school assembly programs or traveling GM motor coach–based exhibits like Futurliner and, after teenagers enrolled, Guild literature arrived quarterly in their mailboxes.[10]

GM advertised the Guild using both internal corporate publications (*Guide Light, GM Folks, GM World*) and mass market publications (*Ladies' Home Journal, The Saturday Evening Post, Air Trails, Popular Science, Model Car Science, Young Men, American Youth* and *Boys' Life*). The results of the competition were reported annually in a youth oriented magazine General Motors produced for young teenage drivers called *American Youth*. Around 1967, GM overseas publications carried the annual Craftsman's Guild scholarship winner results from Venezuela to Norway, as GM had plants and representatives in 22 nations at this time.

The Craftsman's Guild was one of the greatest continuous public relations, advertising and education campaigns ever devised to win the hearts and minds of America's youth, GM's future customer base.

In reality, because the Guild program attracted teenage youths with a special, innate design aptitude combined with great manual dexterity, it appealed to a very select few. So despite the use of mass market sales techniques, the response was not massive. About ½ to 1 percent of the coach era and model car era enrollees actually built a model entry.

An interesting aspect of the Guild was that a major corporate entity recognized, early on, that it had a responsibility to the community and that it was a community partner. This evolved into a process where the needs of the community and the corporation were mutually served; the corporation had jobs for people with the requisite design skills and aptitude and the Guild provided a means to measure design skills and aptitude.

The Craftsman's Guild also was a prototype for modern-day networking, as Guild contacts led to jobs for many, and the network continues today. That network, combined with new technology (the Internet and the World Wide Web), made this book possible.

Purpose of the Guild

A more modern view of the Guild is to look at it as a corporate aptitude test or industrial design prep test, since we know many successful Guildsmen were actively recruited by GM and the other automakers. Educators and psychologists have devised multiple choice tests (for the left hemisphere of the brain) that for years have measured our intelligence quotient (IQ), predicted our future performance in colleges and universities (SAT, CAT), measured primary and secondary school comprehension and achievement (CTBS, Stanford 9), categorized our personality types (Myers-Briggs and Keirsey personality tests), measured self-esteem for the Fortune 500, and measured managerial potential for the federal government (PACE).

There are hundreds of measurable human attributes. The problem is how to measure the qualities GM wanted in its young designers—artistic ability, creativity, imagination, spatial relationship acuity (form, function, balance, proportion, shape), manual dexterity, the aesthetic eye, good taste, propensity for perfection, etc.—that is, many of those attributes ascribed to the right hemisphere of the brain. GM wasn't looking for the average teenager who emulated the automobile designs seen on the street. GM wanted innovators who could foresee and predict the future, as evidenced by their model dream car designs. They wanted the artistic interpretation of blueprints and plans (coach builders) to be supplanted by free-form design and expression (model car making).

The Fisher family's answer was to initiate the Fisher Body Craftsman's Guild, essentially a take-home industrial arts aptitude test. A miniature Napoleonic Coach would require in the range of 1,000 to 1,500 hours to be executed to perfection and a scale model car would require in the range of 250 to 500 hours, or more, to build a scholarship quality model. In 1961, for example, Ronald Will spent 700 hours styling his model dream car for the top national award of a $5,000 university scholarship trust fund.

The medium selected for the industrial arts aptitude test was a serious form of play. Kids from the model car making era, for example, were brought up on an array of realistic toys that prepared them for careers; for example, play stoves for housewives, doctors' and nurses' kits for health care professionals, and model airplane kits, model train kits and Lincoln Logs were popular for young, budding engineers. Two conceived during the depression, just like the Guild, were A.C. Gilbert's Mysto-Erector Set and the All-American Soap Box Derby, geared for aspiring engineers and designers. When the Fisher brothers started the Craftsman's Guild, a reality-based, creative model-making competition, this was consistent with the way Americans would eventually perceive toys, play and fun. Granted, the Napoleonic and Traveling Coach competitions were way ahead of their time, but the model dream cars fit very neatly into this creative play paradigm.

Public Relations Bonanza

It is estimated that 10 million U.S. teenagers enrolled in the Craftsman's Guild cumulatively over its 34 year history and over 32,800 award-worthy coaches and model cars were constructed for the competition.[11] The Fisher Body Craftsman's Guild appeared everywhere, it seemed, including the local newspapers, nationally distributed magazines ads, school assembly programs and live radio broadcasts of the scholarship winners. Both programs (model coaches and cars) had the potential for exposing huge numbers of youth, their future customer base, to General Motors by means of circulating monthly, bimonthly or quarterly Craftsman's Guild publications in the hundreds of thousands.

According to GM Media Archives asset data from 1931, the Napoleonic Coach competition of the 1930s generated 880 million newspaper reader impressions in its first year of existence.[12] The miniature model Napoleonic Coach competition inspired about 145,000 to 148,000 teens to join the Guild in the U.S. for the 1930–1931 competition year and 402,000 to join the Guild in the U.S. and Canada for the 1931–1932 competition year. About 1,350 model coach entries were received in the first year of the competition and about 547 model coach entries were received in the second year.[13] Overall, it is estimated that about 6,000 to 7,200 award-worthy miniature model coaches were made during the Napoleonic Coach competition era (1930 to 1948).

The model car competition of the '50s and '60s had a similar impact, generating almost 1 million inquires and 500,000 to 600,000 enrollees annually, with approximately 25,660 to 26,800 award-worthy model car entries. In the fall of 1966, approximately 804,596 boys and girls (a record) were introduced to the Fisher Body Craftsman's Guild during 1,341 assembly programs conducted by Guild field representatives.[14] The winning models were exhibited at the school venues. After the Guild convention and announcement of the winners, many Guild scholarship winners were spirited off to appear on TV and radio shows. In 1966, for example, winners made 39 TV and radio appearances.

The winning Guild models toured the country, appearing in department stores, hotel lobbies, libraries, state fairs (e.g., Futurliner-type "Parades of Progress") and in the famous GM Futurama and Motorama exhibits. Millions saw the winning coaches, or model dream cars, at such venues as the 1933 Chicago World's Fair, the 1934 World's Fair, the 1939 New York World's Fair and the 1965 New York World's Fair.

Although only as a component part, GM managed to integrate the Fisher Body Craftsman's Guild into practically every one of their key public relations and advertising venues.

Overseas Craftsman's Guilds

Beginning in 1965, the idea of the U.S. Craftsman's Guild program was exported. The GM Overseas Operations division got involved, and Craftsman's Guild competitions were born at Vauxhall (UK), GM Suisse (Switzerland), Adam-Opel (West Germany) and at GM Holden (Australia). Although these were mostly short-lived experiments, the Opel Modellbauer Gilde in West Germany, a coeducational program, was conducted from 1965 to 1979. A few young women such as Gillian Bailey and Ursula Mell-Mellenheim finished among the top 40 model makers in the Vauxhall Craftsman's Guild and the Opel Modellbauer Gilde, respectively. On the average some 1,697 models were entered annually in the Opel Moldellbauer Gilde competition compared to an average of about 3,133 model entries in the U.S. Craftsman's Guild competition.

Lives Changed

The educational movement that the Fisher brothers had envisioned had become an international education program and talent search forum. It helped young people find their way in the world — perhaps an avocation became a vocation or an industrial design career. Maybe their vocational callings switched from auto design to product design to architectural design or from mechanical engineering to architectural engineering, but the Guild got them thinking about their futures and where they fit in. Several combined their engineering degrees with an industrial design, dedicating 6½ to 8 years to a formal design training and education. Some became career automobile designers or executives working at GM, Ford, Chrysler, Nissan, Subaru, Volvo, Mack Trucks, and Thomas Built Buses, reaching, in a few cases, the level of director of design or design executive.

Many became product designers, influencing the aesthetic appeal of the things we use and touch every day, with some specializing in architecture, aircraft interiors, home and office furniture, major appliances, home electronic products, and medical products. They worked for the top design consulting firms like Pelly's Designworks/USA, Teague, and Raymond Loewy International, and many started their own successful design consulting firms.

Lives were affected and changed by the Guild experience. College and university educations previously out of reach were made possible. Many Guild scholarship winners attended the premier Pasadena design school called the Art Center College of Design specifically to become industrial designers specializing in transportation design or product design. The transportation design graduates, sought after by auto companies around the world, became auto stylists and auto designers. This school still provides the world's supply of top auto design talent along with Detroit's College for Creative Studies, the Academy of Art University (AAU) in San Francisco and many others. (See <www.idsa.org> for schools with accredited industrial design programs.) The vast majority of the contributors to this book attended the Art Center College of Design.

Of course, successful Guildsmen did many things other than working in the industry as auto or product designers. They became everything under the sun including architects, architectural planners, architectural engineers, educators, college professors (e.g., of architecture and urban planning, music, history, and furniture-making), model makers, exhibit designers, auto biomechanics experts and scientists, craftsmen, violin makers, mathematical economists, painters, commercial artists and illustrators, and Mattel or Milton Bradley toy designers.) One former Guildsman did the interior design of Wilt Chamberlain's custom Los Angeles home and another designed parts of Disneyland, EuroDisney and a custom home for Michael Jackson in Encino, California.

Tenets, Values and Virtues

Although a far-flung organization made up of disparate individuals, the Guild represented rock-solid values. Participants received satisfaction and a sense of pride from a constructive and positive activity. Perseverance and resourcefulness were essential to completing the project. They learned that hard work was virtuous and that it had tangible rewards (as in money) as well as intangible rewards like praise and recognition. The recognition was the most valuable of all. They learned honesty and integrity by doing their own work to the greatest degree possible. Although there were some highly successful teams of brothers who received multiple national scholarship awards, most Guildsmen worked solo and were generally isolated from one another. Very few Guildsmen actually won a college or university scholarship as only 387 were awarded (1930–1968), but thousands of kids won state level cash awards. Despite the odds of success, it was a win-win situation because of the sense of accomplishment, the joy of working with their minds and hands, and the fact that they learned how to do something constructive.

One of Chuck Jordan's Guild convention speeches summarized the skills taught by the Guild experience:

> Thinking, analyzing, planning; careful thought, perseverance, hours of hard work and how to "stick-to-it"; stretching the imagination; creating new design ideas, making decisions and committing to a new design idea; and the efficient management of time.
>
> There are many scholarships given to boys with outstanding athletic ability or an outstanding scholastic record. ... The Fisher Body Craftsman's Guild offers recognition and reward to boys with imagination who can express their creative ability in 3 dimensions with well defined craftsmanship.[15]

Demise of the Fisher Body Craftsman's Guild

In 1968 all of this came to an end in the U.S. when the corporate leadership concluded that benefits of the Guild did not exceed the costs.[16] Because the number of new GM customers created, the number of cars sold, or the amount of good will generated by the Guild couldn't be measured or quantified, the benefits side of the equation could never be determined. The decision was made that GM was in the business of manufacturing and selling cars and not in the business of teaching America's youth the intricacies of automotive design and the art of craftsmanship. Despite this, the GM Design staff tried, in vain, to rejuvenate the U.S. Guild program by proposing a newer, lower cost approach in 1973.

Perhaps because it was coeducational and formulated for the first phase of women's liberation, the Opel Modellbauer Gilde at GM Opel AG continued to flourish until 1979. This is consistent with other educational institutions that over the years shifted to coeducation. In 1971 the All-American Soap Box Derby, a scholarship program originally sponsored by Chevrolet Division, shifted to become coeducational, and it is still enjoyed by families around the country to this day.

The declining quality of model entries in the 1960s was a clear indicator that U.S. teenagers lacked the disposable time they once could devote to craftsmanship (a key value and virtue of the competition). A burgeoning information society created new competing interests and opportunities for teenagers almost daily. Parallel to this, a paradigm shift had taken place in secondary schools; educational values such as design and craftsmanship were secondary to scholastic achievement and scholarship. The need for skilled craftsmen such as the Fisher brothers had dreamed of for an ever increasing machine age had been replaced by a need for technological information processors, integrators and synthesizers. It is theorized that if GM had modernized the Craftsman's Guild program by making it coeducational and diverse, emphasizing automotive design values and virtues and deemphasizing the time consuming and demanding craftsmanship, the Craftsman's Guild might have survived. It could have been just as effective an advertising and recruiting tool.

Unanswered Questions

Many questions about the Guild are difficult to answer because (1) the Guild was a far-flung assembly of disparate individuals and participants and not organized in any formal manner; (2) Fisher Body Division ceased to exist in 1984 due to a GM corporate reorganization; (3) key people from the various Guild eras have passed away or did not write a definitive history of their experiences; and (4) key memorabilia is in a deep glacial sleep in basements or attics, waiting to be discovered. Future generations will be able to write a more definitive story. Some of the unanswered questions about the Guild are as follows:

1. Who actually designed and constructed the two master models for the miniature Napoleonic Coach competition and where are the master models located today? Who designed the 1934–35 Traveling Coach and the set of scale blueprints? Where is the master model for the Traveling Coach competition, if one ever existed?

2. How did 12- and 13-year-old boys perform at the master craftsman level, winning top scholarship awards? How did a few individuals defy the odds and win top national scholarship awards on their first attempts?

3. Where are the top national scholarship award winning models stored and preserved — the ones purchased from contestants by Fisher Body Division, particularly during the 1950s? Is there a secret vault? Who has the key?

4. GM and its subsidiaries had exclusive ownership of the ideas submitted by the Guildsmen. Did GM adopt any of the ingenious ideas submitted by the creative teen contestants in the model car competition, and were these ideas ever mass produced?

5. For how many of the participants was the promise of the Guild fulfilled with employment at one of the automakers, designing cars for a career?

6. Which famous personalities from the automotive world were connected to the Craftsman's Guild program?

7. Who were some of the organizations that embraced the Craftsman's Guild's philosophy and tried to emulate this successful industrial education program? Which organizations adopted and institutionalized the Guild's literature?

8. Assuming the number of model entries annually was the bottom line for these programs, why were the overseas Craftsman's Guilds more efficient than the U.S. Fisher Body Craftsman's Guild in terms of (1) model entries per enrollee and (2) promotion dollars (Deutsche marks, pounds) spent per model entry?

9. A new, higher speed model-making technique was demonstrated to the press corps in August 1967 by Davis P. Rossi, design sculptor from GM Styling, using polyurethane rigid foam and the commercial polymer Liquitex modeling paste. This technique was consequently introduced for the 1967–1968 Craftsman's competition year. If the Fisher Guild had continued beyond August 1968, would this method have saved enough time for kids to focus on craftsmanship, and in general, have revolutionized participation in the Craftsman's Guild program as a whole?

10. Why was the Detroit Craftsman's Guild competition discontinued in 1968, while the overseas Guilds flourished, at least the Modellbauer Gilde in West Germany, from 1965 to 1979?

11. Would the international Guild competition under consideration in 1967 (where the top Senior winners from Opel, Vauxhall, Holden, Suisse, and Fisher guilds would compete for gold, silver and bronze medallions and be honored with a New York banquet and feted by a host of international guests) have boosted the stature of the program, thus saving the Craftsman's Guild paradigm from being abandoned?

12. Did General Motors ever wake up, realize what it had thrown away, and try to revive the Fisher Body Craftsman's Guild?

Fisher Body Craftsman's Guild
Time Line and Milestones

1908	Fisher Body Company founded on July 22, 1908, by Frederic J. and Charles T. Fisher of Norwalk, Ohio.
1920–22[17]	Fisher advertising agency designs new trademark, logo, and emblem.
1922	First bas-relief brass emblem with Napoleonic Coach and words "Body by Fisher" screwed to right-hand side of cowl of Fisher bodies.
1926	Fisher Body Corporation becomes Fisher Body Division of GM.
1927–29[18]	Craftsman's Guild foundation idea conceived by the Fishers' advertising agency as a means to nurture, among the North American continent's youth, the skills of craftsmen needed in a growing machine age.[19] The program was also needed to sell Fisher bodies. If future purchasers of automobiles (the contestants) understood craftsmanship at some personal level, then the obvious craftsmanship in Fisher Body products would be automatically appealing.
1930	Craftsman's Guild educational program begins. 32 chapters of the Guild are formed across the country by top market newspapers in support of the Fisher brothers' university trust fund program. Frank C. Riess and Walter C. Leuschner design the master blueprints. Two master model coaches are constructed from May to October 1930 at the Fleetwood Auto Bodies plant in Fleetwood, Pennsylvania.
1930–31	First year of Napoleonic Coach competition; Albert W. Fischer, Raymond S. Doerr, Donald C. Burnham, and Howard Jennings win top awards of

Fisher Body Craftsman's Guild History Time Line

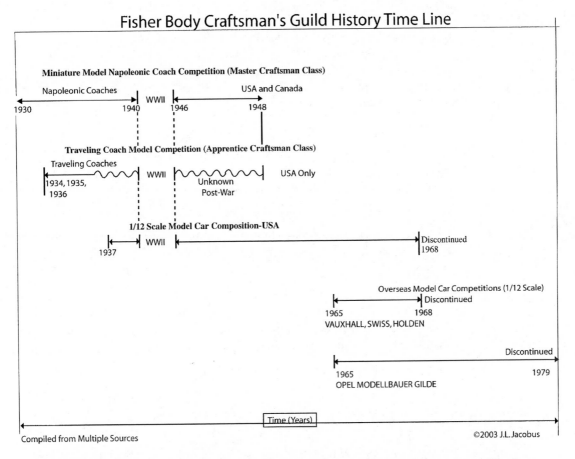

Compiled from Multiple Sources   ©2003 J.L. Jacobus

Fisher Body Craftsman's Guild time line (1930–1968). The Craftsman's Guild was operated by the Public Relations and Advertising Department, Fisher Body Division. This chart shows the program components and the time periods over which they functioned including the Guilds that were exported overseas through the GM Overseas Operations division.

	$5,000 each. 104 state winners are feted at the General Motors Building Auditorium.
1932	Petite Napoleonic Coach cardboard cutout, slot-and-tab promotion toy (with its own competition) is sponsored by chapter newspapers, contingent upon purchase of a six-month subscription.
1932	Canadians join Napoleonic Coach competition, introduce 140 district awards, two national scholarships and three designated cities for judging (Regina, Montreal and Toronto).
1934–35	*The Guildsman*, official magazine of the Fisher Body Craftsman's Guild, is published and distributed to Guildsmen.
1934	Traveling Coach (probably designed by the Leuschner-Riess team) and Apprentice Craftsman Class idea are introduced. Master Craftsman Class idea is introduced for those building Napoleonic Coaches. Canadians offer six national scholarship awards for the Napoleonic Coach competition.

1934	Nine Regions are introduced for the Traveling Coach competition along with nine designated regional locations for judging (Boston, New York City, Washington, D.C., Atlanta, Dallas, Omaha, Seattle, Los Angeles site 1 and Los Angeles site 2. Organizing the states into groups or regions is embraced throughout the model car competition (1937–1968) and ensures a fair distribution of the awards.
1936–40	*Guild News Letter* published and distributed.
1937	Model car competition (four-door sedans) introduced concurrently with coach competitions. Teddy Mandel (age 14) wins first-place national scholarship, junior division, a $5,000 award.
1937–53	Contestants turn 1/12 scale wheels or tires from wood on homemade lathes.
1937–54	FBCG is discontinued temporarily during World War II, suspending activities by 1940 and starting again in 1946. Fisher Body Division builds war materiel (e.g., B-25 and B-29 components, tanks, shells, and Bendix and Sperry navigational instruments for bombers).
1946–53	Model car (four-door sedans only) and miniature model Napoleonic Coach competitions continue simultaneously. Napoleonic Coach competitions ends in 1948.[20] Two-door sedan body style introduced by 1953.
1946–53	*Guild News*, official bulletin of the Fisher Body Craftsman's Guild, is published.
1953–68	*Guildsman*, official publication of the Fisher Body Craftsman Guild, is published.
1954	Model car competition is expanded to include two-door and four-door sedan, hard top, convertible, sports car and station wagon body styles.
1954	1/12 scale hard rubber wheels are offered free to Guildsmen with signed coupon from parents or guardian.
1955–56	Transition year, as the number of scholarship awards is increased from eight worth $20,000 to 18 worth $38,000. (Before 1955–56, there were two awards each (junior/senior division) of $4,000, $3,000, $2,000 and $1,000 for a total of eight national scholarships and after the change there were two awards each of $5,000, $4,000, $3,000 and $2,000, and ten styling scholarships worth $1,000 each.)
1958–59	Both junior and senior age brackets are expanded to boost the number of target population teenagers by as much as 20–25 percent. The junior division is changed from 12–15 to include 11–15 year olds and the senior division was changed from 16–19 to include 16–20 year olds.
1959–60	The 20 regions as established in 1953–54 are completely overhauled to better accommodate the geographic distribution of winners (based on the number and quality of model entries) and to incorporate the new states of Alaska and Hawaii. Wreath from Cadillac's emblem or badge adopted as the Guild insignia on trophies and booklets.

1963   The Open Competition, or Open Category C, is added to the model car competition to allow Guildsmen to explore new wheelbase and body configurations, to further stimulate the imagination and to boost the number of participants. In addition, there is Category A, for regular, conventional wheelbase designs, and Category B for sports car or small car designs. Boys could compete making any one of 11 different body styles.

1968   Although teenage interest remained piqued, the Fisher Body Craftsman's Guild is discontinued because the benefits do not exceed the costs. GM doesn't want to be in the auto design education business anymore. The number of awards being made is decreasing, as is the quality of model entries. Overall, only 13 percent of the model entries are considered award-worthy in 1963 and 1966. The solitary pursuit of design and craftsmanship by teenagers wanes in favor of a multitude of sports and social activities, with an emphasis on high SAT performance and scholastic excellence.

1965–67   Vauxhall Craftsman's Guild (VCG) operates in England.

1965–79   Model Builder's Guild operates in West Germany under Adam-Opel AG.

1966–69   Holden Craftsman's Guild (HCG) operates in Australia under GM Holden.

1965–68   Model Auto Competition operates in Switzerland under GM Suisse.

1984   The Fisher Body Division of GMC is phased out in a GM corporate reorganization along with the General Motors Assembly Division (GMAD). Fisher Body Division and Guide Lamp Division are combined to make the Fisher-Guide Division. Roger B. Smith, chairman of GMC, announces in *Automotive News*, August 20, 1984, that the famous Fisher Body Napoleonic Coach emblem will continue to be worn (on the door sills of GM products) despite the passing of the Fisher Body Division into corporate oblivion.[21]

II

Napoleonic Coach
Competition (1930–1948)

Introduction

The man who can work surely, swiftly and deftly with his hands is always preferable in any employment [*Crafts Guilds, Their History and Influence*].

This chapter describes the Fisher brothers and the Fisher family; the family's legacy of philanthropy; the origins and purpose of the Fisher Body Craftsman's Guild; the miniature Napoleonic Coach competition initiated August 25, 1930; advertising, promotion and incentives for the program; judging and scoring; ingenious and creative ideas; coach kits; labor hours required; and the Traveling Coach competition inaugurated in 1934–35.

The Fisher Brothers

The seven Fisher brothers, in descending order by age, were Frederic J., Charles T., William A., Lawrence P., Edward F., Alfred, and Howard A. Six were involved in the automobile body manufacturing business, but Howard was only involved in the real estate side of things, notably projects like the construction of the Fisher Building located on West Grand Boulevard across from the GM Building.[1] Lawrence Fisher, their father, owned and operated a carriage business. The outdoor sign on his place of business in Norwalk, Ohio, said, "L. Fisher Carriage Factory, Repairing and Horse Shoeing, Carriage Painting."

No doubt this business required the skills of a true craftsman, such as leatherworking, upholstering, and woodworking as well as forge and foundry skills to make harnesses, axles, and springs. Following the family tradition of carriage making, it makes sense that the trademark the brothers adopted for their auto body business in 1922 would be a royal coach — a symbol of craftsmanship equivalent to a BMW or Lamborghini in the carriage trade. Also, up to 1926 and beyond for many years, the automobile bodies built by Fisher were handcrafted from wood, eventually becoming a composite of wood and metal and finally all metal (called Unisteel body construction). The Fisher Brothers innovated the closed automobile body, which paved the way for all-weather utility and made the automobile more marketable to women.[2]

Philanthropy

The Fisher family acquired wealth when GM bought a majority (three-fifths), but not controlling, interest in Fisher Body Corporation in 1919. In 1926 the remaining two-fifths was purchased for a total price of $234.7 million. Although the Fisher family may have seeded the initial Guild program, called a foundation in the 1930s, over the long term it was clearly financed by the trustees at General Motors' bank — the National Bank of Detroit. Only one of the seven Fisher brothers apparently had the advantage of a formal college education, and that may be why a university scholarship program was so appealing to them as a family. The other brothers had either technical school or business educations, and succeeded by sheer hard work and determination.

Before 1929, the Fisher brothers had become captains of industry; the toast of Wall Street, wealthy, successful and powerful, business-savvy people. By 1917 they headed one of the largest automobile body manufacturers in the world, selling 500,000 touring and runabout bodies (with 80,000 closed body styles by 1920) and by 1924 there were 44 Fisher plants with 40,000 employees. During the 1925–26 period, they capitalized their own investment firm, the Fisher Company, Inc., with a $25 million stake. Their portfolio was flush with all the automotive manufacturers as well as Texaco Oil, New York Central Railroad, IT&T, Sperry, RCA, Westinghouse, GE, Anaconda Copper, and U.S. Steel, as well as banks.

The Fishers were not margin players, but owned their stock outright at full face value. Investors scrutinized their Wall Street plays and emulated their moves. They enjoyed yachts, one, custom-built in New York, named after their beloved mother, Margaret. They had their own Fokker trimotor. They enjoyed the company of the rich and famous like the Herbert Hoovers, the Harley J. Earls, the Charles F. Ketterings, the Alfred P. Sloan, Jrs., and the Col. Charles A. Lindberghs. They got away and relaxed in style in their private digs like the Flamingo Villa in Miami. In short, they had become important socialites, the nouveau-rich and Detroit's toast of the town.[3] Needless to say, when the market collapsed, they took a bath and suffered huge paper losses.

The Craftsman's Guild was part of a long series of Fisher family philanthropic and charitable activities such as the Burther Fisher Home (Little Sisters of the Poor), the Nurses' Home at Old Providence Hospital, Sarah Fisher's Home for Children, the Fisher YMCA, the Fisher Titus Memorial Hospital, and Larry Fisher's Grayhaven Home (for actors and other thespians). There was charity of another sort in their hearts as at least one of the Fisher brothers visited their mother, Margaret, each and every day.[4,5]

Fisher Body "Royal Coach" Trademark

It is surmised that some humble artist at GM's advertising agency (possibly Batten, Barton, Durstine and Osborn), penned the original logo design in 1921 or thereabouts.[6] The artist's design was chosen as the official Fisher Body trademark in 1922, the application to register this logo was filed August 9th of that year, and the symbol became the official company trademark on July 10, 1923. Beginning in 1922, rectangular brass plates or emblems containing the coach trademark and the words "Body by Fisher" appeared on the right-hand side of the cowl down at the fender line.

 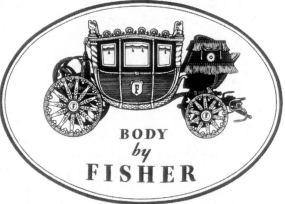

Left: The royal coach symbol from the 1920s shown in this Fisher Body Division trademark conveyed the image that Fisher bodies were built to the highest standards of craftsmanship and that the interiors were elegant and luxurious, befitting royalty. *Right:* A new, modern Fisher Body Division trademark was generated by the initiation of the Fisher Body Craftsman's Guild. Fisher Body magazine ads began to carry the new line drawing of the Walter Leuschner/Frank Riess designed Napoleonic Coach around 1932 or 1933. *General Motors Corporation.*

Napoleonic Coach Trademark

For the Craftsman's Guild educational program, the Fisher Brothers wanted a new, modernized Napoleonic Coach design. Again, their ad agency's artist in consultation with a Fleetwood employee named Walter C. Leuschner, or Leuschner alone, decided to combine the best design features of two famous European coaches into one complete coach model.[7] The two coaches were Napoleon Bonaparte's ornate, gilded Sacred Coach used for his coronation as emperor, and the delicate La Topaze Coach used for his marriage to the Hapsburg beauty Marie-Louise, the archduchess of Austria, on April 2, 1810.[8] The two coaches were probably the two finest examples of their types ever built. Hence the name "Napoleonic" was given to Leuschner's new hybrid two- and three-dimensional coach designs. Frank C. Riess, a Detroit public school industrial arts teacher, was responsible for preparing the technical blueprints in collaboration with Leuschner so that artisans and craftsmen at Fleetwood could make two master models of the miniature Napoleonic Coach and possibly other prototypes for exhibition or advertising purposes. The "gold standard" or benchmark for the coach competition would be the two master models and their respective blueprints. The judges would actually compare the contestants' model entries to the master models as a reference.

The three-dimensional FBCG coach model Leuschner and Riess designed adopted numerous features of Napoleon's Sacred Coach such as ornate gold leaf adorning spoked wheels, folding steps, gold braided trim around the bottom and side of the coach body, and a luxurious interior of fine white silk and gold thread trimming. The exterior design was cleaner and more simplified like the La Topaze Coach.

In the process of creating the three-dimensional Napoleonic Coach for the Craftsman's Guild, Leuschner and Riess also succeeded in redesigning the coach line drawing on the trademark. By 1932 or 1933 the new coach silhouette started to appear in magazine ads. The new two-dimensional line drawing would be used with the famous "Body by Fisher" logo to form a new, modernized trademark design for Fisher Body Division. The new Napoleonic Coach design would be the symbol the Fisher Brothers chose to convey the image of the finest craftsmanship, elegance and luxury available in closed automobile bodies and would appear in magazine print ads and on door sill emblems of Fisher Bodies up to 1984.

Youth Scholarship Program

After the stock market collapsed on October 29, 1929, over $50 billion in stock value evaporated in two short years. The Fisher brothers' portfolio took huge paper losses. Ten months after this economic disaster was precipitated, because of the family's charitable nature and their obsession with quality craftsmanship, the Fisher brothers decided to go ahead with their idea of a foundation, or unique educational scholarship program, for youth to compete and test their natural skills, abilities and ingenuity by building a miniature model Napoleonic Coach from scratch. The Napoleonic Coach, for what was called the Master Craftsman Class, would be used to test skills in recreating the coach design of the Fisher trademark in three dimensions. The three-dimensional miniature Napoleonic Coach would be the centerpiece of the Fisher Body Craftsman's Guild competition, announced August 25, 1930, in the *Detroit Times*.

A simpler miniature model Traveling Coach, to be introduced in the 1934–35 competition year, and which had a striking resemblance to the La Topaze Coach, was designed for the Apprentice Craftsman Class to attract beginner coach modelers. Both the Master Craftsman Class and the Apprentice Craftsman Class would have the competition age brackets: 12 15-year-old entrants for the junior division and 16 19-year-old competitors for the senior division.

Source of Inspiration

The Fisher brothers' college scholarship competition got its name from the craftsmen organized into guilds (the forerunners of modern trade unions) in Brussels, Zurich, Paris, London and other European cities in the Middle Ages. A teenage boy left home at age 16 to become an apprentice in a guild and work under a master craftsman (e.g., vintners, curriers, fishmongers, grocers, ironmongers, skinners, girdlers, blacksmiths, goldsmiths, carpenters, salters, fletchers, merchants, brewers, cloth workers, and coach makers, among many others). Craftsmen in a guild survived because they were taken care of from cradle to grave. After seven years as an apprentice, followed by ten years as a journeyman, a man could become a master craftsman.

The theme of the Guild Hall Square that had existed in Brussels in the Dark Ages was carried over to the Fisher Body Craftsman's Guild convention banquet hall in 1931, and later years, with stage scenery showing the façade of a medieval town, surrounding the 104 Napoleonic Coach state winners being toasted by candlelight and served by waiters in doublet and hose. The same medieval theme adorned the grand exhibit hall where the winning scholarship coaches, up on pedestals, were displayed for the press and the public.[9]

Napoleonic Coach Designers and Creators

With Walter Leuschner as the technical director and Frank Riess as chief draftsman, a set of master blueprints were drawn up so that two master models of the miniature model Napoleonic Coach could be professionally constructed. These were most probably handcrafted at Fleetwood Metal Body Company in Fleetwood, Pennsylvania, between May and October of 1930. Fleetwood built the finest custom automobile bodies in the world and these were chosen by U.S. Presidents, Andrew Carnegie, the Vanderbilts, the Rockefellers and movie stars like Mary Pickford, Rudolph Valentino, Theda Bara and Harold Lockwood. Each custom body was assembled on an engine and chassis that had been shipped to Fleetwood by rail.

Leuschner supposedly was a descendant of a family who had opened their own coach factory in Berlin, Germany, around 1833. Mr. Leuschner himself was once a major in the Imperial German Army and was also a noted, and one of the last, royal coach builders. As the story goes, the Leuschner family built flawless coaches for famous individuals such as the king of Italy, the empress of China, the czar of Russia, the king of England, Kaiser Wilhelm of Germany, and the emperor of Japan, to name a few.[10]

This was the story that appeared in thousands of Guild brochures or *Plans and Instructions* books concerned with building the model Napoleonic Coach. The *Detroit Times* pictured Walter C. Leuschner, a bald, older gentleman with wire-rimmed glasses, promoting the Guild program, and stated that his Detroit address was 2649 Montclair Avenue. In a particularly noteworthy 1930s *Detroit Times* photo, he was shown with one of his Napoleonic Coaches (presumably one of the two master models) and several young contestants. The caption stated that he (or his family) had built coaches for one of the Russian Czars and a former Kaiser as well as many other notables. (This only proves that the newspaper read the same Guild brochures as everyone else.) His picture appeared in numerous 1934 and 1935 Guild publications standing bent over, supervising other judges involved in scoring the Napoleonic Coach entries. But was Walter Leuschner a public relations ploy (or actor) used to promote the Guild's Old World craftsmanship theme, or was he really a coach expert and former technical director of a famous Berlin coach builder?

Fleetwood Metal Body Company, where Leuschner was supposedly an employee, was acquired by Fisher Body Corporation in 1925 and made custom automobile bodies for Cadillac among other famous marquees. Hence, the badge Cadillac Fleetwood evolved. Recently, background information was obtained on the Leuschner family from a Berlin technical library. Apparently, Walter C. Leuschner had lived in Berlin, Germany, in the mid– to late '20s where he and his father Max had been technical directors of the Louis Ruhe Royal Coach Factory. They manufactured custom automobile bodies, just like Fleetwood Metal Body Company, and built coach bodies, carriages and even an experimental airplane. Walter Leuschner was laid off by the owners when the factory went out of business in the mid–1920s. That's probably when Walter Leuschner emigrated to America, settled in Pennsylvania Dutch country and got a job, presumably, at Fleetwood Metal Body Company (Berks County, Pennsylvania).

The author tried to verify whether Leuschner was an actual Fleetwood employee, but this inquiry quickly ran into a dead end. The Fleetwood Area Historical Society (per Ms. Lillian S. Walter) said they'd never head of him. Mr. Leuschner's 1930 Census record gives his address as 1224 Virginia Park, Detroit, and shows that he was a draftsman in the auto body industry. While suggestive, this does not prove he was actually working for Fleetwood.[11]

So, the lineage and heritage of the Louis Ruhe Royal Coach Factory may have gone back to the 1830s, but when the Leuschner family got involved, or how long they were involved, is unknown at this time. It's quite possible their company had made ceremonial coaches for the Russian Czars (the last, Nicholas II, abdicated in 1917) and for the German Kaisers (1871 to 1918) in the late teens or early twenties, but further research would be required to verify these facts.

The design and construction of the miniature master models would not have been possible without Riess, a former head of the industrial arts department of a Detroit high school. Leuschner was to supply his expertise in coach building and Riess was to lend his expertise in drafting, dimensioning, scaling, cross-sectioning, and blueprint making. Riess produced a master set of plans or blueprints, a copy of which still exists today at Skip Geear's FBCG Foundation and Mini-Museum in Eagle Point, Oregon.[12]

Master Model Coaches

When the Fisher brothers announced the creation of their Craftsman's Guild on August 25, 1930, the *Detroit Times* article stated that "two scale models of the Napoleonic Coaches will be made and sent around the country to be viewed by contestants." Although these were probably the two master models built from Frank Riess' exacting blueprints, other prototype coach models must have existed in the late '20s to promote the program.[13] Nothing gets sold in Detroit without prototype models for visual study by executives and scaled blueprint plans to explain ideas. Another *Detroit Times* article, dated October 24, 1930, stated that "completed parts" and a "Master Miniature Coach Model" would be displayed Friday and Saturday at the Times Building, 1370 Cass Avenue, Detroit, Michigan.

Ms. Lillian S. Walter, daughter of one of the founders (Alfred Schlegal) of Fleetwood Metal Body Company, claims to have seen miniature Napoleonic Coach models being made in the shops when she was a teenager. She believes, and her father told her, that they were the master models being made. Regrettably, the Leuschner family name was not familiar to her.

The Fleetwood Area Historical Society (FAHS) displays a full-scale, blueprint drawing (front, rear, top and side views) of the miniature Napoleonic Coach which was dated "7/30" in the sign-off box, and initialed by WCL (presumably meaning July 1930, Walter C. Leuschner). Also, ten 8" × 10" black and white photographic negatives show hundreds of scale model coach parts waiting to be assembled. The Leuschner-designed ornate royal coach is reproduced on the FAHS literature and is a part of Fleetwood's proud history.

A closeup black and white photograph of a miniature Napoleonic Coach adorns the back of a recently published FAHS calendar. The caption at the bottom of the photograph states,

> One of the final projects built at the Fleetwood Metal Body Company before closing its Fleetwood doors and moving to Detroit, was the construction of a coach similar to the Napoleon Coronation Coach. It was the model for the coach logo affixed to all Fisher Bodies. Following its completion, a national contest was held offering college scholarships to those who could produce the best copies of the coach constructed by the Fleetwood artisans.

This is believed to be one of two master models made of the miniature model Napoleonic Coach designed by Walter C. Leuschner and Frank C. Riess for the Fisher Body Craftsman's Guild. It is believed that the master models were made by the craftsmen and custom coach builders at the Fleetwood Metal Body Company in Fleetwood, Pennsylvania. *General Motors Corporation.*

An article by K.H. Stauffer refers to the crest with the letter "F" mounted on the door of the miniature model Napoleonic Coach. He mentions "the detailing evident in these photos, so characteristic of all bodies that so proudly wore the Fleetwood crest." Stauffer was mistaken, as the crest in question is the Fisher Body crest (with the letter "F" for Fisher) identical to the ones seen on the wall in photographs of Guild banquets.[14]

It is also known, from written historical accounts of the Fleetwood Metal Body Co., that they had been commissioned by Fisher Body headquarters in Detroit to build three miniature Napoleonic Coaches between July 1930 and December 1930, that is, six months before Fleetwood Metal Body Co. ceased to exist. Starting January 1, 1931, the Fleetwood technical and design staff would be moved to Detroit. Several articles about Fleetwood published in various auto club magazines describe miniature model Napoleonic Coaches being made. These articles never made clear if they were talking about the two master models or promotional models to be used for exhibitions, photographs or advertisements.

An article by Truman S. Fuller, Jr., about Fleetwood discusses the model coaches they made. He stated, "The original coach was 6 months in the making (from May 1930 to October 1930) and several copies were constructed following acceptance of the original model. … The original model made at Fleetwood is displayed at Fisher Body's General Offices in Warren, Michigan."[15]

The "original" model discussed was probably one of the master models, and in 1967 when the T.S. Fuller article was published, Fisher Body headquarters had a Master Model on display in their lobby. The original model, or master model, was generally believed to have cost many times the price of the finest Cadillac. As indicated in a letter from Norman E. May, general director of Fisher Body Public Relations, to Lillian S. Walter (August 18, 1978), two master models were made and in existence at that time. Mr. Fuller does not mention a second master model being made at Fleetwood.

It would seem logical that the Fisher brothers would have needed one or two prototype Napoleonic Coach models, plans, and public relations and promotion materials much sooner than August 25, 1930, in order to sell GM upper management on the program. The article "General Motors' Fisher Body Emblem Has a Royal Background," which appeared in the in-house newsletter *Fisher in the News*, noted that two scale models of the royal Napoleonic Coach apparently were created and available in the late 1920s. Since the newsletter was dated 1984, the author believes these are the same two master models made at Fleetwood being referred to and the same ones referred to by Norman E. May.

There is good evidence that Walter Leuschner (either as a Fleetwood contractor or employee) was responsible for technically directing the construction of the master models needed for public scrutiny by October 1930. There are several accounts (T.S. Fuller, L.S. Walter and the FAHS archivist) describing Fleetwood as the source of the original or master model miniature Napoleonic Coaches. There is evidence of an initialed blueprint as proof that a Walter C. Leuschner was involved in the design process at Fleetwood in July 1930. (He was definitely a good draftsman, because his detailed coach component illustrations appeared in every Fisher Body publication telling kids how to build his miniature model Napoleonic Coach.) There are ten black-and-white negatives showing miniature model coach parts probably made by Fleetwood craftsmen.

Walter C. Leuschner probably followed in the footsteps of his father, Max, and became the technical director, or chief engineer, of the Louis Ruhe Royal Coach Factory in Berlin in the teens and '20s. He came to this country in 1928 with his family Gertrude and Kurt after being laid off. The Fisher brothers, learning of the coachwright either on their payroll or as an independent contractor, tapped his skills and knowledge to conceive a hybrid, three-dimensional coach model to modernize their logo and to support the foundation they were planning. The author believes that Leuschner, as a coachwright and technical expert, would have been familiar with the great European coaches past and present. He would have drawn upon his historical coach knowledge. Frank Riess converted these ideas to standard blueprint plans. Leuschner was also an excellent illustrator who was able to explain his coach construction ideas visually. Fleetwood had 350–400 Old World craftsmen who handcrafted custom automobile bodies for the rich and famous, who easily could have made the master models from technical blue prints.

Where are the Leuschner-Riess master models today? One master model is believed to be on display at the FBCG Foundation and Mini-Museum in Eagle Point, Oregon, and the other master model is believed to be located at the GM Heritage Center, Sterling Heights, Michigan.

Plans and Instructions

After the two prototype coach models were built, a more simplified set of plans (based on the master set, but not as elaborate) and instructions were drawn up. This set of plans and instructions were distributed to young boy contestants to build their models.

Combining the instruction manual and three large blueprint sheets drawn actual size with a nationwide advertising and promotion program, the Fisher Body Craftsman's Guild was officially off and running in early 1930. By the 1931–32 competition year, this complicated set of prints had been replaced by a book called *Plans and Instructions for Building a Miniature Model Napoleonic Coach* (12" × 20" laid flat, 25 pages), which consisted of full-size drawings and a full-scale color schematic (front view, rear view and side view). Four basic, brushable Duco paint colors would be applied by contestants (a vermillion, a blue-black or dark blue, a light blue called Lilac Blue, and white).[16] The scale of the Leuschner miniature model Napoleonic Coach was approximately 1/18 (1" equals 1.60') and the finished model measured approximately 18" × 8" × 10" (L × W × H).

Guild Purpose and Organization

PURPOSE

The Guild was a foundation throughout the 1930s, then became an educational program for the development of craftsmanship and creative ability among boys, and finally, it became an educational movement, spreading to other parts of the world, and described in GM publications worldwide. But there were broader, more idealistic, corporate visions for the Craftsman's Guild.

A Guild print ad in the *Saturday Evening Post*, November 15, 1930, stated, "It is the sincere desire of the builders of Bodies by Fisher that tomorrow shall see this country peopled by men to whom honor can be given for their ability to design well and build soundly wherever their generation may require."

The small sales booklet given to contestants in 1930 stated, "The man who can work surely, swiftly and deftly with his hands is always preferable in any employment" (*Crafts Guilds, Their History and Influence*, 1930).

A Guild print ad appearing in *Ladies' Home Journal*, June 1931, stated, "The Fisher Body Corporation sponsored this inspiring movement believing that this exercise in creative talent, this quickening of the hand of youth, are essential steps toward the development of high ideals—that only through training the coming generation can fine craftsmanship be perpetuated and superior coachcraft assured."

To quote William A. Fisher, GM vice president, Fisher Body Division's general manager, and president of the Guild, from *The Guildsman* (1934): "Above all, it is only the fully trained and competent craftsman which can carry this machine civilization to higher levels of efficiency and service to mankind in the future. ... And so I tell you that the one crowning need of the world today is for craftsmen — men who are trained, men who are masters of every detail of their jobs. ... The skill of mind and hand together is the way to happiness."

William A. Fisher called it an educational movement in 1934. Print literature and sales brochures called it an educational foundation up through 1937, when it was taken over and institutionalized by the corporation.

ORGANIZATION

The Craftsman's Guild was organized with William A. Fisher (third eldest of the seven Fisher brothers) as Guild president and Daniel Carter Beard, commissioner of the

Boy Scouts of America (BSA), as honorary Guild president. GM Canada Ltd., called the Canadian or Maple Leaf Section, had a similar structure. Frank Riess was the Guild technical director and Walter C. Leuschner was on the technical staff. They presided at both U.S. and Canadian judging venues, supervised their working judges and directed the scoring of the coach entries.

There was an international board of judges consisting of GM leaders such as Charles F. Kettering and Harley J. Earl as well as leaders from top U.S. educational institutions (e.g., MIT, Caltech, Georgia Tech, Carnegie Mellon, Penn State, Notre Dame, the universities of Michigan and Alabama, Ohio State and the Polytechnic Institute of Brooklyn) that approved the final scholarship award recommendations from the working judges. Also, there was an advisory board consisting of top educators as well as public and vocational school superintendents from across the U.S. and Canada. As the presidents of some of the most prestigious universities in America, such as MIT's Dr. Karl T. Compton, and Rhodes scholar, Nobel Prize winner, and former Caltech president Robert A. Millikan, their job was to advocate the values and virtues of the Guild. They promoted this public relations program as though it were an educational institution.

The Fisher alliance with the Boy Scouts was essential to the Guild's success, as not only did they promote common skills and philosophies (woodcraft, handicrafts, and the mind and hands working together), but coach building time and labor would be competing with Merit Badge time and labor. A strong endorsement of educators would also be needed, as coach building would be competing with the time needed for high school course work.

Advertising, Promotions and Incentives

Local Exhibitions

On October 24, 1930, the *Detroit Times* Chapter of the Fisher Body Craftsman's Guild had one of the master models on display at the Times Building, 1370 Cass Avenue, Detroit, Michigan. Boys and their parents could stop by to inspect the master model coach and hear Walter Leuschner and Frank Riess explain details of the model's construction. Mr. Leuschner was kept busy telling the boys and their parents how to form and assemble the various parts and how to paint and add trim. The miniature Napoleonic Coach was displayed in a plate glass case. Boys who decided they were interested right away received (free of charge) a full set of plans and instructions, a bronze Guild pin, a membership card signed by Daniel Carter Beard, the color prints or color schematic for painting the coach, specifications and a booklet containing the rules. Boys were told to watch the *Sunday Times* for instructions on building a coach.[17] Raymond Doerr stated in a *Detroit Times* interview conducted August 26, 1931, after having been named one of the top $5,000 scholarship winners just a few days earlier, that seeing the master model was a critically important step in his success.

Promotions

All of GM's motor divisions were involved. Young boys could go with a parent to their local Chevrolet, Buick, Oldsmobile, Cadillac-LaSalle, and Oakland-Pontiac dealer

All of GM's divisions were involved in promoting the miniature Napolenoic Coach competition and boys could go to their local Chevrolet, Buick, Viking, Oldsmobile, Cadillac-LaSalle, or Oakland-Pontiac dealership to enroll. The 25" × 28" full color window poster, shown in the window of a Buick dealership (circa 1932), announces the formation of the Fisher Body Craftsman's Guild, with the miniature model Napoleonic Coach Competition and $75,000 in awards. *General Motors Corporation.*

and pick up a detailed set of plans, an official Guild bronze pin and a Guild membership card. Direct mail played an important part in the advertising of the Guild as well as advertising in large-circulation newspapers and nationally distributed magazines.

Along with the GM dealer network, newspapers, magazines, direct mail, radio and various other aspects of the advertising world were used to promote the Guild's scholarship program. For example, all of the GM dealers put up window posters to attract young boys' attention. When "Dad" would come in to look at a new or used car, "Junior" was told about the Guild by the salesman, and thus a new potential contestant was signed up.

There were large (25" × 28") full color window posters for the dealers to promote the Guild. One 1932 poster said, "BOYS!! $75,000 in Awards, Fisher Body Craftsman Guild offers 4 University Scholarships of 4 years each and 1,120 other awards. DON'T DELAY … ENROLL TODAY (10 Awards for Seniors and 10 Awards for Juniors in every State and Canadian Guild District)."

In 1930–31, the first year of the competition, the newspaper publicity measured by Fisher Body and recorded in GM Media Archives photographs (GM asset 089698) showed 32 metropolitan newspaper sponsors, with a total circulation of 5,500,000, or 22,000,000 readers (four readers per paper). This translated into one million lines of publicity generation and 880 million reader impressions. Along with all participating GM dealerships, this generated 145,000–148,000 youth enrollees and 1,350 coach model entries in the first year. By the second year, 402,000 kids had enrolled but produced only about 547 coach models.[18]

In 1931 the embroidered emblem containing the diamond-shaped Guild insignia

The diamond-shaped Craftsman's Guild insignia, or trademark, first appeared on the "tams" (french beret) in 1931 and was worn by 104 state winners who attended the first Guild convention and banquet in Detroit. Tams were worn in the 1930s and 1940s by state and regional winners at the convention. By the 1950s, the tams disappeared, and the insignia appeared on the breast pocket of the blue blazers worn by the 40 regional winners at the Guild convention and banquet. The wreath from the Cadillac emblem was adopted in the 1960s as the Guild insignia for trophies and booklets. *Author's collection, with permission of General Motors Corporation.*

(with the initials FBCG) appeared on the berets or tams worn proudly by state and regional winners at the Guild convention held each summer in Detroit. All Guild literature throughout the Craftsman's Guild competition, until it was discontinued in 1968, carried the diamond-shaped insignia or trademark.

Also, 32 leading newspapers around the country became official sponsors, and each newspaper formed a chapter of the Guild to further promote the contest. As part of their responsibility, the newspapers published a series of weekly lessons, tips, and encouraging success stories (beginning in October of the contest year) to help the young builder sort through the often difficult and critical steps essential to building and completing a winning miniature model Napoleonic Coach. The young contestant could write to his local sponsoring newspaper with questions and the questions with answers would be printed in the paper the following week. Also, any other news pertaining to the Guild was published in the newspapers weekly to keep the young boys posted on what was happening within their chapter.

A long list of major newspapers joined the bandwagon of Guild supporters to help young boys win college scholarships during the height of the Depression. Among them were (as they were known in the 1930s) the *Detroit Times*, the *Wisconsin News*, the *News Bee*, the *Houston Press*, the *Seattle Times*, the *Spokane Press*, the *Dallas News*, the *El Paso Post*, the *Oklahoman*, the *Sun Telegraph*, *San Antonio Light*, *Washington* (D.C.) *Herald*, the *Wichita Beacon*, *Globe-Democrat*, *Baltimore American*, the *States*, *Georgian American*, *Boston American*, *Commercial Appeal*, *San Francisco Chronicle*, *Evening Journal*, *Times-Union*, *Miami Herald*, *Los Angeles Express*, *Portland* (Oregon) *Telegram*, and the *Indi-*

The first four scholarship winners from the 1931 Napoleonic Coach Competition, shown flanking William A. Fisher, president of the Guild. Left to right: Raymond S. Doerr (age 19, senior $5,000 award, from Battle Creek, Michigan), Howard Jennings (age 15, junior, $5,000 award, from Denver, Colorado), Albert W. Fischer (age 18, senior, $5,000 award, from Waukegan, Illinois) and Donald C. Burnham (age 15, junior, $5,000 award, from Pittsburgh, Pennsylvania). *General Motors Corporation.*

anapolis Star. Not only was this good advertising for the FBCG, but it gained great notice for the individual newspapers as well. Maybe a young boy in their community would be a national scholarship winner one day.

On August 24, 1931, the Guild convention banquet hall at the GM Building Auditorium (on West Grand Boulevard) was decorated with stage scenery to look like the medieval Guild Hall Square in Brussels, Belgium, complete with candles for lighting and waiters in doublet and hose. A Who's Who of hundreds of top GM executives came to the Guild banquet to celebrate with the winners. The four top national scholarship winners, two in the junior division and two in the senior division, were announced, namely Donald C. Burnham, junior division (age 15), $5,000 award, from W. Lafayette, Indiana; Howard Jennings, junior division (age 15), $5,000 award, from Denver, Colorado; Raymond S. Doerr, senior division (age 19), $5,000 award, from Battle Creek, Michigan; Albert W. Fischer, senior division (age 18), $5,000 award, from Waukegan, Illinois. Alfred P. Sloan, Jr., president of General Motors, promised jobs for the four young men after they graduated from college. Everyone in attendance sang the Fisher Body Craftsman's Guild song to the tune of "Auld Lang Syne."[19] Syndicated columnists such as Bob Considine interviewed winners and wrote about them, and Arthur Brisbane (master craftsman of the newspaper guild, the highest paid syndicated columnist in 1931) paid tribute to the first four 1931 national scholarship winners. The *Detroit Times* in reporting the Guild banquet called it a "Party by Fisher."[20] Silent film star Colleen Moore posed for photographs with Leuschner, the Fisher brothers and the four top scholarship winners.

At the Guild convention, the 104 winners from the states toured the GM Proving Grounds, Ternstedt, Cadillac and Fisher plants. Ternstedt made hardware (e.g., hinges, door locks, and seat adjustors) for Fisher Bodies. There was a trip to Bob-Lo Island Park via steamer that included a picnic. There was swimming, golf, and dinner at the Orchard Lake Country Club, a Detroit Tigers ball game and time for some autographs, and most important of all, a shopping spree.

In 1931, the *Detroit Times*, which was one of the FBCG sponsoring newspapers, printed the headline "Four Winners Named," and the newspaper explained fully the results of the first competition. It also showed the pictures of the first four top national scholarship winners on the front page. On a follow-up page within the newspaper pictures of all 104 convention attendees were published.

Another highlight was that the four national scholarship winning models would be on private display at the General Motors Building Auditorium, Tuesday, August 25, 1931, for a group of 350 business and industry leaders, followed by public display Wednesday, August 26, through Saturday, August 29.[21] The four top winning models and one of the master models were located in a roped-off area and all the other state winners occupied the remainder of the auditorium. An ad in the *Detroit Times* invited the public:

> EXHIBITION— Miniature Model Napoleonic Coaches, Built by Boys from every State, Members of the Fisher Body Craftsman's Guild, the Four Coaches that earned $5,000 university scholarships for their builders, OPENS TODAY at 2:30 PM and continues daily 12:00 Noon to 9:00 PM through Saturday August 29th. General Motors Building Auditorium, ADMISSION FREE.

The same medieval town scene made with stage scenery that had surrounded the perimeter of the Guild banquet hall also provided a Middle Ages ambiance for this coach exhibition hall.

In 1932, the second year of the Guild competition, Fisher Body introduced the Petite Napoleonic Coach promotional toy, a cardboard cutout project for boys and girls, to promote interest and enthusiasm in the Guild's miniature Napoleonic Coach competition. The intricate petite coach parts were cut with scissors from four-color lithograph card stock sheets and constructed with slots and tabs, glue, tape, and toothpicks. The *Petite Napoleonic Coach* card stock kits were offered by the newspaper chapters of the Guild such as the *Knoxville Journal* and were to be used as toys or decorations. All boys and girls under 16 years of age, within the carrier limits of the *Knoxville Journal*, for example, were eligible to participate. The finished cardboard models were hand delivered to the *Knoxville Journal* editorial offices. There were 34 prizes and $200 in total cash awards ($50, $25, $15 and a lot at $2.50 each) to the best models for neatness and exactness, when accompanied by a six-month subscription.

By 1934 the FBCG had well over 400,000 enrollees (including the U.S. and Canada) involving a far-flung network of parents, manual arts instructors, teachers, school principals, BSA leaders, YMCA leaders, college and university administrators, and vocational education training directors and supervisors.

In 1934 the *Guildsman*, the official magazine of the Fisher Body Craftsman's Guild, was introduced with the following quote: "Behold, The Craftsman of Tomorrow!" ... The boy depicted at work on his coach is symbolic of the youths who are obtaining first-hand knowledge of true craftsmanship through the Fisher Body Craftsman's Guild — youths who will be the craftsmen of the morrow." The back cover had the diamond-shaped Guild insignia.

Name the magazine, and a Fisher Body Craftsman's Guild ad was in it: *American Boy, Youth Companion, Popular Mechanics, Boys' Life, National Geographic, Ladies' Home Journal*, the *Saturday Evening Post*, the *Literary Digest*, and others.

Other forms of communication also promoted the Guild. *The Guildsman* magazine was distributed monthly (1934), then bimonthly (1935), to all potential contestants or enrollees. Leuschner and Riess went on a city-to-city road tour with a master model exhibition to promote the Guild. Winning coaches were displayed at the 1933–34 Chicago World's Fair and the 1939 New York World's Fair, toured the U.S., and were displayed in local department stores. At the annual Guild convention, when the winners were announced, the nationwide radio broadcast was narrated by famous commentators. On their visit to Canada in 1939, the King and Queen of England viewed an exhibit containing the 1935 First National Scholarship, Junior Division, award winning Napoleonic Coach built by Robert Rasmussen of Regina, Saskatchewan. Publicity for this event would have boosted the prestige of the Guild competition.

INCENTIVES

The whole concept of the Guild competition was for the top winners to receive prize money for a scholarship to a college of their choice. What average Americans could afford to send their kids to college during the Depression? For example, in 1931, the prize money consisted of $5,000 for each of the four top national winners (two junior winners and two senior winners), and a total of $50,000 in scholarships and cash prizes, 98 all-expenses-paid trips to Detroit for the Guild convention and banquet, 882 other cash awards and 1,120 gold awards ranging from $15 to $100.

There were ten awards per state for juniors and ten for seniors. A first-place state award was worth $10 and second place $5. The two best coach makers in each state (one junior and one senior) were sent to Detroit at the Fishers' expense and given $50 spending money.

The two best coaches in each state, judged locally by traveling judges in 1931, were shipped to Detroit for exhibition. In the 1932 *Plans and Instructions* book, contestants were told how to build a shipping crate, and it is believed that after that, all entries were shipped by the contestants directly to Detroit for judging by the Leuschner-Riess team. The 98 trips represented one junior and one senior winner from each of the 48 states and the District of Columbia, and in 1931, there were 104 state winners making the trip to Detroit, with 112 in 1932 and 116 in 1934, which included the Canadians' top winners.[22]

In 1932 there were $75,000 in scholarships and cash awards available, of which $30,000 was for six national scholarship awards of $5,000 each. There were four national scholarship winners from the U.S. The Canadians joined the Craftsman's Guild competition in 1932 through the sponsorship of GM Canada Ltd., so there were also two top Canadian scholarship winners in 1932. There were 140 Canadian districts and three regional cities (Regina, Montreal, and Toronto) for judging their coaches. Two boys who build a winning coach in each state and each Canadian district would win $100 and a chance to attend the four-day Guild convention. There were 18 other cash awards available for boys in each state and each Canadian district from $15 to $100.

In 1934, the total U.S. and Canadian scholarship awards available equaled $51,000 and included 16 top U.S. winners, and 8 top Canadian winners. There were 116 all-expenses-paid trips to Detroit for the Guild convention.

Napoleonic Coach Competition, Master Craftsman Class

"One dealer alone enrolled 350 boys and actually had 14 kids enter finished coaches in the competition. … Though they concluded that the average per dealer was only 7 enrollees, it seemed that the general effort was to build "good will" rather than sell automobiles."[23]

One commercial magazine's estimate of the number of model coaches was 500,000 (*Popular Mechanics*, December 1933). An internal GM publication (*Chevrolet Friends* magazine) suggested Napoleonic Coach models numbered two million. A Fisher Body press release from 1966 suggests 600+ coaches were made in the first year, and a 1931 *Detroit Times* article reported 1,350 model entries. The author prefers the latter estimate (1,350), reported by the *Detroit Times* on August 31, 1931. Perhaps 6,000 to 7,200 coach models were made nationwide over the course of the coach building era (1930 to 1948, but excluding the war years 1941 through 1945).

Starting in 1934, coach models that competed in one year could be reentered the following year, although some updating might be needed to conform to any new specifications or requirements. This boosted the annual count of coach model entries and gave kids more time to perfect their work. Robert Russell entered his 1934 coach again in 1937 with the hope that the competition would be kinder. Wilfred McClain entered his 1932 coach again in 1933. Henry B. Larzelere noted that Fisher changed the length and shape of the body hangers in 1936. Many boys entered the competition year after year, some as many as four or five times. Each time was a learning experience and each time their model got better and better until they won a national scholarship award.

Even though many kids enrolled at their local Chevrolet dealers, and despite many sets of coach plans being handed out, not many Napoleonic Coaches were actually built. With a U.S. Guild enrollment of 145,000–148,000 members in 1930–31, 1,350 Napoleonic Coaches (a construction rate of less than 1 percent) were actually built and entered in the 1931 competition.[24] In 1932, it is believed there were 402,000 enrollees and 547 model coach entries, for a construction rate of 0.136 percent. Overall, this means that less than one-half of a percent of the enrollees, on the average, were able to actually build a coach entry, for an average of about 11–28 coaches per state. In the state of Washington in 1932, for example, indications are that over 2,000 sets of plans were distributed to youths in that state, but only 19 coaches were entered in the competition.

Shipping Crate

As of 1932 the *Plans and Instructions* booklet told contestants how to build a packing crate in order to send their Napoleonic Coach by Railway Express "in good condition" to Detroit. The inside dimensions of the shipping crate would measure 20" (L) × 11" (W)

× 11" (H) and be constructed from ¾" thick wood, and constructed with 8- or 10-penny nails. The lid was to be screwed in place with countersunk screws. The coach body was to be cradled and restrained independently from the reach pole chassis.

Judging and Scoring Coaches

For the final judging at the national level, and selection of the top national scholarship awards (two junior and two senior division), a clear-cut and accurate system was devised for judging the craftsmanship of each individual coach. Each judge had a booklet containing eight sheets of information for scoring 200 items for each entry. The total score consisted of the following categories as described in the *Guildsman* (1934): Fidelity to Scale, 100 points; Metalcraft, 75 points (for homemade or home cast metal parts it was 75 points, and minus 25 points if purchased); Woodcraft, 75 points; Upholstery, 75 points; and Paint Craft, 75 points, for a grand total of 400 points. Six to eight judges rescored the same models and the points were averaged for a final score. Frank Riess, technical director, and Walter C. Leuschner, technical staff, advised the other working judges who included industrial arts teachers or crafts experts from the Detroit public school system.

FIDELITY TO SCALE

Fidelity to scale meant determining how close to the blueprint dimensions the model had been built. In order to judge the coaches objectively, a series of 24 metal templates were used to measure many aspects of the finished models. For example, templates or metal gauges were used to measure wheel base distance (12" center to center), window opening location, door pillar width, compound roof and body contours, front wheel and rear wheel camber, front and rear wheel diameter, wheel spoke shape (or "whaleback" design), reach pole center height at the front, and reach pole center height at the rear footman's platform.[25] If a dimension was found to be perfect or within tolerances, such as the front axle assembly, then five points were awarded to the model, but if the dimension was not in tolerance, points were deducted. For every ⅛" error in a particular dimension, compared to the template, one point was deducted. So, if the wheel base was supposed to be 12" long and the contestant's was 11⅞" or ⅛" short, only four out of the possible five points would have been awarded.

There were also areas of the model to be scored that were more subjective; for example, (1) body rope molding twist or pitch, (2) spoke, hub, and toe board pillar joinery, (3) four identical capitals with eagles, which had to be carved from balsa wood and carefully fitted, (4) upholstery and interior coach body trim as well as sewing, which had to be neat, clean and artistically done, (5) the purchased or handmade aluminum trim, which had to be cleaned and chased with engraving tools, (6) the quality of the fine sanding or filing that was needed, as scratches or tool marks on the wooden coach body or metal parts resulted in a loss of points, and (7) the application of several brushable Duco colors, previously mentioned, which had to be done neatly without visible brush strokes.[26] A suspension that allowed the body to list or lean to the left or right lost points. The left side of the coach body had to be symmetric with the right side. The judging of each model was anonymous and each model was known only by a number.

WOODCRAFT AND METALCRAFT

For the Woodcraft judging of the models, seven categories were used as a basis for scoring: wheels, rear axle and footman's board, the body, front axle and front gear, pole, tonneau block, and finally general woodwork. The sides and top of the coach body were compound surfaces (curved in two planar directions) and these were checked by template. All of the moldings were checked for detail including the correct spacing for the wooden molding spindles and correct left-hand and right-hand twist of wire trim. Eleven points were awarded in this area for a perfect score, and 18 separate items were checked just concerning the brackets and clips used.

If the entire coach model, or any part thereof, was built from a kit, points were deducted accordingly during judging to make the competition fair for those boys who worked from scratch. If a metal kit was used, for example, the maximum allowable points were 50 for Metalcraft instead of 75. In other words, the coach maker was penalized 25 points for using the metal kit.

Judging was time consuming as well, and it was not unusual for one judge to take 30 minutes or longer to score one model. In order to choose the four best coach models, the judges had to recheck many of the better models numerous times. The Leuschner master models, the gold standards of the competition, were used as references and benchmarks. *Popular Mechanics*, in their December 1933 issue, suggested that up to two hours per coach was required for the scoring process to be completed.

Some Napoleonic Coach Details

Duco nitrocellulose lacquer (a DuPont trademarked product) was applied by brush (spray paint bombs hadn't been invented yet). Aluminum parts had to be cleaned and chased with engraver's tools, and some metal parts had to be cast in plaster-of-Paris molds using "Woods Metal," a nonferrous, low melting temperature alloy. The *Guildsman* magazine told participants how to make molds in order to cast small parts from molten lead, pewter, antimony or 50/50 solder (oven dry the plaster-of-Paris mold, apply several coats of shellac to the inside of the mold as a sealer, apply a caster oil coat or powdered graphite coat to the inside of the mold surface as a parting compound). Rope molding used on the coach body as trim was made by twisting bare coat-hanger wire, for example, in a helix form, soldering the pieces together and then filing the piece flat to the centerline.

All the coach models were actual working models; the wheels turned, the front axle turned on the fifth wheel, the suspension deflected, passenger steps would slide out and fold down, and the doors opened by miniature door handles. Photographic glass used in the door windows would slide up and down with a strap. The operating door latch (bolt and detent), the door hinges, as well as the four ratchets used to adjust the leather body suspension straps were all handmade. Brass or copper sheet wheel ornamentation had to be stamped from a homemade tool-and-die set in order for so many pieces to be identical. Rectangular blocks of mahogany, maple, pine, and balsa had to be carved into compound surfaces for the coach's body, or seat cushions, or capitals with eagles, and assembled to exacting dimensions ($\pm \frac{1}{16}$" accuracy) in hopes of faithfully reproducing the master model coach.

Coach Builder's Biographic Survey

A biographic survey form was designed and distributed in June 1997 to a random sample of coach builders by Skip Geear of the FBCG Foundation. The survey was concerned with entry years, the number of model entries by each contestant, the awards received, the labor hours invested, tools and techniques used, family support, kit use, military service, occupation, Traveling Coach construction, and confidentiality. Out of 12 responses, one requested confidential handling. At the time of the miniature model Napoleonic Coach competition, the participants ranged in age from 15 to 20 years. The results are used throughout this chapter to complete the coach history.[27]

Some Ingenious Ideas Used to Build a Coach

The contestants had to use their imagination in order to succeed. For example, in the 1933 competition, watch springs were cut down to make door springs, piano wire was found to be adaptable to leaf spring veins, coach body window panes were cut from discarded photographic plates, and silk guitar wire was used to make decorative trim tassels. Often the contestant's workshop consisted of a table and a sewing machine. A dentist's drill and burrs constituted the milling machine and a sewing machine might be adapted to be a jigsaw. Nut picks made excellent burnishing tools. A fine jeweler's saw was needed, and files were made into engraving instruments. In many places miniature nuts and bolts (like old carriage bolts) were used to assemble the coach just as if it were the real thing in the early 1800s.

Charles W. Gadd (1933 scholarship winner) converted a sewing machine to a metal-cutting jigsaw, built a small lathe and forge, and utilized dental methods including the lost wax process to mold parts. His dentist taught him a sheet metal stamping method.

Walter Preston (1933; Los Angeles, California) molded "plastic wood" to replicate wheel trim parts, and similarly, Wilfred McClain (first-place state winner; Lawrence, Kansas; 1931 and 1932) made plaster molds for casting of wheel trim from lead. Robert Russell (North Dakota; 1933, '34, and '37) found the end grain of maple particularly useful for making lead molds for casting pieces of trim. Monroe Bean (first-place state winner, Maine, 1931) built a jigsaw using a sewing machine head. Don Burnham (1931 national scholarship winner) made his own dies to stamp the rope molding in brass, and stamped roof trim moldings from 0.005″ thick brass and filled them with solder. Albert Fischer (1931 scholarship winner) used sheet metal forming dies for making trim. Stanley Knochel (1933 scholarship winner) showed the author the professionally engraved tool and die set he used for stamping a bas-relief pattern into thin brass or copper trim pieces used around the wheel spokes.

William Smith (1933–1937, New York) applied gold leaf, instead of homemade gold paint, as his father was in the picture frame repair business and touched up expensive antique gilded frames.[28] Charles Gadd got the precise name of the gold paint used on the master models when he visited the Leuschner-Riess exhibition when it came near his home of Spokane, Washington.

Napoleonic Coach Kits

Initially each model was to be built from scratch, but the free enterprise system invented coach kits. For example, in the early years of the Guild competition, a kit was available for purchase from the George D. Wanner Company of Dayton, Ohio. The complete kit contained everything needed to build a coach: rectangular blocks of wood cut to size, but not shaped; brass stock and rough aluminum castings; screws, nuts, bolts and washers; upholstery trim and even glue. Glue was available in tubes, but alternatively, glue could be melted in a pot (within a pot of boiling water) on a stove or hot plate. The metal castings were supplied in rough cast form and had to be cleaned, filed, shaped, and chased. All the wood materials had to be hand-carved. Wood materials included mahogany, maple, pine and balsa. The total kit cost $9.75, or individual components could be purchased separately, such as a metal parts kit, a wood kit, a trim kit and a Duco paint kit of nitrocellulose lacquer finishes.

In early 1938, a complete kit assembly was available from the Lewis Model Kit Company, Detroit, Michigan, for as little as $2.50. After the war, however, the coach kits were supplied by H.C. Stubbs Company of Detroit, Michigan, at a cost of $20. H.C. Stubbs Company also supplied individual kits such as: Kit No. 1, Wood ($7.81); Kit No. 2, Metal ($9.01); and Kit No. 3, Trim and Paint ($8.92). Kit No. 1, Wood, contained cement, die-cut sheet, and wood blocks (rough dimensioned wood blocks of white pine, poplar, mahogany and balsa that had to be carved and shaped). Kit No. 2, Metal, contained all castings that would require a minimum amount of hand finishing; material for all metal parts other than castings; and all bolts, escutcheons, pins, nuts, nails and screws. Kit No. 3, Trim and Paint, contained all upholstery trim and paint required for the complete coach. All the lacquer paint needed was contained in the complete coach kit (Lilac Blue, black-blue, vermillion, white, and gold-colored bronzing liquid from E.I. du Pont de Nemours and Co. Inc., Automotive Finishes Division, Detroit, Michigan).

Labor Hours Required

The complexity is revealed in the number of labor hours required. A professional model maker at the time estimated 1,600 hours would be required. The top seven scholarship winners in 1933 (U.S. and Canadian) averaged 1,000 hours (*Popular Mechanics*, December 1933). Examples of the labor hours other national scholarship winners committed to this task include Raymond S. Doerr (1931), 2,150 hours; Albert W. Fischer (1931), 2,000 hours; Stanley Knochel (1933), 1,000 hours; and Donald C. Burnham (1931), 1,000 hours.

The 11 survey forms the author reviewed showed a range of 1,000 to 2,000 hours needed to make a Napoleonic Coach. Completing a competitive Napoleonic Coach model appears to have required one-half to one full man-year of effort. (A full-time employee works about 2,080 hours per year). As reported in the *Detroit Times*, Raymond S. Doerr had a year off between high school and college (University of Michigan) to build his national scholarship award coach.

The Guildsman, *Official Magazine*
of the Fisher Body Craftsman's Guild

The tool used in 1934 and 1935 by Fisher Body to communicate more directly with Guild members was *The Guildsman*, a 12–15 page magazine loaded with facts and information. This was the official "rag" that kept the far-flung organization connected and kept members apprised of upcoming events and deadlines. There were editorials and articles written for the Guild by role models such as Charles F. Kettering, Alfred P. Sloan, Jr., Daniel C. Beard and Brigadier General C.H. Mitchell, and there were well researched and professionally written articles and stories about the history of transportation, transportation technology and automotive research (particularly GM auto technology and research).[29] There were sports and adventure stories for boys, advertisements about GM technology and products. There was a story about child actor Jackie Cooper, a fellow Guildsman building a Napoleonic Coach. In some of the later 1935 bimonthly issues there even were GM automobile ads and an introduction to a new 20 ton press at one of the Fisher stamping plants. Every Guildsman was part of the Detroit "action."

The Guildsman exposed kids to new technology and ideas. For example, in 1934 the new streamlined, high speed Little Zip and Zephyr were revolutionizing rail transportation with stainless steel bodied cars and internal combustion engines. Youth read about aerodynamics and wind tunnel testing, automatic refrigeration processes, and automotive engineering advances such as streamlined auto bodies, the Fisher brothers' all-steel body called Unisteel, the solid steel Turret Top, all-silent shifting, and knee action suspension.

There was coverage of the Guild convention at the 1934 Chicago World's Fair (second season), where the coaches had been judged and displayed for millions of visitors in the GM Hall of Progress. Readers learned about the medieval theme of the Guild banquet and the replica of the guild hall square in Brussels, Belgium, surrounding the Napoleonic Coach winner's banquet hall area. They learned about one of the banquet speakers, General Curtiss LeMay, newspaper coverage by the reporter and columnist Bob Considine, and coast-to-coast coverage by radio hook-up as the top national scholarship winners were selected.[30]

There were brief vignettes by previous Guild scholarship winners and how-to articles and tips written by Leuschner and Riess in their exclusive column called "Coachcraft." Boys wrote in with their technical coach building questions, and answers appeared in *The Guildsman* for everyone to read. Quotations or admonitions from the world's greatest philosophers appeared on the back cover (along with the diamond-shaped Guild insignia), such as the Ralph Waldo Emerson quotation, "Nothing worthwhile was ever achieved without enthusiasm." *The Guildsman* had four monthly issues in 1934 and four bimonthly issues in 1935, and then disappeared without explanation.

Traveling Coach Competition,
Apprentice Craftsman Class, Inaugurated 1934–35

Still considered an educational foundation, in 1934–35 the competition was expanded to include the Traveling Coach competition, for the Apprentice Craftsman Class (beginners). This model was simpler in construction, less intricate and less ornate, representing

Brothers Do It! C. E. Wilson, president of GM, congratulates Michael and Robert Welther after the "grand slam" in the 1947 Fisher Body Craftsman's Guild competition. Michael won the senior division and Robert won the junior division top national awards of $5,000 each. Their father, M. J. Welther, was at the time a foreman in Fisher Body's Process Development Plant in Detroit. Two duplicate awards were made to other contestants because Michael and Robert were both sons of a GM employee. *General Motors Corporation.*

an 1835 vintage coach. As mentioned earlier, the Guild's Traveling Coach had a close resemblance to the La Topaze Coach, a simpler, cleaner design used by Napoleon for his nuptials with Marie-Louise. The master model(s) of the Traveling Coach as well as the *1934–35 Plans and Instructions for Building a Miniature Model Traveling Coach* (a book measuring 9½" × 11⅞" when folded in half) were probably designed by the Walter Leuschner–Frank Riess team. These plans and instructions had no dimensions for parts, but were drawn full scale so the contestant could cut and fit parts to the black design lines.

1934–35 Traveling Coach Competition Regions

The Traveling Coach competition was important because it introduced the idea of regional competition, where the top winner from a group of states eventually competed against other regional winners for the top prize money. This became the backbone of the model car competition of the '40s, '50s and '60s, and was important for maintaining fairness or a level playing field, and assured a nationwide and geographic distribution of scholarships and awards.

For the Traveling Coach competition, two boys (one from each junior and senior division) in each of the designated judging regions shown below, whose coaches received the highest average score, would be selected for 802 state awards (16 per state) and 18 regional awards, which included 18 trips to the annual Guild convention in August 1935.[31] The total cash awards were $25,000 without any university scholarships. The state awards were: first place, $75; second place, $50; third place, $25; and finally five $10 cash awards for runners-up. An Apprentice Certificate of Completion was awarded to all entries. Although the Napoleonic Coaches were shipped by the contestants to Detroit to be judged, Guild regions and cities were set up to handle the judging of the Traveling Coaches. The regions, and their shipping destinations (shown in parentheses), were as follows:

Region 1. ME, VT, NH, MA, CT, RI (Boston)

Region 2. NY, PA, NJ (New York City)

Region 3. WV, VA, MD, DE, DC (Washington, DC)

Region 4. KY, TN, NC, SC, MS, AL, GA, FL (Atlanta)

Region 5. MI, WI, IL, IN, OH (Detroit)

Region 6. ND, SD, NE, KS, MN, IA, MO (Omaha)

Region 7. OK, AR, LA, TX (Dallas)

Region 8. WA, OR, MT, ID, WY (Los Angeles, Site 1)

Region 9. CA, NV, UT, CO, AZ, NM (Los Angeles, Site 2)

Beauty contests were held in these regional sites before the top winners were shipped to Detroit for the Guild convention and announcement of the Traveling Coach competition winners.

According to the C.W. McClellan interview cited above, the war slowed momentum and enthusiasm for the Napoleonic Coaches. By 1948 the miniature Napoleonic Coach competition was discontinued by Fisher Body Division based on a recommendation from the school superintendents that comprised the Guild's advisory board.[32] It is believed no coaches were received or judged in 1948. It is unknown how long the Traveling Coach competition lasted, if it ever became popular, or how many models were made, but presumably it was phased out in 1948 along with the Napoleonic Coaches. The scale model car competition, which had been started in 1937, would be King of the Road.

III

Model Car Competition (1937–1968)

Pre–World War II Model Car Competition (1937–1940)

INTRODUCTION

> The coaches meant following instructions—strictly a matter of craftsmanship—no creativity involved. The car design competition the following year was much more interesting [Tony Ingolia, 1937 second-place state winner, Louisiana, model car maker and career GM designer].[1]

GM and Fisher Body management decided to expand the market appeal of the Guild program and define a new direction with the 1937 1/12 scale model dream car competition. This competition continued concurrently with the Napoleonic Coach competition until 1948, when the coach competition was discontinued.

GENESIS AND INSPIRATION

It is believed that the work of Harley J. Earl, head of GM's Art and Colour Section (the forerunner of the Styling Section, GM Styling and GM Design), if not the man himself, was the primary inspiration for creation of the scale model car competition. Lawrence P. Fisher (then president of Cadillac) and Alfred P. Sloan, Jr. (the president of GM), hired Harley Earl, a custom automobile body designer and builder, and brought him to Detroit from Hollywood. The success of the 1927 LaSalle, which Earl designed for Larry Fisher and GM, demonstrated the potential for exterior aesthetics as a future consideration in the design and commercial success of automobiles. (At the same time, Mr. Earl inadvertently invented the field of automobile styling.) As proof of their belief in him, GM made Harley J. Earl head of Sloan's newly created Art and Colour Section.

Beginning around 1932, Earl regularly staged three-dimensional design competitions among his stylists (using scale clay models) to bring out their best ideas. Earl and the Fisher brothers judged these competitions and winners were often awarded expense-paid vacations.[2] In 1933 Gordon M. Buehrig participated as a GM designer in these competitions before going to work for Auburn-Cord-Duesenberg as chief body designer.

In addition, Harley Earl is credited with conceiving the idea of the futuristic show car or dream car, as in 1937, and probably before, he was hard at work on the 1938 Buick Y-Job. The Buick Y-Job would be the world's first show car and would be unveiled at GM's Futurama Exhibit at the New York Auto Show to get public reaction to ideas (engineering and design features) they were working on. Some of the features on the Y-Job were ten years ahead of their time, including the power drive convertible top, power windows, front fender line integrated into the door and body line and concealed running boards.[3]

Of course, Harley J. Earl wasn't the only one thinking about advanced, futuristic automobile designs. So were the Fisher brothers. Having successfully sold their family's Fisher Body Corporation to General Motors for $234.7 million, they wanted to produce their own automobile and were anticipating the acquisition of the Hudson Motor Company. By 1934 Frederic J. and Charles T. Fisher had retired from their GM management positions. At that time, Charles T. Fisher secretly commissioned Roscoe C. (Rod) Hoffman, a Detroit consulting engineer, to develop several prototype automobiles (including one for destructive testing) of a four-door, rear engine, streamlined, Chrysler Airflow–like fastback design called the X-8. These were the very latest in automotive design ideas at the time. Even though the deal with Hudson was never consummated, the Fisher brothers weren't thinking about advanced Napoleonic Coaches in the mid–1930s, but rather, advanced futuristic automobile designs. (The "Patron Saints" of the X-8 were not known until about 1978 and one of the prototypes still exists in the Brook Stevens Collection.[4])

MODEL COACHES VS. MODEL CARS

The Napoleonic Coach competition was a technical model-making contest. Although perfectionism, craftsmanship, and artist ability were essential, the key technical skill for success was the interpretation of two-dimensional blueprints and specifications and the conversion of that into three-dimensional parts and pieces. Tony Ingolia (1937 second-place state winner, Louisiana model car competition; and career GM designer) indicated that it didn't appeal to him because it looked more like following instructions.

In a February 1981 *Special Interest Autos* interview, Chuck Jordan stated that until the model car competition began, "no individualized characteristics or personal creativity were sought — the coach was in the strictest sense a craft project, with no variation sought or accepted, saving excellence in detail or finish."

The model car competition would test perfectionism, craftsmanship, and artistic ability, but most importantly, aesthetic design skills. The model car competition was a more open, creative design experience. In the February 1981 *SIA* interview Chuck Jordan discussed the automobile design contest: "The elements of innovation had entered in, and one can imagine that nothing would have been more exciting to the average car-oriented youth than to visualize his own version of John Tjaarda's 'Starkenberg' or William Stout's 'Scarab.'"

According to Peter Wozena (1937 state winner from Detroit and career GM designer), the 1937 model car competition specifications were inspired by William B. (Bill) Stout's streamlined Scarab designs of the 1930s.

If the long range purpose of the Guild was, among other things, to identify youth with an aesthetic eye, with potential for an automotive design and styling career, then a model car competition might be the better long term proposition. The decision was made to phase in the model car competition right alongside the Napoleonic Coach competition. This would be a market test for their new program idea.

The cover memo sent with the 1937 model car plans to each contestant made the

Fisher brothers' intent quite clear: "There are few schools in the country, where it is possible for a boy to learn motor car design. It is our hope, through the new Guild program, to discover any individuals who may be especially gifted for the work, and to take a hand in their training. You may be one of those individuals."[5]

The Fisher brothers surmised, and rightfully so, that future car designs would be capturing the imagination of America's youth, not Napoleonic Coaches. The 1937 model car competition was founded on ideas popular at the time. The ideas of a rear engine, air cooling, and streamlining were being looked at with favor, in some cases experimentally, by designers throughout the world. Raymond Loewy was concerned about "reduced air resistance at high speeds" in his 1934 Hupmobile designs. Dr. Ferdinand Porsche was working on a rear-engine, air-cooled design that one day would be marketed in the U.S. as the VW Bug or Beetle. The 1934 Chrysler Airflow, although it had a front engine mount, embodied the idea of a streamlined exterior. In 1934–35 Hans Ledwinka (automotive engineer and designer) at Ringhoffer Tatra-Werks AG was the first to combine them all (a fastback, four-door passenger car, with a rear engine, and air cooled) into an experimental automobile design called the Type 77 or "Tatra Scarab."

These advanced automotive ideas, along with conventional automotive ideas, were incorporated into the 1937 model car competition plans and instructions, as viewed in GM Media Archives images; the 1937 model car images in the *Detroit Times*; *Automobile Quarterly*, vol. 25, no. 2, 1987; and *Special Interest Autos* #61, February 1981.

1937 TO 1940 MODEL CAR COMPETITIONS*

A 1/12 scale, four-door family sedan was to be designed by the contestants with either a front or rear engine mount, consisting of a wheel base of 10", a tire track width of 5", an overall body width of 6" and 5½"overall body height with wheels. Interior seating, visibility and other and human factors considerations, were to be based on a 69" tall, 150-pound, seated male. The materials suggested for use in construction included balsa wood, white pine, California redwood, cypress and bass wood. Shellac and clear lacquer sealers were recommended, along with brushing lacquers for color, quick-dry color enamels, ordinary house paint and even spray paint. Contestants could fabricate their own wheels, 2⁵⁄₁₆" in diameter, from wooden rings and cardboard. For judging and scoring, originality and artistic merit were weighted with 33 percent of the available points, followed by proportion and balance (13 percent), workmanship (13 percent), paint and color application (13 percent), practicality of the design (13 percent) and scale fidelity (13 percent). Contestants were told to employ practical and safe ideas. The deadline for the competition was July 1, 1937, with an August convention planned for Detroit, Michigan.

A total of $47,350 in scholarships and cash was offered in 1937 consisting of two $5,000 four-year university scholarships (one each in the junior and senior divisions) as well as 686 state awards of first place, $100; second place, $75; third place, $50; and four runner-up awards of $25 each (for both junior and senior divisions). The same nine regional designations for the states used for the Traveling Coach, Apprentice Craftsman

---

*It is difficult to find any guild documentation dated 1938–1940. Don Burnham reports in his essay in Chapter IV that he gave a guild convention speech in 1939 or 1940. Walter Leuschner is believed to have died during this period and there may have been a lapse in the coach competition. The author theorizes that the guild operated continuously from 1937 to 1940, but evidence is sparse. In 1938 the Lewis Model Kit Company was producing a Napoleonic Coach kit.

The top Guild scholarship winners are shown with GM executives at the 1937 Guild banquet. The airflow model car on the table (middle) was made by the top senior division scholarship winner, Charles Bangert, Jr. (age 19), of London, Ohio, who won a $5,000 award. Theodore (Teddy) Mandel (holding his model) was the top junior division scholarship winner (at age 14) with a $5,000 award. The three youths (standing on the left of T. Mandel) cannot be identified, but were probably other scholarship winners. The three GM executives on the right examining the 1937 winning model entries were (left to right) Charles F. Kettering, director of research, William S. (Bill) Knudsen, GM president and William A. Fisher, GM vice president and Guild president. *General Motors Corporation.*

Class Competition, and discussed in Chapter II, were employed in the first model car competition, and 18 regional winners were given all-expenses-paid trips to the August Guild convention in Detroit.[6]

Boys ages 12 to 19 were eligible to participate, in age brackets similar to those employed for the other coach competitions. There was a junior and senior division as in the Napoleonic Coach competition. It appeared that teenagers from the U.S. and Canada were eligible to compete in the 1937 to 1940 model car competitions, as the 1937 competition brochure indicates a desire to promote handiwork and craftsmanship among boys of the North American continent, which would include Canada. Universities located in Toronto and Montreal were represented on the honorary board of judges. In addition, the Canadians were participating in the Napoleonic Coach competition through the Guild's Maple

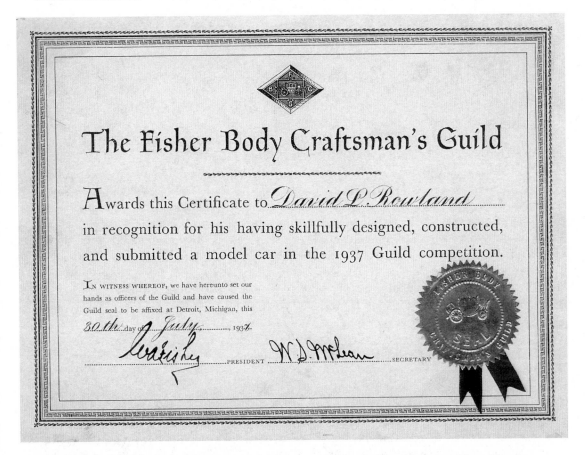

The Fisher Body Craftsman's Guild

Awards this Certificate to *David L Rowland*

in recognition for his having skillfully designed, constructed, and submitted a model car in the 1937 Guild competition.

In witness whereof, we have hereunto set our hands as officers of the Guild and have caused the Guild seal to be affixed at Detroit, Michigan, this 30th day of July, 1937.

PRESIDENT   SECRETARY

Each participant who built a scale model car in 1937 received a certificate in recognition of having "skillfully designed, constructed and submitted a model car." This evolved into a "Certificate of Design and Craftsmanship" given to every contestant who built and submitted a model car design in the 1940s, 1950s and 1960s. Upon the receipt of this piece of paper the contestant officially became a Guildsman. The certificate shown was awarded to David L. Rowland, July 30, 1937, and signed by William A. Fisher, Guild president, and William S. McLean, Guild secretary. *Author's collection, with permission of General Motors Corporation.*

Leaf Section. The memorabilia the author has shows teenagers from Detroit, New York City, and the town of London, Ohio, with their 1937 winning model cars. The model car regional winners came to Detroit to share the same stage at the Guild convention as the Napoleonic Coach first-place state winners and the Traveling Coach regional winners.

There were conventional front power plant designs as evidenced by the 1937 design by Byron Voight (second-place state award) (SIA #61) which looks almost like a 1940 Ford, and there were experimental rear power plant designs as evidenced by the designs made by Tony Ingolia (1937 state award) and Richard Arbib (1937 first-place state award, New York).[7]

By 1937 the honorary board of judges for the Craftsman's Guild model car competition included William A. Fisher, VP of GMC and founder of the Fisher Body Craftsman's Guild, Harley J. Earl, VP of GM Styling Section, and Charles F. Kettering, director of research. Top educators were also on the honorary board of judges and included representatives of prestigious institutions like Carnegie Tech, Georgia Tech, MIT, Ohio State, University of Michigan, Drexel, Penn State, Notre Dame, Caltech, University of

Toronto, and École Polytechnique de Montréal. William S. McLean was the Guild secretary in 1937 and one of the lowly working judges for the 1937 model car competition was Virgil M. Exner, Sr., a young man from South Bend, Indiana, who had been recruited by Harley J. Earl for the GM design studios.

The top 1937 national winner (junior division) was Theodore M. (Teddy) Mandel (age 14) from Detroit, Michigan, who received a $5,000 university scholarship. Teddy Mandel's design was a conventional motor mount, fastback, four-door passenger car with aerodynamically sculpted fenders, no running boards and a two-tone paint job. It had an unusual V-notched roof line at the windshield.

Although Tony Ingola's 1937 model car was rear-engined, his design was strongly influenced by the Cord (a front wheel drive design). It had a split windshield, a "widow's peak" and a pair of wing-like air louver patterns on the rear deck lid. Another important 1937 participant was Peter Wozena, a Detroiter and state winner who enjoyed a long successful career with Tony Ingola at GM Design staff as an automobile designer. (His brother John Wozena, another GM designer, was a 1948–49 Guildsman.) During the winter of 1938, Byron Voight (1937 second-place state award winner and GM engineer) and another Guildsman (Bob Irvin) were invited by GM to work in New York City on a huge diorama called "The City of Tomorrow," designed for the New York World's Fair by Norman Bel Geddes.

The top New York state winner in the 1937 model car competition was Richard Arbib. Hundreds of models from the 1937 competition, including Arbib's model, were displayed at the Museum of Natural History in Manhattan by the Fisher Body Craftsman's Guild. Arbib's fastback model car, named "Emperor," was a rear engine design with integral front fenders, air vents at the front of the rear quarter panels, no running boards, and folding or retractable head lamps. Richard Arbib studied automotive styling at Harley Earl's design school (the Detroit Institute of Automobile Styling), worked on GM's Futurama exhibit for the 1939 New York World's Fair, and at one time ran Harley Earl's industrial design firm, the Harley Earl Corporation. He became a prolific industrial designer with a 45-year career in product design and was considered a "blue sky" designer and true futurist when it came to automotive design.

It is believed that the Craftsman's Guild competition was discontinued around or before 1940 due to the war in Europe, and possible U.S. involvement, and 1946 was the first year of Guild awards after the war.[8]

Post–World War II Model Car Competitions (1946–1968)

We were very interested in the model car you submitted in the 1955 Fisher Body Craftsman's Guild competition. As we always do, we looked the models over carefully, — and felt your work showed definite merit and originality. This indicates to us that you may have the talent and creative ability necessary to become an automobile stylist. ... We would, therefore, like to know if you are considering a career in design" [William L. Mitchell to Guild winners].[9]

PURPOSE

The Craftsman's Guild transformed from an educational foundation throughout the 1930s (with a North American focus) to "an organization for the development of crafts-

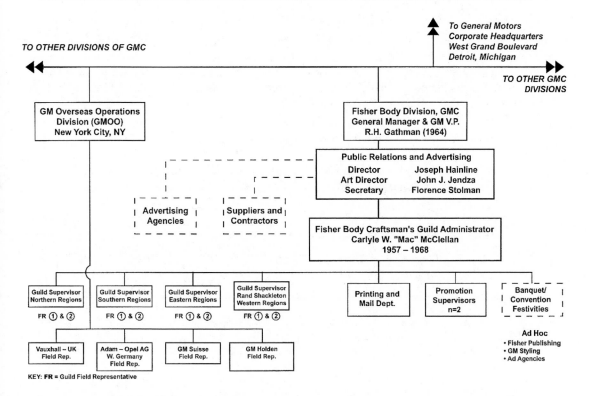

This chart shows how the various operations and functions of the Fisher Body Craftsman's Guild program were organized under the Fisher Body Division's Public Relations and Advertising Department (circa 1965). ©*2003 Jacobus.*

manship and creative ability among boys" in the 1950s to "an organization for the development of craftsmanship and creative ability in American youth" in the 1960s.[10,11]

MODERN GUILD ORGANIZATION

The day-to-day responsibility for Craftsman's Guild operations, based on a mid-1960s "snap shot," was the director of public relations and advertising, Fisher Body Division, in Warren, Michigan. Under this budget line item ($700,000 per year), the Guild functioned with an administrator (Carlyle W. "Mac" McClellan), a group of four Guild field supervisors, two promotion supervisors, a printing and mailing operation, and an ad hoc Guild convention and banquets operation. These were supported by top notch advertising agencies as well as other Fisher Body suppliers and contractors. The four field supervisors had two field representatives each, responsible for making a series of Guild program pitches at high schools in the northern, southern, eastern and western regions of the United States. This is how the winning contestant's schools were awarded trophies and new Craftsman's Guild enrollees or members were recruited. Fisher Body had a staff of approximately 40 people who worked exclusively on this activity.[12] This group had a large clerical force putting information on IBM cards, printing millions of pieces of mail and coordinating and controlling at least five or six major nationwide mailings annually (the quarterly newsletters, free-wheels requests, and shipping and receiving instructions). A fabulous *Guildsman* newsletter, the cornerstone of this correspondence course in industrial design, auto design and aesthetics, had to be designed, planned, written, edited and printed. This was the glue that kept the far-flung membership together and informed. Then there were the thousands of individual pieces of correspondence that had to be handled annually, as Guildsmen wrote to the Guild technical department (the same group of folks) and received a personal hand-typed letter in return answering the writer's questions. Each Guildsman received very individualized and personal attention. In the middle of all of this action, and running the show, was the director's secretary, Florence "Flossie" Stolman, and the art director, John J. Jendza. Without Flossie and Johnnie, there would have been no Guild.

In the mid–1960s (1965 to 1968) the organization chart would also have shown a box at the top called GM Overseas Operations Division, at the same latitude as the Fisher Body Division, showing four overseas Guild field representatives (UK, West Germany, Switzerland and Australia). Chuck Jordan had exported the Craftsman's Guild to Opel AG in West Germany, when he was director of design, and the Guild had proven to be so successful that other nations of the world were queuing up to embrace the Guild's tenets, values and virtues. The generalized organization chart on page 51 shows where the Fisher Body Craftsman's Guild fit into the Fisher Body Division organizational structure.[13]

The acknowledgments section of this book gives the names of many individuals who contributed to this organization.

Contest Incentives

From 1946 to 1953, eight top national scholarship winners were selected from a field of 40 designs that were tops in their regions (20 from the junior and 20 from the senior division), and $65,000 was available in scholarships and cash awards. During this time, the top scholarships ranged from $4,000 to $1,000 for both junior and senior division contestants. For 1954 and 1955, $90,000 in scholarships and cash awards were available from "the General." In 1956, the number of national scholarship winners was increased to 18, with $117,000 in scholarships and cash awards available. During this period the top scholarship awards ranged from $5,000 to $2,000 for both junior and senior division contestants. Ten styling scholarship awards worth $1,000 were also awarded for excellence in design, regardless of state award level, age or division.

The most important part of the regional award prize was the four-day all-expense-paid trip to Detroit. At the banquet and before, winners personally met GM's design executives and designers, got to see the other winning models and meet and befriend other kindred spirits, soak up new design and styling ideas in the flesh and on the drawing board, sign their scholarship trust agreements, and — most of all — talk and sketch cars. In addition to all the educational tours, the regional winners in the mid-'50s were treated to ticker tape parades, a new, sharp-looking Guild blazer, and shopping sprees, and they were pampered with first class accommodations at Detroit's ritziest hotels.

Promotion of the Model Car Contest

General Motors employed a variety of approaches to promote and advertise the model car competition. These included internally and externally distributed publications, the GM dealer and plant network, the popular press and commercial publications, presentations by the Guild field representative at school assemblies, nationwide radio broadcasts of the convention banquet, and traveling exhibits, loaner films and newsletters.

To be closest to the newest driving population, hence the newest target population contributing to or making the car buying decisions, General Motors published and distributed a magazine called *American Youth,* targeted to reach a population of 9,240,000 high school age men and women and about 1 million college freshmen.[14] Articles of interest to youth included topics such as good driver tips, Annapolis plebes, nurses' aids, how to look sharp, voting, horseback riding, skiing and university scholarship opportunities (e.g., the Fisher Body Craftsman's Guild). The magazine periodically contained articles about the Guild model car competition and the university scholarships that had been awarded that year or the previous year.

Another magazine published by General Motors that described the Craftsman's Guild competition was *General Motors World,* written for the Overseas Operations Division. Articles appeared periodically describing the results of the annual Guild competitions at Fisher Body in the United States, Vauxhall in England, at GM Suisse in Biel, Switzerland, Adam-Opel in West Germany and GM Holden in Australia. The articles covered the top overseas Craftsman's Guild winners and their ten-day trip to the USA to attend the Guild convention in Detroit along with their U.S. counterparts. The overseas Craftsman's Guild programs were initiated around 1965, but were phased out around 1968 along with the U.S. Guild, except for the Adam-Opel program in West Germany that ran successfully through 1979. Through GMOO (General Motors Overseas Operations) the Craftsman's Guild program was known around the world including in South Africa, Venezuela, Mexico, New Zealand, Italy, Norway, Argentina, Austria, Belgium, France, Sweden and Peru. In 1965 Guild programs were being planned in Italy, France and Norway (*General Motors World,* September 1966).

GM Dealers and Chevrolet Dealers

The GM dealership system saw the Guild as an opportunity to build warm and enduring community relations and to build good will among its current and future customer base. (It is estimated there were roughly 2,000 GM dealers at the time.)

Mr. W.E. Fish, a general sales manager in the Chevrolet Central Office, stated that their promoting the Guild was "cultivating the youth of the nation ... Building warm and enduring community relations ... PAYS BIG DIVIDENDS IN GOODWILL ... and that dealers were to order Guild literature and enrollment cards with 'the enclosed yellow post card.'" He continued, "The General Motors' dealer can make many loyal friends in the community simply by helping local boys to enroll in the Guild competition ..., and the more the dealer, his staff, facilities can do, ... the greater will be the return in goodwill. ... There is no finer way for the General Motors dealer to make warm and enduring friendships with people who are, or may be, his customers" (Memo to all Chevrolet dealers, November 27, 1951). It is presumed that the approach prescribed by Mr. Fish was promoted among the other motor divisions and the entire network of GM dealers.[15]

GM and Fisher Plant Network

Plant publications and the Employee Program Section helped market the Guild to the sons of GM employees and non–GM employees. For example, Guide Lamp Division, GMC (Anderson, Indiana) published *Guide Light,* a plant magazine, which periodically advertised the Guild program with full-page ads and enrollment coupons or described the program and its winners, especially when they were the sons of plant employees.

The *Guide Light* issue of November 23, 1951, featured a full-page, rear cover, orange and black color advertisement dedicated to the Guild, with the headline, "Your Boy Can Win a College Education in the Fisher Body Craftsman's Guild MODEL CAR COMPETITION, 734 Awards Totaling $65,000 for Boys 12 through 19." The accompanying futuristic auto design (a bulbous, bathtub design with a clear canopy) was probably inspired by Richard Arbib.

The Christmas 1952 issue of *Guide Light* ran an article titled "Design by Youth, $65,000 in Awards to Young Designers," had a full-page photo showing two of the top $4,000 award winning national scholarship winners (William Morgan and Gerald Grabcheski) with Nobel Prize winner Robert A. Millikan, former president of Caltech, and Karl T. Compton, Chairman of MIT Corporation. Both men were members of the honorary board of judges. The article stated that both national scholarship winners planned to become engineers.

There was a network of plants that supported the Guild through the GM Employee Program Section. Plants could use a GM order blank to obtain Guild literature to refill their display racks through the Employee Program Section, 15-260 GM Building, Detroit, 2, Michigan.

They could order copies of the how-to manual *Designing and Building a Model Automobile*, *Guildsman* newsletters, posters, and the brochure "Your Son's Future, A Greeting to You, Parent of a Member of the Fisher Body Craftsman's Guild." The latter included testimonials from role models such as top scholarship winners Robert W. Henderson, Donald C. Burnham, Dr. Henry B. Larzelere, and testimonials provided by parents and contestants. Future possible job opportunities were touted.

One 1962 internal publication, titled "Expressway for Your Future, Written for the Men and Women of GM," was designed to motivate employees to enroll their sons. Mac McClellan, Guild administrator, stated, "Some three hundred thousand [Guild booklets] will be distributed to General Motors employees through our Information Rack Services on December 26, 1962. ... The population explosion has reached the Guild. ... It looks like we will go over the 600,000 enrollment figure for the first time. ... Now all we have to do is find more *Jordans*."[16]

There were also circulars, GM employee son enrollment cards (buff or manila color) and non–GM employee son enrollment cards (white color). The information rack circulars sometimes contained year-to-year Guild rule updates, and often contained messages from role models and executives such as Harlow H. Curtice, president of General Motors. Curtice spoke at the 1953 Guild banquet saying,

> Hand in hand with this confidence in yourself goes an equally valuable trait of character — the will to see the thing through. In the world today there is a great need for men who have an abiding belief in their own ability to do something better than it was done before, and the plain fortitude to finish what has been started.
>
> This is a great combination to bring to the threshold of manhood. It is something we in General Motors can use, for machines can not design themselves, and new products can not design themselves. It takes men to make things happen in industry, in science and in government.[17]

It's assumed that other GM plants and Fisher Body plants, in particular, similarly promoted the Guild in their plant publications and worked with the GM Employee

Program Section. Since Fisher's body assembly plants and the motor division engine and chassis assembly plants were conjoined, so to speak, Guild literature could have informally migrated from plant to plant.

Popular Press and Commercial Magazines

When Guildsmen submitted their models they enclosed in the shipping crate a signed Official Guild Pledge Card, a birth certificate and a photograph of themselves. In July each year, the Guild promoted itself when their public relations people contacted the local newspapers of the state and regional winners and provided the Guildsman's photograph, name, age and address. Short articles appeared with headlines such as "Two Local Teenagers Win Car Body Design Awards."

The major market newspapers periodically wrote about the Guild. The *New York Times* anticipated the excitement of the 1967 competition and the headlines read "600,000 Youth Work on Autos of Tomorrow." The accompanying picture showed Dale A. Gnage, 1966 first-place national scholarship winner, junior division, and his award winning model, with a General Motors vice president, Harold G. Warner.[18] The writer Edward Hudson stated, "Guild judges were preparing for the deluge of models soon to be arriving for the 1967 Fisher Body Craftsman's Guild competition." They were anticipating "1,500 to 1,800 model entries. ... The Guild seeks to encourage one of Detroit's sought after talents— styling."

Roy Boyer, a General Motors official and former supervisor of the Craftsman's Guild, was quoted in the same article:

> The talented person in this field is always difficult to find. ... We are always looking for creative people, and this is one way of encouraging a continuing source of talent, not only GM, but for the entire industry. ... Many of the winners eventually have gone to work for such companies as American Motors, Ford, Chrysler in addition to GM, where nearly half of the creative designers are said to be ex–Guild members. ... Chuck Jordan, in-charge of GM's automotive design was a top winner in 1947.

Edward Hudson continued,

> Inventiveness is given free reign. The only requirements are that the design be of a wheeled vehicle for two to six passengers built to 1/12 scale. The models are 12 to 18 inches long, and usually cost the owner from $5 to $15 to build. After the contest they are returned to their creators. ... The model competition is open only to boys— a tradition that goes back to the notion that designing automobiles is a man's job. But, Detroit has women designers these days and Fisher Executives may eventually ask girls to take part.[19]

Model Car Science magazine, a model maker's hobby rag available at hobby shops across the country and by subscription, "scooped" the Guild winners and all the competition action annually. Their coverage could be excellent, featuring the top winning models along with the contestants' names, addresses, labor hour estimates, prior numbers of entries and awards, and future college aspirations. Sometimes the coverage was weak, with the models identified only by the state's name. But, overall, coverage was balanced, because the designs of the average, struggling contestant were covered as well as those of the truly successful Guildsmen.

Young Men, *Motor Trend*, *Popular Science*, *Air Trails*, and *Boys' Life* magazines ran periodic briefs on the winning models in fall issues after the announcement of the winners (see *Young Men*, February 1956; *Motor Trend*, October 1954; and *Popular Science*, October 1965). If you were lucky your college alumni magazine would do a story about you such as "Tomorrow's Car, Prize Winning Model Designed and Built by Charles Jordan '49." Articles such as this in *Popular Science* (October 1965) sang the praises of the Guild's accomplishments: "A remarkable 90% have earned or are studying for a college degree. ... Craftsman's Guild alumni make up half of the GM Styling Staff.[20]

This is consistent with 1963 and 1966 published lists of Guild award recipients, which show 81 percent of the successful contestants or awardees coming from high schools and colleges. Vocational-technical high school students made up few, if any, of the awardees.

Fisher Body magazine advertisements typically noted that the Boy Scouts of America's "Model Design and Building" merit badge (#3280), was automatically earned by building and submitting a Guild model. This is no surprise, as the roots of the Fisher Body Craftsman's Guild and the Boy Scouts of America went back to the early 1930s. BSA Commissioner Daniel Carter Beard was the honorary guild president in the early 1930s, as was BSA Commissioner Dr. George F. Fisher in the mid–1950s. The 1964 and 1985 editions of the merit badge book called *Model Design and Building* were an exact copy of the Guild's how-to manual, *Designing and Building a Model Automobile*.[21]

As of 1964 Fisher Body had granted copyright to BSA to adapt its "Holy Grail" for use in a new merit badge called "Model Design and Building." This copyright was extended by GM in 1985. Even during the Napoleonic Coach era, the submission of a miniature model coach to the competition automatically counted toward parts or pieces of ten different merit badges.

In 1993 the "Model Design and Building" merit badge was revised to include all types of model building (e.g., buildings, bridges, railroads, ships, and automobiles). The Guild, as an institution, had disappeared by this time.

Guild Field Representatives

During the 1950s and '60s, one of the primary sources of enrollees was the school promotion programs, or assembly hall presentations, by Guild field representatives. In the mid–'50s and '60s Guild reps visited 800 to 1,000 public and parochial junior high and high schools each fall. Edward Hudson, a *New York Times* reporter, suggested that as many as 1,300 schools were typically visited during the fall (*New York Times*, April 1967). According to Chuck Jordan in *Special Interest Autos* #61, "Full-time Fisher employees would take station wagons, and some visual aids, and go around the country to schools and drum-up interest."

Rand Shackleton, who was hired out of college in the 1960s by Fisher Body public relations and advertising at $400 per month to be a Guild field representative, stated that the initial job of traveling the country and visiting high schools was part time, lasting four months, but that with luck a representative would get promoted to one of four Guild field supervisor positions and a permanent paycheck of $600 per month. Mr. Shackleton stated the Fisher Guild college campus recruiters were looking for personable, outgoing people to be Guild field reps. Preferably, they were college communications majors, articulate and imaginative speakers, with good extemporaneous speaking abilities.[22]

Potential candidates came to Warren, Michigan, for a speaking competition, or showmanship test, for the Guild supervisor staff, Guild management and the Guild administrator. Candidates had to think fast on their feet to pass this test, as they were given various topics to be addressed in front of everyone at that moment. The candidate had to project his personality. There was the "three ball story" test where he had three balls in his hands, of various bounce factors, and he had to make up a three minute story using the three balls as props. Or, they had the "model car story" test, and they handed him a winning Fisher Guild model car, and he had to describe this magnificent object, enthusiastically, in complete detail, for three minutes as if he were on the radio.

Rand Shackleton passed the test, and eventually became a field supervisor in the western regions, making $7,200 a year. Life was good. He said that he and the other Guild field supervisors spent the 1967–68 year, just prior to the decision to abandon the Craftsman's Guild, justifying the youth program and its benefits for Fisher and GM upper management. He stated he was there when the "shoe dropped" and the final decision was made. As the story goes, Carlyle W. McClellan gathered everyone together and said, "Boys, the Guild's received a kick in the [pants]." This aspect of GM's youth outreach program would be discontinued, but the Previews of Progress, an outreach component that trumpeted the virtues of GM technology, would be retained.

Rand Shackleton, like many of the Guild field representatives and supervisors, moved on to a successful public relations and advertising career. Another, Joel Higgins, became a movie actor and starred in the TV sitcom *Silver Spoons*. Several became top GM executives and one a GM vice president. Mr. Shackleton worked in the PR and advertising field for years and today is an independent filmmaker currently working on a project to retrace the steps of his famous relative (a distant cousin), the South Pole explorer Sir Ernest Shackleton. The Fisher Body Craftsman's Guild apparently launched industrial design careers for many of the winning contestants as well as successful public relations careers for the Guild program's young managers.

According to a 1963 *Guildsman* newsletter, there was a 12-man field crew that went on a 12-week tour of 32 states making assembly presentations to as many as 1,100 junior high and high schools across the county. (This averages out to one or two school visits per day, excluding weekends.) From this activity as many as 450,000 youths enrolled in the Guild program annually with another 150,000 coming from renewals. In 1963, representatives logged 140 minutes of TV time at 19 TV stations in 15 states. By February 1964, during the 1963–64 Guild competition year, the four Guild field supervisors would go out on a 12-week tour, scheduling assembly programs for the following fall. It took Guild field reps a three month tour, three years in a row, to cover all the major metropolitan areas in the United States (*Guildsman*, vol. 11, no. 3, fall 1963).

This program won high praise from principals and teachers. It generally included a full-color, educational motion picture (e.g., *Getting Started*), a "chalk talk" dealing with automobile design, and instructive insights into the way the automobile industry worked and their plans for the future. After discussing the Guild scholarships, the highlight of the program was when the winning Guildsman from the school was called from the audience to the stage. Other students could see that one of them could be successful in the Guild.

Trophies were awarded to the school in the case of national, styling, regional and state winners. Two Guild trophies were presented — one to the Guildsman and the other to the school's principal. The size of the Guild trophies were graduated according to the size and level of the award. If a national scholarship winner, the school received a huge trophy. Two arms were needed to tote it around. In addition, a scholarship award winning model from a prior year's Guild competition would be exhibited on the stage for the students to closely examine, so they could understand the high quality of workmanship required to win. The enrollment cards were handed out, passed among the students in the audience, and collected before the assembly of students was dismissed. Although the Guild pitch was geared toward an all male audience, coed audiences also participated. The direct student one-on-one contact explains the Guild's huge enrollment figures, as thousands of students were able to quickly enroll on the spot following these highly motivating and professional presentations. Undoubtedly, there was pressure on the Guild field reps to accumulate higher and higher enrollment figures as this was probably a yearly performance measure.

Scholarship Winners Announced by National Radio Broadcast

Only the state and regional winners in the annual Fisher Body Craftsman's Guild competition were made public in local newspapers. The national scholarship winners were kept secret until they were announced at the Guild convention banquet. This news was broadcast live by national radio hook-up from the General Motors Building Auditorium in Detroit (in the 1950s) or the Fisher Body headquarters' auditorium in Warren (in the 1960s).

In 1947 as many as 35 ABC radio affiliates were hooked up for the announcement of the national scholarship winners from New York to Los Angeles. Hundreds of thousands probably listened to the broadcast. In 1949 NBC hosted the broadcast.

High profile personalities were emcees at the Guild banquets, such as Bob Considine (1949; syndicated columnist and author of *30 Seconds over Tokyo*), Bert Parks (1950; Miss America Pageant emcee), Robert Young (1951; screen star who would be best known for his *Father Knows Best* TV sitcom), Walter Cronkite (1957; *Nightly News* anchor of the '60s), and Lowell Thomas (1964; world traveler and commentator).

Newspaper Coverage

The press followed the lives of some of the national winners. Writing about the World War II exploits of Guild alumni such as Robert W. Henderson (1934), Ralph Schreiber (1936), Donald Burnham (1931) and Stanley Knochel (1933), syndicated columnist Bob Considine noted that J. Edgar Hoover had commented favorably on the aid this program had been to the cause of fighting juvenile delinquency ("On the Line," August 21, 1947).

Referring to the contestants, Considine wrote, "Many had worked nearly a year on their models, pledged not to receive any kind of aid — even to the sewing of miniature seat covers and upholstery, the carving of wheels that had to be correct to the thousandth of an inch, before being turned over to a trial selection board headed by the renowned President of MIT — Dr. Karl T. Compton." Referring to the model cars, he continued, "The average U.S. motorist would give an arm to have a car as sleek, as utilitarian and as advanced as the designs submitted by any of the finalists."

Traveling Exhibits

In the 1950s, GM had the "Parade of Progress" public relations program in which 12 General Motors motor coaches were converted to what were called Futurliners, with built-in exhibits extolling the virtues of GM's technology. One bus had a Fisher Body Craftsman's Guild exhibit. This traveling caravan stopped at state fairs across the county.

Beautiful exhibit cases (called "coffins," because of their cross-sectional shape), built by H.B. Stubbs and Company of Detroit, Michigan, held six models each and had rotating platforms at each end for at least one model, to show off the new winning Craftsman's Guild model car designs made by the scholarship winners. The sides of exhibit case glass were set at oblique angles so the viewer could get a closer look. These exhibits traveled all over the United States, making stops at the GM buildings in Detroit and New York, department stores such as Golds in Lincoln, Nebraska (described by Terry R. Henline below), conferences and conventions of school principals and superintendents (e.g., the North American Association of School Principals), and World's Fair venues such as the 1965 New York World's Fair.

According to Terry R. Henline (1958 second-place national scholarship, senior division, $4,000 award winner), a traveling Guild exhibit came to his home town of Lincoln, Nebraska, announced by GM press releases. He stated,

> This photograph was a part of a press release which went out to many news papers at the time. Shown is my winning second place senior model with the General Motors Firebird Three. I have included a photocopy of the actual text that accompanied the photograph. The reference to "Golds" pertains to a department store which was located in Lincoln, Nebraska, my home town at the time. "Golds" was one of the stores which displayed the Craftsman's Guild models on a tour around the country at that time.[23]

Part of the press release read as follows:

> FOR IMMEDIATE RELEASE— One of the 30 award-winning scale models cars of the future which are on display this week at "Golds" is compared to General Motors' newest experimental gas-turbine car, the Firebird III. ... The exhibit, now on a nation-wide tour, is sponsored by the Fisher Body Craftsman's Guild which annually awards $115,000, including 18 scholarships ranging from $1,000 to $5,000 each to young car designers from 12 to 20 years of age. ... Even though the two cars vary in design theme, they both represent futuristic thinking which is vital to progress in the automotive field [General Motors press release, fall 1958].

A letter from Guild administrator C.W. McClellan to Allen T. Weideman of Salt Lake City, Utah, an 18 year old with 1955 and 1956 Guild competition experience, stated that "a special exhibit of approximately 30 award-winning model cars from past Fisher Body Craftsman's Guild competitions is scheduled for J.C. Penney in Salt Lake City from June 3 through June 8. ... It may be that a few Salt Lake City winners in past Guild competitions may be called on to assist in some way in bringing the display to the attention of the public."

Public Information and Education

The Guild loaned a 16 mm movie titled *Getting Started* to clubs and organizations (e.g., Boy Scouts, 4-H Club, YMCA) to show boys how to design and build model cars. Private, public and parochial schools were eligible for the short-term loan, and the Guild would pay the postage. There were other great Guild films such as *Tomorrow Is Here Today*. A new color film was expected for preview August 14, 1967, called *Designing and Building a Model Car*, and was coordinated with the famous Guild how-to booklet of the same name. It is unknown what happened to this film or if it was ever released to promote the Craftsman's Guild.

COMMUNICATIONS WITH GUILDSMEN

Guildsmen had four key items: (1) the how-to instruction booklet titled *Designing and Building a Model Automobile*; (2) the specifications in Drawing A (Regular Wheelbase Category); Drawing B (Small Car or Sports Car Wheelbase Category); and Drawing C (Open Competition Category); (3) a good sketch pad and pencils; and (4) the quarterly Guild publications.

Specification Sheets

The specification sheets included the "Scale Fidelity" parameters or guidelines (minimum roof height, maximum model length and width dimensions, minimum ground clearance, head height and visibility requirements for passengers, maximum model wheelbase length, front and rear departure angles, and maximum front and rear overhang dimensions). This made the contestants think about the real world and ensured that they adhered to basic practical automotive design proportions.

Newsletters

The quarterly bulletin called the *Guild News* (1946–1953) and the quarterly publication called the *Guildsman* (1953–1968) were distributed to all enrollees. Like the *Guildsman* magazine of 1934–35, the *Guild News* and *Guildsman* kept the far-flung network of disparate craftsman connected and kept them abreast of significant events.

The best information was personalized. For example, national scholarship winners were featured periodically and described, in their own words, how they built their winning entry (e.g., Benjamin B. Taylor, 1950 winner, and Arthur Russell, 1956 winner). In 1956 Art Russell had 15 how-to photographs, taken by his friend Bill Moore, published in the *Guildsman*, describing step by step how he made his 1956 styling scholarship winning model.

• Ideas and Inspiration

Pictures of the winning scholarship models and information about their makers were published at least annually, in the Convention Issue of the *Guild News* or the *Guildsman*. This is where Guildmen saw the advanced design cues and design ethic approved by GM management. Not only did Guildsmen emulate what they saw on the street, at dealerships and in show rooms, but they tried to emulate the design principles depicted in the published pictures of the winning scholarship models.

If Guildsmen of the late '40s and early 1950s needed futuristic four-door sedan design ideas, they had Virgil M. Exner, Jr.'s 1946, Chuck Jordan's 1947, Elia Russinoff's 1949, Gale Morris' 1949, Ronald C. Hill's 1950 and Edward F. Taylor's 1951 designs for inspiration. Ed Taylor's had clear plastic windows all the way around with a finished interior, whereas the others had what the Guild Judges called solid-tops.

The subtle design cues from convertible sports cars and roadsters exemplified by Gary Graham's 1954, Bill Moore's 1956, Art Russell's 1957, Gary Law's 1958, Paul Tatseos' 1958, Terry Henline's 1958 and William R. Molzon's 1959 top national scholarship award winning designs were emulated in the following years by young Guildsmen across America.

Other serious and highly motivated Guildsmen tried to predict the future, innovate, and do something new. The Open Competition Category (Drawing C) allowed this with new fresh designs by Ronald E. Pietruska (1964, 1967), Richard Lee Beck (1964), John D'Mura (1964) and John M. Mellberg (1966).

The designs of other Guildsmen in the Convention Issues generated ideas for young readers. The Convention Issue also presented the rewards of being one of 40 regional award winners and convention benefits, including a first class tour of the GM Styling studios, looks at advanced vehicle design renderings and clay models, and private viewing of GM's experimental vehicles and show cars that had appeared at auto shows and in auto magazines and newspapers. Also, the Guild banquet provided announcements of the winners and a chance for the Guildsman to speak briefly to one of the Judges about his specific model entry. Of course, a regional winner had to contemplate the possibility, no matter how remote, of winning a national scholarship!

Techniques were described telling how to create a high luster, flawless paint job (remove all surface defects, seal with shellac, coat with primer-surfacer, spray high pressure lacquer primer coats and then high pressure lacquer color coats, wet sand in between coats, apply hand rubbing compound). There were paint flaw diagnostics, causes and cures (e.g., bubbles, blisters, cracks, orange peel, sags and runs). The scoring criteria to be used by the Guild judges were discussed as well as how to obtain free rubber wheels (beginning with the 1953–54 competition year), build a shipping crate and complete an Official Guild Pledge Card.

• *Planning Business*

Each year new enrollees had to be told, and Guild veterans reminded, of the importance of early planning. A serious decision had to be made, before the start of the school year, about the entry category (A, B, or C), the type of model to be constructed (solid top, convertible, bubble top), and the materials and tools that would be needed. The prospective Guildsman also had to consider how to commit the time needed to meet the early June deadline nine months away. An even bigger question was what new design ideas the model would present — and if there were none, why enter?

The Craftsman's Guild program typically overlapped the school year from September 1 to June 4 or 5. The age of the contestant as of September 1 determined which age division of competitors (junior or senior) the model would ultimately face in the ring. By the middle of July the judging and scoring process had been completed and contestants notified by mail. Checks were distributed at this time to state winners with a cover letter stating whether they were a regional winner and had won a free all-expenses-paid trip to Detroit. By the last week of July or early August the Guild convention and banquet were held and the scholarship winners' names announced over the radio for all to hear from coast to coast.

Unbeknownst to the Guildsman or his parents, the Official Guild Pledge Card was a very important piece of legal business, as the contestant had to attest to doing his own work and had to guarantee his age and his state of residence. These were the primary eligibility requirements which established the pool of competitors. This was critical for GM and Fisher Body from a legal point of view as it assured integrity, fairness, and survival of the program.

• *Guild Technical Department*

There was also the "Craftsman's Corner" for questions and answers. Names and addresses of Guildsmen were freely published. Guildsmen were encouraged to write directly to the Guild technical department with their questions.

Model Body Styles, Dimensions, and Construction Methods

1946–1953: Two- and Four-Door,
Six-Passenger Sedan, and Make Your Own Wheels

From 1946 to 1953 contestants were limited to constructing a conventional front engine, two- or four-door, six passenger sedan, which was reminiscent of the 1937 to 1940 competitions. Using the Guild's famous handbook, boys were encouraged to first make multiple sketches and scale drawings of their design before proceeding to make a clay model. The designing process, they were taught, was concerned with simplicity, proportion, form and unity. The overall allowable model dimensions at this time were 16¾" long (maximum), 6½" wide (maximum) and 5" high (minimum).

For the 1951 plans, Drawing A, for example, had partial front, side and rear views drawn to 1/12 scale and a partially squared-off grid system so that ideas could be explored by a Guildsman with tracing paper. In 1954 Drawings A and B were introduced for six possible body styles, and by 1963, with the addition of Category C (Open Competition), there were Drawings A, B and C for eleven possible body styles.

The two- or four-door passenger sedan was a tough design challenge and has always been a styling challenge. Highly complex compound surfaces were involved in order to execute the project correctly. Some excellent examples of four-door sedan models were designed for the Craftsman's Guild competition by Virgil M. Exner, Jr., 1946 first-place national scholarship winner (cast plaster); Chuck Jordan, 1947 first-place national scholarship winner (white pine); Harvey E. Whitman, 1948 first-place national scholarship winner (cast plaster); Elia Russinoff, 1949 first-place national scholarship winner (mahogany); Gale P. Morris, 1949 third-place national scholarship winner (balsa wood); and Stanley Carl Waechter, 1949 (cast plaster).

1954: Body Style Expansion and Free Scaled Hard Rubber Tires

In the 1953–54 model car competition year, the number of body styles was expanded to include the family sedan, six-passenger hardtop and convertible; the convertible and hardtop sports car; and the station wagon. There were optional wheelbase specifications for a rear engine powered design. On the Official Guild Pledge Card that accompanied the model when shipped to Detroit via Railway Express, the Guildsman had to indicate the body style so the judges knew which overall dimensions and specifications applied.

Models with the clear canopies and finished interiors were judged as convertibles to give the builder full credit for the extra interior design work required. There were specific convertible design requirements (seats, steering apparatus, an instrument panel, and finished interior walls and other surfaces). "Ragtop" stowage area had to be indicated. There could be a five-passenger convertible or a two-passenger sports convertible. The working score sheet for a convertible was slightly different from that of a solid top. The score sheet for a convertible had 30 more points available in the Workmanship subcategory to help the builder to earn more credit for all his extra work, but at the same time, the available points in the other subcategories were reduced or redistributed. The total points available, whether convertible or solid top, was still a maximum of 450. By building a convertible model the Guildsman set a higher performance standard for himself because if the workmanship was poor, or some of basic convertible requirements were missed, he might end up losing 30 points.

Beginning with the 1954 competition year, the Guild began to offer hard rubber

THE 1952 MODEL CAR COMPETITION

FISHER BODY CRAFTSMAN'S GUILD

$65,000 IN AWARDS

GRAND NATIONAL AWARDS

EIGHT UNIVERSITY SCHOLARSHIPS, total value $20,000, consisting of trust funds for university training, to be created by General Motors Corporation in the following amounts:

TWO $4,000 SCHOLARSHIP AWARDS — One Junior • One Senior

TWO $3,000 SCHOLARSHIP AWARDS — One Junior • One Senior

TWO $2,000 SCHOLARSHIP AWARDS — One Junior • One Senior

TWO $1,000 SCHOLARSHIP AWARDS — One Junior • One Senior

AND 686 STATE AWARDS

equally divided between Juniors and Seniors as follows:

1st Senior State Award........$150 cash	1st Junior State Award........$150 cash
2nd Senior State Award.......$100 cash	2nd Junior State Award.......$100 cash
3rd Senior State Award........$ 50 cash	3rd Junior State Award.......$ 50 cash
AND four honorable mention awards of Model Builder's Tool Chests.	*AND four honorable mention awards of Model Builder's Tool Chests.*

PLUS 40 TRIPS TO GUILD CONVENTION

One Junior and One Senior whose models receive the highest score

of those submitted in each of the following regions:

REGION No. 1 — Maine, New Hampshire, Vermont	REGION No. 11 — Illinois, Indiana
REGION No. 2 — Massachusetts, Rhode Island	REGION No. 12 — Wisconsin, Minnesota
REGION No. 3 — New York, Connecticut	REGION No. 13 — North Dakota, South Dakota, Nebraska
REGION No. 4 — New Jersey, Delaware	REGION No. 14 — Iowa, Missouri
REGION No. 5 — Pennsylvania, Maryland	REGION No. 15 — Louisiana, Arkansas, Oklahoma
REGION No. 6 — West Virginia, Virginia, District of Columbia	REGION No. 16 — Texas, New Mexico, Arizona
REGION No. 7 — North Carolina, South Carolina, Georgia	REGION No. 17 — Colorado, Utah, Kansas
REGION No. 8 — Alabama, Florida, Mississippi	REGION No. 18 — Idaho, Wyoming, Montana
REGION No. 9 — Kentucky, Tennessee	REGION No. 19 — Washington, Oregon
REGION No. 10 — Michigan, Ohio	REGION No. 20 — California, Nevada

This Craftsman's Guild print ad was published in GM plant magazines and factory newsletters, on the back of Guild "how-to" booklets and in Craftsman's Guild newsletters to make parents and potential Guildsmen aware of the $65,000 in awards available in the 1952 competition. *Author's collection, with permission of General Motors Corporation.*

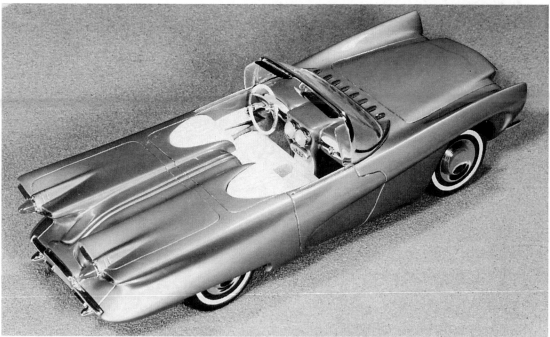

This 2-seat convertible model made by Ronald C. Pellman (age 18) of Snyder, New York, won a 1958 first state New York, senior division award and a regional award (New York/Connecticut). His design captured 198 out of a possible 200 points for "craftsmanship," but overall the design earned 386 out of a possible total 450 points or 85.7 percent. The body was constructed from glass reinforced polyester resin, the windshield from stretch formed (heated) acrylic, the trim from chrome-plated brass and the paint was green metallic acrylic lacquer. This entry earned Pellman a $150 cash prize and an all-expense-paid trip to Detroit for the four-day Guild convention. *Ronald C. Pellman.*

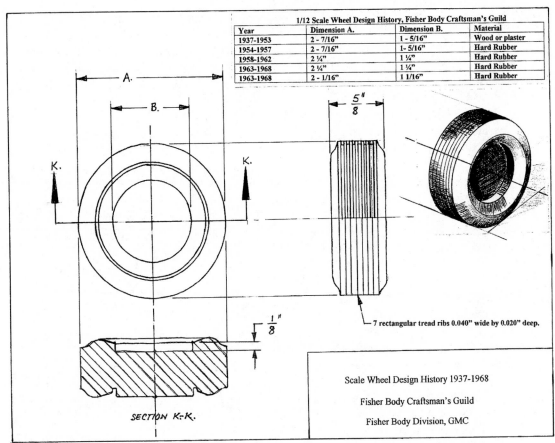

1/12 Scale Wheel Design History, Fisher Body Craftsman's Guild			
Year	Dimension A.	Dimension B.	Material
1937-1953	2 - 7/16"	1 - 5/16"	Wood or plaster
1954-1957	2 - 7/16"	1- 5/16"	Hard Rubber
1958-1962	2 ¼"	1 ¼"	Hard Rubber
1963-1968	2 ¼"	1 ¼"	Hard Rubber
1963-1968	2 - 1/16"	1 1/16"	Hard Rubber

7 rectangular tread ribs 0.040" wide by 0.020" deep.

Scale Wheel Design History 1937-1968

Fisher Body Craftsman's Guild

Fisher Body Division, GMC

SECTION K-K.

© 2003 John L. Jacobus

This illustration shows the changes in the dimensions for the hard rubber wheels used by contestants over the lifespan of the Craftsman's Guild program. Beginning in 1954, 1/12 scale hard rubber wheels were given free of charge to Guildsmen. Before 1954, Guildsmen had to make their own wheels. *Illustration by author.*

wheels of exacting scale (2⅞6" O.D. [outside diameter], ⅝" width, 1⅚6" hub cap I.D. [inside diameter] by ⅛" depth) free of charge to Guildsmen. The availability of properly scaled wooden or rubber wheels (with rectangular grooves for tread) had always been an impediment to participants since the model car competition began. Contestants had had to make their own wheels from the beginning in 1937. The Guild how-to booklet told how to make wheels on a homemade lathe or from plaster. From 1954 forward, Guildsmen had to send in a form signed by their parents, or a photograph as proof, in order to receive a set of four wheels (the assumption being that a model had to be well along in construction). Wheel design evolved to a smaller O.D. and hub cap I.D. by 1958 (2¼" O.D., ⅝" width, and 1¼" hub cap I.D. by ⅛" depth).

Beginning in 1954 the Guild flourished because the variety of body styles available to the contestants got the "creative juices" to flow. America's love affair with the automobile was clearly evident in these models as the Guild came into its own. The youths who entered the Guild in the '50s especially loved cars, had a special rapport with automobiles and were passionate about their Guild model designs. With the introduction of the Corvette in 1953, all bets were off. Convertibles and roadsters captured the imaginations of Guildsmen. The designs made by Gary Graham, 1954 first-place national scholarship winner; James Garner, 1954 and 1955 regional award winner; Ronald C. Pellman, 1958 regional award winner; Bill Moore, 1956 first-place national scholarship award winner; Art Russell, 1957 first-place national scholarship award winner; and Bill Molzon, 1959 second-place national scholarship award winner, exemplify the '50s-era love affair with automobiles and the winners' love of model making.

Station wagons were very rarely seen in the Craftsman's Guild model car competition. Richard R. Sylvester's 1956 styling scholarship design and William Hope's 1960 styling scholarship design are two outstanding examples of station wagon design efforts that succeeded at the national level. These were as rare as hen's teeth. Station wagons, like four-door sedans, given the Guild specifications for practicality, were a tough design proposition. It is interesting to note that few four-door sedan designs won national awards in the 1950s with the exception of the design by John B. Di Ilio, 1957 third-place national scholarship, junior division, award winner.

1963 Open Competition

By the 1962–63 model car competition year, the body style design categories changed again to include Category A, Regular Wheelbase Designs; Category B, Sports Car and Small Car Designs and the Category C, Open Competition, for a total of 11 design categories. The Open Competition accommodated two- to six-passenger vehicles, new wheelbase configurations, new seating arrangements, and new door opening arrangements. Designed to expand the appeal of the Guild to more free-thinking teenagers without an added cost burden to the Guild, it was announced July 31, 1962, in time for the 1962–1963 competition.[24] Contestants in this popular category created wild, far-out models that helped keep the program relevant and vital.

Two wheel sizes were also available at this time (2¼" O.D., ⅝" width, and 1¼" hub cap I.D., ⅛" depth; and 2¹⁄₁₆" O.D., ⅝" width, and 1¹⁄₁₆" hub cap I.D., ⅛" depth). The former size was for use in the Regular Category A; the latter size was used for the Small and Sports Car Category B. Both size wheels could be used for the *Open Category C* (the Open Competition). The Open Competition was set up to help the young designers explore new, exciting occupant-packaging arrangements, and in return, Fisher Body relaxed some of the rigid "practicality" requirements. Successful Guildsmen in the Open Competition include Richard Lee Beck in 1964 (third-place national scholarship winner, senior division), John D'Mura in 1964 (national scholarship winner, junior division), John M. Mellberg in 1966 (second-place national scholarship winner, senior division) and Ronald E. Pietruska in 1967 (fourth-place national scholarship winner, senior division).

The competition rules did not allow light truck and van (LTV), motorcycle, or dragster designs. There was no opportunity for Guildsmen to innovate designs like the minivan or sport utility vehicles (SUV).[25]

Practical Design Considerations

Roof height, interior headroom and driver visibility had to be accommodated and could not be less than indicated by the ergonomic specifications on Drawings A, B or C. The feet of the rear passenger were tucked under the front seat for conventional packaging purposes. Head support was needed for seats that reclined more than normal. The Guildsman had to consider getting in and getting out of a reclined passenger seat.

Real-world vertical wheel jounce and suspension movement as well as front-steer wheel movement had to be accommodated in the fender designs. Exposed front wheels, partially exposed front wheels, enclosed front wheels, and rear wheels had specific maximum and minimum clearance dimensions between the wheel edge and body edge. Front or rear air-cooling apertures had to be accounted for depending on the placement of the power plant. Front and rear engine designs had different maximum wheelbase dimensions. The hood, rear deck or luggage compartment, convertible top storage, door openings, concealed headlights, and other parts had to be indicated by lines consisting of a scored square ½" groove. In plaster models, this was scored with the edge of a steel straightedge or machinist's ruler. For fiberglass models, a ½" square brass rod was sharpened to make a cutting tool to just pierce the gel coat.

Front and rear bumper protection, headlights and taillights were necessary, as well as license plate attachment areas (e.g., recessed body, recessed bumper or brackets). The headlight diameter and height for single or dual headlamps was specified; alternatively, recessed headlights would be scored based on practicality and scored line workmanship. There were ground clearance specs for passenger ingress and egress and undercarriage clearance. Unlike the miniature Napoleonic Coaches, none of the parts on the model cars had to operate.

Materials Used by Guildsmen

Guildsmen loved cars and loved to work with their hands and experiment with a wide variety of materials. A Guildsman never met a material he couldn't file, carve, sand, bake, bend, glue or drill and adapt to complement an award winning design. Some of them were as follows:

Plaster: casting plaster, gauze, room temperature vulcanizing rubber (RTV), and associated parting compounds—soap, Vasoline™ and silicone spray.

Wood: basswood, mahogany, poplar, balsa wood, pine (clear, white, yellow and sugar), cherry, maple, marine plywood, apple wood and fruit crate wood.

Metals: brass, copper, soft aluminum, molded molten lead, tin, solder (50/50), steel, nickel, chrome, rhodium, sterling silver, and silver solder.

Plastics: acetate, styrene, vinyl, fiberglass and polyester resins, rigid polyurethane foams, polyester body filler (Bondo™), and acrylic plastic (Plexiglas™).

Woven Fibers: silk, silk span, velvet, and corduroy.

Paint: lacquers, lacquer thinners, enamels, and model airplane dope.

Finishing: wet emery paper or cloth, pumice powder, rubbing compound, and wax.

Adhesives: Elmer's White glue, Duco Cement™, and two-part epoxies.

Miscellaneous: Naugahyde™ (simulated leather), patent leather, Plastic Wood™, and Wood's Metal™ (a low-temperature-melting pot metal).

Tools and Equipment Used by Guildsmen

Required: The designing process required tracing paper and pencils to work out ideas. A good mechanical drawing of the 1/12 scale model design was needed and required a mechanical drawing set, steel scale (ruler) divided into thousandths, a compass for drawing circles as well as a T-square and triangles (45 degree and 30–60 degree). For Elia Russinoff (a 1949 winner) a dozen sets of drawings were worked out and discarded before a satisfactory design emerged.[26]

For working in wood, the Guildsman needed dividers, a compass, a steel scale, right triangles, an X-ACTO KIT™ (with saw and knife blades), ¼" and ½" wide chisels with honing stone and can of 3-in-1 oil, various hand-saws (e.g., hack saw, coping saw, keyhole saw), work bench and vice or large-jaw wood clamps, various grit sand papers (#100, #180, #200 and #240), fine jeweler's files and saw, manual drill with bits (up to ¼" chuck), electric drill (¼" chuck), and brace and bit with large diameter wood bits.

Optional: A drill press, a table sander, a jigsaw or band saw, a gas or electric oven for heating plastic, vacuum forming equipment, high pressure portable spray paint equipment, a small portable jeweler's lathe or 4-in-1 bench lathe, a polishing wheel and various grits of jeweler's rouge, and a propane torch for soldering.

Trim from Common Household Items

Miniature car building took skill at improvising as well as designing. There were no such things as stock parts or mass produced kits. Everything was made from scratch for a few bucks. Each piece of the model was tailor-made or adapted from available household materials.

The model cars utilized a surprising variety of materials. If a young designer decided that his scale model car should have wire wheels, he had to make them, and so he might use common straight pins from a sewing box. Straight pin heads could be used to indicate the pushbutton for door or trunk handles. The sewing box provided headlight bezels hacksawed from the rim of a thimble and mother-of-pearl buttons were filed and polished for headlight lenses.

A Guildsman would cut up kitchen drawer handles to make bumper parts or salvage a pair of old kid gloves to make genuine leather upholstery for a model convertible. Toothpaste caps provided a variety of round, fluted, red taillight lenses. Red thermoplastic toothbrush handles were cut, shaped and polished for intricate taillight lense designs. Radiator grilles were often cut from pieces of window screen, and smooth, concave hubcaps cut from chromed drawer pull knobs. Stainless-steel chair gliders (Domes of Silence™ chair gliders) also made a good set of convex hubcaps; a stack of concentric washers worked just as well. Ice cube trays provided a convenient supply of aluminum for window trim, dashboards or instrument consoles.

But there was a much more serious side to all this. The serious Guildsman intent on a scholarship made wire wheels from scratch using brass wire, brass tubing, and solder, and then had them chrome plated. These were inserted in the hollowed-out rubber tires.

Guildsmen didn't mess around. They turned parts on the lathes at their high schools, like hub caps and wheel covers, used a polishing wheel to buff aluminum parts with various grits of polishing rouges, and had parts plated with various metals locally. Peter G. Wiinikka (1960 first-place national scholarship winner) and Anthony V. (Tony) Simone (1961 first-place national scholarship winner) cut down beveled gears on a lathe and had them chrome plated for wheel covers.

If you didn't know how to seamlessly solder brass parts together with a propane torch, you weren't really a Guildsman. Art Russell and Bill Moore assembled brass parts using silver solder. If regular lead- and tin-based solder had been used, the chrome finish would be dulled at those joints.

The Guildsman had to know how to heat a piece of clear plexiglass and shape it into a symmetric windshield or canopy using a male mold, or a wood male and plaster female mold die-set, and you had to know how to polish acrylic plastic to remove any and all scratches. You had to be a pattern maker in order to make the molds to make the plastic parts.

So, when the Guildsmen decided to make a convertible model they embarked on a whole new set of problems in acrylic plastic shaping, forming, and polishing not encountered by a Guildsman making a sedan with what was called a solid top greenhouse. These problems were multiplied when the hard top, sports car model maker wanted a clear acrylic windshield and side windows as well as a hollowed out and finished interior. These required fabrication of a clear acrylic bubble top, but with the further step of incorporating a solid roof area and an interior ceiling, not to mention the intricate interior assembly.

The Guild booklet taught how to make a clear plastic windshield by forming and shaping a flat piece of oven heated acrylic plastic over a wood or plaster male mold. They did not teach how to make a bubble top. This required real technical expertise to accomplish and perfect and employed an industrial process called vacuum forming.

Metal Trim and Brightwork

No award winning model was complete without "bright work": either hand-painted plywood, polished soft aluminum or chrome-plated brass trim in the bumper areas, around the windows and on the wheels (e.g., the wheel covers or hub caps). The Guild literature taught the idea of cutting a groove or slot in the body of the model for flush mounted, inlaid metal trim parts, especially those around the windows of the greenhouse. There was to be a seamless line between the bright metal trim and the color of the body. Guildsmen really had to use their ingenuity here. The men were separated from the boys in this area. Judges scored how flawlessly the trim was polished and applied to the model under the Workmanship subcategory of Craftsmanship.

Aluminum wire filed flat, HO gauge brass track cut at the webbing, or flat aluminum sheet could be cut, filed, and polished to create metallic trim parts. In the mid-'50s, the Guild technical department recommended Chrome-O-Lac, Chrome Finish #21 or Plastic Metal #22F (with Thinner #1) to simulate chrome over a metal, wood or plastic substrate. Later in the program, as Guildsman got more sophisticated and the competition more intense, homemade brass parts were rhodium plated, nickel-chrome-plated, or chrome-plated.[27] Like vacuum forming, these plating activities were essentially industrial processes. In the later years of the program, Pep Boys' chrome tape became popular for simulating metallic trim parts. The fitting of the polished aluminum parts, or chrome-plated brass parts, was all done in advance of any primer or paint.

Kits containing soft aluminum bars, plates and rods could be purchased by Guildsmen from an approved Guild vendor. For example, H.B. Stubbs and Co. of Detroit sold three different kits (I, II and III) to Guildsmen for a nominal fee.[28] The soft aluminum bars could be cut and filed to make front and rear bumpers. The rods came in ½", ⅝", ¾" and 1¼" diameters. The ½" and ⅝" diameter pieces could be used for single or dual headlight mounts, respectively, and the 1¼" diameter bar stock was the right size for bright polished wheel covers. Other sophisticated Guildsmen headed to their high school metal shops for the engine lathe to make their own or to the local tool and die shop, where a skilled machinist could be located, and had wheel covers of their own design cut and polished from that 1¼" soft aluminum bar stock.

Paint

Primer and lacquer paint from pushbutton cans, or low-cost spray equipment, was recommended for the painting task (around the 1960s). The Guild advocated the automotive touch-up spray-paint bombs available from auto supply stores or dealer service departments for the best possible finish on the model cars. An automotive supply store spray bomb could cost about $1.89, with one can of primer and three cans of color lacquer being adequate for a Guild model. Of course, the number of coats of paint needed depended on the condition of the model's surface, the thickness of each coat, and the skill of the painter. Some Guildsmen applied 25 coats of color lacquer in order to achieve an award winning finish, and this is where the project could get more expensive. The Guild technical department would provide a list of spray-bomb suppliers in the Guildsman's area.

As alternatives, the Guild technical department suggested other low-cost methods, such as a continuous-pressure garden spray gun, a small touch-up spray gun that operated from cans of compressed air from the local auto accessory store, a high quality, hand pumped insect gun or vacuum cleaner spray gun equipment. With the latter methods, the Guildsman could mix the lacquer and thinner from the local auto body shop. Because some of these methods took longer for the paint to dry (due to larger paint particles), a dustproof box had to be lowered into place immediately to cover the model car just painted. Although the hand pump bug sprayer was recommended, Elia Russinoff (1949 first-place national scholarship winner) opted for the family Hoover canister-type vacuum cleaner (with spray paint attachment), as it had a negative pressure end for vacuuming and a positive pressure end for spray painting.

Of course, it would have been nice to have had access to high pressure spray paint equipment, and a spray booth with continuous air circulation and a ventilation system. Some Guildsmen solved this problem by approaching commercial body shops for help or purchasing high pressure spray paint equipment of their own from Sears, Roebuck and Company. The optimum was a 30–40 psi spray paint system for very fine atomization of paint particles and quick drying.

Construction Materials and Methods Used[29]

The following are typical examples of the materials from which winning Craftsman's Guild models were constructed.

CHARLES M. JORDAN, 1947 FIRST-PLACE NATIONAL SCHOLARSHIP WINNER, SENIOR DIVISION, $4,000 AWARD, AGE 19

This model was started in the winter of 1946 of Jordan's sophomore year and involved scale drawings or blueprints of the design and a clay model to work out details. The construction of the model from white pine was done at the MIT Hobby Shop for students from January to June 1947. All metal parts were carefully shaped from brass, chrome plated, and set into the wood. The model required 35 coats of paint and measured approximately 16" × 6¼" × 5" (L × W × H). The model required 700 hours of work and was delivered by the June 15, 1947, deadline.

ELIA RUSSINOFF, 1949 FIRST-PLACE NATIONAL SCHOLARSHIP WINNER, SENIOR DIVISION, $4,000 AWARD, AGE 18

Russ' father, Even P. Russinoff, a die designer at Fisher Body Central Engineering Division, brought home a block of soft mahogany from the shop, which was used to make the body of this 1949 national winner. The white plastic headlamps were home-made. Brilliant front-end fixtures of chrome-plated brass were filed by hand. Eleven coats of paint were applied using a Hoover vacuum cleaner spray gun attachment. Russ made the wooden wheels on a 4-in-1 tabletop lathe.[30]

BENJAMIN B. TAYLOR, 1950 FOURTH-PLACE NATIONAL SCHOLARSHIP WINNER, JUNIOR DIVISION, $1,000 AWARD, AGE 15

The construction details for the Ben Taylor model were as follows: body—balsa wood, bumpers—marine plywood inserts, wheels—white pine from fruit crates, windows—painted sheet aluminum, window trim—aluminum paint, hub caps—ends of scotch tape rolls, headlights—thimbles, headlight rims—mop handle ends, paint—25 coats of lacquer.

ANTHONY S. HENDRICK, 1951 THIRD-PLACE NATIONAL SCHOLARSHIP WINNER, JUNIOR DIVISION, $2,000 AWARD

This 1951 model was constructed from plaster; the wheel covers, bumpers and trim were aluminum; the wheels were attached via axles on a wood subframe; and the paint was Oldsmobile Fiesta Red.

ROBERT C. RELYEA, 1952 FOURTH-PLACE NATIONAL SCHOLARSHIP WINNER, JUNIOR DIVISION, $1,000 AWARD

The body was pine and balsa wood, the wheels were apple wood turned on a lathe by the contestant, and the bumpers were coated with plastic metal and finished to a chrome-like appearance.

GILBERT MCARDLE, 1955 REGIONAL WINNER FROM UTAH

The body was basswood and the trim was chrome plated brass. The taillights and headlights, respectively, were red and white plastic. The canopy was shaped from a solid block of acrylic plastic (without a finished interior). There was aquamarine color trim on the sail panels and over 20 coats of black lacquer on the body.

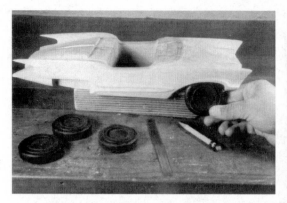

Bill Moore checks the clearances of a 2⁷⁄₁₆″ diameter front wheel in the fender-well of his 1956 Guild model carved from solid poplar. *Above right:* The finished clay model made by Bill Moore for the 1956 Guild competition. Designing and sculpting an accurate clay model was essential to succeeding in the Craftsman's Guild program. *William A. Moore.*

WILLIAM A. MOORE, 1956 FIRST-PLACE NATIONAL SCHOLARSHIP WINNER, SENIOR DIVISION, $5,000 AWARD

The body was made from one piece of poplar after cutting clear through and under the dash. Nineteen pieces were made of wood, aluminum or chrome plated brass to make up the interior components. The steering wheel was one piece turned on a lathe, like a funnel, then cut open leaving the spokes and column. The transmission console was

Art Russell's 1956 model carved from poplar is shown on the left with headlamp trim pieces, hard rubber tires and wheelcovers. Also shown is William A. Moore's 1956 model (right) carved from poplar with headlamp trim pieces, pleated seat tops and floor sub-assembly. Bill and Art were high school friends from Venice, California, who encouraged and supported one another through the arduous Guild design process. Note that for his final 1956 entry, Bill redesigned the headlight mount areas in favor of flush, concealed headlights for a cleaner, more aerodynamic look. Bill won the top senior national scholarship in 1956 with this convertible design. *E. Arthur Russell.*

made of aluminum, and hacksaw grooves allowed the white electrical wire to be flush wrapped for décor. The front bumper was made from a solid block of brass, then chrome plated. The rear bumper was made of three pieces of brass, which were joined with silver solder and chrome plated. The windshield molding was formed from brass tubing, filed in half, fit to the curved plexiglass and then soldered to a recessed bottom piece. The brass hubcaps were turned on a lathe and chrome plated. The model was finished in 1955 Buick Titian Red lacquer with white trim.

William F. Marks, 1957 Second-Place National Scholarship Winner, Senior Division, $4,000 Award, from Twin Falls, Idaho

Bill Marks recently described the design and construction of his award winning 1957 model:

> Wedge and sculptured styling of automobiles was new then and I combined both in my model car. This made for surface complexity. So I decided to make the car of Plastic Wood applied over an armature of balsa wood with many bulkhead or section "formers" to accurately define the plan and profile cross sections, fin outline, etc. (like the fuselage of a model airplane). This eliminated the time-consuming clay model stage and allowed changes in the surface development to be easily made. I made the side panels separately and glued them on. They were covered in "Sculpmetal" to make a brushed aluminum finish which was also applied to indicate the windows. The car was two-tone: a metallic green paint with brushed aluminum. I knew the plastic wood putty would continue to shrink a bit over the years, but it would look fine for the judging. And it still looks OK. A few cracks are now seen at the section "former" locations. The wheel covers were made from aluminum measuring spoons that came, one each, in pancake flour boxes. The grill/bumpers, license plate and tail light bezels, parking lights, window frames, and antennas were carved from aluminum bars that I bought as a kit from a Guild source. These have dulled over the years from oxidation of the aluminum.
>
> From design sketches to finish, the car took about 700 hours. I had never seen another Guild model and, looking back, to earn more craftsmanship points, I should have cut out the air intakes in the wheel covers and scored the body panel shut lines instead of using black decals to indicate them. I would now eliminate the few remaining straight lines and change the grille/bumper as well (I should have mocked it up before carving it out). Forty years later the wedge look is still in, sculpturing is replaced by subtle surface development, and antennas stay retracted until needed.[31]

George W. Aschen III, 1957 Certificate of Design and Craftsmanship, Kirkwood, Missouri

This unsophisticated balsa wood model with a large black area indicating a bubble top was painted in three tones: two with ordinary house enamel (aquamarine and off-white) and the third a silver, metallic paint to accent the rocker panels and valence panels and bumpers. This model, which was recently recovered at the AACA Flea Market at Hershey, Pennsylvania, in 2000, had streamlined headlight cowlings that housed huge headlights mounted in the hood, obviously inspired by the 1955 Chevrolet Biscayne show car, and rear quarter panel intaglios or accent scoops.

David C. Byram, 1958 Styling Scholarship Winner, Senior Division, $1,000 Award, Age 19

The body was made of clear pine finished with sealer, primer and lacquer; the bumpers, light housings, and windshield supports were polished aluminum; and the wheel covers were polished brass. The interior of this two-door sports car was hollowed out and finished with a clear plastic windshield and side windows. The maroon paint job and brass wheel covers were very complementary.

Patrick B. Saturday, 1961 Styling Scholarship, $1,000 Award

The construction of this convertible requiring 560 hours was as follows: roof—clear acrylic dome that was vacuum formed over a plaster model the contestant had made; body—1" thick laminated poplar hand-carved with cardboard templates, and three coats of fiberglass resin; paint—10 coats of lacquer primer, 11 coats of color lacquer, and hand compounded final coat; metal trim—parts made from brass were nickel plated and then chrome plated; wheel covers—made of brass turned on a lathe; taillights—red and clear plastic cut, glued together, and buffed to fit; interior floors—felt paper; and dashboard graphics—a photographic negative scaled to fit.

James W. Green, 1961 Third-Place National Scholarship Winner, Junior Division, $3,000 Award, Age 15

The construction consisted of balsa wood covered with fiberglass, an amber colored, translucent canopy, chrome plated trim, enamel paint, and a hollowed-out and finished interior with full-canopy enclosure.

Richard J. Johnson, 1962 Styling Scholarship, $1,000 Award

The model was constructed from wood with six coats of primer and nine coats of color lacquer. The chrome-like trim was polished aluminum, and the trim around the windows was chrome plated steel wire.

Wolfgang Rueckner, 1963 Regional Winner, Massachusetts

The body for this two-seater convertible was carved from red cherry, with a clear acrylic windshield. The bumpers were filed from solid aluminum stock; the grille and trim fabricated from copper wire, brass shim stock and plastic; the seat and dash board were covered with metallic simulated contact paper; and the paint was metallic brown enamel.

Michael B. Antonick, 1964 Second Place National Scholarship Winner, Senior Division, Age 19

This 1964 model was an Open Competition (Drawing C) entry that required 600 hours to construct. It was a two-seater painted midnight blue, with a white canopy and brightly plated brass trim.

Secrets of Success

READ THE DIRECTIONS

If all else fails, read the instructions! Although a Guildsman could read the quarterly newsletters and how-to booklets containing step-by-step illustrated text, there was still a lot of missing information only experience could teach — or, if he was lucky, he had a mentor or a friend who could interpret the technical instructions. William A. Moore indicated that he simply followed the techniques and procedures in the Guild printed materials and that helped him win the first-place national scholarship at age 19 in 1956. But there were other secrets to his success. Bill Moore had entered the competition in 1955. He and his buddy Art Russell, another Guildsman, drove to Detroit to examine the Craftsman's Guild entries on display and talked to a Fisher Guild judge about their model designs. At that point Bill concluded, "I can do this!"

The two friends worked together in Art's workshop. Art's father, Elwin Russell, was the perfect mentor, a tool and die maker by trade. John M. Mellberg had the perfect mentors, his grandfather being a tool and die maker by trade and his father an engineer. In Chicago, the Mellbergs lived above the father's machine shop. John knew how to use every tool in the shop early on in his life.

MULTIPLE MODELS

Although there were a few notable exceptions, Guildsmen had to construct multiple models in order to succeed at the national award level. Some constructed seven, eight or even nine models in as many consecutive years. To win a national scholarship award in the first attempt required exceptional design genius and talent, as the contestants theoretically worked their way up the ladder from the first-place state award level to the regional award level and then finally to the national scholarship level. Each level demanded a further commitment of their time to craftsmanship and design. The following examples show the number of years of experience and success levels achieved for some specific Guildsmen.

One Time

Charles M. Jordan won the 1947 first-place national scholarship, senior division, $4,000 award, at age 19 on his first attempt at the competition.

Gale P. Morris won the 1949 third-place national scholarship, junior division, $2,000 award, at age 13 on his first attempt.

Charles W. Pelly won the 1954 second-place national scholarship, junior division, $4,000 award, at age 15 on his first attempt.

Patrick B. Saturday won a 1961 styling scholarship, $1,000 award, on his first attempt at the competition.

Robert E. Davids won the 1963 first-place national scholarship, senior division, $5,000 award, on his first try.

Thomas H. Semple won the 1964 first-place national scholarship, senior division, $5,000 award, on his first attempt.

Two Times

William A. Moore won the second-place California state award in 1955 and in 1956, the first-place national scholarship, senior division, $5,000 award.

Adrian A. Bruno won the third-place New York state award in 1954 and a second national scholarship award in 1955.

Patrick O. McKittrick won the first-place Indiana state award in 1956 and a national styling scholarship in 1957.

Three Times

Elia Russinoff won a $250 award, among the sons of GM employees, for his 1947 four-door sedan model entry, the third-place Michigan state award in 1948, and in 1949 the first-place national scholarship, senior division, $4,000 award.

Anthony Hendrick won the third-place New York state award (junior division) in 1949, the second-place New York state award (junior division) in 1950, and the third-place national scholarship (junior division) in 1951.

John T. Williams won the first-place Texas state and regional awards all three years he participated: 1956, 1957 and 1958.

Kenneth H. Kaiser (deceased) entered the Guild competition three times (1956, 1957 and 1958) culminating in a 1958 fourth-place national scholarship, senior division, $2,000 award.

Henry F. Rom built three models for the Guild. The first two were in the junior division. The third model won the 1953 fourth-place national scholarship, senior division, $1,000 award.

Newell Bringhurst won three first-place state awards, three regional awards (1958, 1959 and 1960) and a national styling scholarship award.

Richard B. Lee entered three times (1964–1966) and won a regional award in 1966 on his third try.

Spencer L. Mackay won first-place state and regional awards in 1966 and 1967, respectively, and won a national styling scholarship in 1968.

Four Times

Gary Graham entered four times (1951, 1952, 1953 and 1954). His 1954 model won the first-place national scholarship, senior division, $4,000 award.

David P. Onopa began at the bottom with an honorable mention (junior division) in 1963, a regional award (junior division) in 1964, a third-place state award (senior division) in 1965 and a regional award (senior division) in 1966.

William A. Keyser (Pennsylvania) entered the competition four times (1949, 1950, 1951 and 1952). He began as a second-place state winner in 1949, was a third-place state winner in 1950, won a first-place state and regional award in 1951, and finally, won a second national scholarship, junior division, $3,000 award in 1952.

Five Times

Noland Vogt entered the competition in 1948, 1949, 1950, 1951 and 1952 and won four first-place state awards, one second-place state award and two regional awards.

James Garner entered the competition five times 1951 through 1955. His 1954 and 1955 models won regional awards. Talking to judges at the awards banquet, he learned that his 1955 model missed winning a national scholarship by only a few points.

Six Times

Edward F. Taylor (Oklahoma) entered the competition six times from 1946 to 1951. At age 12 he earned a second-place Oklahoma state award with a four-door sedan made from balsa wood and painted with enamel. During the years he participated, the Guild rules only allowed four-door sedan designs. In the next four years he won first-place state and regional awards (three in the junior division and one in the senior division) with balsa wood and lacquer models, a plaster and lacquer model and then in 1951 a mahogany and lacquer model. This last model, featuring clear translucent windows and windshield, won a third-place national scholarship award, senior division, $2000 award. Taylor was only 17 years old. He competed in Region 15, made up of Louisiana, Arkansas and Oklahoma. One year he arranged to use his father's employer's workshop to refine his Guild project.

E. Arthur Russell began competing at age 13 in the 1951 model car competition with his first entry, a sedan, winning nothing. His second entry at age 15, a sedan, in 1953 won a third-place California state, junior division, $50 award. Art's third entry in 1954 at age 16, a convertible sports car, won an honorable mention, senior division, $25 award. His fourth entry at age 17, a hardtop sedan, in 1955 won an honorable mention, senior division, $25 award. With his fifth entry, at age 18 in 1956, he won a second-place California state, senior division, $100 award, and because of excellence in design he won a styling scholarship worth $1,000. Art began professional training for his career at the Art Center School at this time. He took a semester off from school and at age 19 in 1957 he won the first-place national scholarship, senior division, $5,000 award.

John M. Mellberg of Park Ridge, Illinois, built six models (1961 to 1966) of which five were regional winners and one was a 1966 second-place national scholarship winner, senior division. One year this hot shot Guildsman submitted two models.

Seven Times

Roy R. Dickey of Kansas City, Missouri, made seven entries for the Craftsman's Guild model car competition, first winning in 1956 a first-place state award and finishing in 1962 with a first-place national scholarship, senior division, $5,000 award. Three times he won second-place state awards and two times he won third-place state awards.

Geza A. Loczi, from Scottsdale, Arizona, entered the competition seven times. On his seventh try, in 1965, he won the first-place national scholarship, senior division, $5,000 award. With a boost from the Art Center School, he had come a long way, as in 1963 he was only a third-place Arizona state winner.

Larry K. Eby of Vancouver, Washington (deceased), entered from 1962 to 1968, winning a 1967 styling award ($1,000) and a 1968 second-place national award, senior division, $4,000.

Eight Times or More

Michael R. (Bobby) D'Mura entered the competition eight times from 1957 to 1964. He was a regional winner six times and a styling scholarship winner once in 1962.

Richard Lee Beck of Louisville entered the competition eight times (making ten models) and won seven regional awards, including a styling scholarship and a national scholarship. His brother, Thomas L. Beck, entered the Guild competition as well.

Richard and his brother Tom dominated Region 7 (later reorganized into Region 9) with their model-making skills and innovative designs. Richard Beck had a successful career at Ford Motor Company as an interior and exterior designer and his brother Tom had a successful career at General Electric's Appliance Park in Louisville, Kentucky, in the area of computer aided design.

Stuart Shuster entered the competition nine times from 1952 to 1960, winning state awards. The first two entries were from Pennsylvania and the last seven entries were from Kentucky.

DON'T MESS WITH A GOOD THING

Because there were so many variables in this competition there was no sure formula for success. There are several examples where the axiom "don't mess with a good thing" was applied.

In 1955 Murray A. Milne won the first-place Michigan state award with a two-seat convertible. In 1956 he won a second-place national scholarship, senior division, $4,000 award, with an almost identical design. (Murray became an architectural professor at UCLA.) Except for the color, the 1956 would appear to be a perfected copy of the 1955 model. Paul Tatseos did the same thing. His 1957 styling scholarship award winning design was perfected with an almost identical two-seat convertible design in 1958, winning a third-place national scholarship, senior division, $3,000 award. (Paul became chief designer at Buick Interior Design Studios.) The styling scholarship for excellence in design represented a score of 90 percent or better of the available 225 points in the Design category. Paul just needed to perfect the Craftsmanship side of the equation, which he obviously did in 1958 to win a national award. Both scores had to be at least 90 percent or better to win a national award. GM set a very high performance standard.

In 1957 James T. Sampson of Terra Haute, Indiana, won a national styling scholarship and in 1961 Kaizo Oto of Fresno, California, won a national styling scholarship. In the following year's competition both contestants won top national scholarship awards by entering what appears to be the same design (not necessarily the same model). In 1958 James T. Sampson won the first-place national scholarship award, senior division, and in 1962 Kaizo Oto won the third-place national scholarship, senior division, $3,000 award. (Kaizo designed safety cars for Raymond Loewy International.) Each person improved or perfected what was already a sound design.

Bob D'Mura, either out of superstition, or a "don't mess with a good thing" philosophy, painted nearly all the models he entered the same color (1957 Chevy Sierra Gold) and won many regional awards and trips to Detroit between 1957 and 1964.

BE A REGIONAL WINNER AND ATTEND THE GUILD CONVENTION

Attending the Guild convention in order to see and inspect the other models, meet the other competitors, and exchange ideas with peers was a milestone for success in the Craftsman's Guild program. As a future contestant, it was necessary to see how high the competitive bar was raised and understand the reality of the program.

The quarterly black and white Guild publications (*Guild News* and *Guildsman*), which contained small pictures of winning models (½" × 1" images), did not adequately communicate the exacting precision represented by each model. The editors of the publications could never describe for the beginner what the competition was really all about.

Guildsmen used their cash awards to upgrade their tools and equipment in order to make better models. After attending the 1961 Guild convention, talking to other Guildsman, and studying the award winning models, Kaizo Oto returned to his home in Fresno, California, and purchased spray paint equipment to obtain a better paint job and a jeweler's lathe to make better parts such as wheel covers. One year Ed Taylor bought a spray paint gun with his Guild prize money.

ACHIEVE HIGH PERFORMANCE STANDARDS

A very high performance standard was set by GM in order to be a national winner.

The number of points for Craftsmanship and Design were about equal, so the contestant had to perform well in both areas. The Guildsman had to balance design originality, practicality and artistic merit for maximum points under the Design scoring category. In addition, scale fidelity, workmanship, and painting and finishing had to be combined for maximum points under the Craftsmanship scoring category.

A contestant's design would have to be awarded 50–60 percent of available points to receive a minimum state award. To be considered for a national award, first the Guildsman had to win a first-place state award, in either the junior or senior division, in the state where he resided. (The age divisions ensured that contestants of similar experience and maturity competed against one another.) This required winning 60 percent to 75 percent or more of the available 450 points awarded by the judges. For example, in 1955 Allen T. Weideman won 62 percent of the available points for a first-place Utah state award, and in 1962, John L. Jacobus won 342 points out of 450 (76 percent), for a first-place Maryland state award and $150.[32] All the first-place state winners competed for the regional awards, junior and senior division. At least 85 percent of the available 450 points had to be earned in order to be considered for a regional award.

In 1957 Allen T. Weidemen won 387 of the available 450 points (86 percent) for first-place Utah state and regional awards (Colorado, Utah, Kansas), while in 1958, Ronald C. Pellman won 384 points out of 450 (85 percent) for first-place Connecticut state and regional awards (Connecticut, New York). To be a regional winner was to be one of the top 40 model-makers in the country.[33]

Finally, the top national winners, who won university trust funds, were selected from the 40 regional winners. In order to do this, a model had to win 90 percent or more of the available 450 points. E. Arthur Russell's 1957 first-place national scholarship, senior division, award winning design earned 92 percent of the available 450 points. The judges agreed this model was close to perfection. He achieved 93 percent in Craftsmanship and 92 percent in Design. Similarly, Robert E. Davids' 1963 first-place national scholarship, senior division, award-winning design earned 90 percent in Craftsmanship and 94 percent in Design.

The 1955–56 competition was the transition year from eight top national scholarship awards (four senior division and four junior division) to 18 top scholarship awards (four senior, four junior, and ten styling scholarships for Excellence in Design). The styling scholarship awards did not have to come from the top 40 models, but could be from any level of the competition. The Guildsman had to earn at least 90 percent of available points in the Design category. For example, Bruce Claypool, a 1967 styling scholarship winner, achieved only 70 percent in the Craftsmanship category, but 93 percent in the Design category.

A lowly state or regional winner could conceivably win a styling scholarship, and this actually occurred on numerous occasions. In the case of Paul Tatseos in 1957, he was not a first-place Massachusetts state winner, yet he won a styling scholarship because of a high score in the "Design" category. In 1966, the ten styling scholarship awardees

This 2-passenger sports car designed by Harry E. Schoepf (age 19) of Manchester, New Hampshire, won a 1961 styling scholarship worth $1,000, being cited for excellence in design. His design also won the first state New Hampshire, senior division, and regional awards from Region No. 1 (Maine, New Hampshire, Vermont). *General Motors Corporation.*

included four regional winners, one first-place state winner, three second-place state winners, and two honorable mentions. Another example is Dennis A. Little from Lyndhurst, Ohio, whose design received third-place state honors in the senior division, but was awarded one of the ten styling scholarships in 1967 (*Model Car Science*, October 1967).

The winning models were built to high model-maker standards (± ⅟₁₆″), almost perfection, and combined a fluid sculptured design, metal brightwork and a mirror-finish paint job. Polished metal surfaces were flawless and integrated into the body design. Inlaid trim was flush with the paint. Lacquer was hand rubbed, or hand compounded, to a brilliant luster. The model was perfectly proportioned to 1/12 scale. Turned wheel covers of intricate design complemented the overall body design. Brass parts were chrome plated. Vacuum-formed acrylic canopies or windshield parts were trimmed with brightwork, and plastic surfaces were buffed like new. There was no evidence of glue to hold the canopy or windshield to the body. Overall, and most important, the model had to conform to GM's design principle of crisp design lines, and had to exemplify simplicity and beauty.

SIMPLICITY AND BEAUTY, NOT COMPLEXITY

The working mantra of the Guildsman was KISS (Keep It Simple, Stupid). One idea embraced by naïve Guildsman was that a complex model would win. Unfortunately, as many participants learned, an overreaching, complex design that could not be executed to a high level of perfection was not the answer.

A simple design idea expressed as a solid-top model, and executed to a high degree of perfection within the nine-month competition period, had a high probability of suc-

This model designed by Stewart D. Reed of Traverse City, Michigan, won the 1964 first state Michigan and a regional award. This is an example of a clean, sculpted design called a "solid top" which represented the least amount of construction complexity for a Guild model. Mr. Reed is an independent automobile designer. *Theodore A. Becker.*

cess. Some Guildsmen took this minimalist approach, working with a simple body shape with sculpted design lines and balanced proportions and cast as one solid piece out of plaster or resin. Few, if any, metal trim parts other than a unique set of lathe-turned wheel covers were used for brightwork. Although the model was a pure sculpture or speed form, high attention would be paid to scale fidelity, symmetry and workmanship (e.g. accurately scored door-opening grooves, ½" square) and a flawless paint job. This is all that was really needed.

Other Guildsmen took a more complicated approach such as the convertible sports car that required a finished interior with steering wheel, transmission console, seats, instrument panel, etc. This involved more parts and pieces that had to be finished to perfection. Some simplified this idea by finishing only the driver's side of the two-seat sports convertible. Despite its level of complexity, the convertible was by far the most popular body style built by Guildsmen, because they loved cars.

Another rarer group of Guildsmen raised the bar further by creating clear bubble-top canopies for two-door sports car or four-door sedan designs or creating hardtop designs with clear windshields and side windows as well as hollowed-out and finished interior. Even in the late '40s, hardtops with finished interiors, or designs with Richard Arbib–style bubble top canopies, appeared on the Guild competition scene. This is an extraordinary level of complexity. If not executed to a high level of perfection the model would not be successful in the competition.

This model designed and constructed by Thomas H. Semple from Medford, Oregon, won the 1964 first national scholarship, senior division, $5,000 award. This is an example of the "hardtop" with finished interior, which was the most complex type of model made for the Guild competition. Mr. Semple spent 900 hours planning, sketching and constructing this magnificent ebony-black sports coupe complete with finished tan interior for the 1964 competition. Thomas H. Semple became President of Nissan Design America (formerly Nissan Design International). *Theodore A. Becker.*

Models designed with a clear acrylic windshield and side windows or models with clear plastic bubble-top canopies, in which the finished interior could be viewed by the judges, periodically won high awards. Edward F. Taylor, 1951 third-place national scholarship award winner; Gilbert McArdle, 1955 regional award winner, whose model was a solid block of clear shaped acrylic; David C. Byram, 1958 styling scholarship award winner; Anthony Simone, 1961 first-place national scholarship, junior division award winner (clear bubble top) are examples. The national scholarship award winning models made by Robert Davids (1963), Walter Peeler (1964), Tom H. Semple (1964) and Richard Lee Beck (1964) are additional examples of hardtops with hollowed-out and finished interiors.

Subcontractors

Access to family or other outside know-how would prove critical to the Guildsman's success.

In addition to subcontracting vacuum-forming and chrome-plating tasks, Guildsmen would sometimes subcontract tasks such as paint jobs to the local auto body paint shop; but this was only part of what had to be done. Wet sanding with a fine grit paper was required between each paint coat, and there could be 15 to 20 coats. Grooves for trim,

This 2-door convertible model designed by Thomas L. Covert won a 1962 second national scholarship, senior division, $4,000 award. After the "solid top" model, the convertible model represented the next level of construction complexity with multiple parts and pieces finished to perfection and assembled flawlessly. Tom Covert is a career GM designer. *General Motors Corporation.*

or scored indicator grooves, had to be cleaned after every coat of paint. Different colors such as white, gray or black paint (traditionally used by Guildsmen to indicate windows) had to be masked and remasked from the body color, or vice versa, during the painting process. This would have required close family support, as multiple paint coats, with wet sanding in between, would be needed to achieve a high mirror-like finish. The lacquer had to be hand rubbed (with the soft palm of the hand) using rubbing compound for a final mirror finish.

The local engraver's shop, tool and die shop, or machine shop might be tasked to produce a set of intricate wheel covers. Chrome plating had to be performed by an outside vendor, but the preparation of the brass parts was the Guildsman's job. One Guildsman described nickel plating followed by chrome plating of brightwork for his model. Another Guildsman reported rhodium plating of brass for his brightwork. But, trial and error was the biggest teacher, and multiple experiences entering the competition were the largest determinant in the Guildman's success.

Guild Clubs

There were high school Guild clubs and GM plant clubs where adult advisers were available to help young model makers. There was a "Guild Instructor's Guide" for the adults. There were Guild clubs sponsored by Delco Remy and Guide Lamp in Anderson, Indiana, and these clubs provided access to shop facilities for boys at local junior high schools. The Department of Trades and Industry of Anderson's Public Schools supported this program (*Guide Light*, Dec. 21, 1951, p. 6). In 1967, the Guild club at Delco-Remy Division of GMC produced John F. Faust, first-place national scholarship winner, junior division, age 15.

Many Guild scholarship winners attended the Art Center School (ACS) in Los Angeles (renamed the Art Center College of Design [ACCD] in 1966) to study industrial design with a major in transportation design. One such scholarship winner from 1950 was Ronald C. Hill. In this photograph, Hill (circa 1954) studies the skill of Joe Thompson, a revered automobile design sculptor and his teacher at ACS. *Ronald C. Hill.*

There were Craftsman's Guild clubs in Marion, Warren, and Dayton, Ohio, because the GM and Fisher Body plants nearby promoted the Craftsman's Guild for the sons of employees. GM Styling representatives, including Mr. Jordan, addressed parents and sons at such venues as the Fisher Body plants in Hamilton and Euclid, Ohio; the AC Spark Plug plant in Flint, Michigan; and the Mid-Michigan SAE's Father and Son Dinner at Central Foundry in Saginaw, Michigan. As indicated earlier, hundreds of thousands of Guild booklets were published annually for plant information racks in the hope that a GM employee's son would be a top national winner. There were special color-coded sign-up cards especially for the sons of GM employees.

There were also non-factory related clubs. Fueled by the success of the Guild's commercial advertising program, there must have been high school clubs in 1963, for example, at Compte-Creston High School in Louisiana, with nine Guild model entries winning awards; at Alta Vista High School in Virginia, with seven Guild model entries winning awards; Central High School in Altus, Oklahoma, with four Guild model entries winning awards; and Canton High School in Canton, North Carolina, with six Guild model entries winning awards.

GM Dealers

In the 1950s Chevrolet dealers were encouraged to let aspiring young Guildsman, who they had just signed up, work in their shops. The assumption is that this same message was given to all the GM dealers to encourage customers' sons' participation in the Craftsman's Guild. The Guild distributed their literature through the dealership network. Dealers were given order forms for literature to refill their Guild displays or information racks.

Art Center College of Design

The Art Center College of Design in Pasadena, the famous school that produces the world's supply of top quality automobile stylists and designers, was represented regularly, at some level, in the Guild winner's circle. According to Stanley F. Parker, a chief designer at GM, one-third of the designers at GM in the 1960s were graduates of the Pasadena school.[34]

In the 1960s ACCD taught Model-Making 101, a three-credit course, to their freshman industrial design students. Model-making would be a regular part of the industrial designer's life, because they expressed themselves in three-dimensional terms. The first semester of courses at ACCD addressed many of the problems in designing and building a successful Guild model. The drafting of compound surfaces and cutting of sections (or what was called surface development) was taught as a mechanical drawing class. This was the most important skill to learn as automobile surfaces are not flat, but are subtle compound surfaces. They are curved or convex in the longitudinal direction as well as in the lateral direction. The skill of surface development requires knowledge of how compound surfaces are joined, how they transition from one to the other, and how light's reflection off these surfaces guides the designer's hand.[35]

Two Guild scholarship winners and ACS students with their award winning model car designs (circa 1958) are *(left)* E. Arthur Russell, 1957 first national scholarship, senior division, $5,000 award winner, and *(right)* William A. Moore, 1956 first national scholarship, senior division, $5,000 award winner. Art and Bill have remained lifelong friends and still talk cars. *E. Arthur Russell, with permission of Russell and William A. Moore.*

ACCD Model-Making 101 taught clay modeling (templates, drags and cams); how to make Hydrocal plaster molds and apply silicone release agents; and how to apply gel coats, fiberglass lay-up, high pressure sprayed lacquer (30–40 psi), and palm-of-the-hand compounded lacquer surfaces. This first semester did not guarantee success, but it provided the tools and techniques to be successful. The Guildsman had to apply these tools and techniques.

Stylist's Genes, Pedigrees and the "Right Stuff"

Some contestants had the automobile stylist's "gene," such as Virgil Exner, Jr. (a 1946 national scholarship winner at age 13), whose father was Virgil Exner, Sr. (destined to become VP of Styling at Chrysler Corporation in the '50s). Also, there was Patrick O. McKittrick, whose uncle was the famed classic Duesenberg and Cord designer Gordon

M. Buehrig. McKittrick won a 1956 first-place Indiana state award and a 1957 styling scholarship, $1,000 award. Mr. McKittrick stated, "Being born in Auburn Indiana, home of the Auburn and Cord automobiles and having a famous uncle named Gordon Buehrig, who was highly active in the automotive design arena, I was quite steeped in its history and present day (1950s) posture. So, I went into the field of architecture instead of a Stylist's career."[36]

Thomas C. Goad won the 1948 first-place national scholarship, junior division, $4,000 award, making his father, Lewis C. Goad, executive vice president and director of General Motors, very proud.[37] For Tom Goad this was clearly a mixture of auto executive genes and having the "right stuff."

Elia Russinoff, whose father, Even, was a Fisher Body Central Engineering die designer, won several state awards in 1947 and 1948 before winning the 1949 first-place national scholarship, senior division, $4,000 award.

David H. Koto of Birmingham, Michigan, son of Robert Koto, a Ford designer, was a big winner with a 1956 styling scholarship, $1,000 award, and a 1957 fourth-place national scholarship, senior division, $2,000 award.

Top: Clay is applied to an armature made from scrap wood for Art Russell's 1956 design. The design ideas Guildsmen had sketched on paper could be better visualized three-dimensionally when sculpted by hand. Although most Guild participants had access to oil-based clays from the hobby shop or hardware store, Guildsmen could also contact professional automotive styling clay suppliers by writing to the Guild technical staff. *E. Arthur Russell. Bottom:* The finished clay model made by Art Russell for the 1956 Guild competition. Designing and sculpting an accurate clay model was essential to succeeding in the Craftsman's Guild program. *William A. Moore.*

Project Planning

Planning was another factor that made the difference. A Fisher Body competition model was not completed by luck or chance. The model had to be conceived in an integrated manner either on the drafting board with scale drawings and/or a 1/12 scale clay model or pattern. The *Guildsman* laid out in detail a 24-week (6-month) schedule each contestant could follow from September to June. For the procrastinators, the *Guildsman* also laid out a 17-week step-by-step (4-month) schedule.

Guildsmen had to read the instructions in the design booklet and adhere to the minimum and maximum allowable dimensions depending on the body style. A system using templates from the clay model, or a home made marker gauge or stylist's bridge, had to be employed in order to achieve any semblance of symmetry. The greenhouse or solid-top for the driver and passenger occupants might be carved and finished separately, then assembled to the body with pins or pegs. The metal trim parts and pieces were cut, filed and fitted a thousand times to the plaster or wood grooves or slots before any paint or primer was applied. Pins to hold the metal parts in place without epoxy glue showing had to be provided. Wheels were located and fitted with wood screws far in advance of any paint or primer as well. Hood, truck and door openings all had to be scored in advance. Once the wood body parts were painted, and metal parts were polished or chrome plated, the parts and pieces all fit into preplanned locations. Tasks had to completed in a logical, sequential manner, overlapping and simultaneous tasks had to be identified, long

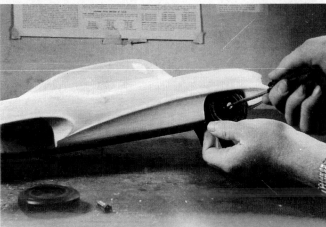

Top: Using a ruler, dividers and a pencil, Art Russell located the front and rear axles longitudinally on the bottom of his 1956 model and then transferred them vertically within each wheel well. The center of each attachment point is pre-drilled with a starter hole for the wood screws. *Bottom:* The hard rubber wheels (2⁷⁄₁₆" diameter) given by the Guild to contestants are preliminarily attached with wood screws by Art Russell. Ground clearance, departure angles, and fender-to-wheel clearances (front and rear) had to be checked. The wheels are removed until all metal work and painting tasks are completed, then reattached at the very end to finish the model. *E. Arthur Russell.*

lead times had to be identified, and each step had to be completed on schedule, or the June deadline might be missed. A mental flow diagram was needed.

Family Know-How

Family know-how was critical, as evidenced by the number of successful Guild families that competed. In many cases the father had an applicable area of expertise (e.g., machinist, upholsterer, tool and die maker, woodworker, cabinet maker, model-maker, engineer, or auto designer). An older successful brother often passed on his knowledge to the younger brother. Guild participation became a family tradition. This phenomenon also explains how boys in junior high aged 12 and 13 won top national awards. The following list of awards show how effective and successful the families were in the competition.

WHITMAN BROTHERS, JACKSON, MICHIGAN

David W. Whitman	1946 third-place national scholarship, senior division, $2,000 award.
Harvey E. Whitman	1948 first-place national scholarship, senior division, $4,000 award.

TETER BROTHERS, ELKINS, WEST VIRGINIA

Roger D. Teter	1949 third-place national scholarship, junior division, $2,000 award.
H. Keith Teter	1948, 1949, 1950 first-place West Virginia state, $150 cash award; 1951 first-place West Virginia state and regional winner.

RAUTH BROTHERS, NEBRASKA

In the Rauth family, five brothers participated from 1937 to 1956:

John F. Rauth	1937 first-place Nebraska state award.
Vincent J. Rauth	1946 first-place national scholarship, senior division, $4,000 award.
Phillip J. Rauth	1947 second-place national scholarship, junior division, $2,000 award.
R. Joseph Rauth	Early 1950s second-place Nebraska state award, senior division.
Herman I. Rauth	1955 first-place Nebraska state award; 1956 styling scholarship, $1,000 award.

McDONNELL BROTHERS, STOCKTON, CALIFORNIA

Thomas A. McDonnell	1953 third-place national scholarship, junior division, $2,000 award.
Robert F. McDonnell	1955 second-place national scholarship, senior division, $3,000 award.

ANTONICK BROTHERS, MT. VERNON, OHIO

Milton J. Antonick	1955 first-place national scholarship, senior division, $4,000 award.

Michael Antonick   1964 second-place national scholarship, senior division (age 19), $4,000 award.

GREENE BROTHERS, MEDINA, WASHINGTON

Thomas F. Greene   1955 first-place national scholarship, junior division, $4,000 award.

Joseph F. Greene, Jr.   1956 fourth-place national scholarship, $2,000 award.

Daniel C. Greene   1957 first-place national scholarship, junior division, $5,000 award.

LAW BROTHERS AND FAMILY, FLORIDA

Gary W. Law   1956 and 1957 second-place state awards, Miami, Florida; 1958 second-place national scholarship, junior division (age 15), $4,000 award.

Norman Law   1957 styling scholarship, $1,000 award, Miami, Florida.

Bonner W. Griner   1963 styling scholarship, $1,000 award, Hialeah, Florida (cousin).

FERRAIOLI BROTHERS, BROOKLYN, NEW YORK

A remarkable family of model-makers who earned national scholarships at age 15 or earlier.

Joseph Ferraioli   1958 national scholarship, junior division (age 15), $2,000 award.

Bill Ferraioli   1959 second-place national scholarship, junior division, $4,000 award.

Tom Ferraioli   1960 first-place national scholarship, junior division, $5,000 award.

HELD BROTHERS, LIVONIA, MICHIGAN

Donald F. Held   1960 second-place national scholarship, junior division, $4,000 award.

Richard K. Held   1961 third-place national scholarship, senior division, $3,000 award.

PIETRUSKA BROTHERS, STAMFORD, CONNECTICUT

Richard, Michael, Ronald and Robert were born with hammers in their hands, so to speak, being brought up in the family upholstery business, and being taught quality craftsmanship by their parents.

Richard Pietruska	1963 first-place national scholarship, junior division (age 15), $5,000 award.
Michael A. Pietruska	1965 second national scholarship, junior division (age 12), $4,000 award.
Ronald E. Pietruska	1964 styling scholarship, (age 15), $1,000 award; 1965 regional winner (age 16), Region 4 (Connecticut, New Jersey); 1967 fourth-place national scholarship, senior division (age 18), $2,000 award.
Robert K. Pietruska	1966 regional winner, junior division (age 11), John J. Ryle elementary school; 1968 third-place New York state award, junior division (family moved to Pound Ridge, New York).

SIMONE BROTHERS, PROVIDENCE, RHODE ISLAND

The boys made 15 models, all winners of some sort.

Gerald Simone	1958 styling scholarship, junior division, $1,000 award; 1962 regional award, senior division.
Eugene Simone	1960 fourth-place national scholarship, junior division, $2,000 award.
Anthony Simone	1961 first-place national scholarship, junior division, $5,000 award.

HAGEN BROTHERS, MINNESOTA

Raymond Hagen	1963 second-place national scholarship, junior division, $4,000 award.
Glen Hagen	1965 styling scholarship, $1,000 award.
Larry Hagen	1966 third-place national scholarship, junior division, $3,000 award.

D'MURA BROTHERS AND FAMILY, FLAGSTAFF, ARIZONA

The father, Michael, was a 1933 Napoleonic coach builder. Sons Bobby and John were model car makers, as was their cousin Joseph Wayne who lived in East Gary, Indiana. Michael D'Mura (father) entered the 1933 Napoleonic Coach competition, winning the first-place Indiana state award for Painting and the second-place Indiana state award for Woodworking. Michael R. (Bobby) participated from 1957 to 1964 and was a regional winner 6 times. In 1962 his entry won a national styling scholarship, $1,000 award.

| John M. D'Mura | 1964 second-place national scholarship, junior division (age 13), $4,000 award. |
| Joseph Wayne D'Mura | 1964 first-place Indiana state and regional winner; 1966 fourth-place national scholarship, senior division, $2,000 award. |

BECK BROTHERS, LOUISVILLE, KENTUCKY

Richard Lee Beck	1957 regional award, junior division (2 models submitted); 1958 regional award, junior division (2 models submitted); 1959 regional award, junior division; 1960 styling scholarship, senior division, $1,000 award; 1961 first-place state award, senior division (age 17); 1962 regional award, senior division (age 18); 1963 regional award, senior division (age 19); 1964 third-place national scholarship, senior division (age 20), $3,000 award.
Thomas Beck	Entered the competition in the shadow of his brother Richard and won various Kentucky state awards (actual awards are unknown).

PEELER BROTHERS, REELSVILLE, INDIANA

Walter Peeler	1963 second-place Indiana state award; 1964 national scholarship, junior division (age 15), $2,000 award.
Raymond W. Peeler	1964 Indiana state award; 1968 first-place Indiana, senior division, and regional winner.

CATALANO BROTHERS, CHEEKTOWAGA, NEW YORK

They made nine Guild models between them.

David G. Catalano	1965 first-place New York state and regional award (age 11); 1966 third-place New York state award (age 12); 1967 fourth-place national scholarship, junior division (age 13), $2,000 award.
Joesph W. Catalano	1964 styling scholarship, $1,000 award.

Top 18 Guild Brother or Family Scholarship Teams

Guild Brothers or Family Teams	Family Residence	Total Scholarship Funds
1. 4 Pietruska brothers (out of 5)	Stamford, CT	$12,000
2. 3 Greene brothers	Medina, Wash.	$11,000*
3. 3 Ferraioli brothers	Brooklyn, N.Y.	$11,000*
4. 2 Welther brothers (Napoleonic Coach builders)	Detroit, Mich.	$10,000*
5. 2 Antonick brothers	Royal Oak, Mich.	$ 8,000*
6. 3 Simone brothers (made 15 models)	Providence, R.I.	$ 8,000*
7. 3 Hagan brothers	Minnesota	$ 8,000*
8. 5 Rauth brothers	Nebraska	$ 7,000
9. 4 D'Mura family	Flagstaff, Ariz.	$ 7,000*

10. 2 Held brothers	Livonia, Mich.	$ 7,000
11. 2 Whitman brothers	Jackson, Mich.	$ 6,000*
12. 3 Law family	Miami, Fla.	$ 6,000*
13. 2 Larzelere brothers (Napoleonic Coach builders)	Flint, Mich.	$ 6,000*
14. 2 McDonnell brothers	Stockton, Calif.	$ 5,000*
15. 2 Beck brothers (made 18 models)	Louisville, Ky.	$ 4,000
16. 2 Catalano brothers	Buffalo, N.Y.	$ 3,000*
17. 2 Peeler brothers	Reelsville, Ind.	$ 2,000
18. 2 Teter brothers	Elkins, W.V.	$ 2,000

These are all model "dream car" makers, except for the Welther and Larzelere brothers who were Napoleonic Coach builders, shown for comparison.

This list includes individuals and families who have corresponded with the author and contributed to the book. There are undoubtedly many other brother and family teams who participated. The above are the most famous and most commonly mentioned among the rank and file. The table shows only total university trust fund amounts and excludes any cash winnings. For example, the Simone brothers made 15 models for another $1,500 (minimum) in cash, and the Beck Brothers made 18–20 models for another $1,800 (minimum) in cash.

*The affectionate moniker "family dynasty" was given when the same family names were repeated year after year in the regional or national award-winner's circle, and especially when all brothers won Guild scholarships.

Labor and Time Commitment

Looking at a sample of 14 1964 and 1967 national scholarship award winners for which published labor hour estimates are available (and as reported by the contestant), a top winning Guild model car consumed 480 hours (average) to complete, or a range of 200-900 hours. The average represents about one-quarter of a man-year of effort where a man-year is about 2,080 labor hours. Walter Peeler indicated in a letter to the author that he kept a record of the labor hours logged to build his 1964 fourth-place national scholarship, junior division, $2,000 award winning model and came up with a total of 238 hours. His was the most complex model design possible, with a hollowed-out and finished interior and a clear canopy with a hardtop roof. Mr. Peeler concluded that, based on his experience, most of the published cumulative labor hours about the Guild models may have been exaggerated.

In 1961 Ronald Will (age 18) of Hobart, Indiana, won the first-place national scholarship, senior division, $5,000 award. He built an asymmetric sports car convertible that consisted of 54 miniature wood and metal parts and took 700 hours to complete. A television reporter asked Will at the time about the amount of time consumed in the model car. Will replied, "I spend 3 hours every night consistently. I planned the work and knew it would take 600 hours to complete my model" (*Guildsman*, vol. 9, no. 1, September 1961).

Here are some examples of hours worked by some of the top national award winning Guildsmen, showing a range of 238 to 1,000 labor hours or an average of 671 hours. These times were reported in newspapers or magazines, by the contestants, at the time they won.

Charles Jordan, 1947 first-place national scholarship, senior division, 700 labor hours.

Harvey E. Whitman, 1948 first-place national scholarship, senior division, 800 labor hours.

Elia Russinoff, 1949 first-place national scholarship, senior division, 500 labor hours.

William F. Marks, 1957 second-place national scholarship, senior division, 700 hours.

Ronald J. Will, 1961 first-place national scholarship, senior division, 700 hours.

Robert E. Davids, 1963 first-place national scholarship, senior division, 1,000 hours.

Walter Peeler, 1964 fourth-place national scholarship, junior division, 238 labor hours.

Thomas H. Semple, 1964 first-place national scholarship, senior division, 900 labor hours.

John F. Faust, 1967 first-place national scholarship, junior division, 500 labor hours.

Shipping Container

Not only did the Guildsman have to design and build an award winning, original, scale model automobile, but he had to ship the fragile, handcrafted piece of art safely, in one piece, to Detroit or Warren, Michigan. The wooden crate or shipping container was a key piece of a winning strategy. The idea was to design the interior packing of the box to cushion against impact or shock and to prevent severe damage. The Guild recognized that the model cars, whether they were made of wood or casting plaster, were fragile and adorned with small, delicate parts and pieces.

Many dreams would be shattered if parts fell off a dream car while in transit. To prevent this, the Guild's technicians at the shipping and receiving depot faithfully repaired damaged models the best they could so they could be scored and judged. The condition of the models as they arrived at the designated shipping and receiving location was recorded and reported to Guild headquarters. Just because things fell apart or were damaged, or the paint hadn't dried, or the suspension collapsed, did not eliminate the model entry from being scored and included in the competition. The chrome plated brass suspension system the author made for his 1965 model (Open Category) collapsed during shipping. Guild technicians sent a black and white photograph showing what had happened. Despite this setback the model was awarded a first-place Maryland state award.

Models were returned to the contestant in the same shipping crate shortly after the judging was completed in August or September. The regional and scholarship winning models, however, might be purchased, leased or borrowed from some of the contestants for exhibition around the country. The borrowed models were eventually returned to their owners.

Deadline

The model car contest coincided with the public school year (typically September 1 through June 4) and the deadline for shipping the completed models to Detroit (later to Warren, Michigan) via Railway Express, or hand-delivering them by car, loomed large around the first week of June. This happened to be just around final exam time in many high schools and colleges.

If a contestant was preparing a model for the competition he had to notify the Guild with a "Final Check-up Card" to obtain shipping instructions (how to ship and where to ship). This coupon was cut from one of the quarterly *Guild News* or *Guildsman* issues. The shipping instructions included shipping tags (addressed to the proper receiving point), "Handle with Care" stickers, a self-addressed, return postcard receipt from the receiving point, a few "Fragile" stickers, and an Official Guild Pledge Card. The shipping kit eventually included the four identification tags for the ingenious tag system.

Some Guildsmen took extreme measures to meet the deadline. To accelerate the drying process, Virgil M. Exner, Jr. (1946), tried baking his model in the family's oven, but this actually cracked the paint job. The Guild deadline was barely met.

Noland Vogt (1948–1951) remembered the last hours and minutes of efforts to make the deadline — even one year when the paint was still wet and he didn't realize the damage until in Detroit at the Guild banquet dinner, when he was handed his model. He was horrified to see that the finish had been completely destroyed by the imprints of the wax paper with which he had wrapped the model as it was put in the pine shipping crate. That was tragic for a teenager.

The family of John M. Mellberg took this step of the process very seriously (after his first model was damaged in transit) and hand-delivered each model entry to the receiving point by driving from their Chicago, Illinois, home to Detroit. It was a matter of family pride. Why take any chances?

Judging and Scoring

WORKING JUDGES

Three pairs of working judges studied and scored each model for state and regional awards and made national scholarship winner recommendations. In the 1960s their work was reviewed and approved by the executive in charge of exterior design (Charles M. Jordan) and the V.P. in charge of styling (William L. Mitchell). The honorary board of judges, made up of some top GM executives and university leaders, approved the final selection of scholarship winners. The judges' decisions were final and the scholarship winners were not announced until the banquet.

From the mid–1950s forward, the working judges for the model car competition consisted of three two-man pairs of professionals, who would take on the task of selecting the winners from the thousands of entries.[38] Each working judge team consisted of a GM stylist who would appraise each model for its styling features or Design (originality of design, artistic merit, and practicality of design), while the second member of the judging team (usually a secondary school industrial arts teacher from the Detroit school system) would judge the entries on Craftsmanship (scale fidelity and workmanship).[39]

The working judges had a set of portable tools to work with: a rotating table and surface gauge to check the height of left and right points; a pair of calipers to ensure compliance with maximum allowable width and minimum allowable height; a wooden wedge to check minimum front and rear departure angles; and a scale to measure for maximum allowable wheelbase length and front and rear overhang. An adjustable rectangular wheelbase fixture helped check wheelbase dimensions, wheelbase width, overhang dimensions, and front and rear axle alignment.

A sample of the "brain trust" represented by the Guild's honorary board of judges who gathered for the final approval of the college scholarship awards in July 1963 with William L. Mitchell, GM vice president in charge of Styling staff (with model in hand). Robert W. Henderson, a 1934 Guild scholarship winner, vice president of Sandia Corporation and top scientist in U.S. nuclear weapons research, was a member that year and is believed to be the tall executive with glasses, looking on intently over Mitchell's left shoulder. Other executives on the honorary board of judges that year (who regrettably cannot be identified by name in this photograph because of the passage of time) were the vice president of GM Research Labs, the chairman of MIT, the past president of the American Association for the Advancement of Science, the vice president of Tulane University, and the presidents of Cal Tech, Purdue, Georgia Tech, Stanford, Penn State and Carnegie Mellon universities. *General Motors Corporation.*

HONORARY BOARD OF JUDGES

In 1954, for example, the honorary board of judges included Charles F. Kettering, GM director; Harley J. Earl, vice president of GM Styling; the presidents of Georgia Tech, MIT, Cornell, University of Michigan, Purdue University and Tulane University; and the heads of the National Science Foundation and the University of Notre Dame College of Engineering.

In 1958 the honorary board of judges included Robert W. Henderson (a new member), who had been a 1934 Napoleonic Coach scholarship winner. He had been the head of the atomic bomb engineering group at Los Alamos, New Mexico, in 1945 and in 1958 was the V.P. of Sandia Corporation, which did engineering development and research for the Atomic Energy Commission.

In 1964 the honorary board of judges included William L. Mitchell, GM vice president in charge of Styling, and Robert W. Henderson, executive vice-president, Sandia Corporation, among others. In 1967, the honorary board of judges included the presidents of Rensselaer Polytechnic Institute, Georgia Tech, Purdue University, Penn State, Tulane University and Carnegie Tech. Also included was the Lawrence R. Hafstad, GM vice president of Research Laboratories.

ADVISORY BOARD

An advisory board made up of secondary school superintendents from across the country had overview responsibilities for the Guild program. In 1967, for example, the advisory board included superintendents of schools from Portland, Detroit, Washington, the District of Columbia, Miami, Kansas City, Cincinnati, San Francisco, Memphis, Dallas, Richmond, and Chicago. They ensured that the Guild program was viewed as a credible, legitimate educational activity for high school age young men.

SCORING CRITERIA

The primary categories used by the working judges to score each model car entry were Craftsmanship and Design, and the available points for each subcategory are shown below. Although objective measuring tools such as a rotating platform, a wheelbase jig, dividers, a scale or ruler, and a 1/12 scale side-view seated manikin were used by the judges, the scoring criteria were predominantly subjective. When their model cars were returned to them in September, entrants received a "Report to Contestants," or score sheet, showing the maximum allowable points for each criteria and the points actually awarded. This feedback provided an opportunity for the Guildsman to improve his next entry.

The following table shows that in the **Craftsmanship** category, 40 percent of the available points were for Workmanship and in **Design**, 40 percent of the available points were for Originality of Design. *Workmanship* and *Originality of Design* were the two largest scoring subcategories Guildsmen faced.

Points and Percentage Allocation of Available Points for Craftsmanship and Design on 1956, 1957, 1958 and 1962 Score Sheets

Craftsmanship	Percent	Design	Percent
1. Scale Fidelity (50 pts.)	25%	Originality of Design (100 pts.)	40%
2. Workmanship (80 pts.)	40%	Artistic Merit (80 pts.)	32%
3. Painting and Finishing (70 pts.)	+ 35%	Practicality (70 pts.)	+ 28%
Subtotal (200 pts.)	100%	*Subtotal* (250 pts.)	100%
Total Points = 450			

On 1956, 1957, 1958 and 1962 score sheets, which show the available points for each category, Craftsmanship had a subtotal of 200 points and Design a subtotal of 250 points for a total of 450 points. This was a 44%/56% weighting scheme. Design was given a slightly higher weight overall. By 1962–63 competition year this weighting was changed to 50/50 so that Craftsmanship and Design were of equal weight, or a subtotal of 225 points each, as shown in the table on page 98.

Points and Percentage Allocation of Available Points
for Craftsmanship and Design on 1963–1968 Score Sheets

Craftsmanship	Percent	Design	Percent
1. Scale Fidelity (50 pts.)	22%	Originality of Design (92 pts.)	41%
2. Workmanship (90 pts.)	40%	Artistic Merit (72 pts.)	32%
3. Painting and Finishing (85 pts.)	+38%	Practicality (61 pts.)	+27%
Subtotal (225 pts.)	100%	*Subtotal* (225 pts.)	100%
Total Points = 450			

Life had become more complicated for the judges as the competition's options expanded to make the program more appealing to youth. A score sheet from the 1963–1968 period showed a box for the model's identification number, a check-off box for "Junior" or "Senior," and a series of check-off boxes pertaining to design category A, B or C and 11 model body styles (Category A included the six-passenger convertible, six-passenger hardtop, sedan, and station wagon; Category B included the hardtop sports car and convertible sports car as well as the compact sedan, compact station wagon and compact convertible; and Category C was the Open Category).

SPECIAL FEATURES

Originality of Design was an important subcategory in the judging. Sometimes, however, the judges found that the purpose of new features was not clear. To ensure full credit, it was recommended that the Guildsman write a clear description of his novel ideas on a small card and attach it to the bottom of his model. This way judges would better understand what the new feature was, how it would work, and what it would mean to passengers and drivers if the car was ever manufactured full size (*Guildsman*, vol. 4, no. 5, 1956). Although some features did not physically exist on the model, the Special Features card or label gave contestants to chance to express their forward thinking ideas.

Virgil M. Exner, Jr.

This 1946 first-place national scholarship winner noted that his model had rectangular polaroid headlamp lenses, radiator vents or grilles at the front of the rear quarter panels, and an air intake nose cone. (Polarized headlight systems in conjunction with polarized windshields to reduce headlight glare are being researched even today.)

Charles M. Jordan

The special features of Chuck Jordan's 1947 first-place national scholarship winning rear engine design included many new ideas, as reported by the MIT *Tech Engineering News*, December 1947.

The rear engine was mounted on a sub-chassis so that it could be easily removed for overhaul and a temporary service unit could be installed. When the original engine was ready for use it could be replaced.

The windshield extended up into the roof to permit the driver and passengers to see the tops of high mountains and skyscrapers as they toured the country. An adjustable shade was mounted on the interior header, so that it could be pulled down as far as the driver wished. "The driver looks out through a polarized windshield made of unbreakable plastic."

Tubular headlights were mounted parallel to the bumpers and protected by them.

"These throw out a wider and more brilliant illumination of the road ahead than do those in current use."

Another feature of the Jordan model was body panels divided into two sections to reduce repair or replacement costs ("Tomorrow's Car").

It is interesting to note that polarized headlight lenses were mentioned by Vigil M. Exner, Jr., and polarized windshield glass was mentioned by Chuck Jordan, as special features in 1946 and 1947, respectively. These were popular safety ideas at the time to reduce oncoming headlight glare for drivers. In order for this idea to work, polarized headlights and polarized windshields would be required to work together.

Gale P. Morris

This 1949 third-place national scholarship model, with custom metallic green paint job, featured a V-8 engine, a girder box-type frame and girder reinforced roof and sail panels, torsion bar suspension, hood and trunk hydraulic lifters, pushbuttons to opens doors, and bumpers mounted on shock absorbers.[40]

George W. Aschen III

Aschen, of Kirkwood, Missouri, won a 1957 certificate of design and craftsmanship for his efforts. The Special Features card still taped to the bottom of the model reads: "transparent plexiglass roof, high ground clearance, rear mounted turbine engine, large front trunk area, and high mounted taillight assembly for better visibility." A very similar high mounted stop light, or Dole Light as it was called, was mandated by Secretary of Transportation Elizabeth Dole in 1984 and has appeared in all cars sold in the United States since the 1986 model year.

Ronald C. Pellman

Ron Pellman, 1960 second-place national scholarship winner, submitted a scale drawing of his model with a typed description of each special feature for the judges to read. The model had a white body with twin blue plastic canopies. It was designed to be a high performance sports vehicle of small size and light weight employing aerodynamic principles such as a reduced frontal area. Access to the rear engine, transmission and differential was gained through the rear deck, through removable panels behind the seats and from underneath the car. The rear engine was a horizontally opposed, air-cooled type like a Corvair engine of the 1960s. The twin clear canopies, one for the driver and one for the passenger, were tinted for sun protection. The headlights were retractable. Interior ventilation and engine ventilation were clearly noted as were engine, transmission and differential packaging.

Ronald J. Will

Will, a 1961 first-place national scholarship winner, stated what his model's special features were in a September 1, 2003, email to the author.

> My explanation sheet on the bottom said that the bumpers and grilles were designed to absorb energy. The doors had fingerprint locks. There was no steering wheel, but a steering knob that moved right or left. It had a padded control panel that pulled over you to serve as a restraint device and a control panel. This panel also served to protect the door in a side collision. All controls were flush with their mounting surfaces. A high performance, low weight Wankel-type engine would be used as a

power plant. Interesting predictions for a 17-year-old kid in 1960. I still think the control panel is a good idea.

Wolfgang Rueckner

This 1963 regional winner built a two-seater sports car with a sweeping bubble windshield and continuous rear brake light lenses across the full width of the rear (similar to what we see today on some cars). This design would have provided access to the trunk from inside the car through a sliding door between the seats (another feature common on today's cars).

Tristram Walker Metcalfe

This 1963 regional winner was concerned with air pressure and ground effects from the front and rear bumpers as well as streamlined efficiency and high speed control. At the Guild convention the judges advised the young Syracuse University student that style and appearance were far more important than efficiency and performance.

John M. Mellberg

This 1966 second-place national scholarship winner was a three-wheel configuration, named the Scorpion, designed for Category C, the Open Competition. Carved from REN board (a synthetic wood) this model was designed as a high speed, aerodynamic emergency medical dispatch vehicle and had actually been wind tunnel tested. There was one small handmade 1" O.D. wheel in the front and two outrigger, regulation size tires on each side. There was tandem seating (one person behind the other) and a pair of turbine engines mounted on each outrigger wheel-assembly with variable air inlet cones. (The cones incorporated headlight assemblies as well). There was photochromatic light adjusting glazing, and there were pop-up air brakes behind the cockpit canopy. The outrigger rear wheels were connected by negative lift stub wings with taillights in the trailing edges. The aerodynamic body had negative lift silhouette for road holding enhancement. The single front wheel retracted at high speed with the body riding on a cushioned "ground effect" shock wave.

CURVE BALLS

Since highly creative and fertile minds were involved in this competition, the judges had to contend with special cases such as partially completed convertible interiors, partial solid-top canopies, canted front wheels, simulated convertible top and folding mechanisms, real chrome-plated spoked wheels and hollowed-out hardtops with completed interiors.

There was the case of the partial interior. One example was a convertible model with only the driver-side completed to convertible specifications and the passenger side opening indicated by scored lines. This was done with great success by Gary Law (1958 second-place national scholarship winner), Joseph Ferraioli (1958 fourth-place national scholarship winner), Ronald J. Will (1961 first-place national scholarship winner) and Michael R. D'Mura (1962 styling scholarship winner). Ronald J. Will indicated to the author in an email that the 1960 Ghia Plymouth XNR show car by Virgil M. Exner, Sr., made this an acceptable method of design presentation.

The teenage designers also adopted this idea and innovated the partial solid-top or greenhouse in which only the driver's side above the belt line was defined and the passenger side was only indicated by scored lines. Roy Dickey's 1962 first-place national scholarship, senior division, award winner was a good example of how this was done.

There were Guildsmen who canted the front wheels a few degrees (as if to indicate motion) such as Tristram W. Metcalfe's senior regional winner, shown in a 1964 banquet brochure; Dennis A. Little's 1965 design, shown in *Popular Science* (October 1965); John F. Faust's 1967 first-place national scholarship winner, junior division); and the design by Robert Kohler, the top senior 1968 winner from Geneva, Switzerland (GM Suisse, Biel, Switzerland).[41] The latter two were shown in *Model Car Science* (October 1967) and *GM World* (October-November 1968). This added a further level of sophistication to the models being designed. If executed flawlessly, this type of feature could result in added points, but would play havoc with a judge's rectangular, but adjustable wheelbase jig and fixture.

And there were asymmetric body styles enough to eliminate the need for a judge's styling bridge, such as Allen Weideman's award winner (1958 first-place Utah state and regional), Ronald J. Will's design (1961 first-place national scholarship, senior division) and Ron R. Steinhilber's 1962 regional award design. Asymmetric design elements had to be skillfully and artistically executed or a lot of points could be lost very quickly. Allen Weideman's design with dual solid-top white canopies had an off-center, metallic trim piece down the driver's side of the hood curving down to the asymmetric grille. Mr. Weideman reported that his design was well received at the Guild convention and received high praise. Ronald J. Will, inspired by the asymmetric features of the 1960 Ghia Plymouth XNR show car, employed complementary, asymmetric design themes generously on the front and rear decks, as well as side panels, of his 1961 award winning convertible sports car and achieved what he called the Wow Factor.

Here is what Ronald J. Will said recently about the use of asymmetry in the Guild competition:

> As for the asymmetrical car, it worked only once. The following year the judges said I created a nightmare of asymmetrical designs that looked like bad accidents or like some just got caught in a blender. Yes, every panel in my 1961 design was different, so I had left and right templates from my clay model. I think Virgil M. Exner, Sr.'s show car design (XNR) allowed me to get way with only a one-sided passenger compartment. I explained that the passenger-side windshield could "pop-up" when the tonneau was removed.[42]

In 1962 Gerald Simone's regional winning design raised the canopy competition further when he submitted a simulated convertible "rag top" with folding top mechanism, open side windows, finished interior and chromed wire wheels. (These were not fake hubcaps, but actual wire wheels.)

By 1964 this accomplishment was equaled by designs, mentioned previously, in the "complexity" competition (Walter Peeler, 1964; Richard Lee Beck, 1964; and Thomas H. Semple, 1964), which featured two-door hard tops with finished interiors, as well as clear acrylic side windows and windshield. The competition was fierce.

Quantity of Model Entries for Selected Years

An estimate of the number of model car entries, for selected years, was obtained from a variety of sources: (1) GM publications, (2) published news media and magazine accounts of the Guild, (3) Guildsman literature, (4) the original competition score sheets former Guildsmen sent the author, and (5) antique banquet brochures. The competition score sheets contained the four-digit sequence number or model identity numbers (located in the upper right-hand corner) assigned at Fisher Body's shipping and receiving site and written on the bottom of each model with a marker, or written on a tag and stapled to the bottom of the model. The sequentially assigned model number, or tag number, was designed to anonymously identify for the judges, but accurately identify for Fisher management, the owner of each model entry as it was processed, evaluated and scored by the Guild working judges. The four-digit sequential numbers are probably the most accurate indicators of the quantity of model entries submitted to the competition by year. They were available for a few selected years including 1954 (4,916), 1955 (1,483), 1957 (1,889), 1958 (1,925), 1959 (4,186), 1962 (4,075), 1963 (4,137), 1964 (2,833), 1965 (2, 932) and 1966 (2,949). In the case of the Guild convention banquet brochures, these were the highest four-digit sequence numbers observed. In the case of the personal score sheets these were the only numbers observed. The numbers in any given year easily could be higher. The data in the table below yields an average of about 3,133 model car entries annually, based on the ten years for which data were available.

Model Entry Estimates for the FBCG Model Car Competition for Selected Years (1954–1967)

Year	Estimated Number of Entries	Source
1954	4,916	Stuart Shuster's score sheet, Model No. 4916
1955	1,483	Allen T. Weideman's score sheet, Model No. 1483
1957	1,889	Allen T. Weideman's score sheet, Model No. 1889
1958	1,925	Ronald C. Pellman's score sheet, Model No. 1925
	2,000+	Guild color brochure with 1958–59 competition pictures
1959	4,186	Stuart Shuster's score sheet, Model No. 4186
1962	916	SIA #61 interview with Chuck Jordan
	2,566	John Jacobus' score sheet, Model No. 2566
	4,075	John F. Mercer, banquet brochure, Model No. 4075
1963	4,137*	Estimated from the proportion of awards in 1963 vs. 1966
1964	2,833	Glen Garrett, banquet brochure, Model No. #2833
1965	1,200+	*Popular Science*, October 1965
	2,932	Larry Fogarty, banquet brochure, Model No. 2932
1966	1,200	*General Motors World*, September 1966 GM Overseas Operations Division
	2,949	Edwin L. Wilson, Jr., banquet brochure, Model No. 2949
1967	1,500–1,800	*New York Times*, April 2, 1967; number of models expected or anticipated by the Guild for 1967 competition.

*The number of model entries in 1963 was estimated using proportions. The numbers of awardees in 1963 and 1966 were known from other reliable sources. The reasonable assumption was made that the number of awardees was proportional the number of model entries in any given year. The number of model entries in 1966 was estimated at 2,949 based on the 1966 banquet brochure and Edwin L. Wilson, Jr.'s Model No. 2949. Appendix I shows how this proportion was set up and how the calculation was made.

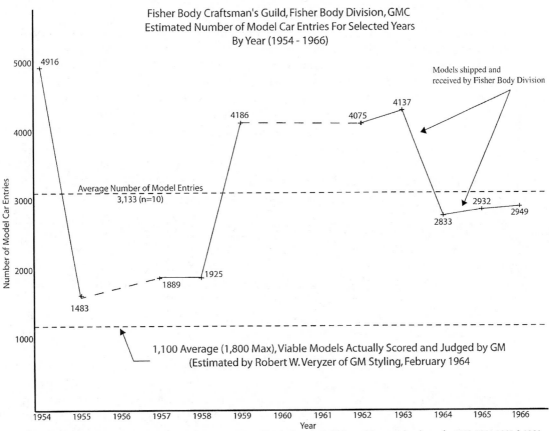

Fisher Body Craftsman's Guild, Fisher Body Division, GMC
Estimated Number of Model Car Entries For Selected Years
By Year (1954 - 1966)

Source: Numbers are Maximum Model Tag Numbers in Any Given Year As Seen in Guild Annual Banquet Brochures for 1962, 1964, 1965, & 1966 as well as Score Sheets randomly selected for 1954, 1955, 1957, 1958 and 1959. 1963 Was Estimated.

This graph shows the estimated number of Fisher Body Craftsman's Guild model entries by year for selected years (1954–1966) as well as the average number of models entered in the famous Detroit model car competition for selected years.

It is reasonable to assume Fisher Body used a sequentially ascending number system in order to identify each model with a unique four-digit identifier. This is the customary practice for inventory and control processes. At shipping and receiving, a sequence number was stapled or written on the bottom of each model via prenumbered tag or indelible pen. This number was transferred to the score sheet and ensured that the contestant was anonymous to the judges. An ingenious tag system implemented in 1950 had a preprinted and fixed four-digit number. Since these were printed by machine, the numbers had to be sequential ascending numbers (e.g., 0001, 0002, 0003, 0004, 0005,...). It is highly unlikely that Fisher Body management would have opted for a random numbering scheme for inventory and control of the models as this would have eventually led to chaos. The sequential numbering system appears to have been correlated to the order of the alphabet with states like California having low numbers and states like Washington having very high numbers. Some years this correlation was perfect, as in 1956. Other years the correlation could be poor.

However, it should be noted that internal GM Styling staff memos contradict the above approach of counting and estimating the number of model entries. For example, a letter dated February 21, 1964, to Mr. C.M. Jordan from Robert W. Veryzer (Design Development Studio and 1955 FBCG judge) suggests 1,100 average annual model entries with a maximum of 1,800. The author's average annual estimate is three times higher than Mr. Veryzer's estimate. In a handwritten note to William L. Mitchell (circa 1965), C.M. Jordan mentioned "500 models in Switzerland compared to 1,400 models for us." Another letter dated June 13, 1968, to William L. Mitchell from C.M. MacKichan, GM Styling staff, suggests only 900 entries in 1967.[43]

Externally published information also contradicts the sequence-number system of counting the number of model entries. In the February 1981 *Special Interest Autos* interview with GM Design staff members, a figure of 916 model entries was suggested for 1962. Although the other numbers in the table for 1965 (1,200+ models), 1966 (1,200 models) and 1967 (1,500–1,800 models anticipated) come from reliable sources (e.g., *Popular Science*, *GM World* and the *New York Times*), they are much lower than the assigned sequential model numbers and different from the entry counts from internal memos.

Although these differences are impossible to reconcile, it is known that models were inspected upon receipt for being oversize or undersize, meaning they could have been eliminated from the judges' workload through an initial screening for lack of scale fidelity. It is also known that models were damaged or destroyed in the shipping process, and some of these were probably eliminated. Models arriving made out of oddball materials inconsistent with the program, such as clay or paper-mâché, were probably eliminated immediately from further consideration. So, the lower counts above probably represent the working number of award-worthy models received or the number of models that were actually judged and scored. In addition, there's another subpopulation of models that fell below the 50–60 percent of points, or some minimum threshold level, needed for a minimum state award. These models may have been factored into the model entry numbers GM and Fisher used for public consumption. Therefore, it is concluded that the Veryzer estimate of 1,100 average annual model entries probably represents the judges' actual work load or the award-worthy population of models capable of achieving 50–60 percent or more of points.

Judges' Workload

Looking at it from a time and motion perspective, and accepting the Robert W. Veryzer number (1,100 average model entries annually), three teams of judges scoring 1,100 models over 20 actual working days (in 1958 it was 9 A.M. to 5 P.M., June 23 to July 23) would have to score 55 models per day or slightly over 18 models per team per day. With 420 minutes available per seven-hour day (including a one-hour lunch break), that's 23 minutes per model. The stylist had about 11.5 minutes to assess the design aspects and the industrial arts teacher had about 11.5 minutes to assess the craftsmanship aspects of each model. A contestant might spend 480 hours (average) on a model viewed for less than ½ hour during the scoring process.

GM Sons' Presence

In 1946 the sons of GM employees submitted 19 models and won four prizes, and in 1947, the sons of GM employees submitted 44 models and won 12 prizes. In that year, the two Welther boys, Robert and Michael, ages 15 and 16 respectively, sons of a Fisher Body plant employee, won top prizes of $5,000 each in the Napoleonic Coach competition. This was an expensive proposition because duplicate awards had to be made in this case. In 1947 Fisher Body Division Central Engineering awarded three of their own sons special awards, including a $250 check to Elia Russinoff. In 1949 *GM Folks* magazine (October 1949, vol. 12, no. 10) featured the article "Awards to 26 GM Sons Totaling $9,365." One son was Roosevelt Harris, an African-American from Kansas City, Kansas. In 1953, 11 GM sons from 9 divisions won state level awards. In almost every year of the Guild competition, duplicate cash awards or duplicate trips to Detroit or duplicate scholarships had to be awarded at every level because of the awesome model-making capabilities of the GM employees' sons. A GM son dynasty was Leonard Constance (1966 fourth place, junior division) and his brother David Constance (1968 first place, junior division) of Flint, Michigan.

1963 and 1966 Competition Demographics (Age, Education) for Awardees Only

The following table shows that in 1963 and 1966, 81 percent of the Guild award winners were in the senior division (ages 16–20) and attended high school or college. Sixty-five percent were enrolled in high school and 16 percent were enrolled in colleges or universities. Ninety-two colleges and 66 universities were represented by Guildsmen in 1963 and 1966, respectively. Only a few vocational-technical trade schools were represented in the 1963–66 winners. The top national winners tended to be contestants 19 or 20 years old who had built multiple Guild models. The Guild competition appealed to this dominant age group, who were older and more experienced as model makers.

Education (Age) Distribution of Award Winners for 1963 and 1966 Competitions

School Type	Age Interval	1963	1966
Elementary	11 years old	0.972%	2.21%
Junior High	12–15 years old	17.51%	16.57%
Senior High	16–18 years old	65.76%	64.63%
College/University	19–20 years old	15.76%	16.57%
Total		100%	100%

Source: Two documents entitled "The Fisher Body Craftsman's Guild is pleased to announce the STATE, REGIONAL AND NATIONAL AWARD WINNERS IN ITS 1963 [1966] MODEL CAR COMPETITION." These critical vintage documents contained the contestants' names, cities, schools, and award levels and amounts, but were for the award winners only. Unknowns were redistributed where school type was not indicated.

Only 17 percent of the award winners in 1963 and 1966 came from the junior division (11–15 age group). This group could have had a large number of entries, but fewer were probably worthy of an award (i.e., met GM's minimum threshold). In the junior division, despite their inexperience as model makers, some national scholarship awards were made to 12 and 13 year olds. For example, in 1964 John D'Mura was a 13-year-old national scholarship winner and in 1965 Michael A. Pietruska was a 12-year-old national scholarship winner. Normally, however, the top junior division national scholarship winners were 15, or at the top of the bracket, having worked their way up. The Ferraioli brothers were all junior division national scholarship winners, being 15 years old or less.

Program Diversity and International Scope

The Fisher Body Craftsman's Guild program was predominantly a middle class endeavor for families aspiring to send their kids to a university for a degree. The background of the participants was diverse, as the potential for winning a college scholarship attracted young people from all walks of life. Persons with Italian-American roots (e.g., Simone, De Fazio, Caracciolo, Ferraioli, Bottarelli, Loczi, Catalano and Baldini), German-American roots (e.g, Fisher, Goetz, Herr, Herzog, Stein, Stumpf, Ulmschneider, Von Loewe, Von Delden), Bulgarian-American roots (e.g., Russinoff), Swedish-American roots (e.g., Mellberg), Chinese- or Asian-American roots (e.g., Wu, Yeh and Wong), African-American roots (Roosevelt Harris), Japanese-American roots, (e.g., Kaizo Oto), Dutch-American roots (Jacobus), and Pacific Rim American roots (e.g., Jared Kanemaru and his brother) were attracted to the Guild program. And, of course, many kids with English-sounding family names (e.g., Beck, Davids, Garner, Graham, Graves, Hill, Jordan, Kelly, King, Miller, Moore, Morris, Norton, Powers, Ray, Reed, Russell and Smith). Some highlights from this diverse population of Guildsmen are as follows:

1947: Richard H. Conibear (a Lakeland, Florida, Napoleonic Coach builder), wheelchair bound with poliomyelitis, having won a regional award, arrived in Detroit for the Guild convention with his mother. Richard had long been a model maker and builder and continued to compete in the model car competition through 1951.

1949: Roosevelt Harris (African-American) from Kansas City, Kansas, won an honorable mention (GM Folks, October 1949, volume 12, number 10).

1952: William Endow (Asian-American) won a third-place national scholarship, junior division, $2,000 award.

1955: Yen Yeh (Asian-American) from Lawrence, Kansas, won a junior regional award; Jen Yeh, either a brother or a relative, 1956 Kansas state winner.

1961 and 1962: Kaizo Oto (Japanese-American) from Fresno, California, won a styling scholarship worth $1,000 and the third-place national scholarship, senior division, $3,000 award.

1965: Jared Kanemaru from Wahiawa, Hawaii (Region 19), won a styling scholarship worth $1,000. He was a regional winner in 1966. His brother, Lester Kanemaru, won the second-place Hawaii state award in 1966.

1966: Karlin Wong from Torrance, California, won a styling scholarship, $1,000 award; David S. Wong, brother or relative, from Torrance, California, 1967 junior regional winner and 1968 second-place California, senior division winner.

The Craftsman's Guild, at various brief periods of time, was international in scope, with Canadians, Englishmen, West Germans, Swiss and Australians participating.[44]

Age Bracket Expansion

In the early 1960s Fisher Body Division expanded the age intervals for the junior and senior divisions. The junior division was expanded from 12–15 to 11–15 years old and the senior division was expanded from 16–19 to 16–20 years old. Based on 1960 U.S. Bureau of Census data, this would have boosted the potential number of eligible male youths by some 25 percent, or about 2.8 million boys and young men, a significant increase. An increase of this kind would have been a dream come true for any Guild manager intent on steadily increasing enrollments, increasing the number of quality models and boosting the recognition power of GM's "Mark of Excellence" in the youth market.[45]

Despite the fact that Fisher Body expanded the age range of the junior division to accommodate 11 year olds, only 1–2 percent of the award winners came from this part of the population. But this explains the number of elementary school students seen in the junior division ranks and helps explain the presence of Robert Pietruska, one of the four famous Pietruska brothers from Stamford, Connecticut, winning a regional award at age 11.

Fairness

The models were judged anonymously and were only known by a four-digit identification number during the scoring process. If the highest scoring model belonged to the son of a GM employee, a duplicate award was made to the next highest scoring model. This explains why some years there were 42 or 45 regional winners and sometimes additional national winners. The awards were well distributed, as the number of states represented in the 1957, 1963 and 1966 competitions were 29, 31, and 27, respectively, or 60 percent of the states.

Judges were not obligated to award all of the available cash prizes and all the judges' decisions were final (*Guildsman*, Vol. 12, No. 2). The working judge's decisions were subject to approval by the honorary board of judges. An earlier analysis by the author (*Automotive History Review*, no. 34, spring 1999) had incorrectly assumed that all Guild entries received a cash award of some kind. Looking at historical data, it appears that the number of models submitted exceeded the number of awards available by a factor of four or five easily. This means all of GM's awards would have been consumed. But in 1963 and 1966, despite a flood of model entries, GM left cash awards unclaimed. This could mean that some states had a low participation rate or poor product quality, or it could mean that GM had a minimum threshold score below which a model was designated as not award-worthy. It would appear that about 50–60 percent of the available 450 points was the threshold.

Purchased or Duplicated Models

The model entries remained the property of the contestant and were returned by late August or September. In the early '50s, the Guild technical department built reproductions of some of the top national scholarship winning models for exhibition purposes. GM also purchased some of the winning models for promotion purposes, paying Gary Graham (1954) $1,000 and Robert F. McDonnell (1955) $650 for their designs. Some received about $150 for their models. In the 1960s GM changed this policy and leased the models and returned them to the contestant. Whether the model car design was purchased or leased, GM and its subsidiaries had all the rights to reproduce any aspect of the young entrant's design.

Some others who had models purchased by GM included Thomas A. McDonnell (1953 third-place national scholarship, junior division, $2,000 award), Henry F. Rom (1953 fourth-place national scholarship, senior division, $1,000 award), Milton J. Antonick (1955 first-place national scholarship, senior division, $4,000 award), James L. Garner (1955 regional award winner), Ronald C. Pellman (1956), and James T. Sampson (1957 styling scholarship, $1,000 award).

These models were used to promote the Guild in traveling exhibits or by Guild technical representatives for display purposes when visiting the hundreds of high schools nationwide to make the Guild award presentations. The models were also used in traveling exhibits, as discussed earlier, to promote the goals and purposes of the Craftsman's Guild.

The Regional Awards System

In order to ensure a fair geographic distribution of Guild awards, the states were organized into groups or regions. Because Fisher had performance data (e.g., the number of model entries) from various geographic regions, states and metropolitan areas, the regional system was overhauled in 1960–61. This prevented the Midwestern states clustered around Michigan, home to many GM and Fisher plants, and where the interest was most keen, from dominating the competition. Another theory often repeated by Guild folks is that without the regional awards system the Southern California kids would have dominated the awards.[46]

Despite the regional awards system which was designed to assure the fair distribution of awards, and the appearance of objective impartiality, there was some variation in how the national scholarship award winners were distributed geographically within the United States. A total of 158 scholarship winners from 12 years (1946, 1947, 1951, 1953, 1955, 1956, 1957, 1960, 1961, 1962, 1963 and 1966) were examined for which complete data was available by state and region. This represented only 40 percent of the total scholarships awarded.

The number of scholarship winners, and their geographic distribution, is a reasonable surrogate measure for regional popularity. In the most active area, the contestants in the Midwestern states clustered around Michigan (including Iowa and Missouri) were highly interested and involved in the Guild competition. Called the "Iron Belt," this is where the GM and Fisher Body plants were mostly located. Iowa and Missouri churned out an unusually high number of scholarship winners (17 percent of the region),* but Michigan dominated the Midwest with 29 percent of the region's scholarship winners.[47]

The second most successful area in the competition, and the second most popular

*The percentages refer to the proportion of each respective geographic region, not the whole or total. These figures show which states had the most successful contestants in each regional section of the country.

Craftsman's Scholarship Winners
by Geographic Location in the United States

U.S. Geographic Region	Success and Popularity Rank	Number and (%) of Awards (n = 158)		Craftsman's Guild Regions Involved After 1960–61 Reorganization
Mid-West	#1	59	(37.34 %)	9, 10, 11, 12, 13 and 14
West Coast	#2	36	(22.78 %)	18, 19 and 20
Northeast	#3	32	(20.25 %)	1, 2, 3, 4, and 5
Southeast	#4	17	(10.76 %)	6,7, and 8
Southwest	#5	10	(6.33 %)	15 and 16
Northwest	#6	4	(2.53 %)	17
		158	(100.00 %)	

recruiting ground for the Guild, was the West Coast, with Californians accounting for 56 percent of the scholarship awards in the region. Washington was another West Coast state with a high interest in the Guild, producing 17 percent of the region's national scholarship winners. In terms of total number of individual scholarships by state, California (20) exceeded Michigan (17).

In the Northeast, the third most popular major market area for the Guild, Massachusetts and Rhode Island had an unusually high number of scholarship winners at 31 percent of the whole region.

All the remaining areas produced a small number of scholarship winners that were about evenly distributed.

Competition Integrity

The Guild encouraged its members to seek advice, criticism and suggestions from other people, but required that the actual work be done by the boy who entered the model car in the competition. The purpose of this rule was to ensure fair play and provide each Guild member with a full measure of the most important benefits of the program, namely the development of craftsmanship and creative ability.

The Official Guild Pledge Card was one of the keys to the competition's integrity and this was completed by the Guildsman and his parent and mailed with the model in the shipping crate to Detroit. This affirmed that the work being submitted to the competition was that of the contestant himself and assured compliance with the other eligibility requirements such as age and U.S. residency. This provided a legally sound basis for disqualification, if this became necessary. For example, if the judges were faced with what appeared to be a professionally-made model, such as made by a "ghost" model maker, GM and Fisher Body had the legal means to challenge the contestant and seek disqualification.

The Guild employed the honor system. The Guild management was primarily concerned that the contestants were U.S. citizens, eligible based on age, and that they did their own work. Not only did the Guildsman provide his date of birth on the Pledge Card, but he had to prove it by submitting a copy of his birth certificate, baptismal certificate or a statement giving the correct birth date signed by a pastor, teacher or principal. GM also needed to know if the contestant was the son of a GM employee. By signing the Official Guild Pledge Card, the parent or guardian asserted and guaranteed the accuracy of the information provided.

On the Pledge Card after 1954, Guildsmen had to check off the body style being entered, such as sedan, six-passenger convertible, convertible sports car, hardtop sports car, six-passenger hardtop, or station wagon. This told the judges which set of scale fidelity specifications to apply during the scoring process.

Although personal pho-

This is the 1966 telegram from Carlyle W. "Mac" McClellan, Guild administrator, to John M. Mellberg notifying him he was a state and regional winner in the 1966 model car competition, which implied he was one of the top 40 model car designers in America and eligible for a scholarship award. The names of the scholarship winners were held confidential until announced at the Guild convention and banquet in Detroit. *John M. Mellberg.*

tographs were normally requested of regional winners only, during the '50s it became routine for the Guildsman to submit a personal photograph along with the Pledge Card and proof of date of birth. As a way for the Guild to promote itself, the photographs were published in the winning Guildsman's local newspaper announcing the good news to friends and neighbors. The photos also could have been used by Guild transportation staff to locate regional winners traveling alone at train stations and airports or at the Detroit Guild convention. This may have been a low-key, subtle integrity check. The Guild management took reasonable steps to ensure they were conducting a fair, amateur model-making competition. All of the above did not make for an ironclad system of integrity checks, but created a highly problematic situation for "ghost' model-makers (*Guildsman*, vol. 4, no. 5, 1956).

A second key to the competition's integrity was the anonymous scoring system supported by an ingenious four-card tag system. The anonymous review and scoring of each model guaranteed the unquestionable impartiality of the team of judges. Part one of the tag system was a sequential four-digit number that was stapled or taped to the bottom each model. The second tag was a name and address label that was attached to the shipping crate or box. The third tag was sent to Guild headquarters from shipping and receiving, giving the builder's name and address and describing the "as received" condition of the model. And finally, the fourth tag, giving the model number and identity of the builder, was placed in a sealed envelope and kept under lock and key in the office of the superintendent of the Detroit School System (*Guild News*, May 1950, volume 5, number 5).

In the 1960s this was presented to the contestant as a four-in-one colored card. A 1966 set of tags was a single piece of card stock divided into four parts, with perforated

Only 40 regional winners were invited, with all expenses paid by GM, to the Guild convention and banquet. At the July 1966 banquet, shown in this photograph, Harold G. Warner, Group Vice President, General Motors Corporation, made 19 scholarship awards before 800 guests at the Fisher Body Central Engineering Auditorium in Warren, Michigan. Four junior division scholarships (age 12–15), four senior division scholarships (ages 16–20), one duplicate scholarship and 10 styling scholarships were awarded. *John M. Mellberg.*

dividing lines, and a four-digit number at the top of each section, preprinted by a machine. The name and address was filled in on one of the four tag pieces by the contestant and placed in the shipping container with the model along with the Official Guild Pledge Card.

National Guild Convention and Banquet

The highlight of the Craftsman's Guild competition was the four-day, all expenses-paid trip (worth $890 in 1966 dollars) to Detroit for the 40 regional winners (20 junior division and 20 senior division winners), the banquet and radio announcement of the national scholarship winners, and an all-star line-up of festivities.[48] Guildsmen arrived in Detroit by train, knowing only that they were first-place state and regional winners. The

Photographs of the scholarship winners with one or more GM executives were printed in the *Guildsman* newsletter after the Guild convention and distributed nationwide to Guildsmen. This photograph shows the 1966 Guild scholarship winners with Harold G. Warner, General Motors Vice President. Back row *(left to right)*: Kenneth A. Kelly (18), third senior, $3,000, St. Petersburg, Florida; Joseph W. D'Mura (20), fourth senior, $2,000, East Gary, Indiana; Warner; Ovid O. Ward (21), first senior, $5,000, Roanoke, Virginia; John M. Mellberg (20), second senior, $4,000, Park Ridge, Illinois. Middle row *(left to right)*: Dale A. Gnage (15), first junior, $5,000, Rochester, New York; Leonard A. Constance (15); fourth junior, $2,000, Flint, Michigan; Bruno N. Bottarelli (16), second junior, $4,000, Chicago, Illinois; Carl L. LaRoche (15), fourth junior, $2,000 (duplicate), Franklin, New Hampshire; Larry T. Hagen (13), third junior, $3,000, New Brighton, Minnesota. Front row *(left to right)*: Styling scholarship winners John F. Faust, junior, $1,000, Anderson, Indiana; Michael G. Czyzewski, senior, $1,000, Detroit, Michigan; Lance D. Prom, senior, $1,000, Vancouver, Washington; and Karlin Wong, senior, $1,000, Torrance, California. *General Motors Corporation.*

names of all the scholarship winners were held confidential until read by the president of General Motors on banquet night.

Detailed travel arrangements, including spending money, were made for each regional winner by the Guild secretary. Some would be traveling away from home by themselves for the first time, and some traveled four or five days (round trip) to attend the four-day event called by the *Detroit Times* the "Party by Fisher" in 1931. Accommodations were top flight at the Book-Cadillac and other elegant Detroit hotels at the time.

After a day of sightseeing in Detroit, the first agenda item for the 40 regional winners was the convention banquet at the GM Building or the Fisher Body Auditorium

Publicity photographs like this one, showing Guildsmen with a famous GM executive, were used to promote the Craftsman's Guild program in newspapers and magazines. Charles F. "Boss" Kettering, famed inventor, researcher and director of General Motors, is shown carefully scrutinizing the models built by two top national award winners in the 1957 Fisher Body Craftsman's Guild model car competition. The two boys each won $5,000 university scholarships to the schools of their choice. They are, left to right, Arthur Russell, 19, of Los Angeles, and Daniel C. Green, 15, of Medina, Washington. *General Motors Corporation.*

in Warren, when the names of the national scholarship winners were announced on national radio. This was that eye opening moment when they got to see all the other designs, sitting on the table in front of them, and could size-up the competition. Following the announcement of the scholarship winners by one of Guild emcees (Robert Young, Bert Parks, Walter Cronkite, Lowell Thomas, and others) there was gut wrenching disappointment for half, and sheer euphoria for the other half of the Guildsmen present.

The 40 young men were aligned at a long table across the hall, models in hand, dressed in matching blue Guild blazers with the diamond-shaped breast pocket insignia (1950), or light blue Palm Beach sports jackets (1960s), facing an audience of 800–900 guests consisting of Fisher vendors (suppliers and ad agency personnel), GM division managers, Fisher plant managers, newspaper columnists, and noted scientists and

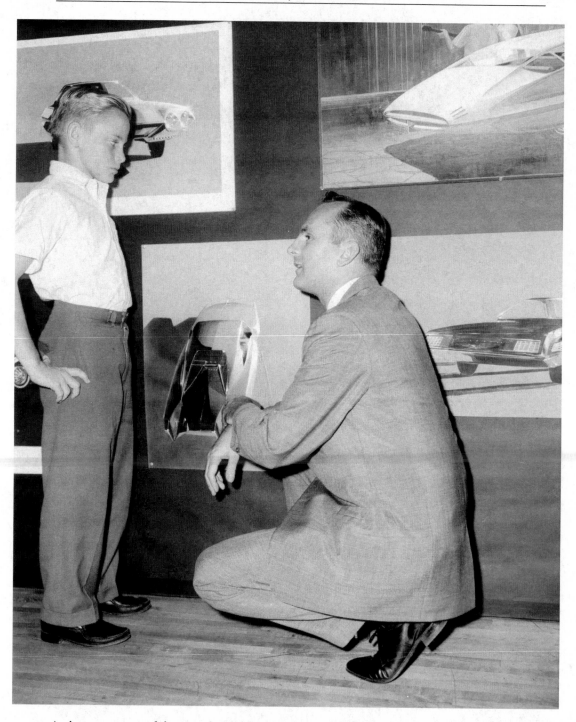

An important part of the annual Guild convention and banquet festivities was for the 40 regional award winners to tour the GM Styling Studios, to meet the professional auto designers and to learn about new design trends and ideas. Some of the regional award winners were very young. Larry W. Fogarty (age 12), a 1963 regional junior winner from Bay Haven Elementary School in Sarasota, Florida, is shown meeting with Charles M. Jordan, Executive-in-Charge, Automotive Design, General Motors Styling. *General Motors Corporation.*

educators. These had all been assembled by Fisher Purchasing to fete these bright young Guildsmen. Behind the Guildsman's table was a long line of GM's leadership — vice presidents, Guild leaders, etc. — in white dinner jackets (1960).[49] In 1966, as each winner's name was being called, an image of his winning design was flashed on an overhead screen for all to see. A GM vice president, or the GM president himself, always made the scholarship award presentation to each Guildsman.

Afterwards, as consolation, Harley Earl, Bill Mitchell, Chuck Jordan or one of the Guild judges might stop by to chat and discuss the particulars of non–scholarship winners' scores and give a pat on the back, encouragement and assurance for the next year's competition. In the 1930s and '40s, scholarship winners wore white tam headwear to distinguish themselves, and in the 1950s, a military style shoulder cord was adopted and worn with the blue blazer as their mark of achievement.

The Guildsmen were indulged in all the things that teenagers love to do. Trips were made to nearby Selfridge Air Force base, the GM Proving Grounds at Milford, Michigan, the Libby-Owens-Ford Glass plant in Ohio, the Oldsmobile assembly plant in Lansing, and the Fisher plant in Livonia, Michigan. The high-water mark for the regional winners was the tour of the GM Styling studios at the Tech Center that included a visit with and career pep talk by Chuck Jordan, personal introductions to GM's stylists, a private viewing of experimental cars like the Firebird III or the Mako Shark and time to preview 1/5 scale clay models as well as renderings. A sketch pad at the ready, this is where new styling and design ideas were stimulated for future competitions. In the 1950s, Guild convention planners had ticker tape–like parades set up with a caravan of GM convertibles, and there were several "Guild Specials" where dining and coach cars were reserved for the round trip train ride between Detroit and Lansing with a chance to see the movie *Around the World in 80 Days.*

Before the end of the four-day event, the scholarship winners signed their scholarship trust fund agreements. There was always time for a swim in Lake St. Clair and a buffet dinner at the Bloomfield Hills Golf and Country Club. Life was sweet! Most importantly, however, this is where Guildsmen met kindred spirits and a network of friends was formed. Some who met at the Guild convention have remained friends for life.

Being a National Scholarship Winner

> I entered the Guild contest in 1949 and won the third grand national award ($2,000 scholarship) in the junior division. I was fourteen years old at the time. This scholarship paid for approximately one half of my college education at West Virginia University (1952-1956) [Roger D. Teter, former Guildsman].[50]

The terms of the scholarship trust fund agreement executed by scholarship winners at the Guild convention were very generous.[51] The funds were to go for care, maintenance, support and education of the beneficiary and/or his dependents while enrolled in a college or university. Alternatively, the funds could be used for high school or college preparation expenses, for expenses due to illness or disability, or paid to his estate in case of death. After graduation the remaining unconsumed funds went to the beneficiary. Alternatively, at age 27 all unconsumed funds reverted to the beneficiary or scholarship winner. The trustees allowed Bill Moore to use some of his trust fund for a new transmission for his car so he could get to classes each day at the Art Center School. The trust funds definitely could not be used for a down-payment on a new Corvette.

Consolation Prize: Certificate of Design and Craftsmanship and Score Sheet

No matter what their score, and regardless of the award, each Guildsmen received a Guild Certificate of Design and Craftsmanship with the hand-lettered name of the contestant.

Along with their Certificate of Design and Craftsmanship, the contestants received a Report to Contestants (the actual score sheet used by the Judges), along with a cover memo from the administrator of the Guild:

> It is a pleasure that the Fisher Body Craftsman's Guild can say, "Congratulations for a job well done. ... The Certificate of Design and Craftsmanship express our feelings to a degree, however, enough can not be said about your ability and determination to see a project through to completion. ... Possibly you did not win an award, however, the fact that you successfully completed your model car evidences a quality of talent, character and ability.

The score sheet showed the grade the contestant received in each category. The letter from the Guild administrator told craftsmen to review the one to two areas where improvement was needed:

> Should your score be low, be concerned but not discouraged. ... It is a rare occasion for a model entry to achieve the maximum scores stated. ... The judges to the best of their ability, have evaluated your model, and every model in your region was judged under an equal criteria [Form letter to J. Jacobus about September 1963 from C.W. McClellan, administrator, Fisher Body Craftsman's Guild].

Several months later, the contestants would typically receive a formally printed list of the individuals who had received awards in the Guild competition that year. This included the name, city and state, school name and award level for each person who submitted a viable, award-worthy model.

Demise of the Fisher Body Craftsman's Guild

There is serious doubt that the corporate tax advantages of donating millions in college scholarships and cash as well as of other potential Guild write-offs, could possibly have outweighed the costs of operating the Guild. Based on a $710,000 Guild budget figure for 1967, it is estimated that it cost Fisher and GM $10 in expenses for every dollar given away.[52] By 1968 when the Guild was terminated, 387 scholarships had been awarded to individuals and $2.4 million in scholarships and cash had been distributed.[53] Ten million teens had enrolled and made about 32,800 viable coaches and model cars for the competition.[54] Given that these cost figures are shown in 1966 economics, and employing the 10 to 1 ratio, GM might have spent up to $24 million on administering the Guild over the life of the program. Since it would not have been possible to quantify the number of

Guild youths who became loyal GM customers, or the percentage of showroom traffic or vehicle sales generated by Guild field reps visiting high schools with the film *Getting Started*, or the amount of good will generated, it is easy to see how GM executives, headed by James M. Roche, chairman of the board, could have concluded in 1968 that the program was not cost-effective. After reigning 34 years (excluding the World War II years), one of the most successful public relations, advertising and education programs in corporate America had come to an end.

Although there appears to have been high interest in the Guild right up to the end (as indicated by model entry counts), there were clearly model quality problems. As evidenced by the 1963 and 1966 model car awards data, discussed in Appendix I, only 65.3 percent (571/874) of allocated state awards were distributed in 1963, and an even lower 46.6 percent (407/874) were distributed in 1966. Six regions had reductions of 50 percent or more in the number of awardees between 1963 and 1966, representing some 43 percent of the states in the contest. Overall, only 13 percent of the model entries from 1963 to 1966 received a cash award of some type (cash, trip or scholarship).

Although the sea of models the judges faced were made of a plethora of materials such as fiberglass, Bondo, plastic wood, laminated wood, cast plaster, paper-mâché, and polyurethane foam, they were unprepared for the aluminum casting made by one young stylist in his father's foundry.[55] And they must have been caught flatfooted by the mocking, pop-art design consisting of a tree branch with windows and four crude wheels nailed on with large spikes.[56]

In addition to the GM executive's position that benefits did not exceed costs and a few practical problems like the poor quality of entries, there are other theories as to why the Guild program was terminated.

(1) The conditions of the Depression that spawned the Guild no longer existed, when youth had an overabundance of time, prosperity was low and everyone was short of cash. A time when there was this tremendous determination to be resourceful enough and ingenious enough to make a coach (e.g., make your own lathe with a washing machine motor, or make your own jigsaw from a sewing machine head).

(2) In an affluent society youths don't need to craft their way to a college scholarship, they just had to be smart enough and test well enough to qualify for one.

(3) Teenagers had too many other things competing for their free time in the '60s (TV, school sports, homework, Boy Scouts, school youth clubs, social activities like dating and drive-in fast food restaurants), and "stick-to-it-tivity" (Bill Moore's spelling) or how to "stick-to-it" (Chuck Jordan's spelling) was a thing of the past.

(4) Kids lacked scratch-building know-how, as there were few reinforcing institutions other than the Boy Scout merit badge "Model Design and Building" and the Cub Scouts' Pinewood Derby, in which some 2.5 million youths participate annually.

(5) America was moving from a hands-on, do-it-yourself, know-how society to an information sharing and technology driven society, and educational emphasis had shifted to higher SAT scores, scholastic performance and academic excellence.

(6) The last Fisher brother (Edward F. Fisher) retired from the GM directorate in 1969 and William A. Fisher, the first president of the Guild, passed away that year. The Guild was no longer a sacred cow, as there were no namesakes or champions in high places to protect it.

(7) The multimillion dollar plastics hobby and model industry undercut the interest in scratch-building taught by the Guild.

(8) There were probably additional management concerns about the cost efficiency of the Guild program. For example, Adam Opel AG spent $90,000 on their Guild program with 90,000 enrollees ($1.00 per enrollee) and got a response of 1,500 models, whereas in the U.S., GM spent $710,000 for 600,000 enrollees ($1.18 per enrollee) with only 900 viable model entries in 1967. Vauxhall Motors spent only $45,000 for 103,000 enrollees ($0.44 per enrollee) and 1,117 model entries in 1967.[57]

(9) The time had come to include girls and young women in the program and perhaps the corporation was unwilling to make this move. The coeducational Opel Modellbauer Gilde in West Germany, promoted by Chuck Jordan as director of design at Opel (1967–1970), thrived from 1965 to 1979 with the number of entries equaling the number of U.S. Craftsman's Guild entries in some of the later years. The All-American Soap Box Derby, another scholarship program started by GM, would become coed in 1971 and survives today in communities all across America.

(10) A more simplified auto design contest, emphasizing design and deemphasizing craftsmanship, could have kept the Guild around for many more years and could have been just as effective a PR tool. But design and craftsmanship were the fundamental tenets and backbone of the Craftsman's Guild program. The pool of potential contestants in the mid- to late 1960s apparently lacked the necessary interest and disposable time for the "craftsmanship" part of the bargain. This was evidenced in a reduction in the quality of the entries circa 1963 and 1966. The Guild had become a well-respected recruiting tool within the industry as a whole, and an auto designer had to have both design and craftsmanship abilities. GM and Fisher management were unwilling to compromise and give up what the Fisher brothers loved and cherished most — craftsmanship. Therefore, rather than compromise, they terminated the program.

Can't Keep a Good Man Down

As of July 1970, two years after the Guild was discontinued, Fisher Body's public relations and advertising administrator was still receiving 200 Guild inquiries per month. Even as of July 1973, five years after the Guild was discontinued, 60–75 inquiries per month continued to arrive.[58] When the author inquired about writing an article about scratch-building that would include mention of the Guild, Norman E. May of Fisher Body public relations and advertising stated, "We would appreciate your also noting its [the Craftsman's Guild's] discontinuance to prevent a flood of inquiries regarding the program."[59]

And 16 years later, the presence of the Craftsman's Guild was still felt, as indicated by the following excerpt from a 1984 letter from Fisher Body Division:[60] "We know that there are several thousand coach models still existing, many of them with the original builders and others with the builder's family. We seldom hear from owners of the model cars. We also know that there are coach models still being built because we furnish plans to those who are interested. Many of them are men who say they started that coach when they were a boy ... never finished it ... and now have the time to try it again because they're retired."

Despite the fact that the Craftsman's Guild had been discontinued as a Fisher Body Division public relations and advertising budget line item, outside interest remained keen and unchecked. Because the tenets, values and virtues of the Craftsman's Guild movement were so fundamentally strong and appealing, the Fisher brothers had started something that couldn't be stopped by an executive edict. It was so institutionalized and so much a part of people's lives that the grassroots folks wouldn't let go of it. Many of the essays that follow in Chapter IV show that nostalgic feelings and emotions are still strong for the "days of yore" when the Guild reigned supreme in their lives.

Legacy

The Guild was an advertising bonanza and its prime purpose was to generate good will. In fact, it was so successful that Ford Motor Company tried to imitate the Fisher brothers' pride and joy with a short-lived model car competition of their own. Far more successful was the Ford Industrial Arts Awards Program in the early 1950s, which mimicked many features of the Fisher Body Craftsman's Guild, but catered to vocational-technical high school students. The intangible value of the public relations generated by the Guild and the resultant talent identified and recruited cannot be quantified. This book has tried to qualitatively highlight the benefits and achievements of the Craftsman's Guild by focusing on its people.

The Fisher brothers had built a positive image and introduced the idea, long before it became popular, of corporate responsibility to the community by providing college scholarship opportunities. In return, the program they started was used as a direct means of identifying and recruiting many young, creative and talented people needed for the automobile industry. The raw creative design talent identified was hired and trained by GM initially, but eventually migrated to work at Ford, Chrysler, AMC, Nissan, Subaru, Mack and Volvo trucks, Volvo cars, Thomas Built Buses and many other vehicle manufacturers as well as industrial design firms such as Chuck Pelly's Designworks/USA, Walter Dorwin Teague Associates (called Teague), and Raymond Loewy International. Many Guild participants, after formal training, became independent, self-employed, successful industrial design consultants.

The program was international in scope, including Canada initially and later was exported overseas by the GM Overseas Division, to include GM subsidiaries like Adam-Opel in West Germany, Vauxhall Motors Ltd. in the UK, GM Holden in Australia and GM Suisse in Switzerland. By the mid–1960s, the program became an international and coeducational design competition with a few girls finishing among the top 40 (in the UK Gillian Bailey was the top 1966 female winner, and in West Germany, Ursula Mell-Mellenheim was the 1970 second-place junior division winner with a DM 2,000 award). The Europeans embraced the Craftsman's Guild idea, and between 1965 and 1979, the Opel Modellbauer Gilde produced 1,697 (average) model entries annually compared to the U.S. with 3,133 (average) model entries annually.

The overall model construction rate in the U.S. Guild based on viable, award-worthy models was 0.38 (32,800/10,000,000) percent, with 0.25 percent to 1.0 percent for certain years of the '50s and '60s, whereas in 1967 the four overseas guilds combined had a model construction rate of 1.79 percent.[61] In 1970, the Modellbauer Gilde participation rate alone was 5.8 percent (1,759/30,227). Although these rates are not directly

The 1965 Overseas Craftsman's Guild winners are shown checking out a 1964 styling scholarship model built to Category C specifications for the Open Competition and made by Ronald E. Pietruska of Stamford, Connecticut. *Left to right*: Heinrich L. Jakob, age 18 (W. Germany); Jean-Claude Guggisberg, age 17 (Switzerland); and Terence John Kirk, age 20 (United Kingdom). *General Motors Corporation.*

comparable because they were measured at different times, they provide some idea of overall U.S. and overseas participation.[62]

Although there were many creative design ideas submitted during the model car competition, the boys usually emulated the automobile designs they saw on the road, in popular magazines, at their local dealerships, or at auto shows. But there were some young people who were innovative, who went beyond the ordinary, and could forecast the future with their model designs. Because this raw talent was so rare, GM pursued these people, saw to it they were trained and hired them. Robert E. Davids, the 1963 first-place national scholarship winner, was put on a two-year GM training program that included management course work at Macomb College, and ended up working personally for William L. Mitchell in Studio X, Mitchell's personal design studio.

We don't know, but maybe, just maybe, a few of those model car ideas reached a GM designer or stylist's eyes/ and stimulated a whole flow of new ideas, illustrations or clay models. Gary Graham, the 1954 first-place national scholarship winner, believes his "horizontal fin" ideas were incorporated into the 1956 Buick Centurion show car and the production 1959 Chevrolet. Stephen J. Derezinski believes his 1957 third-place Michigan design inspired the split grille of the production 1959 Pontiac (www.fisherguild.com website, Guest Book, May 4, 2004). Similarly Eugene Simone thinks his 1960 scholarship winner may have inspired a whole generation of fastback body styles. Of course, GM wasn't alone, as many Guildsmen mimicked the national winners' design ideas in future models.

It is known that GM valued the multitude of ideas submitted by American and European youth, as the winning designs were professionally photographed by the GM photographic section. Some years, particularly during the mid-'50s, all the model entries were photographed. Several views (side view, ¾ front view and ¾ rear view) of each model were taken to fully describe the Guildsmen's creations. Although this is pure speculation, these ideas may have been reviewed periodically by GM stylists or designers for potential design themes. Many of these images still exist in computer files at GM Media Archives as a record of the Guild's creativity, but the Guildsmen's names and award levels are held confidential.

The contest rules stated that GM and its subsidiaries owned the ideas submitted. We know GM purchased many of the winning model cars, not so much to copy and own the design ideas involved as to promote the Guild with traveling exhibits and Guild field reps. First, they had GM model makers duplicate some of the winning model designs, then they purchased some of the winning models, and finally, they leased the models from winning contestants. Some say that the models purchased in the 1950s era have long since been sold at auction and are being enjoyed by collectors.

Some nostalgic Guildsmen who yearn for the days of yore would like to recover the scale model dream car designs they sold to GM many years ago. No one at the time could foresee the possibility that Fisher Body Division, GMC, might be reorganized out of existence in 1984 and that the GM-purchased Guild models would be sold at auction to Guild enthusiasts, memorabilia collectors and people who care about cars.

About $2,400,000 in university scholarships and cash was awarded by GM during the life of the Guild to 387 deserving youth. Tens of thousands of dollars in cash awards were made to thousands of youths. Another thing we know for sure is that, although it looked like work, the boys had a lot of fun participating! Over 10 million youths enrolled over the life of the Guild and many lives were touched, some very profoundly.

Postscript

Up to and including 1968, there were new program ideas on the drawing board such as a new four-color litho Guild manual, a new modeling clay design kit, a new quicker and faster construction technique, the potential for a new Guild chapter in Norway, an International Craftsman's Guild Award, a proposed Guild name change and change in organizational responsibility, and a new, rejuvenated Guild called the Fisher Body Design Competition.

GM Styling's proposed new Guild manual was to be similar to a GM Styling book entitled *Styling — The Look of Things*, and use a four-color lithograph process. C.W. McClellan said, "The present Guild manual costs $11,699 and according to GM Photographic's cost study the new manual would cost $55,000 for 700,000 books or approximately 5 times the cost of the present book."[63] This book was never produced.

A modeling clay design kit was being proposed as of October 7, 1965. It was to contain ruled contact paper with section lines (for a baseboard), five pounds of Chavant™ auto modeling clay, a styrofoam block for an armature, a ½" thick base block, a set of four vacuum-formed wheels, two wooden tools, a bottle of glue, cardboard for section templates, and a scaled instruction sheet with graph paper for front, side and rear elevations ($7.95 postage prepaid, Chavant Clay Models, Inc., 1 McAdoo Avenue, Jersey City, New Jersey).[64] This kit was never distributed.

In August 1967, Dave Rossi, design sculptor from GM Styling, demonstrated a new faster and speedier model-making technique (using rigid polyurethane foam and the polymer Liquitex modeling paste) to 64 members of the press at the GM Burbank Training Center. This technique was new for the 1967–68 competition year. A Guild advertisement in *Model Car and Science* (October 1967) proclaimed, "New space age polyurethane blocks speed up building of your 1968 Fisher Body Craftsman's Guild model car!" The Modellbauer Gilde at Adam-Opel AG may have owed its success to the discovery of this streamlined modeling technique.

GM Continental, GM France, GM Italia, GM Portugal and GM Norway (all GM Overseas Operations divisions) were interested in starting Guild programs. GM Norway was expected to announce a Guild program in time to participate in the 1966–67 competition year.[65] None of these things ever happened.

Internal memos reveal that the GM and Fisher Body proponents of regaining young people's interest in automobile design tried to resurrect and rejuvenate the Craftsman's Guild with a number of ideas that never publicly materialized.

Guild movers and shakers proposed an International Craftsman's Guild Award among the top senior winners from Vauxhall, Opel, Holden, GM Suisse and the FBCG competitions. Selection of the top three recipients would have been by William L. Mitchell and staff using secret ballets. There would have been gold, silver and bronze medallion awards with a New York City banquet and international cadre of attendees. The medallions had already been designed by GM Styling. (See Stuart Shuster's essay in Chapter IV; he did the design work on the proposed international trophy and medallions.) Also proposed at the time was transfering the Fisher Body Craftsman's Guild to GM Styling staff and calling it the General Motors Craftsman's Guild.[66]

Charles M. Jordan noted that in the 1960s, well over half of the members of the GM Design Staff had participated in the Guild and that many of them held responsible positions within GM Design. He also noted that an academic study (a Master's Thesis) found that students selected the industrial design profession because of their exposure to the Craftsman's Guild. Jordan suggested raising the college scholarships for first place to a minimum of $10,000 to keep up with the current cost of an education. Another idea he had was for the top winner of all the Guilds to spend the summer at GM Design developing full-size drawings and a large scale model with staff professionals.[67]

On July 3, 1973, a Fisher Body Design Competition was proposed internally to be structured similar to the Carrozzeria Bertone model design competition in Turin, Italy, open to all Europeans. This was a two-dimensional design and rendering competition rather than a 3-D model competition. Bertone had about 1,064 entrants completing all four parts of the competition's requirements and 5,374 partial entries total from across European nations.[68]

The new Fisher Body Design Competition would have been open to U.S. residents, with a junior division (ages 15–18) and senior division (ages 19–22). Scale line drawings, a color appearance rendering and a special features report would be required from each entrant. The 1973 proposal had three design categories: land transportation, home appliances and automotive interiors. The first place regional and national awards for both

It was William L. Mitchell's dream to have an international Guild competition among all the first place national winners of all the Guild programs (USA, UK, West Germany, Australia and Switzerland). Stuart Shuster of GM Styling created this rendering of a trophy for the General Motors International Craftsman's Guild competition to be awarded at a New York City gala event. Regrettably, Mitchell's dream never came true. *Stuart B. Shuster.*

junior and senior divisions would have been $6,000. Total regional and national scholarship awards proposed were in excess of $106,000. The new youth design competition would have cost about $500,000 to operate and promote annually.[69]

Despite the fact that none of the above ideas saw the light of day, talent searches for gifted innovators have continued, such as those sponsored independently by *Automobile Quarterly* magazine (1987–1991 Car Design Contests) and *Motor Trend* magazine's 2003 Car Design Contest, currently sponsored in cooperation with the Academy of Art University in San Francisco (and formerly in cooperation with ACCD in Pasadena) and the California International Auto Show.

Although the Craftsman's Guild touched contestants' lives only briefly, it left an indelible mark when a scholarship was awarded. The winners' lives were changed forever. An avocation became a vocation. Chapter IV, "The Search for Guildsmen," contains a series of autobiographical and biographical sketches written by and about many of the scholarship winners. These essays describe what it was like to participate in the Guild, what it meant to win a scholarship, what winners did with their university trust funds and what they accomplished in their chosen fields of endeavor.

1931 Napoleonic Coach made by Wallace Lench of Flint, Michigan. He took the coach with him as a résumé for his interview at the Flint Chevrolet plant, was hired (Apprentice Class of 1936) and became a journeyman die maker working at Chevrolet for 40 years. The author purchased the Wallace Lench coach from an online auction house and was able to locate the Lench family via Internet. *Author's collection.*

This model, made by Michael D'Mura, won the 1933 first state Indiana award for Paint Craft and the second state Indiana award for Wood Craft. Michael D'Mura's sons were very active in the Guild with Michael R. (Bobby) D'Mura and John M. D'Mura winning Guild scholarships. Cousin Joseph Wayne D'Mura also won a scholarship. *Dr. Michael R. (Bobby) D'Mura.*

Fisher Body Craftsman's Guild reunion of coach builders at Eagle Point, Oregon, June 1996. The front row attendees (*left to right*) were Carl E. Joyce (1933, Indiana), Emmett E. Day (1931, Texas), Charles W. Gadd (1933, Washington, Grand National winner) and William R. Smith (1933–1937, New York). The back row attendees (*left to right*) were Karl Moldenhauer (1932–1933, New York), Richard H. Berge (1933, Minnesota), Wilfred McClain (1931, Kansas), Laurence Jayne and Carl L. Timpe (1938, Missouri). *Skip Geear and Jerry Turner.*

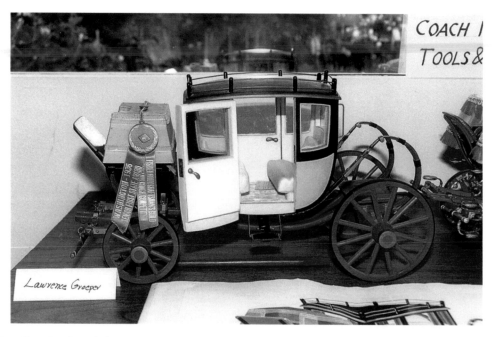

This Traveling Coach made by Laurence Groeper won the 1936 first-place state award in Washington in the Fisher Body Craftsman's Guild, Apprentice Craftsman Class. The Traveling Coach was introduced in 1934–35 Craftsman's Guild competition as a way for teenage youth to gain experience and encouragement before attempting a miniature Napoleonic Coach model. The Traveling Coach was supposed to be a simpler and easier model to build. *Skip Geear, FBCG Foundation and Mini-Museum, Eagle Point, Oregon.*

Vincent J. Rauth is shown at a 2004 Guild reunion with his 1946 first national scholarship, senior division, $4,000 award winning Guild model, a rear engine fastback design. Vince Rauth attended Notre Dame, studied architecture and worked for Minoru Yamasaki from 1963 to 1979. One of their projects was the World Trade Center in New York. *Photograph by author.*

Charles M. Jordan, Guildman, MIT engineer, automobile designer, vice president of GM Design (retired 1992) and Automobile Hall of Fame inductee. *Charles M. Jordan.*

This Guild model entry, displayed at a 2004 reunion, was made by Tom Goad and won a 1948 first national scholarship, junior division, $4,000 award. Tom Goad was manager of Pontiac Division's Special Vehicles Program from 1985 to 1996. *Photograph by author.*

Above: This Guild entry made by Harvey E. Whitman (age 18) won the 1948 first national scholarship, senior division, $4,000 award. Some construction details are as follows: Body — plaster casting from a rubber mold; bumpers and grille — cast aluminum; scored lines — edge of a steel scale used as a cutting tool; wheels — turned on a lathe from maple; paint — auto paint and used service station spray paint equipment. *Harvey E. Whitman.*

Below: As a high school student in Cincinnati, Stanley C. Waechter saw a Fisher Body Craftsman's Guild ad in *Boy's Life* magazine and decided to give it a try. Using a clay model and casting plaster, he designed this 4-door passenger sedan for the 1948–1949 competition year. This model has metal trim around the windows, silver painted trim around the bumpers, and a plywood bottom to which the wooden wheels are attached. He made one Guild entry. *Photograph by author.*

This balsa wood model constructed by Gale P. Morris (age 13) won the 1949 third national scholarship, junior division, $2,000 award. Gale Morris was involved in the first of the corporate industrial design offices, and as part of that new trend, coordinated the appearance and ergonomics of all new Tektronix, Inc., products. *Gale P. Morris.*

Above: Robert A. Cadaret won the 1950 first national scholarship, senior division, $4,000 award at age 19. Cadaret, shown with his wife Phyllis Ann circa 1994, was considered the most important auto designer of his time other than Harley Earl. He attended the Art Center School in Los Angeles with Ron Hill and Chuck Pelly in the early 1950s. *Michelle Cadaret-Schulz.*

Below: Elia "Russ" Russinoff (age 18) won the 1949 first national scholarship, senior division, $4,000 award with this 4-door sedan design. A dozen sets of drawings were discarded before this satisfactory design emerged. This soft mahogany model featured sculpted head lamps, an intricately designed and chrome-plated brass grille and wooden wheels turned on a 4-in-1 home shop lathe. The scale model required 500 hours and 8 months of labor to complete. *Elia "Russ" Russinoff.*

Despite not being a top state or regional award winner, this 2-door convertible sports car designed by Paul Tatseos of Boston, Massachusetts, won a 1957 styling scholarship, $1,000 award, for excellence in design. *Paul Tatseos.*

This sports car model won E. Arthur Russell (age 19) of Los Angeles a 1957 first national scholarship, $5,000 award. Art took a semester off from his Art Center School studies to complete his Guild entry. Some construction details are as follows: Body — poplar wood; trim — chrome-plated brass, silver-soldered brass parts; windshield and tail-lights — acrylic pastic; paint — nitrocellulose lacquer. *E. Arthur Russell.*

This model made by Edward Frasier Taylor (age 17) won the 1951 third national scholarship, senior division, $2,000 award. Some construction details for this model are as follows: Body — laminated ¾" thick mahogany, clear pastic windshield and side windows formed over plaster molds; bumpers, moldings, wheel discs — aluminum; headlamps and taillamps — pastic; and paint — lacquer. *Edward F. Taylor.*

Above: This model made by George R. Chartier won first state Wisconsin and a $150 award in 1953. The next year he entered two model cars in the 1954 Guild competition and one of the 1954 designs won a second state Wisconsin, $100 award. George always regretted not being able to compete in 1955 because, by then, he was too old. *George R. Chartier. Below:* This Guild model was made by George R. Chartier and won 1954 second state Wisconsin, $100 award. George made two model entries for the Guild competition in 1954, but according to the rules, only the highest scoring model could receive a prize. This model scored 88.5 percent. *George R. Chartier.*

This convertible sports car made by Paul Tatseos of Boston, Massachusetts, won the 1958 third national scholarship, senior division, $3,000 award. Carved from a solid block of poplar and finished with multiple coats of automotive lacquer, it required about 700 hours to complete. Metal parts were hand-made from solid pieces of aluminum, except the wheel discs which were turned on a lathe, hand-filed and then polished. Plastic parts were made from solid blocks and hand-polished. The windshield was heated in an oven then molded over a wood bock shaped to fit the body. The grille was fine aluminum screen. *Paul Tatseos.*

Similar to the Thomas H. Semple model, this model by James W. Green, age 15 (1961 third national scholarship, junior division, $3,000 award), is a highly complex design with an amber colored acrylic canopy and hollowed-out, finished interior. The construction details are as follows: Body — balsa wood covered with fiberglass; canopy — amber colored acrylic; trim — chromed plate and aluminum; paint — enamel; and interior — miscellaneous fabrics. Green became vice president of an architectural engineering firm. *James W. Green.*

This model made by John B. Di Ilio from College Station, Pennsylvania, won the 1957 third national scholarship, junior division, award worth $3,000. It was constructed from laminated bass wood with 5 coats of primer and 10 coats of lacquer. The color coat was a 1956 Buick production color, Tahiti Coral, and the window areas were painted Castle Grey. This design was one of the few 4-door sedans to win a national award and the only one in the 1956–1957 competition year. *John B. Di Ilio.*

This model designed by William A. Moore (age 19) won the 1956 first national scholarship, senior division, $5,000 award. An accurate clay model was made to work out the design ideas before starting the wood model. This model was carved from a single piece of poplar and silver-soldered, chrome-plated brass trim parts were applied. *William A. Moore.*

William F. Marks, 1957 second national scholarship, senior division, $4,000 award. Bill Marks had a challenging career at du Pont solving client product design problems using plastics. *William F. Marks.*

Gerald A. Simone's highly detailed 2-door sports sedan featured a simulated convertible top, a convertible top mechanism, authentic chrome wire wheels and a drop-away interior dash pad. In 1962 it won first state Rhode Island and regional award. *Gerald A. Simone.*

This convertible sports car model made by Patrick B. Saturday won a 1961 styling scholarship award worth $1,000. The construction of this convertible requiring 560 hours was as follows: Roof — clear acrylic dome that was vacuum formed over a paster model the contestant had made; body — 1" thick laminated, poplar hand-carved with cardboard templates and sealed with three coats of fiberglass resin; paint — 10 coats of lacquer primer and 11 coats of color lacquer (with hand compounded final coat); metal trim — parts made from brass were nickel plated and then chrome plated; wheel covers — made of brass turned on a lathe; taillights — red and clear plastic cut, glued together and buffed to fit; interior floors — felt paper; and dashboard graphics — photographic negative scaled to fit. *Patrick B. Saturday.*

This convertible model designed by Ronald J. Will of Hobart, Indiana, which featured an asymmetric design theme, won the 1961 first national scholarship, senior division, $5,000 award. According to Will, no two surfaces were alike. An interesting feature of Will's 1961 model was the partially completed interior. This was a model-making shortcut, but was supposedly legitimized by Virgil M. Exner, Sr.'s full-scale "XNR" show car for which only the driver's side compartment was completed. *Ronald J. Will.*

This station wagon design displayed at the 2004 Guild reunion in Detroit was constructed by Jerome A. Grunstad from Ortonville, Minnesota, at age 17. His model won a 1962 second state Minnesota $100 award as well as a 1962 styling scholarship, $1,000 award. Jerome Grunstad received his bachelor's degree in industrial design from Auburn University and has pursued a successful design career with Harley Design, a consulting firm, and Phillips Plastics Corporation of Minnesota. *Photograph by author.*

These Guild models crafted by Theodore A. Becker won a 1964 third state Illinois, senior division (left) and a 1965 second state Illinois, senior division (right) award. Becker became manager of industrial design with Maytag Cooking Technology, and is now retired. *Theodore A. Becker.*

 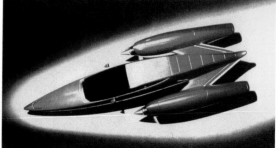

John M. Mellberg's 1966 model, which won the second national scholarship, senior division, $4,000 award, was designed to Category C specifications for the Open Competition. This side view shows the unique shapes possible in the Open Competition. The overhead or top view shows the turbine pods connected to the main body by stub wing surfaces. An exact scale drawing was made of this design integrating each component. The model was carved from REN board (i.e., solid blocks of polyester resin filled with mahogany sawdust). *General Motors Corporation.*

This model designed by Thomas L. Covert won a 1962 second national scholarship, senior division, $4,000 award. This photograph was taken in 1962 in the lobby of Fisher Body Central Engineering in Warren, Michigan, where the scholarship winners were on exhibit for the public. After graduation from ACCD in 1968, Tom Covert had a career at the GM Design Center as a designer and recently was the lead designer on the Hummer SUV/SUT program. *Photograph by author.*

Richard Pietruska (age 15) of Stamford, Connecticut, won the 1963 first national scholarship, junior division, award worth $5,000 with this design. The model was made of laminated clear pine with lacquer finish and aluminum wheels and bumpers. Pietruska attended the Art Center College of Design (ACCD) as a student and works there today as an instructor, noted for his fine art automotive sculpture and illustrations. *Michael A. Pietruska.*

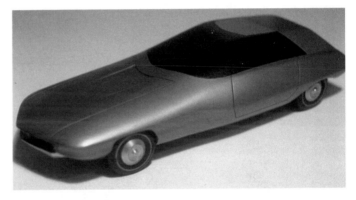

Michael A. Pietruska (age 12) of Stamford, Connecticut, won the 1965 second national scholarship, junior division, award worth $4,000 with this design. This model was built of laminated clear pine with lacquer finish and aluminum wheels and bumpers. It featured a stainless steel roof. Pietruska studied at the ACCD and has worked as an exhibit designer as well as a toy/game designer for Milton Bradley. *Michael A. Pietruska.*

This model made by Michael R. (Bobby) D'Mura of Flagstaff, Arizona, won a 1962 styling scholarship award worth $1,000. This model also won the 1962 first state Arizona and regional senior division awards. Note the partially completed interior (e.g., driver's side interior is completed in detail with a windshield, but passenger-side compartment's outline is indicated by scored lines). D'Mura became a prosthodontist. *Dr. Michael R. (Bobby) D'Mura.*

C-14　*Below:* A sea of scale models await the three pairs of judges for the 1966 Fisher Body Crafsman's Guild Model Car Competition at the Fisher Body Central Engineering auditorium in Warren, Michigan. About 3,000 or more model entries were received that year. The author's 1966 entry is the red, 2-door sports coupe with black indicated side windows and windshield seen in side view in the lower left foreground. This model was made using a finely detailed surface development drawing (scale mechanical drawing), Sears Roebuck & Co. polyester boat resin, and fiberglass cloth, and painted with Macco automotive lacquer. The model won a first state Maryland, senior division, $150 award. The prize occasioned a family celebration at Haussner's Restaurant, one of Baltimore's most famous establishments. *General Motors Corporation.*

Dale A. Gnage of Rochester, New York, won the 1966 first national scholarship, junior division, $5,000 award at age 15. The construction is as follows: Body — three pieces of laminated cherry wood; bumpers — chrome-plated brass pegged in place; paint — Nassau Blue acrylic lacquer. Gnage's first entry won the 1965 second state New York, junior division, $100 award. Gnage is a retired engineer from Rochester Products Division, GMC. *Dale A. Gnage.*

Below: Three working Guild judges at the 1966 competition in Warren, Michigan: *(left to right)* Roy V. Lonberger, James Bisignano and Russell Orr. All were GM stylists. The model cars on the table were made by *(left to right)* John M. Mellberg (second national scholarship, senior award), Joseph Wayne D'Mura (fourth national scholarship, senior award) and Kenneth A. Kelly (third national scholarship, senior award). The model on the rotating pedestal is that of Ovid Ward (first national scholarship, senior award). *General Motors Corporation.*

This model made by Ronald E. Pietruska (age 18) of Stamford, Connecticut, won a 1967 fourth national scholar-ship, senior division, $2,000 award. This model was designed to Category C specifications for the Open Competition which accommodated designs with unusual wheelbase configurations. Note that this design had two steered wheels in the rear. *Michael A. Pietruska.*

This Open Competition, rear engine, 2-door sports coupe designed by Terry P. Graboski of Miami, Florida, won the 1967 first state Florida and regional awards and a styling scholarship award worth $1,000. This model received 94 out of a possible 110 styling points and was carved from balsa wood, covered with fiberglass resin and finished with a metallic blue automotive lacquer. The chrome window trim was made from solid silver wire, glued into grooves and sanded flat. The racing stripes on the rear of the model were used to conceal damage from a last minute traumatic fall from the workbench. *Terry P. Graboski.*

This model made by Tom W. Graboski of Miami, Florida, won a styling scholarship award worth $1,000 in 1968, the last year of the competition. Constructed from fiberglass resin over rigid polyurethane and painted dark metallic green, this model was built to Category C specifications for the Open Competition. This electric pow-ered urban minicar featured a very short wheelbase as well as a wide front track and narrow rear track. The Gra-boski brothers (Tom and Terry) have had successful industrial design careers in the field of environmental design. *Tom W. Graboski.*

IV

The Search for Guildsmen

In this chapter, autobiographic and biographic essays describe some of the coach builders (1931–1948) and some of the model car-makers (1937–1968), where they came from, what years they participated, the scholarships and awards they won, their university educations and subsequent training, and the vocations they pursued.

Napoleonic Coach Builders

My experience in building my coach and winning the subsequent scholarship has had a profound influence on my life. While it has helped me to make a good living and make some important contributions to society, this is not the point I want to make. I have been retired since 1972 and have occupied my time with violin making. This is very demanding craft and I think I am good at it. My background as a craftsman is still serving me well.[1]

The following sketches about the coach builders were derived using a variety of sources and references, such as essays written by the coach builder himself or contributed by a relative or family member; telephone or personal interviews or correspondence with the coach builder; and old newspaper, magazine, or *Guild News* articles; written about the individual many years ago.

Using a form designed by the author and modified by Skip Geear, a biographic survey was conducted in 1997 by the FBCG Foundation, Eagle Point, Oregon, in which 12 coach builders participated.[2] This survey included three of the four 1931 national scholarship winners (Howard F. Jennings, Albert W. Fischer, and Donald C. Burnham), the top 1933 national scholarship winner (Charles W. Gadd), and the top 1936 national scholarship winner (Henry B. Larzelere). One of the 12 individuals desired confidential handling of his biographic information, but the other 11 indicated on the form that their information could be used to write about the Guild. All of this immensely valuable survey information was used in the coach chapter to describe how the coaches were made and the ingenious tools created but was also used to fill in details in some of the biographic essays. An example of the Coach-Builder's Biographic Survey Form is shown in Appendix C.

NAPOLEONIC COACH BUILDERS' REUNION, JUNE 22–23, 1996

On June 22–23, 1996, an FBCG reunion of Napoleonic Coach builders was held in Eagle Point, Oregon. Forty-eight people gathered including family, friends and neighbors to remember the Guild. Having studied, read and written about these very valuable coaches for several years and labored over the Guild blueprints and instruction books on many occasions trying to understand how they were made, the author finally met several history-making coach builders and got to see the exquisite models they had made so many years ago.

In attendance were Karl Moldenhauer (1932 and 1933 New York entry), Richard H. Berge (1933 Minnesota entry), Wilfred McClain (1931 Kansas senior division winner), Laurence Jayne (who completed his coach in 1976), Carl L. Timpe (1938 Missouri), Carl E. Joyce (1933 entry), Emmett E. Day (1931 Texas Junior Division winner), Charles W. Gadd (1933 national scholarship winner, from the state of Washington), and William R. Smith (1933, 1934, 1935, 1936, and 1937 New York state winner, now deceased).

Eight former Guildsmen in their late seventies and early eighties as well as other coach builders, enthusiasts and groupies came from across the country to show off and talk about the scale model coaches they had handcrafted in the 1930s. They drove or flew with a spouse, son or daughter, some under their own steam, in order to meet and make new friends and reminisce with others who had spent the 1000–2000 or more grueling hours to make one of these magnificent models. The models they made were awesome works of art and the coach builders, themselves, were delightful people. It has always been hard to understand how a 12–19 year old could have ever made one, but as the author had learned from talking to people on the phone, and confirmed at the reunion, it was a family affair—dad, mom, brothers, sisters and skilled relatives were all involved. The contestant became the prime contractor, so to speak, and his family members subcontractors. This was the accepted practice at the time.

Mr. Charles Gadd, a 1933 national scholarship winner, had received a wonderful college education that otherwise might not have been. Mr. Gadd spent his career at GM Research in the field of biomechanics and automobile safety. A biomechanics head injury criteria used around the world in the early 1970s bears his name: the Gadd Severity Index.

Mr. William Smith, a first-place winner from the state of New York in the years 1933–1937, described how he'd applied gold leaf to his coach trim, instead of homemade gold paint, because his father restored gilded picture frames for a living and could show him how. They all concurred that photographic plate glass was the only glass that had just the right thickness to make the movable sliding window work. The author wondered how Bill Smith had the reserve energy and moxie to make so many coaches from 1933 to 1937. There is a reasonable explanation. As it turns out, in 1934, the official Guild rules made it possible to resubmit a previous year's coach provided the current competitions year's new specifications were met.

I met some very wonderful and generous people at that reunion. I still remember Laurence Jayne showing me the box of rejected parts and pieces from his coach, as trial and error were often needed to perfect a part. The overall message received was that these coaches are very valuable (worth thousands), highly prized, family heirlooms and, quite frankly, the only way you'd ever own one would be to build one yourself.

The author had never really appreciated the miniature model Napoleonic Coaches until that 1996 reunion. After meeting and speaking with the coach builders and meeting their families, the author had a whole new perspective on those beautiful old model coaches that required such creativity, ingenuity, skill and genius to build. In fact, the author grew so fond of the idea that he purchased one in May 2000 from eBay that had been made in 1931 by Wallace Lench of Flint, Michigan.

Retirees are still finishing their Napoleonic Coach models. During the '70s and '80s, one of the most frequent requests at the Fisher public relations office was from retirees seeking copies of the Napoleonic Coach *Plans and Instructions* book from the 1930s.

COACH BUILDERS' BIOGRAPHIC PROFILES

Brief profiles are provided for the following individuals. Donald C. Burnham (1931), Raymond S. Doerr (1931), Albert W. Fischer (1931), Wallace Lench (1931), Gordon L. Drummond (1932), Emmett E. Day (1932, 1933), Stanley Knochel (1933), Charles W. Gadd (1933), Myron Webb (1933), Michael D'Mura (1932, 1933), Robert W. Henderson (1934), Henry B. Larzelere (1936) and Leo C. Peiffer (1946).[3]

Donald C. Burnham

1931 First-Place National Scholarship, Junior Division, $5,000 Award

Donald Burnham was the son of a gasoline station operator in West Lafayette, Indiana, and spent 1,000 hours building from scratch (except for a few purchased parts) his award winning Napoleonic Coach.[4] He was 16 years old at the time.

In an article he wrote a few years later (1937) titled "How I Built My Coach in 1931," he described the upholstering process:[5]

> The upholstery was one of the most interesting parts of the coach for me. I made little shallow boxes of the shape of the seat cushions. Then, I made the shape of the seat out of sponge rubber. Then, I glued the silk velvet to the front and back of the seat cushion. I had previously laid out on the velvet where the French knots were to come. When the glue had dried, I pulled the cloth down with a thread at each point where a knot was to go. Then, I went over it again running a thread along each place where a crease was to go. This made the tufts distinct. Then, I went over it and put in the gold French knots after which I glued the silk velvet down at the ends of the cushion. Then, I put white leather on the bottom to cover the stitching, and then last, I put the brocade around the front and sides of the cushion.

Mr. Burnham commented further about the coach build process:

> On carving the eagles, one on each corner of the coach, I spent one day on each eagle. One of the hardiest things that I had in the line of tools was a set of little hand carving chisels that were given to me several years before, which I had no use for, until I made the coach. They were a gouge, a skew and a straight chisel. I sat out on the porch of my grandmother's house at 353 Chauncey Avenue in West Lafayette, Indiana, and worked on those eagles. I had, as a model, the aluminum eagles that came in the coach kit of materials. I could have used the aluminum ones, but I decided to carve my own. They looked pretty good. The first eagle was easier than the others because you had to end up making them all look just alike. By carving my own, instead of using the aluminum kit eagles, I was able to achieve potentially a higher score.[6]

Mr. Burnham studied mechanical engineering at Purdue University using his Guild scholarship trust funds. As a young "up and coming" GM employee, and an important role model for Guildsmen, he made the following speech to the 1940 Guild national convention at age 25:

Building one of the Napoleonic Coach models is about the best example of all around craftsmanship that can be obtained today. It is easy to see how the principles taught in building the model coach can well be applied to the tasks of everyday life. In fact, the processes gone through in building a coach are directly comparable to a person's life itself.

When you craftsmen who have built coaches first looked at the plans, things seemed rather complicated and you hardly knew where to start. That is just the way life seems when a young man looks forward and tries to see what he wants to be in the world. As you read further in the plans, the clouds begin to clear a little. That set of plans is like your education. In the schools we learn how to do things, but it is up to us to use this knowledge later.

There are many obstacles encountered as we piece our lives together just as there were in building a coach. Parts had to be made over and over again to get them perfected and just as we never gave up trying on the coach, we should never give up when we get a hard knock in life. Personally, I believe that the greatest lesson one learns from craftsmanship work is to stick to the job until you get it completed and this very important principle should be carried over into every day life.

If you have built your coach like a true craftsman it will not be set off in a corner to collect dust; it will be a center of interest for along time. And when you have completed your life, if it has been built along the principles of craftsmanship — honesty, stick-to-it-iveness, patience, and an ambition to do ones best, you will not be forgotten, but will live on in the eyes of the world.[7]

Initially working for the AC Spark Plug division, he worked his way up through the ranks of General Motors Corporation, becoming manufacturing manager by age 32 at the Oldsmobile division. In 1953–54, at age 39, he was Oldsmobile's assistant chief engineer. After a 17-year career at General Motors he moved to Westinghouse and eventually became the CEO and chairman.[8,9]

In November 1993, Mr. Burnham donated his award winning coach to the Smithsonian's Guild collection at the National Museum of American History in Washington, D.C. The remainder of Mr. Burnham's Guild memorabilia (silver loving cup, tam, and other items) resides at the FBCG Foundation and Mini-Museum in Eagle Point, Oregon.[10]

Raymond S. Doerr

1931 First-Place National Scholarship, Senior Division, $5,000 Award

Mr. Doerr is a retired mechanical engineer, former GM employee and expert violin maker who donated his national scholarship award winning Napoleonic Coach to the University of Michigan School of Engineering, his alma mater. The coach is on permanent display at the Transportation Building.

Rummaging among his things he found three photographs of his coach which were taken before color photography. He did the original photo finishing himself and still preserves the negatives. He also found his 1931 scrapbook containing newspaper clippings when the *Detroit Times* (August 26, 1931) interviewed him, stories about the first four Napoleonic Coach winners, and congratulatory cards from friends and associates.[11]

The scrapbook, which now resides at the Smithsonian's National Museum of American History, indicates that Mr. Doerr spent 2,050 hours building his award winning coach. (Another Raymond S. Doerr scrapbook and photo album resides at the FBCG Foundation and Mini-Museum in Eagle Point, Oregon.)

Graduating in February 1931 from high school, he was encouraged to pursue the coach competition rather than a job. He worked with bulldog-like determination 12–14 hours a day until it was completed. Ray Doerr came from a family of craftsmen: his father was employed as a pattern maker for a plumbing company and both his grandfathers were woodworkers.

Mr. Doerr wrote in 1985,[12]

> My experience in building my coach and winning the subsequent scholarship has had a profound influence on my life. While it has helped me to make a good living and make some important contributions to society, this is not the point I want to make. I have been retired since 1972 and have occupied my time with violin making. This is very demanding craft and I think I am good at it. My background as a craftsman is still serving me well. I am 72 years old; I have completed 15 violins and have 250 more in process. I am almost ready to publish a book on violin making.[13] I am currently teaching a class once a week in the art of violin making. God willing, I hope to pursue this old craft for many years to come.

Mr. Doerr sent the author photographs of a restored and refinished Stradivarius violin (circa 1728) he had worked on.[14]

In an interview with the *Detroit Times* on August 26, 1931, Mr. Doerr said,

> I am grateful to the *Times*, for without its weekly instructions the result would have been a different story. ... I read the *Times*' step-by-step instructions every Sunday and then clipped and kept them filed where I could refer to them as often as I had to. They straightened out much of the confusion about different details, and suggested many practical ways of getting the hard parts finished. ... Then, when the "Master Model" was displayed in the *Times*' lobby, Dad drove me and my brother over to study it at close range. I can truthfully say that visit made a tremendous difference to me for it gave me a real picture of what the finished job was to be. But, the *Times* kept encouraging its chapter members to keep at it, and so I did.

The *Detroit Times* writer commented,

> Doerr compared the Fisher Body Craftsman's Guild to the Boy Scouts organization pointing out that both have eliminated artificial bars to progress, and put every member on an equal footing, in which individual merit counts. ... But even individual merit he believes might not have carried him through without the occasional aid of encouragement from outside ["Thousands See Winning Model"].

Albert W. Fischer

1931 First-Place National Scholarship, Senior Division, $5,000 Award

Mr. Fischer grew up in Waukegan, Illinois, and at age 18 won state, regional and national scholarship awards with his first attempt at building a Napoleonic Coach. The project consumed 2,000 hours of time and employed a purchased coach kit. His father bought him a table saw, 4" joiner, jigsaw and lathe when he was 16. In addition, he had to make a tool and die set to punch out copper pieces for the trim of the coach wheels and spokes. According to Mr. Fischer, his parents were getting by with 8 children (there was no welfare assistance in those days), and the family had to raise their own vegetables in a garden. There was no money for college and the Guild was his only chance. In responding to a 1997 survey of former Guildsmen, Mr. Fischer said, "I graduated with

$1,500 to spare and gave $1,000 to a younger brother to get a degree in chemistry. We were the only ones to go to college." He worked at GM Research and received a draft deferment for the work he was doing for the war effort. He eventually became a development engineer in electromechanical instrumentation. In 1939 he had purchased a violin making kit and got hooked on making violins as a hobby. Albert has made many award winning musical instruments. Many pieces of Mr. Fischer's Guild memorabilia reside at the FBCG Foundation.

Wallace Lench
1931 Certificate of Craftsmanship and Bronze Pin

Wallace Lench was born in Antioch, British Columbia, Canada, in February 1916 and died April 1980 in Flint, Michigan. He married Genevieve Cole on July 12, 1941, who at age 84 still lives in Flint, where they made their home and raised a family. Wallace Lench built a Napoleonic Coach in 1931 when he was 15 years old and entered it in the Guild competition. He was an average participant who won a Guild Certificate of Craftsmanship and a Guild pin. But he did win big time; several years later, using his completed coach as a resume, he was hired into the Flint Chevrolet plant, was a member of the second graduating apprentice class of 1936 and worked for 40 years as a journeyman die maker.

In May 2000, the author acquired the 1931 Napoleonic Coach (also the Certificate of Craftsmanship and diamond-shaped Guild pin) made by Mr. Lench from the online auction company eBay. According to the seller in Wisconsin, the coach had originally been sold at auction in Flint, Michigan, possibly by the widow of the builder. The author tracked down Lench family addresses via an Internet search and contacted the only one in Michigan. Raymond D. Lench, son of Wallace Lench, wrote back and confirmed that the color photographs the author had sent were of his dad's coach.

The Lench coach has been preserved by the author in a clear acrylic exhibit case with a thick "butcher block" base. A repair had to be made when this coach was received via UPS as the aluminum "reach" pole, or primary suspension structure, had sheared off at the fifth wheel pivot point. This is precisely one of the vulnerable, weak points coach builders were warned about under "Shipping Instructions" in a 1934 issue of the *Guildsman*. But this particular shear failure had existed for many, many years, as the red paint around the shear plane had been chafed or abraded away. The Lench family had apparently re-fit the two pieces together many times so the coach had the proper regal bearing. Because the author had also collected a copy of the Napoleonic Coach Plans and Instructions book many years earlier, the aluminum reach pole could be drilled and pinned together with a 0.060" piece of brass rod, fixed with Super Glue and restored to its original design position. The author tried to get the exact 12" center-to-center wheelbase, but it just wasn't to be. Wallace definitely lost points on that one in 1931 (Raymond D. Lench letter, August 18, 2000).

Gordon L. Drummond
1932 First-Place National Scholarship, $5,000 Award

Gordon L. Drummond was a first-place state winner from Washington, D.C., in 1931 and won the top national prize in 1932. On both occasions he received an all-expenses-paid trip to Detroit for the annual Guild convention and an inscribed silver loving cup. His 1932 miniature model coach was placed on display in the Arts and Industries Building, Smithsonian Institution, in Washington, D.C., and was seen by thousands of visitors.

To duplicate the four eagles at each corner of the coach roof, he carved a left and right wood pattern and made molds from the wood patterns. Hard rubber castings were made from the molds for the finished parts. Samples of the trial castings from his effort reside at the FBCG Foundation.

Mr. Drummond was trained in engineering at the University of Michigan and worked as a model builder for the General Motors Futurama exhibit at the 1939 New York World's Fair, and as a Fisher Body employee before the war, gained extensive auto body manufacturing experience. During World War II he was engaged by the Detroit naval arsenal.

In the early 1950s he worked with Theodore M. Mandel (1937 first place national scholarship winner in the first year of the model car competition) to help duplicate Guild scholarship winning model cars at the Fisher plant at Piquette and Oakland streets. These were built by the Guild technical department and used for exhibition pur-

Gordon L. Drummond (circa 1931) was a state winner from Washington, D.C., in the 1931 Napoleonic Coach competition and the 1932 first national scholarship winner, $5,000 award winner. Gordan studied at the University of Michigan, worked as a Craftsman's Guild supervisor and enjoyed a long career at Fisher Body Central Engineering Headquarters in Detroit. *General Motors Corporation.*

poses. At this time he was assistant technical supervisor of the Guild. Mr. Drummond spent his automotive career at the Fisher Body Division of GMC at the Tech Center in Warren, Michigan.

One of his friends was Stanley Knochel of Baltimore, 1933 first-place national scholarship winner, junior division. Gordon Drummond passed away April 30, 1982.[15]

Emmett E. Day

1931 and 1932 Texas State Winner

Mr. Day, from Commerce, Texas, used the miniature model Napoleonic Coach kits. State awards were in the $25–$75 range, not enough for college. According to Mr. Day, he loved to make things with his hands and the coach competition was a great challenge. He was pretty much on his own, as there was no school shop or Scouts organization where he grew up. His sisters were art teachers and they were helpful on aesthetic aspects of the coach design. Everything was handcrafted, because he had no shop equipment other than a hand scroll saw, a small vise, a few files, a soldering iron, a pair of tin snips, a hammer, sandpaper and pliers. Mr. Day believes that the Guild led to his graduating in mechanical engineering from MIT and his teaching engineering for 38 years at the University of Washington. His Napoleonic Coach was seen at the 1996 FBCG reunion. It was in good condition and well preserved in a glass case. In June 2001, Mr. Day donated his coach to Texas A&M University in Commerce, Texas.

Stanley Knochel

1933 First-Place National Scholarship, Junior Division, $5,000 Award

The author had the wonderful opportunity to interview Mr. Knochel on Father's Day, June 16, 1985, when he was 67 years old, in his Baltimore home where he grew up. He won the Maryland first-place state award in the coach competition in 1932 (when he "learned the tricks of the trade," he said) and in 1933 won the first-place junior national scholarship when he was 15 years old. (In the 1930s this was triple what a man earned in a year and in the 1940s a three-bedroom single family dwelling could be yours free and clear for the same amount. In 1940, the median family income in the U.S. was only $1,231.[16]) He showed me the cigar boxes full of remnants of materials from his winning coach. Mr. Knochel was a craftsman, engineer, designer, draftsman, inventor, patriot, and entrepreneur; a very creative and ingenious person.

He used his $5,000 scholarship to attend the University of Louisiana and worked in the Baltimore area at Bendix Corporation, Aircraft Armaments, Inc. (AAI) and Glenn L. Martin Co. These were principally aerospace defense contractors. At Martin's he was a member of the "200 Club"— an elite group of inventors with 200 or more patents to their credit. While there, during World War II, he helped build the Martin Marauder (B-26) and perfected a method of testing aircraft carrier cables for the navy that cut that tedious process by ten times.[17] From 1950 to 1955 he ran his own tool and die shop.

Mr. Knochel had a complete machine shop in his basement while growing up, and his father (chief draftsman at Baltimore Dry Dock) taught him how to use it to advantage. They used it together, and father taught son. Just for fun, they made a fully operational, dual cylinder, gas, model airplane engine. Flying models in those days were scratch-built (no die-cut or laser-cut parts or kits were available). A model boat propeller was carved from wood using a cam and template system, and using this as a pattern, was cast in brass. They also constructed miniature lead batteries to operate model boat motors. It can be seen from this resume that Stanley Knochel was fully qualified to build a Napoleonic Coach.

The spoke wheels on the coaches consisted of at least 50 parts each. The chances of fabricating a wheel that ran true were one in a million. In order to achieve perfectly aligned spoke wheels for the coach, with zero run-out or side-to-side variation, the Knochels cast their wheel rims in aluminum and then machined them on an engine lathe to plus or minus 5 thousandths of an inch tolerance. Some of the aluminum trim Stanley had purchased from GM was flawed, but no problem here. They recast the aluminum parts using Woods Metal (having a low melting point) and a mold made from room temperature vulcanizing (RTV) rubber. The rubber allowed flexibility from negative draft, or undercuts, in the trim which would otherwise lock the part in the mold. Also, the GM-supplied medallions, needed around the spoked wheels, lacked crisp definition. Again, no problem in the Knochel household, because new ones were stamped from copper sheet using brass dies that had been engraved by a local professional artisan.

There were no hobby shops as we know them today and no spray paints—you made your own glue from celluloid and acetone, made "gold" paint by mixing brass filings with clear lacquer, and melted down toothbrush handles to mold parts of your own design.

Mr. Knochel made it clear that family support and involvement was essential to successful coach building. The whole family was involved. According to Knochel, the color of materials contained in the purchased Trim Kit were not true to the colors of the GM-supplied coach plans, so his mother worked with the local millinery shop to remedy the situation. His mother and sister did a lot of the sewing tasks required for the interior of the coach body (embroidery, needlepoint and the cutting and finishing of materials such as silk and rabbit's fur) and the exterior tassels and tonneau trim.

Later in life, Mr. Knochel lost an arm. But this was not an impediment to an inventive person. He designed and built a mechanical drafting board and jigsaw system for disabled persons so he could continue to do the projects he enjoyed. This is fundamental Yankee perseverance, self-reliance and know-how. He lived in an era when if you didn't make it yourself, you didn't own one.

Unfortunately, he sold his award winning coach to GM in 1968 for $3,000, so all he had to show me were a few black and white snapshots. Years earlier, realizing his mistake, Mr. Knochel tried to locate his heirloom model, but to no avail. One theory is that Mr. Knochel's coach sits in a display case at some suite of GM executive offices somewhere. However, Gordon L. Drummond, a 1932 coach builder and winner, who was working at the Fisher Body Division in 1968 and may have brokered the deal, advised Stanley that his coach had met an untimely end and that the model's finish has been inadvertently ruined. Mr. Knochel passed away in 1994.

Charles W. Gadd

1933 First-Place National Scholarship, Senior Division, $5,000 Award

Mr. Gadd built three Napoleonic Coaches, winning first-place Washington state awards three years in a row; and in the third year of the competition, 1933, he won a national scholarship. His coaches were built from scratch, but relied upon purchased trim and upholstery kits. He was 17 years old and an honor student when he won the highest Guild award. Mr. Gadd had been studying engineering by correspondence courses to advance his education (via Washington State College), but the Guild scholarship allowed him to attend Massachusetts Institute of Technology (MIT) and formally take up the study of mechanical engineering. He graduated from MIT in 1937.

His father made a modest income and could not afford to help with college. During his boyhood he delivered papers by bicycle to earn spending money. His father had built basic power carpentry tools for the home workshop, but gave no help to Charles with building the coaches. But his parents were very encouraging and allowed him to use the kitchen stove to heat his soldering iron and the living room stove to make castings. Charles converted a sewing machine to a metal-cutting jigsaw, built a small lathe, and

This miniature model Napoleonic Coach was built for the Fisher Body Craftsman's Guild competition by Charles W. Gadd (age 17) and won the 1933 first national scholarship, senior division, $5,000 award. Although kits were available, this coach was scratch-built. Charles Gadd used his scholarship to attend MIT, and after graduation, he worked at the General Motors Research Laboratories in automotive structures and biomechanics research. This model coach is preserved at the Henry Ford Museum and Greenfield Village in Dearborn, Michigan. *Photograph by author.*

used dental methods such as the lost wax process to form metal castings for body trim moldings. Mr. Gadd said, "I am convinced that I, or anyone, wishing to succeed in Engineering will do best if he (she) has some background of working with his (her) hands and brain to develop a mechanical aptitude and skill in the designing of products. The Fisher Body Craftsman's Guild did this."

Mr. Gadd was not called to active duty during World War II because of his expertise in the design of aircraft engines (the Allison V12 engine). He worked for GM Research for 39 years.

In 1956 Mr. Gadd was a supervisor of vibration and stress analysis at GM Research, particularly suspension system experimental stress analysis. In that year, as a Guild role model, he wrote a column in the *Guildsman* (vol. 4, no. 3, fall 1956) advising participants to pursue math and science in their educational endeavors and making clear that math and science were the keys to success in a professional life.

Primarily he worked in the field of automotive biomechanics and studied automobile injury mechanisms and automobile safety improvements, including the energy absorbing steering column.[18] The Gadd Severity Index, an acceleration based measure of head injury potential in automotive crash research, was world famous in the 1970s. Mr. Gadd donated his national scholarship winning Napoleonic Coach in recent years to the Henry Ford Museum in Dearborn, Michigan, where it is seen and enjoyed by thousands annually.

Myron Webb

1933 First-Place National Scholarship, Junior Division, $5,000 Award[19]

Myron Webb lived in Arkansas City, Kansas, and built a Napoleonic Coach for the 1931 and 1933 competitions. His second coach was judged the finest in the U.S. and Canada. He attended Guild conventions as an alumnus in such cities as Cleveland, Chicago, Detroit and Quebec over the years, using stream powered transportation. Mr. Webb was quoted in 1983 as saying about his coach, "The door windows moved up and down in tracks by means of pull straps similar to the method adopted for the Model T Ford. ... The coach body suspension springs had leather straps attached the body with belt buckles and miniature ratchet adjustors for fine tuning the body/chassis alignment. ... Each wheel was assembled like a real-world wagon wheel, each wheel containing 100 parts" ("Craftsman Remembered").

Myron Webb remembered that at this time in our history (the Depression), time was more plentiful than money, so the whole family helped out with the coach project. Myron's mother, Alma, had at one time worked in a millinery shop designing and making hats and did beautiful handiwork. She did the sewing on the interior trim of the coach body. There is a magnificent sunburst she hand-stitched on the silk roof lining. Myron's father, Paul, had designed and constructed many things and was an excellent craftsman and teacher. Paul and his brother, Frank, operated a carbide manufacturing plant and worked with tools every day. Myron grew up with tools and learned how to make things. While in the fifth or sixth grade, he built a working electric train and track. Myron has passed along his crafts abilities to his daughter (Sherrylin), grandchildren (Lori and Juli) and son-in-law (David).

Michael D'Mura

1933 Indiana State Winner

Michael D'Mura's Napoleonic Coach won the first-place Indiana state award for paint craft and the second-place state award for woodcraft in the senior division. The photographs of the model in *Automobile Quarterly* (vol. 25, no. 2, 1987) reveal how fierce and competitive the Guild competition must have been in 1933, as this model, just a state-level winner, had exquisite craftsmanship. Even though the model was 52 years old when the *Automobile Quarterly* photographs were taken, it was in immaculate condition and well preserved by the D'Mura family. Michael D'Mura is the father of Michael R. (Bobby) D'Mura and John D'Mura (Flagstaff, Arizona, contestants from the 1960s) who successfully participated a generation later in the FBCG model car competition (see their biographies later in this chapter). The father passed along his know-how, passion and enthusiasm for the program and created a family legacy. The boys' cousin, Joseph Wayne D'Mura from East Gary, Indiana, also won a 1964 regional award and a 1966 fourth-place national scholarship, senior division, $2,000 award. One year, the two brothers and their cousin went to the Detroit Guild convention together. The D'Muras earned the moniker of "family dynasty" with two sons and a cousin winning Guild scholarships.[20]

This is the miniature model Napoleonic Coach made by Robert W. Henderson for the 1934 Guild competition for which he won a 4-year college scholarship. Robert W. Henderson had a career as a top nuclear weapons engineer and scientist. *Dr. William G. Henderson.*

Robert W. Henderson

1934 National Scholarship Winner

In the following 1 minute and 35 second speech, most probably delivered at a Guild convention one summer in Detroit, the great American scientist and engineer Robert W. Henderson expressed what the Craftsman's Guild meant to him:

> I grew up on a citrus ranch in Riverside, California, where in addition to the regular outdoor activities of ranch life, I intensively pursued the hobbies of building model airplanes and boats, and of sail boat racing during the summer months. In 1931, I first heard of the Fisher Body Craftsman's Guild and its annual competition encouraging boys to build a model Napoleonic Coach. I entered the competition and began work shortly thereafter, using as my work bench a table set up in the kitchen which kept me close to the family and their continued active interest. My own tools were supplemented by the facilities of the high school shops, the automobile repair shop of a friend, and a dental laboratory. This was a difficult task, but my coach was awarded second place in the California state competition. I was determined to try again the following year, profiting by my experience. After many more evenings spent at the work table, the second coach finally was completed, winning first place in California. Progress was real, and I was determined to win

one of the university scholarships offered by the Guild as a national award. Consequently, I set out to build my third carriage. The next year, 1934, my coach took national honors and I won my scholarship at age 19. The experience gained from these three years of intensive effort, besides giving me a great deal of pleasure and self-satisfaction, has paid off on numerous occasions since, both in drive to see a job completed on schedule and in the knowledge gained of the precision instrument and tool trade. In retrospect I can say that there is no doubt that the Fisher Body Craftsman's Guild competition helped to a considerable degree in laying the ground work for my career as a mechanical engineer.

Robert W. Henderson attended the University of California School of Engineering on his Guild four-year scholarship and had jobs initially with Standard Oil of California and Paramount Pictures in Hollywood. In 1942 he won an Academy Award for his work on photographic processes and special effects. By the start of World War II, Mr. Henderson had joined the Berkeley Radiation Laboratory under Nobel laureate Dr. Ernest Orlando Lawrence, and from November 1942 to March 1944 was engaged both at Cal Berkeley and Oak Ridge, Tennessee, on design, construction, and performance testing related to the pilot plants of the vast atomic energy (Manhattan) project. Specifically, he worked on the design of a large electromagnet to separate U235 from its parent metal. In 1944, he was transferred to Los Alamos, New Mexico, to work for Dr. Robert Oppenheimer, head of the Manhattan Project, and was teamed up with a world expert on chemical explosions, Dr. George Kistiakowsky. Together, they collaborated on the development of the atomic bomb. As head of the engineering group, he was involved in the engineering details of the Los Alamos Project and the test firing of the first atomic bomb in the Alamogordo Desert (Trinity detonation site), New Mexico.[21] According a Bob Considine article dated August 21, 1947, "Robert W. Henderson was chiefly instrumental in the engineering of the atomic bomb."

After the war, Mr. Henderson was sent to head the Albuquerque branch of Los Alamos called the Z Division, where he recruited top scientific talent to continue work on ordinance and munitions. This became the Sandia Corporation, and later, the Sandia National Laboratory, from which he retired in 1974 having achieved the position of executive vice president.

He appeared in the "Craftsman's Guild Hall of Fame," a special column in *Guild News* featuring the careers of Guildsmen and devoted to rising stars and role models. As vice president of Sandia Corporation, he attended many Guild conventions in Detroit in the 1950s, and at one point, served on the honorary board of judges.[22]

Dr. Henry B. Larzelere

1936 First-Place National Scholarship, Senior Division, $5,000 Award

by Henry B. Larzelere, age 86, September 7, 2003

In my life now as I look back, 1936 seems a long time ago. Yet for all of us it's a very short life. You mentioned a book. Probably now it's too late for me.

I shall try to be brief, yet as I search my memory, I recall sending a very detailed resume to Detroit, Michigan, GMC, regarding my history leading up to August 1936. I shall try to recall various highlights.

I was a Boy Scout and I rose to the rank of Life Scout, only three merit badges short of an Eagle Scout, the highest rank that can be achieved in Scouting. One evening our assistant Scout master, Mr. Olsen (Troop 51, Civic Park School, Flint, Michigan) gave me a copy of the famous Scout periodical called *Boys' Life*. This was around 1932 and I was 15 years old. On the back cover was an advertisement and colored picture of a Fisher Napoleonic Coach. I showed this ad to my father, Benton S. Larzelere, and he said if I wanted to try in the junior division (12–15 year olds) he would buy the coach kit made by Warner Company of Ohio. So, in January 1932, I started, barely finishing my first coach by August 14, 1932. What I didn't know was that the "kit coaches" all had 75 points deducted by the judges, giving an advantage to the scratch-built coaches. Despite this, I won two state awards.

The Larzelere brothers from Flint, Michigan, seen circa 1938, were miniature model Napoleonic Coach builders with Norman *(left)* winning a 1934 scholarship worth $1,000 and Henry *(right)* winning the top 1936 scholarship worth $5,000. Both brothers had careers as doctors. *Henry B. Larzelere.*

The next year (1933) my brother, Norman L. Larzelere, used a coach kit and won two or three state awards. In 1934, Norman went for broke and won a national scholarship, senior division, $1,000 award. As a family, we got a little tired of coaches.

During my sophomore year in Flint Junior College, I would turn 19 years of age, after which I would be too old for the competition. I had enrolled in a pre-medical program and my father talked to me and said, "Henry, I'm paying for your first two years of college. After that, no more. I suggest you become an apprentice at Buick Motor Company and earn your own way to medical school."

Tough words! Knowing just about everything I could know about the Fisher Body Craftsman's Guild, I then decided to "go for broker." This was in December 1935. I dropped out of college and devoted full time to my coach building activities beginning early in 1936. I believe I built the equivalent of two or three coaches by July 1936 — anything that wasn't perfect in my eyes went into the trash basket. In a sort of weird frame of mind, I felt sorry for anyone competing against me. Believe it or not, all wheel spokes were the same within 7/1000 inch (± 0.007"). I made three coach body tops before I learned the secret of keeping it from warping and distorting. And, so it went.

In July, when the competition year was coming to a close, I lived three days and nights with little sleep, no bathing and no change of clothes. I refused to even see my friends and family.

The coach, boxed and packed, got to the Detroit judging center before the deadline

August 1, 1936. I had developed into a very determined, almost hard-bitten young man. This self-discipline crystallized into a permanent type, which helped me during the rest of my life.

The great award night was in August in Cleveland, Ohio, at the Great Lakes Exposition. There were 11 junior division and 11 senior division national scholarship winners in 1936. One chap, I believe named Ralph Schreiber from Faribault, Minnesota, and I won the two senior awards of $5,000 each.

[Dr. Henry B. Larzelere did his medical residency in thoracic and cardiac surgery at Hahnemann Hospital in Philadelphia and had chest and heart surgery practices in Toledo, Ohio, and Philadelphia, Pennsylvania. Dr. Larzelere taught at Temple University Medical School and had a private surgical practice in Lynchburg, Virginia, until 1988. He is a founding member of the Thoracic Surgical Society. Henry stated in a recent letter to the author that he retired from major surgery in 1988, and general medicine in September 2002; and his 1936 coach "still looks as good as ever in his living room."]

Leo C. Peiffer

1946 First-Place National Scholarship, Senior Division, $5,000 Award

by Leo C. Peiffer, September 25, 2003

The upholstery is white, the enamel is red, the footman's step is genuine leather, and the tiny glass windows slide down for the occupants to enjoy the weather.

The coach won first for Leo C. Peiffer, who spent roughly 1,200 hours on the model over a period of eight months. There are over 2,700 pieces in the model. He exercised almost all of the handicraft arts in the construction process: woodworking, metal working, leather tooling, wood carving, plaster modeling, metal casting, and even needlework for the French knots on the upholstery.

The doors have workable brass hinges and latches. The brass suspension springs are adjustable by miniature ratchet mechanisms, there are brass bearings in the wheels, and the harness equipment on the doubletree is complete. There is a tiny leather covered toolbox behind the coachman's seat. The coach body is hard maple. The eagles on each corner of the roof are hand-carved from plum wood which has virtually no sign of grain and took over ten hours each to sculpt by eye. The gold finished molding or trim around the top of the coach body was first carved, in reverse, in plaster, and then molded in lead and soldered together. There are fine lace curtains on the sides of the interior of the coach body and the ceiling is upholstered in white velvet.

One tough problem was that of making the different size rope moldings that serve as trim along the exterior sides of the coach body. A plaster mold failed to stand up to the effects of the hot lead, so two copper wires were twisted together, heated until red hot and then pressed, like a branding iron, into a piece of wood to form a mold. Molten lead was then poured into this heat-hardened mold to get the desired twisted rope pattern.

The first-place national Napoleonic Coach award, a $5,000 university trust fund scholarship, was won by Mr. Peiffer in August 1946 at General Motors in Detroit, Michigan. He attended Iowa State University at Ames, Iowa, in 1946 and graduated with a degree in architectural engineering in 1950. He continued in architecture, along with teaching, and earned a master's degree in 1952. After two years in the U.S. Army Chemical Corps, he was discharged with an Honorable Sergeant E-5 military rating. He returned to his home in Cedar Rapids, Iowa, and started his architectural profession, a prospering business that is now in its fifty-first year. The work of his architectural firm extends approximately 200 miles in each direction from the firm's main office, and consists of schools, churches, luxury single family and condominium housing as well as commercial and private manufacturing and places of business.

A major project was the Five Seasons Center in Cedar Rapids, Iowa, consisting of a 21 story, $20 million hotel, a ballroom with attached multipurpose area, and seating for approximately 7,200. Leo C. Peiffer Architects, PC, has just completed a $15 million Veterans Memorial Baseball Stadium. Another recent project was the new nationally known, multimillion dollar Czech and Slovak Museum and Library. The office has won many awards for excellence in design.

The design and creative ability of Mr. Peiffer was being born and nurtured almost 60 years ago when he built his first-place award winning Napoleonic Coach in General Motors' Fisher Body Craftsman's Guild competition.

He said, "Every moment was worth it, not only because of the grand scholarship award, but the lessons of patience and craftsmanship I learned as well."

[Mr. Peiffer contributed a vintage photograph showing himself (wearing a suit, tie and white tam) between two top executives, with Dr. George J. Fisher, honorary guild president and commissioner of the Boy Scouts of America, on the right and T. P. Archer, GM vice president and Fisher Body Division general manager, on the left. The back of the photo is stamped with instructions on how to order duplicate copies, with the Negative Identification Number #40-353, and address, Fisher Body Photographic, 3-258 (or 3-25E), General Motors Building, Detroit, Michigan.]

Model "Dream Car" Makers

Using old Guild banquet alumni mailing lists, a comprehensive file of public library phone books, a USPS zip code book and personalized, computer generated letters, many former Guild participants were located in 1985 to contribute to the Smithsonian's Guild exhibit. This mailing list was tested in October 1991 with a general mailing that announced the Smithsonian's Guild exhibit in the National Museum of American History, on the Mall near the Capitol.

During the preparation of this book in 2002–2003, this mailing list was updated using the "white pages" and "yellow pages" of the World Wide Web. The old 1991 mailing list was updated and retested, again, and again, this time using email addresses, until a group of Guild book participants were recruited. The focus was on former Guildsmen who had previously sent photographs of their model designs for the Smithsonian's consideration many years earlier, and who proved to be helpful and knowledgeable about the Guild's history. These people, when successfully contacted, were requested to provide autobiographical information, photographs, and other items for this book.[23]

TOP GUILDSMEN WITH CAREERS IN AUTOMOBILE DESIGN

Some of the well known Guildsmen in the automobile design community from the model car competition era include Virgil M. Exner, Jr. (1946), Charles M. Jordan (1947), Elia Russinoff (1949), Galen Wickersham (1948, 1949), Ronald C. Hill (1950), Robert A.

Cadaret (1950), Edward F. Taylor (1951), Charles W. Pelly (1954), Terry R. Henline (1957, 1958), Paul Tatseos (1957, 1958), Bill Molzon (1959), Stuart Shuster (1960), Ronald J. Will (1961), Thomas H. Semple (1964), Richard Lee Beck (1964), Richard Ray (1964), Geza Loczi (1965), David P. Onopa (1966) and John M. Mellberg (1966), to name a few.

Virgil M. Exner, Jr.

1946 First-Place National Scholarship, Junior Division, Age 13

Starting at age 10 or earlier, Mr. Exner wanted to be an automobile designer. He studied fine art at Cranbrook and Notre Dame. In the '60s he became a design consultant to Ghia of Italy and teamed up with his father (Virgil M. Exner, Sr., former VP of Chrysler Styling) to form their own auto design firm. Mr. Exner, Jr., then settled down to become a design executive at Ford Motor Company Design Staff, and is associated with designing the 1970 Thunderbird, 1970 Maverick, 1971 Mercury Marquis, 1971 Pinto, 1979 LTD, 1979 Mercury Grand Marquis, and the 1980 Thunderbird. He is also associated with the Escort, Granada, and the first Ford Fiesta at Ford Europe. Mr. Exner and his wife Janet are retired and living in Florida.

Charles M. Jordan

1947 First-Place National Scholarship, Senior Division, Age 19

Mr. Jordan wanted to be an automobile designer by the age of seven. He studied automotive engineering at MIT. He was a Guildsman, automobile designer, auto industry executive, and automobile hall of fame inductee. Jordan was personally involved in the design of the 1955 Chevrolet Cameo pickup, 1956 Buick Centurion show car, 1958 Corvette, 1966 Oldsmobile Toronado, 1967 Cadillac Eldorado, 1992 Cadillac STS and Eldorado, the new Camero and Firebird and the Oldsmobile Aurora. Just like in the Guild days, Mr. Jordan teaches automotive design to high school students near San Diego, California, and enjoys his family: wife Sally and children Debra, Mark and Melissa along with four grandsons. He also loves Ferraris!

Elia "Russ" Russinoff

1949 First-Place National Scholarship, Senior Division, Age 18

Mr. Russinoff was the son of a Fisher Body Division die designer. After he attended Pratt Institute he was hired by Bill Mitchell of GM Styling (now GM Design) because he had a much sought after and coveted quality—"gasoline in his veins." During his 40-year career at GM as an automobile designer, he worked for Harley J. Earl, William L. Mitchell and Charles M. Jordan, worked at the board and did what he loved to do—"design cars."

Galen Wickersham

1948 and 1949 Regional Winner from Washington, D.C.

Mr. Wickersham's father, Victor Wickersham, was a congressman from Oklahoma so the family lived in the Anacostia section of Washington, D.C. He attended the Art Center School in Los Angeles with Chuck Pelly, Art Russell, and Bill Moore (three very important Guildsmen from the Los Angeles area) and started his career as creative designer in the Pontiac Studios, GM Styling. Later he worked in the Cadillac, Chevrolet and Truck Interior Design Studios and recently completed a 41-year career in automobile design with General Motors Corporation.

Ronald C. Hill

1950 First-Place National Scholarship, Junior Division

Mr. Hill, formerly a GM designer, became chairman of the transportation design department at the prestigious Art Center College of Design in Pasadena, California. As the chief designer at Chevrolet Advanced Studio, his team is credited with the design of the 1965 Corvair. Mr. Hill was assistant design director at Adam-Opel AG under Chuck Jordan, served as assistant design director at Vauxhall in the UK and then was chief designer at the Buick Studios in Detroit. He had a 30 year career in auto design before turning to teaching and education. Mr. Hill is now retired.

Robert A. Cadaret

1950 First-Place National Scholarship, Senior Division, Age 19

Mr. Cadaret was considered the single most important auto designer of his time, other than Harley Earl. He attended the Art Center School in Los Angeles with Ron Hill and Chuck Pelly in the early '50s. His name will forever be associated with the styling of the classic Chevys of 1955, 1956 and 1957 as well as the 1956 to 1959 Corvettes. He was instrumental in designing and naming the Chevy Impala, Chevy Nova and Corvair Lakeside Wagon. Mr. Cadaret held wheel cover design patents on the 1956 Corvette and 1960 Chevrolet. Robert A. Cadaret passed away in recent years.

Edward F. Taylor

1951 Third-Place National Scholarship, Senior Division, Age 17

Mr. Taylor always wanted to work with dream cars. As an exterior designer at GM he was involved in the 1960 Oldsmobile, 1966 Oldsmobile Toronado (*Motor Trend* "Car of the Year"), 1970 Chevrolet Monte Carlo, 1970 Opel Manta, 1970 Opel GT and 1973 Chevy Chevelle. He became an assistant executive designer responsible for five studios and had a hand in designing the 1982 S-10 pickup, 1983 S-10 Blazer, 1985 Aero Astro, 1985 Astro and Safari vans, 1988 GMT 400 pickup (1988 IDSA Design Award), many of the 1988 pickups and the Suburban designs. He was also involved in the 1982 Cavalier body styles, 1982 Camero and 1984 Corvette. As a hobby, Ed and his two sons (Charles and Blair) restored a Lamborghini Miura. Ed retired to California after a 30-year career at GM Design Staff and enjoys teaching and fine arts.

Charles W. Pelly

1954 Second-Place National Scholarship, Junior Division, Age 15

Mr. Pelly founded a highly successful industrial design firm (Designworks/USA, now a subsidiary of BMW) that has worked for GM, AMC, Chrysler, Mazda, Subaru and Magna. They did the 1987 Terrero SUV concept vehicle for Magna and the E2 electric vehicle for BMW. Mr. Pelly has been active in the Art Center College of Design and the Industrial Designers Society of America.

Terry R. Henline

1957 Styling Scholarship, $1,000 Award; 1958 Second-Place
Senior Division, National Scholarship, $4,000 Award

According to Mr. Henline, being an automobile designer was his dream as a youth in Lincoln, Nebraska. In 1960, after studying at the Art Center College of Design, he was a 21-year-old co-op student at General Motors Institute. As a GM rookie, he worked in the Design Development Studio. In 1963 he served as a Guild working judge with two other GM stylists (L. Casillo and D. Swanson). During his 40-year GM design career, Mr. Henline became the chief designer at the Pontiac, Chevrolet and Buick studios; the director of design at GM's Advanced Concept Center in California; head of GM Truck Design Activities; and more recently, director of Hummer design on the 2003 Hummer H-2.

Paul Tatseos

1957 Styling Scholarship; 1958 Third-Place
National Scholarship, Senior Division, Age 19

The 1956 trip to the Guild convention and the ultramodern GM Tech Center designed by Eero Saarinen galvanized Mr. Tatseos' desire to design cars. He was chief designer at Oldsmobile Interior Studios (1972–1974) and chief designer at Pontiac Interior Studios (1974–1975). Paul was head of Buick Interior Studios (1975–1994) and was responsible for all Buick model interiors including the 1997 Park Avenue, Century and Regal. Paul retired from GM Design after 35 years and is currently a design consultant.

William R. Molzon

1959 Second-Place National Scholarship, Senior Division, $4,000 Award

Mr. Molzon combined a mechanical engineering degree from the General Motors Institute (GMI) co-op program with an Art Center College industrial design degree, and runs his own product engineering and design consulting service in the Detroit area. He can solve both sophisticated vehicle handling and stability problems (pitch, roll, yaw) and aesthetic design problems.

Stuart Shuster

1952–1960 Guildsman

Mr. Shuster, a "true-blue" Guildsman, entered the competition nine times, every year for which he was eligible. He attended the University of Cincinnati Design School and worked for Peter Muller-Munk in Pittsburgh before joining GM Styling at the Tech Center and working for Chuck Jordan. Currently, he works with industrial design students in an advanced automotive design program, and as a consultant, recruits new creative design talent for GM Design in Warren.

Ronald J. Will

1961 First-Place National Scholarship, Senior Division, $5,000 Award

Mr. Will is from Hobart, Indiana. He worked at GM in the Corvette-Camaro Studio until 1976. He itched to design his own "wow factor" car — a beautifully designed three-wheel, Honda powered vehicle called the Turbo-Phantom. He has worked at Subaru, contributing to the designs of the Outback and Forester. According to Mr. Will, there was a consortium of about eight consistent Guild participants from Gary, Hobart, and Michigan City, Indiana, notably Guild scholarship winners such as Alan Lee Flowers (1962) and Geza Loczi (1965), who have since played a huge part in the success of their respective companies, namely Nissan Design and Volvo AB.

Alan Lee Flowers

1962 Fourth-Place National Scholarship

An associate of Mr. Semple's at GM Design and Nissan, Alan Flowers is a 16-year GM Design veteran and has worked in every studio except the Cadillac and truck divisions. He became a chief designer at Nissan Design International (NDI) by 1987, in charge of a design studio, and is associated with the Nissan Pulsar NX. More recently he became manager of product design at Nissan Design America (formerly NDI) in San Diego, California. Mr. Flowers also coordinates the student design projects sponsored by Nissan at the Academy of Art University in San Francisco.[24]

Thomas H. Semple

1964 First-Place National Scholarship, Senior Division, Age 19

Currently president of Nissan Design America, Mr. Semple joined Nissan Design International (NDI) in 1980 and was part of the team that designed the 1986½ "Hardbody" truck and Pathfinder, the Infiniti J30 and the 1993 Nissan Quest. By 1987 he was a chief designer at NDI in charge of a design studio. Prior to Nissan, Semple worked at GM Design for 13 years, reaching the position of assistant chief designer for Chevrolet and Oldsmobile divisions.[25]

Richard Ray

1964 Styling Scholarship

Mr. Ray is director of commercial vehicle marketing and planning at Daimler-Chrysler Corporation. GM Styling sponsored him at the General Motors Institute (now Kettering University) in Flint, Michigan. He has been involved in the product planning and packaging of the Jeep Grand Cherokee, Dodge Ram, Dodge Dakota and Durango trucks.

Geza Loczi

1965 First-Place National Scholarship, Senior Division

Mr. Loczi became director of design at Volvo Monitoring and Concept Center (VMCC) in southern California. In 1980 he was the VW design manager at the Michigan studios and in 1983 was a consultant to Volvo via Chuck Pelly's Designworks/USA. In 1986 he became chief designer at VMCC, involved in the 1986 Environmental Concept Car (ECC), contributed to the S80, V70, and S60 production cars and the Safety Concept Car (SCC), a show car.

David P. Onopa

1966 Senior Regional Winner

Mr. Onopa is director of product design at Mack Trucks, Inc. For the past 27 years he has been involved in virtually all Mack products in one way or the other. In an email to the author January 10, 2003, Mr. Onopa stated, "The Fisher Body Craftsman's Guild design competition, and the experiences that it provided me, became critically important in my choice of a design career."

John M. Mellberg

1966 Second-Place National Scholarship, Senior Division

Mr. Mellberg is a creative vehicle stylist who started at GM Styling working on the exteriors for a concept V-16 "E" Body for Cadillac, "F" Body Firebird, "H" Body Pontiac, 1973 Chevy Laguna, and 1974 Chevy Nova hatchback. Since leaving GM he has worked for other automotive and vehicle manufacturers designing agricultural tractors, emergency rescue vehicles (e.g., Emergency One's all composite "E One Daytona" vehicle — John did the interior and exterior), as well as bus vehicles for Freightliner/Daimler-Chrysler/TBB Bus Group (TBB = Thomas Built Buses, High Point, North Carolina).

OTHER AUTO DESIGNERS AND ENGINEERS WHO PARTICIPATED IN THE GUILD

Many GM Design staff members participated in the Guild, including Peter Wozena (1937 winner), Tony Ingolia (1937 state award), Masaji B. Sugano (first-place state award, Wyoming), Byron Voight (1937 second-place state honors), Stanley F. Parker (1947 regional award), Charles M. Jordan (1947 first-place national scholarship, senior division, age 19), Elia Russinoff (regional awards 1947, 1948; 1949 first-place national scholarship, senior division); Robert A. Cadaret (1948, 1949, 1950 regional winner; 1950 first-place national scholarship, senior division), John Wozena (1948, 1949), Galen Wickersham (1948 and 1949 regional awards, from Washington, D.C.), Ronald C. Hill (1950 first-place national scholarship, junior division), Donald Logerquist (1950), Chuck Torner (1955–1957), Edward Frasier Taylor (1946–1951; 1951 third-place national scholarship, senior division, age 17), Stuart Shuster (1952–1960), Stanley T. Denek (1954), Ron Meyer (1955 state award), George Anderson (1955), Charlie Stewart (1951–1955), Paul Tatseos (1957 styling scholarship and 1958 third-place national scholarship), Gordon Brown (1959), Terry R. Henline (1957 styling scholarship; 1958 second-place national scholarship), William R. Molzon (1959 second-place national scholarship), John Adams (1960–1964), Ronald J. Will (1961 first-place national scholarship), Alan Lee Flowers (1962 fourth-place national scholarship), Thomas L. Covert (1962 second-place national scholarship, senior division), Robert E. Davids (1963 first-place national scholarship, senior division), James Bieck (1963 national scholarship), Thomas H. Semple (1964 first-place national scholarship, senior division), George S. Prentice (1965 regional award), John M. Mellberg (1966 second-place national scholarship), Robert L. Menking (1968), and John Folden (1968).[26]

Several retired GM engineers who were formerly Guildsmen include Harvey E. Whitman of Oldsmobile Engineering (1948 first-place national scholarship, senior division)

After receiving their college educations, many Guildsmen were hired by GM Styling to work at the Tech Center facilities. Some spent part or all of their automotive styling and design careers at GM. This photograph shows eighteen of them, circa 1980. *Left to right:* Paul Tatseos, John Folden, Stan Parker, George S. Prentice, Robert Menking, Charlie Stewart, George Gadda, George Anderson, Stuart Shuster, Roy Tiesler, John Wozena, Tom Semple, Chuck Jordan, Kirk Jones, Gordon Brown, Elia "Russ" Russinoff, Chuck Torner, and Dennis Little. *Stuart B. Shuster.*

(retired) and Dale A. Gnage (1966 first-place national scholarship, junior division) an engineer at Delphi Automotive Systems in Rochester, New York (retired).

Recognizing their value, Ford Motor Company employed a number of Guildsmen:[27]

Robert Aikins (1960 styling scholarship, $1,000 award; 1963 fourth-place national scholarship, senior division, $2,000 award)

Richard Lee Beck (1957–1960 first-place regional awards; 1960 styling scholarship; 1961 first-place state award, Kentucky; 1962–1963 first-place regional awards; and 1964 third-place national scholarship, senior division, $3,000 award)

Ben Callaway (1951 first-place state award, Missouri)

Donald Held (1960 second-place national scholarship)

James R. Powers (1949–1951 first-place regional awards, from Texas; 1952 fourth-place national scholarship, senior division, $1,000 award)

Jim Robberts (1954 first-place state award, Virginia; 1956 first-place regional award)

Ken Saylor (1957 third-place state award, Pennsylvania; 1958 third-place national scholarship, junior division, $3,000 award)

Gerald Simone (1962 regional winner)

Other Ford automobile designers who participated in the Guild included:

Dale Berg (1951 third-place state award, Michigan; 1952 first-place regional award)

Vic Bogdon (1954–58 honorable mentions, Michigan; 1959 first-place regional award and $1,000 styling scholarship; 1960–1961 first-place regional awards)

George R. Chartier (1953 first-place and 1954 second-place state awards, Wisconsin)

Bill Dayton (1951 honorable mention, Oregon)

Darwin Hawthorne (1958 second-place state award, Texas; 1959 honorable mention; 1960 first-place regional award and a styling scholarship, $1,000 award)

Frederick "Bud" Magaldi (1961 first-place state award, Massachusetts; 1965 $1,000 styling scholarship)

H. Keith Teter (1949 first place state award, West Virginia, and 1951 regional winner)

Bob Koto's son, David H. Koto, won a 1956 styling scholarship ($1,000 award) and the 1957 fourth-place national scholarship, senior division, $2,000 award. Bob Koto was a Ford designer.

Gary Haas (1957 second place, Colorado; 1958 honorable mention)

James White (1957 and 1958 honorable mention, Michigan; 1959 third place; 1960 honorable mention; 1961 second place)

Many former Guildsmen also worked for Chrysler Styling, AMC Styling, Raymond Loewy International, and Teague (formerly Walter Dorwin Teague Associates) in automobile and product design endeavors, but regrettably, contacts were not maintained adequately over the years to present a fuller picture. Donald Stump (1947 second-place national scholarship winner, the same year as Chuck Jordan), for example, was associated with AMC Styling and Richard Ray worked on the 1990 Jeep product planning (before joining DaimlerChrysler AG). Raymond Canarra (1962 national scholarship award winner) worked at the Chrysler design office. Kaizo Oto (1961 styling scholarship and 1962 third-place national scholarship awards) worked for Raymond Loewy International when they were designing safety cars for the Big Three in the early '70s. Kenneth J. Dowd is currently the VP of Teague Aviation Studios in Everett, Washington. The next time you fly in a Boeing aircraft, look up and around to enjoy the aesthetic environment that Dowd and his team have created for consumers.

PRODUCT DESIGNERS

There were also a number of Guildsmen who became important industrial designers working on products, packaging, graphics and architectural design. They include Richard Arbib (1937), Stanley C. Waechter (1949), Gale P. Morris (1949), Robert F. McDonnell (1955), James Lee Garner (1954–1955), William A. Moore (1955–1956), Charles Gibilterra (1955–1956), E. Arthur Russell (1956–1957), William F. Marks (1957), John B. Di Ilio (1957), Allen T. Weideman (1956–1959), Kenneth J. Dowd (1957–1959), Harry E. Schoepf (1961), Patrick B. Saturday (1961), Richard Pietruska (1963), Michael Pietruska (1965), Theodore A. Becker (1964–1965), and Ronald Pietruska (1967).

Richard Arbib

1937 First-Place State Award, Senior Division, from New York

Mr. Arbib began designing cars for Harley Earl at GM and developed the 1953 Packard Pan American for Henney Motor Company, but ultimately became a prolific consumer product designer in New York City. His clients included, among many others, Hamilton, Swank, Gucci, NY Safety Car Bureau, de Schelds Shipyards, Eureka, and Century Boats.

Stanley Waechter

1949 Ohio, Senior Division

With a BS degree in design from the University of Cincinnati, Stanley Waechter became an industrial designer working initially for Burroughs (now Unisys) and then joined Chevrolet Creative Services (now GM Creative Services), working on Chevrolet auto show exhibits. Some of the other exhibits and displays he designed, or contributed to, were for Cadillac, Delco, Lotus, GMC, GM Canada, GM Overseas, GM Sunraycer and Saturn. In the Guild contest, Mr. Waechter did not receive a cash award but got the Certificate of Design and Craftsmanship.

Gale P. Morris

1949 Third-Place National Scholarship,
Junior Division, Portland Oregon

Mr. Morris, industrial designer at Tektronix, Inc., has contributed to the appearance and ergonomics in the design of their products for some 32 years. He helped establish Tektronix internal industrial design activity. Involved in automobile restoration and building custom cars, he takes pride in doing his own work — upholstery, instrumentation, air conditioning and metal fabrication using an English wheel.

James Lee Garner

1954 and 1955 Regional Winner from Missouri

Mr. Garner's 1955 design missed a national scholarship by just a few points and was sold to General Motors Corporation. Mr. Garner is an artist, engineer, designer and craftsman who loves Corvettes. He designed a 10 foot high water fountain made of copper, brass and bronze located at the Paducah City Hall (Paducah, Kentucky) and has consulted with architects on numerous large sculpture projects. He is currently designing a sculpture for a new building in his community.

E. Arthur Russell

1956 Styling Scholarship Winner; 1957 First-Place National Scholarship, Senior Division

Mr. Russell studied at ACCD and is associated with the prototype design proposals of Craig Breedlove's Spirit of America, with Mattel's Hot Wheels toy line and with Revell, the plastic model kit manufacturer. The company he founded, Russell Product Development, does designs, prototypes, model and patterns and has been a major vendor for Mattel toys. In a telephone conversation with the author, Robert E. Davids stated that Art Russell has created over 1,000 prototypes for Mattel working solely from artist's sketches and possesses a unique creative genius to render rough concepts and ideas into three-dimensional reality. While at Revell he did a proposal for a ½ scale Fisher Body Napoleonic Coach model kit.

William A. Moore

1956 First-Place National Scholarship, Senior Division

Nature, wildlife, ancient cultures, and the Old West are subjects close to the heart of Nevada artist, William A. Moore. After a career encompassing 22 years as a successful designer and commercial artist, Mr. Moore has returned to fine arts for the past 20 years. The recipient of many awards, he is known for his dedication to realism, detail and accuracy. His work has been featured on several Nevada television programs and in numerous national magazines. His paintings are in collections worldwide and in several national museums. Mr. Moore's work was chosen for the 1991 Idaho Upland Game Stamp and Idaho's 1994–1995 Duck Stamp.

In the summer of 1955 Bill Moore and Art Russell drove from Los Angeles to Detroit, in Art's custom 1946 Chevy, to inspect the winning model cars in the 1955 Fisher Body Craftsman's Guild competition. The models were on display at the GM Building. Norman E. May, a Guild employee, arranged for three Californians (Bill, Art and Charles Gibilterra) to meet with a Guild technical judge or GM designer to critique their scale model designs. The Guild technical judge summarized his winning styling and design philosophy with the phrase "keep it crisp." This proved to be an invaluable experience as in 1956 all three won national scholarship awards.

Charles A. Gibilterra

1956 Third-Place National Scholarship, Junior Division

Mr. Gibilterra studied industrial design at USC and has been involved in residential and commercial interior design projects as well as furniture design and product design and manufacturing. As a project designer for KS Wilshire, he was responsible for large interior design projects such as the First City National Bank of Los Angeles and the American Broadcasting Company corporate headquarters in Los Angeles. As a personal friend of Wilt Chamberlain, he was responsible for the interior design for a custom home built by the late basketball star overlooking Los Angeles. Some of his clients include manufacturers such as Vecta, Brueton Industries, Terra Furniture, Brown-Saltman, Sauder Manufacturing, and Brandrud Furniture.

Robert F. McDonnell

1955 Second-Place National Scholarship, Senior Division

Robert F. McDonnell, an architectural designer, worked on parts of Disneyland and Euro Disney, and designed custom homes for the rich and famous in California.

John B. Di Ilio

1957 Scholarship Winner

Mr. Di Ilio is another architect involved in the design of airports and sports facilities.[28]

Allen T. Weideman

1957 and 1958 Regional Winner from Salt Lake City, Utah

Mr. Weideman had offers from General Motors, Philco-Ford, Sylvania, IBM and Raymond Loewy International when he graduated from the Art Center School. After a period with IBM, working on the IBM 360 System, he started his own design service and shifted his focus to product design, graphics and packaging aimed at retail merchandising. In 1997 the Retail Confectioners International Candy Clinic awarded Ingeborg's Truffle Trio (a Weideman client) "Highest Quality" in the Best Packaging category. He runs his own firm called International Packaging Group, Inc., from Forestville, California.

William F. Marks

1957 Second-Place National Scholarship,
Senior Division, $4,000 Award, Twin Falls, Idaho

Mr. Marks was similar to Bill Molzon in that he completed dual degrees, one in Mechanical Engineering (BSME) at Purdue University and another from the Art Center School (BSID) in Los Angeles, California. After design opportunities with McDonnell Douglas and Westinghouse Major Appliances, he settled down for a career designing new products with new DuPont plastic materials in Wilmington, Delaware. A major client of his was Black and Decker, the power tool maker. During his DuPont career, Mr. Marks designed everything from pens to roller blades, car bodies, drafting boards and the key board of a Cray Supercomputer.

Kenneth James Dowd

1957 and 1959 State Winner from Denver, Colorado

Mr. Dowd wanted to become an automobile designer because of the Guild. By devouring issues of *Motor Trend*, *Hot Rod*, *Car Craft* and *Custom Cars* two things came that shaped his life: the Fisher Body Craftsman's Guild and the Art Center College of Design. Mr. Dowd became VP of Teague Aviation Studios in Everett, Washington, and was formerly a Ford senior designer who worked with Larry Shinoda in the Special Projects Studio.

Harry E. Schoepf and Patrick B. Saturday
1961 Styling Scholarship Winners

Mr. Schoepf is an industrial designer, antique car buff and 1913 Model T technical expert working on a book about model making. Patrick Saturday has had nearly a 40-year career in graphic design and printing.

Pietruska Brothers
Richard Pietruska *(1963 First-Place National Scholarship, Junior Division);*
Michael Pietruska *(1965 National Scholarship);*
Ronald Pietruska *(1967 National Scholarship)*

The Pietruska brothers grew up in the family's furniture upholstery business in Stamford, Connecticut, delivering quality craftsmanship to customers from an early age. Richard attended ACCD and is an ACCD instructor and fine arts automotive sculptor; Michael attended ACCD and is known for his Milton Bradley toys and games; and Ronald attended Pratt Institute and is known for his museum quality exhibit designs. **Robert Pietruska**, the youngest brother, was a 1966 Regional winner and today runs the family's upholstery business with a fifth brother who was not in the Guild.

Theodore A. Becker
1964 and 1965 Illinois State Winner

Mr. Becker is a manager of industrial design at Maytag, Major Appliances Division, Cooking Technology Center, with 20 patents to his credit. He is very active in his local chapter of the Industrial Designers Society of America (IDSA).

MEDICAL FIELD

Rowland Kanner (1964 styling scholarship) is VP of technology at Atrion Medical Products in Arab, Alabama; **Dr. Michael R. D'Mura** (1962 styling scholarship) is a dental expert in prosthodontics in Peoria, Arizona; and **Dr. Gilbert McArdle** (1955 regional winner from Utah) is a general surgeon who attributes his success to the early manual dexterity and cognitive learning skills taught by the Guild.

EDUCATION FIELD

Richard Pietruska (1963) is a teacher at the Art Center College of Design; **Dr. Harrell Lucky** (1955–1958) teaches music at Eastfield College in Dallas, Texas; **John M. D'Mura** (1963) is a professor of physics and physical sciences at New Mexico State University; and **Anthony V. Simone** heads an international school in Jakarta, Indonesia.

ENTREPRENEURS

Gary Graham (1954) started out working on aeronautics and astronautics at Boeing and got involved in how to facilitate astronaut exercise while in space capsules. This led to a civilian spin-off. Mr. Graham's Contemporary Design Company manufactures and markets a line of rehabilitative exercise equipment called Shuttle 2000-1, Shuttle MVP, Shuttle MiniClinic and Shuttle Balance.

Ronald C. Pellman (1956–1960) began his career in the Ford Advanced Engineering and Design arena, but became a consultant. He has served as the president of four companies (two of which he founded) and has worked on over 300 new product, new business development, and technology planning projects for leading companies in the U.S. and Europe, many in the automotive field. As a hobby, Mr. Pellman designed and fabricated his own racecars and won seven North East Regional Championships over the span of 25 years of racing with Sports Car Club of America.

Robert E. Davids (1963 first-place national scholarship, senior division, $5,000 award) is a former GM designer who worked for William L. Mitchell personally, worked for Bill Lear in Reno, worked as a product designer for the gaming industry, has designed electronic hand-held games for which he is the inventor, designer and manufacturer (e.g., the Wal-Mart money-maker called Bass Fishin'), and has been a manager, executive, and CEO. Mr. Davids is currently a semi-retired vintner.

ACADEMICS

Richard R. Sylvester (1956, 1957) studied automotive styling at the Art Center School briefly, then acquired an MBA from the University of Southern California, a JD law degree from Loyola and a Ph.D from UCLA. He has settled down to become a mathematical economist.

MODEL CAR MAKERS' BIOGRAPHIC PROFILES

Richard Arbib

1937 First-Place State Award, Senior Division, New York

Richard Arbib built a highly aerodynamic, fastback, four-door sedan, probably with an air cooled rear engine. As was popular at the time, he did away with the running boards and each fender was a sculpted aerodynamic pod. Arbib's model featured folding, recessed headlamps mounted in the nose of the hood. In his career, he was a prolific design genius, highly creative, and an exuberant product designer for over 40 years with more than 300 national and international clients to his credit. He is described by his admirers as ahead of his time, "a blue sky guy" and was the "man to see" for futuristic car designs.

Richard Arbib began work in 1939, a decade after the last generation of industrial design stars such as Raymond Loewy and Walter Dorwin Teague. He studied auto design at Pratt Institute in New York City, and was an early student in Harley J. Earl's Detroit Institute of Automobile Styling (DIAS), completing the program in nine months. While still at Pratt, Arbib was invited to work on GM's groundbreaking Futurama exhibit for the 1939 New York World's Fair. He was an advanced auto stylist at GM before World War II.

During World War II he was an armament specialist for the P-47 Thunderbolt fighter at the Republic Aviation Corporation and designed a jet propelled flying bomb (similar to a cruise missile).

After the war, he returned to run Harley Earl Corp. (HEC), an industrial design firm owned by the GM Styling V.P., with clients such as Argus Cameras, U.S. Royal Tires, Union Pacific Interiors, and Benrus Watches. In 1950 he moved back to New York City to start his own consulting business as a freelance designer.

One of his projects was to restyle Packard cars for the Henney Motor Company, a maker of hearses and ambulances. Henney had had an exclusive contract with Packard since 1939 to be its body builder. The late 1940s and early 1950s are what Arbib called the "bath tub era," and the manufacturers, except for Studebaker, were trying to "out-round" each other. He came up with the 1949 Packard hard-top style Monte Carlo coupe with big, round, bulbous curves. Early in the 1950s Arbib came up with new car designs such as the V-Line Custom Sedan, the Full-Vision Coupe De Ville, and the Turbo Charged Coupe for the Veedol Motor Oil Dream Car Salon.

Richard Arbib created a concept Packard sports car for the International Motor Sports Show, Grand Central Place, New York, March 29, 1952. His design won first prize. Based on Arbib's award winning design, the Packard Pan American was born in 1953, based on the 1951 convertible Packard, chopped and channeled to look low and sleek, incorporating a custom interior and continental kit. Only six were produced. Richard A. Teague called the Pan American "the best Arbib ever did."[29]

Some of Arbib's automotive design innovations include vertical and horizontal four-headlamp arrangements, the narrow white wall on tires, the hood mounted carburetor air scoop, concave rear windows and the clear bubble canopy for the greenhouse. In 1956 he designed and built the futuristic bubble-top car called Astro-Gnome.

He produced a prototype safety car for his client, the New York Safety Car Bureau, in conjunction with the U.S. Department of Transportation, for the sum of $1.

Arbib was more than just the most gifted product artist of his time; he was the man who showed what tomorrow could look like. Arbib's auto images defined the tail-finned, two-tone-with-chrome look of the atomic age.

He was involved in all kinds of products, not just cars. Arbib redesigned the exterior faces for a new line of Hamilton electric watches (elongated triangular faces, skewed trapezoidal faces jutting out asymmetrically) including the 1957 Ventura, Hamilton's first electric, which was a world famous classic. He also designed men's jewelry for Swank and Gucci; a concept cruise ship called the Oceanic with swimming pools on the top deck, for De Schelds Shipyards of Holland; a suitcase shaped design for the Eureka vacuum cleaner. He brought automotive styling to boats like the Century Coronado runabout purchased by celebrities such as Elvis Presley, Liberace, Robert Redford, and Edward Kennedy.[30] He sketched ideas ahead of his time such as the pushbutton phone, removable car radios, and personal water craft (such as the Jet Ski or Skidoo). Richard Arbib passed away in 1995 at age 77.

Virgil M. Exner, Jr.
1946 First-Place National Scholarship Winner

Virgil M. Exner, Sr.
1937 Guild Judge

"A genius of design!" declared Stookie Allen of the *National Associated Newspaper* of Virgil Exner, Jr., who had just won the 1946 first-place national scholarship award

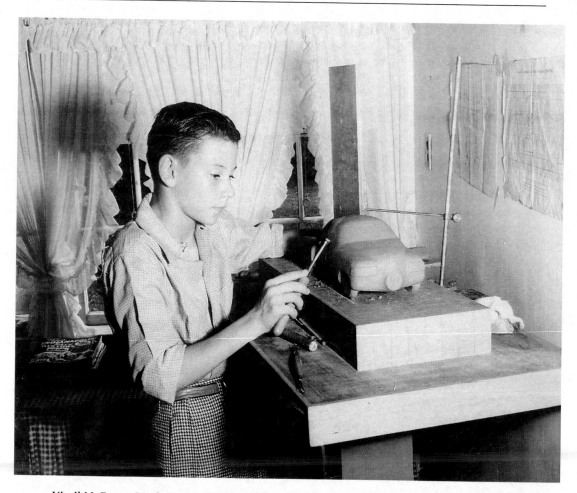

Virgil M. Exner, Jr., designed his 1946 model out of clay as shown. This was a valuable precaution because he made several changes before achieving what the Guild judges termed a "near perfect" example of automotive design. The clay model was cast in plaster of Paris using a special mold design with copper partitions developed by the young Exner. Wheels were turned on his grandfather's lathe using small blocks of pine. The bumpers were made from thick strips of aluminum and were shaped specially for the purpose, running horizontally along the front fenders and vertically along the rear fenders. *General Motors Corporation.*

(junior division) at age 13. Stookie continued, "He startled the experts! ... This 13-year-old lad in South Bend, Indiana, won an auto model-making contest with the above design. ... Several of his features will be on cars of the future and he started only 3 years ago when his Dad gave him a tool set for Christmas."

Allen said that the top awards went to "Robert Hartlieb (16 years old) of Allentown, Pennsylvania, and Virgil Exner (13 years old) of South Bend, Indiana, whose imagination and ability in craftsmanship were so close, the lads were given *duplicate* $4,000 awards" ("Teen-Age Triumph").

Exner's 1946 award winning four-door sedan (cast plaster) featured rectangular, polarized headlight lenses and air scoops in the front of the rear quarter panels to cool the rear engine. (Safety engineers still wrestle with the potential of polarized head lighting, in combination with polarized windshields, as a way to reduce or control oncom-

This model designed by Virgil M. Exner, Jr. (age 13), from South Bend, Indiana, won the 1946 first national scholarship, junior division, $4,000 award. In an article his family wrote in 1946 Virgil stated, "After entering the competition I started to design what I thought would be a smart-looking automobile. I couldn't quite make up my mind on several features so I made 12 different drawings on graph paper before coming to a final conclusion." *General Motors Corporation.*

ing headlight glare.) It had a strange and uncanny resemblance to the 1947 Studebaker production automobile that his father used to win the hearts of postwar Studebaker management over a Raymond Loewy design. Virgil Exner, Sr., having been hired by Harley J. Earl to be a designer in the Art and Colour Section, had the dubious honor of being a Guild judge in 1937, the first year of the model car competition.[31] In 1938 the senior Exner (called "X") moved to New York and worked for Raymond Loewy, who had landed the Studebaker account in 1936, but moved back to South Bend in 1941 to work on the Studebaker premises. Studebaker management (Roy E. Cole, chief engineer) chose Exner's 1947 "Studie" design over Loewy's proposal and put Exner on the payroll.

The Exner family lived in South Bend, Indiana, where Virgil Exner, Sr., was chief designer for Studebaker. As a 13-year-old Guildsman, Virgil Jr. tried to hurry the painting process for his plaster model by trying to cure it in his mother's oven. Unfortunately, baking resulted in terrible cracks in the finish of the model and delayed the whole finishing process. The final midnight shipping deadline was only narrowly met. Virgil Exner, Jr., like his father attended the University of Notre Dame, studying fine arts and transportation design (1952–1957).

There were a number of one-off show cars produced under the direction of Virgil Exner, Sr., and built by Turin of Italy, which turned the public's head and captured imaginations in auto magazines and shows: the K-310 (1951–1952), Chrysler D'Elegance (1953), Dodge Firearrow (1953), Dodge Firearrow convertible (1954), the XNR Roadster and the Falcon Roadster. His mass produced designs generated with the "forward look" made

A profile view of the 1946 model built by Virgil M. Exner, Jr. In his prepared notes for a 1987 *Automobile Quarterly* article about the Guild, Exner wrote that the Fisher Body Craftsman's Guild "inspired study and taught patience in the struggle for creativity and understanding of the basic design process. Whether one completed a model or not, won or not, or chose to even pursue design or crafts in any way — it gave youth incentive and opportunity to experience *trying* a worthwhile and interesting vocation." *Virgil M. Exner, Jr.*

Chrysler profitable and won him a promotion to Chrysler's V.P. of styling, 1957–1962. Virgil Exner, Sr., took an early retirement November 1961 after being replaced at Chrysler by Elwood Engel as corporate styling V.P. However, he remained with Chrysler as a consultant until 1964.

During 1960–61, Virgil Exner, Jr., was a design consultant to Ghia of Italy; his work resulted in the Fiat 2100 Sports Coupe, the Selena II Show Car, the Karmann Ghia VW 1500 and many Renault, VW, and Fiat proposals including the Renault Caravelle.

From 1962 to 1967, the younger Exner and his father teamed up professionally and opened their own industrial design firm to design cars and power boats. They consulted with Ghia of Italy, Pininfarina, U.S. Steel, Duesenberg Corporation, Stutz Corporation of America, the Copper Development Association and Renwall Models. They designed power boats for Riva (Italy) and Buhler Turbocraft of Indianapolis, Indiana. Virgil Exner, Jr., designed the *Motor Trend* magazine "Car of the Year" trophy still used today.

During this time the Exner team invented the retro-designed automobile (today called retrofuturism) long before today's popular Beetle, Plymouth Prowler, Thunderbird or PT Cruiser. In the 1960s they redesigned a number classic automobiles including the Mercer, Duesenberg, Bugatti, Stutz Bearcat and Packard Victoria.

The Mercer-Cobra became a reality. The redesigned Bugatti, built on a shortened

From 1946 to 1953 the Guild model car contestants were required to design either a 2-door or 4-door passenger sedan. Virgil M. Exner, Jr., chose a 4-door, rear-engine design and incorporated special features such as rectangular, Polaroid headlights; windows flush with the outer body panel; a novel air circulation system with the intake vent around a "spinner" (replacing the usual radiator grille); and radiators set along the front edge of each rear fender. *Virgil M. Exner, Jr.*

Type 101 C chassis (supercharged), was unveiled at the Turin Auto Salon in 1965. The prototype 1966 Duesenberg was unveiled at Indianapolis, Indiana, but was never mass produced.[32] The sales brochure produced by the Duesenberg Corporation, 3989 Meadows Drive, Indianapolis, Indiana (1966) stated, "The year 1966 represents a milestone in American automotive history, for this is the year the magnificent Duesenberg automobile makes its reappearance. ... The body and coachwork are hand-crafted in Carrozzeria Italy, SpA. ... The Duesenberg is powered by a 425 hp Chrysler built V-8. ... The automobile is assembled in the modern Duesenberg facility in Indianapolis, Indiana, the birth state of the original Duesenberg."

It was supposed to be a limited production car, with body by Ghia and engine by Chrysler Corp., that would retail for about $19,500. The graceful curved fender lines and chrome radiator-shaped grille were design features most reminiscent of the original Duesenberg.

Charles M. Jordan (age 19) won the 1947 first national scholarship, senior division, $4,000 award with this 4-door sedan. As an engineering student at MIT, he designed and built this model from a set of blueprints he'd drawn and a clay model he had sculpted. The MIT Hobby Shop was his workshop. Design work began in the winter of 1946 and construction of the model, using a block of white pine, lasted from January to June 1947. The deadline was June 15. All the metal parts were carefully shaped from brass, chrome-plated, then set into the wood. Thirty-five color coats of paint were applied. The model measured approximately 16" × 6¼" × 5" (L × W × H). *General Motors Corporation.*

In 1967 Virgil M. Exner, Jr., continued his creative design career with the Ford Motor Company, first in exterior development (1970 Thunderbird, 1970 Maverick, 1971 Mercury Marquis, and 1971 Pinto). From 1969 to 1974 he was assigned as a design executive to Ford Europe in exterior development (Escort, Granda, and the first new Ford Fiesta). From 1974 to 1988 he returned to Dearborn, working in the Exterior Studios (1979 LTD, Mercury Grand Marquis, 1980 Thunderbird, and many advanced car and truck programs) up through the year 2000. He was design manager of Advanced Exterior Concepts Studio in 1987, and finally design manager of 2000X Studio, the Ford Motor Company's experimental computer studio.[33]

In May 1988 he took a normal early retirement package and moved to Florida with his wife Janet, where he continues to be a creative design consultant. (Virgil M. Exner, Sr., passed away December 23, 1973, and was inducted into the Automotive Hall of Fame in 1995.)

Charles M. Jordan

1947 First-Place National Scholarship, Senior Division, $4,000 Award

by Chuck Jordan, September 2002

From early childhood I've had a love for cars and trucks. My first car drawings were done in church at age seven. My mother, who always encouraged my interest in cars, responded to a Fisher Body Craftsman Guild ad. The material the Guild sent gave purpose and direction to my early design and modeling activities.

In high school, my goal became clear. I was determined to be an automobile designer. I studied hard and filled many notebooks with car sketches.

After graduating with honors from high school in 1945, I entered MIT where I studied engineering and design. During my sophomore year, I designed and built a model car and entered it in the 1947 competition. I won the first-place national award and a $4,000 scholarship.

During the FBCG convention in Detroit, I was taken aside and told, "When you finish school, there's a job waiting for you here." In 1949, shortly after receiving a BS degree from MIT, I joined GM Styling as a junior designer.

My first assignment was in the Truck Studio where I soon became assistant chief

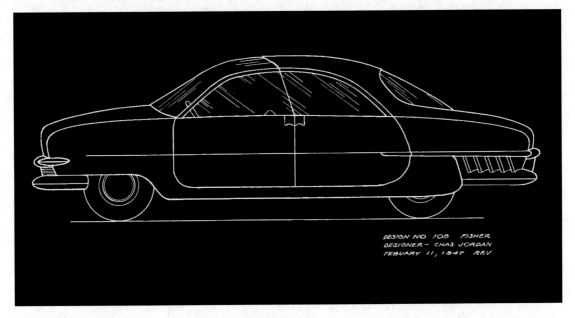

Scale line drawing of Charles M. Jordan's 4-door sedan model which won the 1947 first national scholarship, senior division, $4,000 award. *Charles M. Jordan.*

The top model car scholarship winners with models in hand, ribbons and berets were photographed for publicity purposes at the Guild banquets. These were the 1947 Model Car Competition winners: *(left to right)* Donald A. Stumpf (19) of Buffalo, New York, second national scholarship, senior division, $2,000 award; Charles M. Jordan (19) of Cambridge, Massachusetts, first national scholarship, senior division, $4,000 award; Phillip J. Rauth of York, Nebraska, second national scholarship, junior division, $2,000 award, and James F. Mariol of Canton, Ohio, first national scholarship, junior division, $4,000 award. *General Motors Corporation.*

designer and led the design of the all-new '55 Chevrolet truck line including the trend-setting Cameo Carrier pickup.

In 1952, the Korean War intervened. After a year's service as a lieutenant in the air force, I returned to GM Styling as chief designer of the Special Projects Studio to design a Euclid Crawler Tractor and the GM lightweight Aerotrain.

"Now let's see what you can do with cars," my boss, Bill Mitchell, told me, and I spearheaded the design of the 1956 Buick Centurion show car and the 1958 Corvette. At age 29, during the tail fin era, I moved up to chief designer of Cadillac. Then, in 1962, I was appointed Bill Mitchell's assistant with responsibility for the exterior design of all GM cars and trucks. I'm especially proud of the 1966 Oldsmobile Toronado and the 1967 Cadillac Eldorado.

Also in '62, *Life* magazine, in its September "Take Over Generation" issue, selected

A more informal looking, but highly choreographed, publicity photograph of the 1947 model car scholarship winners and the models they made. *Left to right:* Charles M. Jordan, James F. Mariol, Phillip J. Rauth, and Donald A. Stumpf. *General Motors Corporation.*

me as one of the 100 "Most Important Young Men and Women in the United States." After that, people listened better.

In 1967, I was sent to Opel in Germany as director of design. Three years later, after an invaluable experience running my own design group, I returned to GM as executive in charge of design. In 1977 I was named director of design.

I reached my career goal in 1986 when I was elected GM vice president for design. Together, with a staff of over 1200 people, we made creative waves with trend setting concept cars and leadership production cars like the '92 Cadillac STS and Eldorado, the new Camaro/Firebird and the Oldsmobile Aurora.

In October 1992, I retired. Looking back, my 43 years as an automobile designer were fun, exciting and rewarding—they never quite seemed like work. The awards I received—induction into the Automotive Hall of Fame (1990), Designer of the Year (1992) and an honorary doctorate from both the Art Center College of Design (1992) and

the Center for Creative Studies (2001)—
don't compare to the satisfaction of seeing a design I'm proud of coming down
the street.

My wife, Sally, and I have been married over 50 years. We have three children: Debra, Mark and Melissa, and four
grandsons. Our home is in Rancho Santa
Fe, California—a paradise far from
Detroit's snow and cold.

Since retirement, I've traveled to
China, India and Korea consulting on
automobile design. For three years I
wrote a regular column on design for
Sport Cars International. My hobby is
playing with my Ferraris and teaching
automobile design to students at a leading San Diego high school.

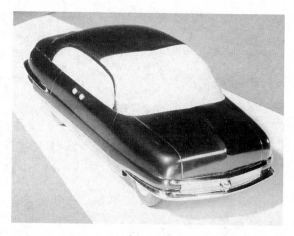

The 4-door sedan scale model made in 1947 by
Charles M. Jordan. A faithful reproduction of this
model is exhibited at the Henry Ford Museum and
Greenfield Village, Dearborn, Michigan.

I've always been grateful for my experiences in the FBCG competition. They have
paid huge dividends. In fact, when I think about it, my life has really become a big FBCG
competition, designing and modeling cars just like I did when I was 19—except these
models are full size and they compete with the best in the world.

[You can look up examples of illustrations by this famous auto designer at www.
CarDesignerArt.com.]

Harvey E. Whitman

1948 First-Place National Scholarship, Senior Division

by Harvey E. Whitman, June 2002

The model was constructed when I was age 18, and entered in the 1948 Fisher Body
Craftsman's Guild competition. The concept and design work was started in late 1947
with modeling and construction finished in June 1948, a total of approximately 800 hours
of work. This model won the 1948 first-place national scholarship award, senior division,
and I received a $4,000 university trust fund.

The design concept was to give the car the appearance and feel of the coming jet age.
The grille, front bumper and rear bumper all created the smooth feeling of a military jet
aircraft.

The construction process began by making numerous concept and design sketches
until a final design was settled upon. This design was then sculpted in clay to make a pattern. The next step was to cast the clay pattern in liquid rubber reinforced with surgical
gauze. This, in turn, was covered with plaster to give the rubbery mold some structure,
but in two pieces, to form a mold that could be separated into sections. The two plaster
structural sections allowed the clay pattern to be removed once the mold had cured. The
rubber skin was then removed from the clay pattern and inserted into the reassembled
mold. Casting plaster was then poured into the new rubber mold and this would be the
final model car shape.

The final cast model car shape was then finished: detailed with scribed lines, fitted

Harvey E. Whitman, director of manufacturing for powertrains, Oldsmobile Division (retired). *Harvey E. Whitman.*

with moldings, and then spray painted with multiple primer and color coats of automotive lacquer. The bumpers and grille parts were cast out of aluminum using wood patterns and sand molds. These parts were then finished by hand and polished to a high luster to simulate chrome.

The wheels were made from wood (hard maple) and turned on a lathe to produce the wheel and tire profile and tread design. The hubcaps were made from chair leg glider buttons and cemented to the wooden wheels. The wheels were then cut to fit the wheel-well openings and pegged and glued to the car. The headlights and taillights were formed from pieces of clear and red plastic and fitted to match the fender contours prior to painting and final attachment.

I became involved with the Fisher Body Craftsman's Guild as a result of my old brother David, who was a national award winner in 1946. He received the third-place national scholarship, senior division, $2,000 award. He studied mechanical engineering at Michigan State College and spent summer vacations working at GM Styling as junior designer. David went on to work for General Motors Styling, but unfortunately lost his life in the

This Guild entry made by Harvey E. Whitman (age 18) won the 1948 first national scholarship, senior division, $4,000 award. Some construction details are as follows: Body — plaster-of-Paris from a rubber mold; bumpers and grille — cast aluminum; scored lines — edge of a steel scale used as a cutting tool; wheels — turned on a lathe from maple; paint — auto paint and used service station spray paint equipment. *Harvey E. Whitman.*

Korean War as a navy jet fighter pilot.

I entered a car in the 1947 competition, but only won state and regional awards. As with the other contestants, the first try and the trip to Detroit to see all the models was a good lesson on how keen the competition was and the kind of craftsmanship it would take to be a national winner. I entered again in 1948 and was fortunate enough to win the first-place national award in the senior division. I used my $4,000 scholarship to attend the General Motors Institute (GMI) in Flint, Michigan, pursuing a manufacturing engineering degree and was sponsored by the Oldsmobile Division of General Motors in Lansing, Michigan.

I had always felt that my brother had more natural design talent than I, and that my strengths lay in the craftsmanship and detail areas. As a result my brother and I had always planned on going into business together as a design-and-build consulting house, with Dave handling the design function and me the manufacturing end. As with many plans this did not work out.

Like my brother, I was also a navy jet fighter pilot during the Korean War. I served on active duty from 1950 to 1955 and continued in the active reserves for another 20 years, eventually retiring as a navy captain. Upon release from active duty with the navy, I rejoined General Motors, finished my education at General Motors Institute (now Kettering University) and went to work for the Oldsmobile Division of GM as a manufacturing engineer and manager of production machining in 1985.

I held various manufacturing engineering and administrative assignments, eventually retiring in 1989 as director of manufacturing for powertrains in Lansing, Michigan.

My activities since retiring center around the family of my four children, a little golf, some fishing and boating, and overseas travel with my wonderful wife.

[Mr. Whitman donated his 1948 model to the permanent collection of the National Museum of American History, Smithsonian Institution, in the late 1980s.]

Stanley Carl Waechter
1949 Ohio, Senior Division
by Mr. Stanley C. Waechter, September 2002

Stan Waechter was born May 9, 1932, in Burlington, Ohio, near Cincinnati, the youngest of four children. Stan's mom painted and his dad was an engineer and inventor and an accomplished sculptor. Fascinated by art and machines at an early age, Stanley produced countless drawings (many of cars). Cereal-box cutouts inspired him to draw cars in four planes on paper, then fold and glue them into three-dimensional toys. That sparked a love of model-making and drawing. His grandfather, a retired wagon maker and amateur oil landscape artist, also carved wooden figures of people and animals and made beautifully detailed working scale model farm wagons and equipment. They intrigued Stan and inspired him to try more advanced model-making.

Although hampered by congenital cataracts, he kept drawing and making things anyway. At ages 10 and 11, operations removed the cataracts. It was perfect timing for serious model-making of wooden World War II planes, ships and jeeps—the kind that had to be cut out, carved, sanded, glued together, painted and finished with delicate decals.

Stanley's interest in an auto design career grew, but he was unable to find advice about how to pursue it. In 1948 or 1949, he saw pictures of the Fisher Body Craftsman's Guild models (probably in a Boy Scout magazine), read the article about the competition and decided to enter. The design deadline looming ahead and his design chosen, Stan had to learn about clay modeling and metalworking tools to go with what he already knew about plaster molds and castings. He attached a spray gun to his Mom's vacuum cleaner to apply the multi-coat lacquer finish. The model was delivered by the deadline.

Stanley C. Waechter as a young Guildsman. He became an industrial designer and retired from GM Creative Services after a 26-year career. *Stanley C. Waechter.*

Though not a prize winner, Stan credits the Guild experience with enriching and focusing his career path.

Graduating from high school in 1951, Stan became a draftsman. After a stint making training aids in the army during World War II, he worked as a detailer and technical illustrator and enrolled in commercial art night classes. He put together a portfolio of car designs and submitted it to GM Design staff, who ruled him not ready, partly for lack of formal transportation design education, and partly for being a bit old to start one. So in 1958, at age 26, he enrolled in a five-year industrial design program at the University of Cincinnati, earning his BS in design in 1963.

Stan's first three years as a professional industrial designer were with Burroughs Corp. (now Unisys). When he learned of a design position opening at Chevrolet Creative Services (now GM Creative Services), he applied for it. This time he clicked at GM and began a 26-year career, not designing cars, but being close to them daily while designing auto shows and exhibits. A fun by-product of the position was occasionally being able to build scale presentation models of the displays. The Guild experience again surfaced, definitely enhancing and improving his skills in model building and presentation.

In addition to his mainly Chevrolet auto show exhibit work at Creative Services, Stan also designed displays for Cadillac, Delco, Lotus, GMC, GM Canada, GM Overseas, the GM Sunraycer (solar car), and Saturn.

Galen Wickersham

1948 and 1949 First-Place State and Regional Winner, District of Columbia; 1950 and 1952 First-Place State Winner, District of Columbia

by Galen Wickersham, June 2003

My family and I moved from Mangum, Oklahoma, to Washington, D.C., in 1941 after my father, Victor Wickersham, was elected to the U.S. Congress. He served his country and home state for nine terms over a period of 24 years. Oklahoma lost population during and after World War II (mostly to California, Arizona and New Mexico), requiring reelection campaigns at home for my father because of the redistricting that occurred. During one term, when my father was not reelected, he purchased real estate

Galen Wickersham shown in 1952 (age 19) posing at the dining room table with the four Guild models he made. He won 1948 *(model at right)* and 1949 *(left)* regional awards in Washington, D.C., and first state awards in 1950 *(rear)* and 1952 *(in hands)*. Galen was a career automobile designer and worked for GM Design for 41 years. *Galen Wickersham.*

in Bethesda, Maryland, and sold houses in Georgetown to John F. Kennedy and his brother Robert Kennedy.

As a teenager, I enjoyed building model airplanes, trains and military vehicles, so it was natural that I would build model cars when I learned of the Fisher Body Craftsman's Guild model car competition. I won first-place state ($150 cash) and regional awards in 1948 and 1949 (free trips to Detroit and $150 cash) and first-place state awards ($150 cash) in 1950 and 1952. I was in Region 6 so I competed against other high school kids from Virginia, West Virginia and the District of Columbia.

For a short period after graduating from Anacostia High School in 1952, I attended General Motors Institute (now called Kettering University) in Flint, Michigan, where I soon found my interests and skills were not in the field of engineering. I returned to Washington, D.C., where I worked as a cartographic draftsman at the Naval Hydrographic Offices in Suitland, Maryland.

I was drafted in 1953 and served two years in the United States Army, after which I attended George Washington University for three semesters in our nation's capital. I learned of the industrial design program at the Art Center School in Los Angeles, California, and I applied for admission. I had a few drawings and illustrations to submit, but I also sent my 1952 Craftsman's Guild award winning model as part of the required art portfolio. Fortunately, I was accepted. I sold my 1956 Ford Thunderbird, bought a 1956 Ford station wagon and with my wife Renee and our 16-month-old son, Glenn, made the long trek to Los Angeles, California.

I attended the Art Center School for eight semesters, majoring in transportation industrial design, and graduated in 1959. Some of my classmates included Dean Beck, Tom Bizzini, Jerry Brockstein, Tom Daniels, Ara Ekizian, Dick Finegan, Wayne Fuerst, Glen Gardner, Roger Hughet, John Jaquish, John Marsh, Syd Mead, Bill Moore*, Dave North, Fred Overcash, Chuck Pelly*, Gerry Post, Art Russell*, Don Wood, Dennis Wright and Diran Yazejian.

Several Art Center School instructors I would like to mention with much appreciation are Bob Cadaret (who also was a regional winner in 1948 and 1949), Joe Thompson, Strother MacMinn, George Jergenson, John Coleman, Ted Younkin, Mary Sheridan, Gene Fleury, Bill Brewer, Joe Ferrer, and Dick Collier.

I interviewed with General Motors, Ford and Chrysler and was offered a position in an interior design studio at GM and a position in an exterior design studio at Chrysler. Because of my Fisher Body Craftsman's Guild experience, I chose the GM offer.

I started as a creative designer in the Pontiac Interior Studio, Styling, at the GM Tech Center in Warren, Michigan, and later worked in the Cadillac, Chevrolet and Truck interior design studios. The last two years of my career were in truck exterior design and I retired in year 2000 with 41 years of service.

I have been a collector of toys, designer lamps, primitive and contemporary paintings, prints and ceramics. I continue to attend auctions and exhibits and I seldom miss the Meadow Brook "Concours d'Elegance" car show or the "Eyes on the Classics" car show (now called "Eyes on Design"), a Detroit fund raiser coordinated by a local eye surgeon for children with special eye needs.

My good friend and fellow collector, Bill Porter, a former chief designer at the Buick Studios, for many years was the resident curator and historian of the GM Design Center.

Also featured in this book.

Bill also taught transportation and history of modern design at the College for Creative Studies and Wayne State University, both in Detroit. He has contributed to this book as have many former GM Design people.

Renee and I will celebrate our golden wedding anniversary this fall (2003). We live in Birmingham, Michigan, and have five children and ten grandchildren, all living in the area with the exception of two grandchildren who live in Oklahoma.

Gale P. Morris

1949 Third-Place National Scholarship, Junior Division, $2,000 Award, Age 13

by Gale P. Morris, November 2002

There were not many hobby stores in Portland in 1943 so the choices were limited. A kit for a model was quite basic in those days. There were no die cast metal parts, no ejection molded or vacuum metal coated parts, no adhesive overlays and no decals with graphics. The kit for a 2½-ton army truck, for example, would consist of a block of balsa wood, ten vacuum-formed wheel shells, and a three-view line drawing mimeographed on newsprint. The wheel forms were made of celluloid and you had to fill the hollow back side with plaster of Paris in order for the wheels to hold up the weight of the finished model. Because of the war effort, the only metal in the kit would be six 4d nails used for axles.

At age 12, I was working Saturdays at a hobby supply store. The war was over and new cars were once again rolling out of Detroit. My attention was focused totally on building model cars at the time. Plastic model kits for automobiles were not on the market yet, so I continued to make everything from scratch. The owners of the mom-and-pop hobby store where I worked introduced me to the Fisher Body Craftsman's Guild and encouraged me to participate. This was a new and welcome challenge to build a model automobile to precise dimensions and specifications.

I glued up a large block of balsa wood from two or three smaller blocks, primarily because large blocks were a little hard to come by and the larger pieces were rather expensive. The body of the model was carved from this.

The features, materials and technology appearing on the new cars were so exciting that I just had to incorporate them into my first Guild model entry. For example, the new metallic paint finishes were so spectacular, I was determined to use them. Brushing the paint on would leave streaks of metallic particles and spray paint would mean paying a commercial paint shop, which was against Guild rules. Guild participants signed a pledge card stating that we did all the work ourselves. So, I set out to build my own spray gun with a hand operated tire pump and a concept observed from my mother's perfume atomizer. After the third attempt, it worked. The paint was gorgeous and probably influenced the judges' award. I won a national scholarship on my first attempt at the competition.

I was probably destined to establish my own auto repair or custom shop, when I discovered the Art Center College of Design. This was a new world for me. This kind of school work was something I wanted to do. Good grades now came easily compared to high school. The Fisher Body Craftsman's Guild scholarship, plus a competitive academic scholarship from Ford Motor Company, made my financial concerns minimal.

Art Center was a "doing things with your hands" place. My instructors stressed that my newly acquired artwork skills would provide my livelihood upon graduation. I was convinced that my ideas were primary, and the artwork was the most effective way to communicate those ideas. If the automobile manufacturers had southern California design studios in 1958 as they do today, I surely would have remained in the auto styling profession. But the quality of life in Oregon beckoned and I returned to Portland rather than move to Detroit.

A new manufacturing company in Portland was making its reputation building electronic tools, primarily oscilloscopes, that were suddenly in great demand

This balsa wood model constructed by Gale P. Morris (age 13) sported a custom metallic green paint job and won the 1949 third national scholarship, junior division, $2,000 award. Gale Morris was involved in the first of the corporate industrial design offices, and as part of that new trend, coordinated the appearance and ergonomics of all new Tektronix, Inc. products. *Gale P. Morris.*

by organizations such as IBM, Standard Oil, NASA and the military. *Fortune* magazine had just published an article about industrial designers. The magazine stressed that the new trend with progressive companies was to form their own internal industrial design departments. When I walked in the door at Tektronix, Inc., that trend was realized. I was with Tektronix for 32 years, and together with the industrial designers I subsequently hired, we coordinated the appearance and ergonomics of all the company's products. If they could not find a component or a process needed for a new product, they would build it themselves from scratch. This approach fit my style as did the unstructured working environment.

With newly acquired skills and refined old skills I now want the challenge and satisfaction of doing it all myself. When asked about details of my current custom car project, I answer that I did all the finishing and painting, the internal engine work, sewed up the upholstery, figured out the electrical schematics, constructed the valves and did the plumbing for the air conditioning. The instruments in the dashboard are made from scratch, or very nearly so. I am currently designing and forming sheet metal body panels on my homemade English Wheel.[34]

I married a girl I met at Tektronix. She understands my creative juices are flowing constantly, at the office or at home, evenings and weekends. And that girl has nurtured my creative soul into a way of life for both of us.

[A detailed article was written about Mr. Morris' participation in the Guild, "Entering the Fisher Body Craftsman's Guild Competition." Mr. Morris generously donated his 1949 award winning design to the Smithsonian's permanent collection at the National Museum of American History.]

Elia "Russ" Russinoff

1949 First-Place National Scholarship, Senior Division, $4,000 Award

by Elia Russinoff, October 2002

It all began when I was about 12 years old, this passion for cars. I was able to name each car, front- or rear-end design. Sketching in the back of my school books kept me from becoming too bored in school. At 16, I noticed an advertisement in *Popular Mechanics* for a correspondence course, which Harley Earl had initiated, for aspiring automobile stylists. What a break! The course taught me the do's and don'ts of car design, à la Harley Earl, the first vice-president of design at General Motors. It was he who put automobile styling on the map.

The opportunity of a lifetime for me was the day my father, a GM die designer, handed me a flyer describing the Fisher Body Craftsman's Guild competition. I chose to design and build a model automobile rather than a coach, since I was more interested in designing something of my own. The Guild manual detailed the approach to the project: first, draw the sketches; next, make a scale drawing; and then build a clay model. After that, templates had to be made from the clay model, and finally, a model was made out of plaster or carved out of wood. Wow!

I accepted the awesome challenge and entered the Guild competition at the age of 16 in 1947. It took me a year to design and build my first model, which was carved from wood. After submitting the rather crude model, I visited the GM building to see all the entries on display, and was flabbergasted! What a rude awakening: the top models boasted chrome moldings and aluminum wheelcovers that were turned on metal lathes. Those models featured bumpers, plastic headlights, window moldings, license plate brackets, hood ornaments, and everything a finished production car would have. My wheels had been

Elia "Russ" Russinoff (age 18) won the 1949 first national scholarship, senior division, $4,000 award with this 4-door sedan design. A dozen sets of drawings were discarded before this satisfactory design emerged. This soft mahogany model featured sculpted head lamps, an intricately designed and chrome-plated brass grille and wooden wheels turned on a 4-in-1 home shop lathe. The scale model required 500 hours and 8 months of labor to complete. *Elia "Russ" Russinoff.*

turned on an inexpensive lathe, which was not very accurate, since the wheels were not exactly round.

This humbling experience prepared me for my second entry. All the metalwork was made out of brass and was chrome plated afterwards. The model was carved out of mahogany and spray painted with 11 coats of lacquer using my mother's Hoover vacuum cleaner spray attachment. The hard work and perseverance paid off and I won a third-place state prize. The two-tone paint job looked great, but I knew I still had a lot more work to do to become a top winner.

The third and final model I entered was a sleek rear engine design with fully skirted front and rear wheels. I thought it looked as if it could travel 100 mph. I was elated to learn I landed first place in the senior division, which meant a $4,000 scholar-

Elia "Russ" Russinoff, GM designer, retired. *Elia "Russ" Russinoff.*

ship! I was 18 years old. This was a very exciting time in my life, and it convinced me I had the talent to become an automotive designer. I knew I wanted to work at General Motors Design.

I'm glad I asked the advice of Homer LaGassey about which design school to attend. He was a GM designer and served as a Guild judge. As a graduate of Pratt Institute in Brooklyn, he felt that Pratt was a good choice for me. I was on my way to Brooklyn in 1951 and enrolled in a four-year course in industrial design. After my school day, I would meet with three or four other students who were also car enthusiasts to talk about and sketch (what else?) cars and more cars.

General Motors offered a student program at its Design headquarters during the summer, and in my fourth year at Pratt (1954), I was fortunate enough to be accepted into the program. I learned that summer that car design is a collaborative effort. Our full-size airbrushed renderings were critiqued by the professionals on the design staff. An unexpected highlight of the summer was a visit by Harley Earl himself! It was great fun.

Bill Mitchell, assistant head of GM's styling staff, came to Pratt during my final year in search of design talent. After seeing my portfolio and model he remarked that I had "gasoline in my veins." I was lucky to be hired by the styling leader, and by General Motors, whose Motorama exhibits led the way. What an exciting time that was!

The Guild experience taught me not to accept failure and to persevere. I spent one year in the basement of our home working on each model car. As a Guild winner, I realized that intense concentration on the project at hand was, for me, very satisfying. This experience has helped me immensely during my 40-year career at General Motors. I was saddened when General Motors no longer sponsored the Fisher Body Craftsman's Guild competition. It was my dream come true, and yes, I still have "gasoline in my veins."

Ronald C. Hill

1950 First-Place National Scholarship, Junior Division, $4,000 Award

by Ronald C. Hill, November 2002

Originally from Pasadena, I grew up in the very exciting time of the forties and fifties that defined the California automotive scene. This prompted me to enter the Fisher Body Craftsman's Guild in late 1949. The model I designed and built won the junior regional award and a trip to the 1950 Guild convention in Detroit. My model/design was chosen the winner of the top national award for juniors that year. The designers I met urged me to attend the Art Center School then located in west Los Angeles.

After graduating with honors in 1954, I was hired as an entry level designer at General Motors styling. After serving a brief apprenticeship I was picked to join the staff in the Cadillac studio. I worked on the 1957 line for Cadillac and was promoted to assistant chief designer in 1956.

Late in 1956 I was drafted and spent the next two years serving in the U.S. Army. After discharge I returned to GM Styling in early 1959.

It was a different era, as Harley Earl had just retired and Bill Mitchell had been appointed vice president for design. I was chief designer in the Chevrolet Advanced Studio and my team received the credit for the 1965 Corvair. In late 1968 I was posted to the General Motors affiliate Adam Opel AG in Germany. I served as assistant director of design under Chuck Jordan, another Fisher Body Craftsman's Guild alumnus. In 1969 I was transferred to Vauxhall Motors Ltd. in the UK where I was also assistant design director. Returning to the U.S. in late 1972, I was appointed chief designer of the Buick studio.

In 1975 I was posted to Brazil to function as assistant director of design at GM Brasil in Sao Paulo. Returning to Michigan in late 1976 I was involved with products for most of the GM brands. When I was running an advanced design studio in the late 1970s my team worked on what became the Pontiac Fiero.

In the early 1980s I was asked to assemble a studio that was to explore fundamental aerodynamics. Also about that time I became involved in researching and implementing computer graphics. I was the first designer at General Motors to demonstrate the software that is now used throughout the industry.

The model shown on the left, which was made by Ronald C. Hill, won the 1950 first national scholarship, junior division, $4,000 award. The 1990s style model on the right is shown for comparison purposes. *Ronald C. Hill.*

In 1985, after 31 years on General Motors staff I accepted the position of department chairman at the Art Center College of Design, now located in Pasadena, California. The transportation design department is a well known resource for designers.

After 15 years I retired from the chairmanship of the transportation design department at Art Center in 2000, marking over 45 years as a professional designer and educator.

In addition to land based mobility products, I have always been interested in water-going vessels. I have a certificate of small craft design from the Westlawn School of Yacht Design and have served them as a consultant.

Happily married for over 40 years, my wife and I enjoy our two grandchildren, our daughter and our son, a senior designer for Porsche. Currently I am painting, teaching, and enjoying life, all this due to a

Ronald C. Hill, former chairman, Industrial Design Transportation Department, Art Center College of Design. Ron was a GM designer for 30 years, working with Chuck Jordan, Elia "Russ" Russinoff and Ed Taylor before embarking on an education career that lasted another 15 years. *Ronald C. Hill.*

decision made in the early 1950s to try to design and build a Fisher Body Craftsman's Guild model.

Robert Arthur Cadaret

1950 First-Place National Scholarship, Senior Division, $4,000 Award

by Michelle Lenore Cadaret-Schulz

Robert Arthur Cadaret was born on September 19, 1931. As a young boy he loved to draw trains, fire trucks and automobiles. That love of cars was finally rewarded in his senior year in high school. He attended Franklin High School in Highland Park, California, where he graduated in 1950. It was there that he entered the Fisher Body Craftsman's Guild competition three years in a row. It was thanks to his woodshop teacher, Hugh Baird, who allowed him to work on his model during class, that he was finally able to design and build the best automobile model in the nation. At age 19, he won the first-place national scholarship and was awarded $4,000.

I had the pleasure of speaking with Bill Sherinyan, who was a close friend of my father's. Bill attended high school with him and remembered some interesting facts. His father, the late William K. Sherinyan, taught mechanical drafting at Franklin High and had Bob as his student from 1947 to 1950. Bill stated, "There were three winners all originating from Franklin High. The first was Ron Hill, who later became the chief designer at Cadillac. The second was Bill Milaken, who won third in state, and the third was Gordon Williams, who won first in state."

Using the award money, Bob attended the Art Center School in Los Angeles, California, and graduated in 1953. He was pre-hired by General Motor's Chevrolet studio.

Bob Cadaret worked side by side with Clare MacKichan, Chevrolet chief designer at that time, and Ed Cole, Chevrolet chief engineer. He also worked for Harley J. Earl, who was a giant in automotive history.

He immediately went to work on the 1955 Bel Air. The goal was to give these vehicles a major facelift and an image that would appeal to youthful people. This included big chrome bombs in front, big fins, a big chrome "V" on the hood and dual gun-sight ornaments on the hood. This youthful image was definitely accomplished as these Chevys are to this day some of America's best loved cars. He also started work on the '56 models, in particular the Nomad station wagon. It had been a show car based on the concept of the Corvette station wagon. While Carl Renner designed most of the upper trim, Bob did the chrome exhaust pipe in the rear fender.

He designed and held patents on the 1956 Corvette wheel covers and well as the hubcaps for the 1960 Chevrolet. He was instrumental in the design and naming of the Chevrolet Impala, Chevrolet Nova and the Corvair Lakeside Wagon. Bob retired in 1987 to care for his wife Phyllis, who was suffering from multiple sclerosis. During those years he produced six original pieces of artwork featuring the 1955, '56, and '57 Chevys, the Nomad wagon and the Corvette from 1956 to 1959. Bob passed away on October 13, 2000, after a long struggle with emphysema. He will always be remembered for his talented contributions to automotive design.

You can look up examples of the famous illustrations made by Robert A. Cadaret at www.RACDistributing.com.

Edward Frasier Taylor

1951 Third-Place National Scholarship, Senior Division, $2,000 Award

by Edward F. Taylor, September 2002

Long before he won a scholarship in the prestigious Fisher Body Craftsman's Guild competition in 1951, Edward Frasier Taylor knew he wanted to work with dream cars. His career at the drawing boards got a jump start when he graduated from the Art Center College of Design in Pasadena and took a job with General Motors in 1956. For the next 30 years, Ed Taylor would have his hand in almost every new product America's largest automobile manufacturer produced, beginning with the 1959 Oldsmobile and continuing through the 1994 Chevrolet Blazer.

The 1960 Oldsmobile was based on sketches Ed had made as an assistant designer. General Motors sent him to Australia in the mid-'60s to add some pizzazz to the Holden, GM's mid-size car sold "down under." Taylor returned to the U.S. just in time to be part of the Oldsmobile Toronado and Cadillac Eldorado design projects. The 1966 Oldsmobile Toronado was *Motor Trend*'s "Car of the Year" and was a major break from tradition both in styling and in engineering concepts.

Ed spent the next three years in West Germany as the assistant design director at Opel. He was responsible for the 1970 Opel Manta and the compact version of the Chevrolet Corvette called the Opel GT. Following his successes in Europe, Ed Taylor was brought back to Detroit to be the assistant director for the Chevrolet Design Studios. During this time he guided the creation of the 1970 and 1973 Chevrolet Monte Carlo and the Chevelle.

In the early 1970s GM sent Ed Taylor to Luton, England, to work on the Vauxhall-Bedford truck designs. Returning the U.S. in 1975 he was named assistant executive director for international designs and traveled frequently to Brazil, Canada, England and West Germany to assist in what was becoming a global series of designs for GM products. The Chevy Chevette and Chevy Cavalier were the first worldwide additions. Then he was involved in the development of the first mid-size, front-wheel drive, Chevy Celebrity (1982) and then rear-drive sports cars such as the 1982 Camaro and 1984 Corvette. As the truck market began to heat up, Mr. Taylor played a role in the design of the 1982 Chevrolet S-10 pickup, the Astro van and the new series of 1988 pickup trucks and Sub-urbans, now known as sport utility vehicles (SUVs).

Both of Ed Taylor's sons started showing signs of interest in

This model made by Edward Frasier Taylor (age 17) won the 1951 third national scholarship, senior division, $2,000 award. Some construction details for this model are as follows: Body — laminated ¾" thick mahogany; clear plastic windshield and side windows formed over plaster molds; bumpers, moldings, wheel discs — aluminum; headlamps and taillamps — plastic; and paint — lacquer. *Edward F. Taylor.*

design, winning high school awards in architectural competitions and then attending the Art Center College of Design to fine-tune earlier desires to become car designers. They both wanted to follow in their father's footsteps. Spending summers restoring the family hobby, a Lamborghini Miura, both Charles and Blair graduated from ACCD. After graduation, Charles spent three years at Opel Design working his way up to assistant studio head, then returned to the U.S. as an assistant at Isuzu California Design U.S. He later started a successful southern California design studio called Aria Group.

His other talented son gained experience in design, animation, and marketing in the movie industry before realizing his first love was also car designing. He's now Volvo's veteran interior design expert. Each son has children who are learning how to draw everything including cars.

Edward Frasier Taylor, assistant design executive, GM Design, retired. Edward F. Taylor.

After leaving GM, Taylor returned to his starting point and taught classes and for seven years lectured at the Art Center College of Design in Pasadena, and more recently, in San Francisco at the Academy of Art University. Sometimes, when called on, he helps his son Charles with Aria design projects and is still interested in sculpture and painting. Last year he finished that other hobby, the family's Lamborghini, in time for the 35th anniversary Miura event at Monterey, California.

George R. Chartier

1953 First-Place State Award, Wisconsin, and
1954 Second-Place State Award, Wisconsin

by George R. Chartier, August 2003

The Fisher Body Craftsman's Guild has fascinated me since I first found out about it in 1952, which was the year I graduated from high school. My first car was entered in 1953 and won the first-place Wisconsin state, senior division, $150 cash award. The second model I made was in 1954 and won the second-place Wisconsin state, senior division, $100 cash award.

In 1953 I competed for a regional award against a young man from St. Paul, Minnesota, named Henry F. Rom. He won the 1953 regional award (Region 12 — Minnesota, Wisconsin) and also won the 1953 fourth-place national scholarship, senior division, $1,000 award. Despite a promising career in automotive design, Mr. Rom became a commercial business owner in Burnsville, Minnesota. In February 1993, June 1993 and February 1994, some of Mr. Rom's exquisitely executed and futuristic scale model automobile designs were pictured in *Collectible Automobile* magazine and I was able to contact him after all these years. It gave me a great deal of pleasure to finally make that connection. He had become a professional model maker in ability, but it was only a hobby. I truly believe he may have missed his calling as an automobile designer.

I used the $150 cash prize from the 1953 competition to finance a trip to Detroit in 1954 in order to review the model entries and size up the competition. After arriving at the GM building in Detroit, I found my way to the Guild exhibit hall just in time to see my 1954 model on the turntable being examined and scored. This two-door scale model has clear plastic windows all the way around. I went back to the GM building the next day after the judging was completed to view all the model cars that were now in display cases. I also met and spoke with many of the winners of the regional and scholarship awards. With my camera in hand and plenty of film, I took pictures of all the model cars that had won an award. Among my pictures was James Lee Garner's* 1954 regional award winning sports car model (1954 first-place Missouri state and regional award (Region 14 — Missouri, Iowa).

I hurried my 1954 second-place state

Too old for the Guild competition in 1955, George R. Chartier built a radio-controlled model to perfect scale featuring a big "V" grille, clear windows all the way around, a finished interior and operating front lighting and rear signaling systems. He traveled to Detroit and showed it to the design managers at GM, Ford and Chrysler. He was hired on the spot by Ford Motor Company and enjoyed a 37-year career as a designer/modeler. *George R. Chartier.*

award winning car because I was afraid I would be drafted into the army before I had a chance to finish it. I sent in my model car three months before the deadline. Then I thought there was still enough time left to design and build another car, so I did. It turned out to be the third highest scoring model in Wisconsin. I was told by one of the judges that only the highest scoring model of the two would be counted. Then he asked me why I hadn't put all of my effort into making just one improved model.

In 1956, as part of our honeymoon trip, my wife and I visited the Tech Center in Warren, Michigan. We found our way into the domed General Motors Design Center where all of the Craftsman's Guild model cars were laid out on tables. The models had not been judged yet but each one had a unique three- or four-digit tag attached to it. I wrote down the numbers of the cars I thought would be the top winners in each of the junior and senior divisions. I had intended to take pictures of these models but I was told to hand over my camera as we entered the showroom. The security guard said I could

*Featured below.

pick it up in the lobby when we were ready to leave. After returning home from our trip, I wrote to Norman E. May, who was a technical supervisor for Fisher Body Craftsman's Guild, and asked him to mail me the numbers of the top winning model cars as soon as the judging was completed. I was a bit surprised to find that I had picked five out of the eight top national winners that year.

I sure wished I had known about the existence of the Fisher Body Craftsman's Guild competition back in 1946 when I was 12 years old. I had only two chances to compete, at ages 18 and 19. If I had had just one more year of eligibility, I think it's possible that I could have been one of the top national winners. To prove to myself that I could design and build a much better model car, I began the design process in the fall of 1954. Knowing that I couldn't enter this model in the FBCG, I took it a giant step further by engineering this one to be a completely operational radio-controlled (R/C) scale model. The body was carved from basswood and had a complete interior with seats and instrument panel. The bumpers and all exterior and interior trim was formed from brass and chrome plated. There were clear plastic windows all the way around, operational R/C with variable forward and reverse speeds, operable steering, a working differential, clutch, independent adjustable suspension on all four wheels, and working lights (headlights, taillights, turn signals, backup lights, interior dome lights) and an audible horn. It took about 3,000 hours to complete this model.

A friend of mine suggested I take the model to Detroit to demonstrate my R/C scale model for design staff at the "Big Three" and in 1962 I did just that. I was surprised when I was hired during my interview at Ford Motor Company. I started as a design modeler at the Ford Styling building in the Advanced Studio. I continued to work for Ford for nearly 37 years as a modeler and enjoyed a wonderful career and comradeship with many very talented modelers and designers.

I did get my camera back from the guards that summer day in 1956, and I'll always wonder how my future would have been affected if I had learned about the Fisher Body Craftsman's Guild five or six years earlier.

Gary Graham

1954 First-Place National Scholarship, Senior Division, $4,000 Award

Gary Graham, from Bellingham, Washington, entered the competition four times and was a was a regional winner in 1951, 1952, 1953 and 1954. His 1954 model won a first-place national scholarship, $4,000 award, and was sold to General Motors for $1,000. *Motor Trend* stated,

> First place winner in the Senior Division, Gary Graham (19) of Bellingham, Washington came up with a car that GM could logically duplicate (full size) for a forthcoming Motorama. Some of the details are not too practical, such as the unusual rear bumper treatment, but then neither are some of the real-life show cars. Details in current favor are the wrap-around windshield and the shrouded headlights, which are so far not part of any production car but a popular accessory. We're not pleased about the disguised wheel openings ["Spotlight — What's New for Car Owners"].

It was a popular styling-studio idea in the early '50s to have partially covered front wheel-well openings and fully covered rear wheel-well openings. Graham's sheet metal

This convertible designed by Gary Graham of Bellingham, Washington, won the 1954 first national scholarship, senior division, $4,000 award. For many years after, Guildsmen all over the country emulated the design lines of this model. Today, Gary Graham designs and manufactures a unique line of low impact aerobic exercise equipment. *General Motors Corporation.*

came down to the center of the front wheel cover and sheet metal shrouded almost the entire rear wheel white wall. The 1951 Nash Rambler carried some of these ideas into production.

Graham believes that GM used the major styling features of his two-seater convertible model (namely the spectacular rear horizontal fins) on the 1956 Buick Centurion show car and the 1959 Chevrolet production car. Even if he had not sold the model design to GM, this was legal, as all automobile design ideas submitted in the Guild competition became the exclusive property of GM and its subsidiaries. Even future Guildsmen's designs emulated this key design feature from Graham's model.

Mr. Graham attended Bellingham High School and graduated from the University of Washington with a degree in mechanical engineering in 1958. He went to work for Boeing Company in Seattle, Washington, and was involved in the early 1960s in the design of the U.S. Air Force space station called the MOL. In addition, he was involved in the preliminary design of Boeing's entry into the Lunar Excursion Module (LEM) competition for NASA and the Lunar Rover that subsequently was used for lunar surface exploration.

After 11 years with the Boeing Company, Graham moved to Glacier, Washington, a small alpine recreational village at the foot of Mt. Baker. At Glacier, he started Graham's Restaurant in 1972 and the Contemporary Design Company in 1985. The Contemporary Design Company has designed a line of rehabilitation and exercise equipment called the Shuttle 2000-1, Shuttle MVP, Shuttle MiniClinic and Shuttle Balance. (For further information, see his web site at www.shuttlesystems.com.) Shuttle products are used by a range of people from geriatric patients in nursing homes to NFL, NBA, and Olympic athletes as well as the army Rangers. Gary's products are distributed throughout the world.

Charles W. Pelly

1954 Second-Place National Scholarship, Junior Division, $3,000 Award, Age 15

Charles W. Pelly, a 40-year veteran of the design industry, has recently left the helm of Designworks/USA, a BMW subsidiary, to start his own design and creative consulting group called Pelly Design Management with his partner Joan Gregor. Pelly continues to consult on projects for BMW Group as well as for other clients. He is cofounder of the Design Academy concept, a multidisciplinary consulting network dedicated to applying design and creative knowledge to corporations, educational institutions and organizations.

This model designed by Charles W. Pelly (age 15) of Los Angeles won the 1954 second national scholarship, junior division, $3,000 award. This was Charles Pelly's first try at the Guild competition. As an Art Center School graduate, distinguished designer and founder of Designworks/USA, Chuck Pelly has designed race cars, snowmobiles, farm equipment, campers, and catamarans as well as vehicles for GM, Chrysler, American Motors, Mazda, Subaru and BMW. *General Motors Corporation.*

Pelly took Designworks/USA from a start-up operation in his garage to one of the top ten consultancies in the world. Pelly developed the unique structure of Designworks/USA with a balance of automotive, transit, product, advanced communications, and graphic consulting to stimulate cross fertilization and thinking among his design team. Headquartered in Newbury Park, California, with an office in Munich, Germany, Designworks/USA became a wholly-owned subsidiary of the BMW Group in 1995 and was instrumental in the design of the BMW X5 Sports Activity Vehicle as well as the award winning BMW 5 Series. In addition, between 1987 and 2000, other development projects included the BMW Electric car, BMW 7-Series interior, BMW 850 seat, BMW Zeta show car, BMW E46 3 Series, BMW 100 and 1200 Touring motorcycles and the BMW Z8, among others.

Mr. Pelly has been involved in the Art Center College of Design since 1968 as a student, teacher, mentor, and lecturer and has received their George Jergenson Design Achievement award for significant contributions. He has been president of the Industrial Designers Society of America. As the designer of the original Scarab sports car for Lance Reventlow, Mr. Pelly continues to contribute to the design profession

This 2-seater sports car model made by James Lee Garner (age 17) of Bloomfield, Missouri, won the 1954 first state Missouri, senior division and regional award. His raked design, with Aztec red exterior and soft white leather interior, featured headlights sculpted and integrated into the front fender lines, a recessed grille, fender skirts integrated into the rear quarter panels, a wrap-around windshield and whitewall tires with wire wheels. The model was constructed with a balsa wood body, plywood floor for wheel support, soft aluminum exterior trim parts, and wheelcover spokes made from chrome-plated pins. The car was sprayed with Duco lacquer. *General Motors Corporation.*

through worldwide lectures, articles and appearances and has received 50 awards of distinction.

James Lee Garner

1954 and 1955 First-Place State Award, Missouri, and Regional Winner

by James Lee Garner, December 2002

The Fisher Body Craftsman's Guild was brought to my attention by an ad in my *Air Trails* magazine in 1950. I wrote to them and received an information pack. I was extremely excited to get started designing and building a sedan model for the 1951 national competition.

This was the beginning of a wonderful dedication for the next five years. I won an honorable mention and the prize was a large X-Acto tool set. My second model in 1952 was more successful. I won a third-place state award and really felt more confident in my ability. I think I won $50. The model car I created for the 1953 competition won a second-place state award and $100 cash, I believe.

For 1954, the Guild included a sports car design category in the competition. I started designing a neat sports car. I worked on the design in the fall of 1953 when I was a senior in high school. I made four views plus a perspective view drawn to scale.

I glued up six blocks of hard balsa wood and prepared to carve the model. Card-stock templates were made from the scale drawings and their shape transferred to the balsa wood block. I carved the model using a homemade designer's bridge, ½" station lines and cardboard templates for symmetry as prescribed by the Guild how-to manual, and spent many hours carving and sanding the body to the final shape. This task required

Dr. W. W. Parker, president of Southeast Missouri State College, making a trophy presentation to arts and science student James Lee Garner of Bloomfield, Missouri. Garner had won a 1955 first state Missouri and regional award but missed winning a national award by just a few points. Dr. Parker formally presented this big trophy in December 1955. *James Lee Garner.*

approximately 60 hours of meticulous work. I checked the car for accuracy and symmetry with templates on my platform designer's bridge.

The convertible cockpit floorboard was made from $\frac{3}{32}$" plywood and seats were built up and shaped from blocks of balsawood. The bucket seats were carved to simulate pleat and roll upholstery. The steering wheel was made from $\frac{1}{16}$" diameter copper tubing. Spokes were soldered to the rim and hub and then filed with needle files to form scale finger grips for the driver.

James Lee Garner shown in his 1978 25th Anniversary Corvette with first place trophy awarded at the 1st Annual Lions Club Car Show held in May 2003 in Bloomfield, Missouri. *James Lee Garner.*

All the chrome trim and bumper parts were made from aluminum. These parts were fitted on the primed surfaces of the model so as to match the body contours. I fitted all parts to the primed model before the final finish.

Aluminum parts were cut, filed and hand-formed, then sanded and brought to a high lustrous finish with a homemade polishing wheel to make the aluminum shine like chrome. Many hours of polishing with various compounds were needed to bring the metal to a fine finish. All moldings, trim and bumpers were drilled; then small jeweler's screws were inserted like pins on the back side to secure the trim pieces to the body upon final assembly.

I did the wheel design layout as a math problem in school. I chose a spoke wheel design and using formulas I was able to derive the accurate geometric location of the spokes.

The instrument panel was recessed for safety. A list of special features was attached to the bottom of the car model with screws.

I remember how much time I spent getting the model all polished and assembled without damage. I photographed the model with an old Kodak and got it all ready to ship. I used the same shipping box I had built three years before and took it to the railroad station five miles away. Over 400 hours of work was invested in that model.

I was thrilled to receive notice of my first-place Missouri state and regional win. I was on the top of the world! The wonderful trip to Detroit was very memorable—being treated like royalty by GM and having a chance for a scholarship was very exciting. I enjoyed meeting all of GM's head people such as Mr. Kettering, Mr. Fisher and Mr.

Above: This Guild model made by Gilbert McArdle (age 17) won the 1955 first-place state Utah and regional award, senior division, $150. The construction details are as follows: Body — bass wood; trim — chrome-plated brass; canopy — solid sculpted translucent acrylic plastic with aquamarine painted sail panels; taillights/headlights — red and white plastic; paint — black and aquamarine color lacquers. *Below:* Rear view of Gilbert McArdle's 1955 model. *Dr. Gilbert McArdle.*

Jordan. I made friends while at the Fisher Body Guild convention and I regretted not winning a scholarship.

I came home from Detroit with a sketch pad full of ideas and notes, determined to design a winning sports car for 1955. Although I was busy as a freshman in college, I started developing a clay model from drawings for the Guild competition. I spent weekends at the home shop working on the sugar pine model and consumed over 500 hours in its construction. Again, I won a first-place Missouri state and regional award. This design lost a university scholarship bid by 2 points. Regrettably, I sold the model to GM.

The Guild instilled in me a greater level of development in design and craftsmanship which I have been practicing all my life.

[Author's notes: Mr. Garner entered the Guild competition five times (1951 to 1955). He is a former appliance product designer turned freelance artist who has devoted his life to fine arts. He regards himself as an artist, engineer, craftsman and designer. As an artist, he works in multimedia.

Some of Mr. Garner's three-dimensional sculptures include *Earth Cradle II — Ecology Study*, a scale model for a large public sculpture; *Variations on the Firebird*, a brass and bronze wall sculpture located at the Rose Theatre, Southeast Missouri State College Campus; *Lunar Tree*, a rotating kinetic sculpture made of brass and bronze; *PODS*, a 10' high water fountain made of copper, brass and bronze, located at the Paducah City Hall, Paducah, Kentucky; *Wind Chimes*; *Reeds in the Wind*; *Lunar Flightscape*; *Structural Improvisation*; and *The Red Balloon*, all made from bronze or a combination of copper, brass and bronze. He loves classical music and jazz. A real independent creative genius.]

Dr. Gilbert McArdle

1955 First-Place State Award, Utah, and 1955 Regional Winner (Region 17—Colorado, Utah and Kansas)

At an early age I was interested in making models of planes, cars and ships. My first attempt to make a car model was in kindergarten. When attempting to cut a piece of 2 × 4 for the body, I inadvertently cut several corners off the wooden steps at the back of the house, which was not appreciated by my father.

In grade school I made numerous balsa stick model airplanes and solid wood model cars and, therefore, was significantly enthused when a representative from the Fisher Body Craftsman's Guild made a presentation at my school about a model car competition sponsored by General Motors.

Over the next four years I made four models for the Guild competition, winning four first-place state awards and two regional awards (Region 17 — Colorado, Utah, Kansas). The two trips to Detroit at age 14 and 17 were particularly exciting, including meeting other boys interested in car modeling, visiting GM's production plants, and being introduced to famous designers and inventors such as Mr. Charles F. Kettering. I should say I was more interested in constructing than in designing model cars and was convinced that I had sufficient skills to win a scholarship with a final model. However, this was not to be. I went away to college and didn't have the time or facilities to finish the model. (I was awarded a Benjamin Franklin academic scholarship to the University of Pennsylvania in 1955.)

During my junior high school and high school years, I had developed an interest in becoming a physician — a surgeon in particular. I have always thought that the mechanical skills I developed while making model cars greatly enhanced and facilitated my ability to learn new surgical skills, which obviously required three dimensional and perceptual skills associated with hand-eye coordination.

I completed my medical degree and surgical training after college and spent several years at Camp Pendleton Marine Base as a

Dr. Gilbert McArdle, surgeon, professional period-vessel model-maker and master craftsman. *Dr. Gilbert McArdle.*

surgeon during part of the Vietnam War (1967–1969). I subsequently practiced general surgery in Gettysburg until my recent retirement.

I married a physician during my medical internship and have five children, all of whom are interested in art and woodworking and three of whom have careers in design and manufacturing (one with a scholarship to Cooper Union).

Over the years, time permitting, I have continued an interest in modeling, but have switched to historic ship modeling and writing magazine articles about their construction. In 1983, I donated a large model of the USS *Constellation* I constructed to the Constellation Foundation. The model is presently on display in their museum at Baltimore's Inner Harbor. I also wrote a book about its construction which was published by the Cornell Maritime Press in 1983. Several years ago, I donated an admiralty model of HMS *Cyane* that I assembled to the USS *Constitution* Museum in Charlestown, Massachusetts. This model was a gold medal winner in the scratch (built) sailing model division of a ship model competition sponsored by the Nautical Research Guild and the USS *Constitution* Museum. I am presently working on a large scale model of the *Sussex*, the lines of which were taken off the original model in the Rogers Collection at the U.S. Naval Academy Museum in Annapolis, Maryland. I hope to publish a book about its construction. In conclusion, I believe that participation in the Fisher Body Craftsman's Guild was the most enjoyable and rewarding experience of my young life.

Robert F. McDonnell

1955 Second-Place National Scholarship, Senior Division, $3,000 Award

by Robert F. McDonnell with his daughter, Bobbie Purdy, March 2003

After winning my Fisher Body Scholarship along with my identical twin brother Tom McDonnell, we both attended Art Center School of Design in Los Angeles, California. Upon completion of Art Center we were both offered positions with General Motors in their automotive design department; however, we declined as we did not want to move to the East Coast where they were located.

I accepted a position with Scott Brothers Sign Company in Stockton, California. I was head of the graphics department and designed logos, signs, interior showcases and concept designs.

After ten years, I decided to explore other avenues and moved my family to southern California, where I accepted a position with Disney. I worked in the graphic arts department creating designs for Disneyland in Los Angeles and Disney World in Florida.

After ten years of working with Disney, I wanted to get more involved in architectural design so I started Robert F. McDonnell Architectural Design Consultants, which is still going strong today.

Often I am contacted by Disney to do consulting work for them on their theme parks. To date, my work exists in each of the Disney theme parks around the world. In 1991, my wife and I spent three months in Paris working on Euro Disney. I designed storefronts and interiors for Main Street and other sections of the park. Originally they had contacted me to design Sleeping Beauty's castle. They were looking for something unique, since castles in France were very common.

Today, I am self employed and enjoy working on custom homes. Some of the homes I have designed are located throughout California and Canada.

In the summer of 1955 Bill Moore and Art Russell drove from Los Angeles to Detroit to inspect the winning model cars in the 1955 Fisher Body Craftsman's Guild competition. Bill Moore *(left)* an unidentified Guild technical judge *(middle)* and Art Russell *(right)* are shown. This proved to be an invaluable experience as in 1956 both young men won national scholarship awards. *General Motors Corporation.*

I still have a passion for automotive design and enjoy attending classic and current auto shows and browsing through automotive magazines. I have restored several vehicles, including a 1963 356 SC Porsche and a 1965 Jaguar Drop Head Coupe, and have enjoyed them very much.

[Robert F. McDonnell passed away April 23, 2003.]

William A. Moore

1955 Second-Place State Award, California,
and 1956 First-Place National Scholarship,
Senior Division, $5,000 Award

Born in Glendale, California, I grew up in the Venice and Culver City area with many of the childhood interests that the school district had to offer. Art, ceramics, science, history, printing, electric and metal-shop classes outweighed most others for me. As an only child (until I was 18), I was always drawing. With paper and pencil I was in my own lit-

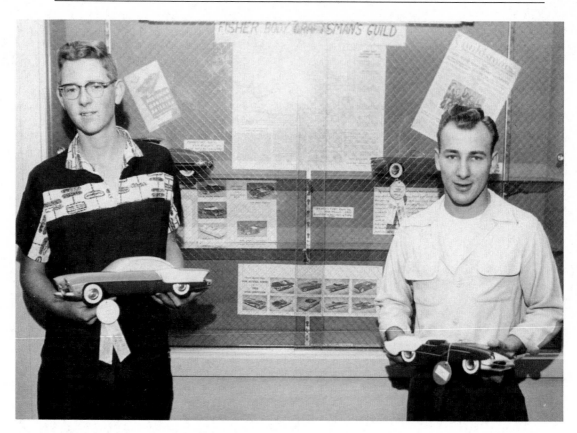

In 1955 Art Russell *(left)* and Bill Moore *(right)* celebrated their Guild success with a Venice High School Guild exhibit. The photograph shows Art Russell (age 17) holding his 1955 third state California award winner and Bill Moore (age 18) holding his 1955 second state California award winner. *E. Arthur Russell.*

tle world. As I approached my teens, I was torn between drawing dinosaurs, a few monsters and cars. I collected fossils and turned a small room in the backyard into a museum complete with paintings of dinosaurs and sculpted habitat groups. As the possibility of getting my first car loomed, a 1941 Chevy Coupe was my choice. So I began drawing lots of customized Chevy ideas. When the time came, a 1942 Chevrolet was the first deal I found. Back to the drawing board. I drove it for 12 years and it was featured in *Rod &*

Bill Moore, 19, is shown test fitting the roughed-out rear bumper to the rear of his hand-carved 1956 model design. These rectangular pieces were hand-filed to fit the contours of the wood body. *William A. Moore.*

Custom magazine, December 1954. While attending Venice High School, I met E. Arthur (Art) Russell. He had a 1946 Chevy coupe and obviously good taste. Art had entered the Fisher Body Craftsman's Guild contest several times and suggested that I give it a try. His father, Elwin, had built a fine shop and offered to let me work there with Art on our hopeful entries.

My first model was a "roly-poly" convertible and brought me a second-place state award for California. Art and I had gone to GM Motoramas and viewed some of the models on display, but we needed to see all the big winners. We decided to drive from Los Angeles to Detroit where they would all be on exhibit. It took a bit of persuasion for our folks to agree that this was a good idea. We flipped a coin to see whose Chevy we took. Art's '46 was the winner. We went over the car mechanically with Elwin's expertise, including "shimming" the rods. This was a great adventure for two young teens and provided us with life-long memories. When we arrived in Detroit, Norman E. May and the Guild were impressed with our drive and set up a critique session with a designer. He evaluated each of our models and gave us great pointers. Three words stuck with me: "Keep it crisp."

I was anxious to get to work

Bill Moore's rear bumper was assembled from several pieces of hand-filed brass and silver-soldered together. The bumper included a license plate mounting area. The whole bumper assembly was polished to perfection and chrome-plated for the competition. *William A. Moore.*

A rear view of Bill Moore's hand-carved 1956 model with the final chrome-plated bumper part mounted for a trial fitting. Chrome-plated brass parts were mounted with pins to ensure fit and reliable attachment after the painting process. In this case, many coats of Titian Red automotive lacquer were applied and then "compounded" by hand to a high luster. The palm of the human hand was the preferred tool for the compounding or for the hand rubbed lacquer finish. *William A. Moore.*

on my next design and made many drawings and finally a clay model to work out the shapes, which I later learned was called surface development. I carved the final model out of poplar wood. Most of the metal parts were made of brass and chrome plated, a couple made of aluminum and buffed. The original plan was to have two inboard headlights with fading hood spears. I wrestled with this feature for quite awhile. Finally I eliminated them in favor of hidden lights with flush covers. This model won me first of state, regional and the trip to Detroit for the scholarship awards banquet. At the dinner, they started with the junior division winners. Then the senior division. When they announced the second place winner, I remember thinking, well it's all over. Then they said, "and first place goes to a young man from California." Afterwards, one of the design judges pointed out that my front blade bumper would slice through other cars. I said, "it's 'crisp.'"

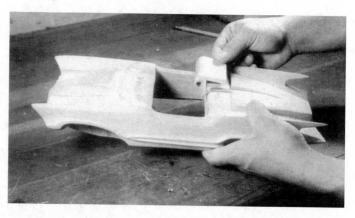

Adjusting and fitting the pleated top seat covers which were hand-carved from poplar for Bill Moore's 1956 model. *William A. Moore.*

After attending the Art Center School in Los Angeles [relocated to Pasadena in 1966, the school is now the Art Center College of Design] on the FBCG scholarship, I worked at Hughes Aircraft for three years, where I did some of the first concept drawings of Surveyor I. Loving cars, I left and established Automotive Arts, designing racecars and products, illustrating for nearly every automotive magazine in the '60s and working on design concepts and presentations for Craig Breedlove's first two land speed record cars. Bill Lear brought me to Reno,

Fitting the hand-filed brass driveshaft cover to the interior of Bill Moore's 1956 convertible design. This part was polished and chrome-plated for the competition. Note the carved seat cushion parts on the table. *William A. Moore.*

Nevada, in '68 to create and head a design department for Lear Motors Corp. and his steam car development program.

The Fisher Body Craftsman's Guild represents some of the finest memories of my

Opposite bottom: The 1956 Guild scholarship winners and the models they made. Selected best in the nation on the basis of craftsmanship and designing ability in 1956 were: Senior winners *(top row, left to right)*: Joseph Greene, Medina, Washington ($2,000); Murray Milne, Detroit ($4,000); Bill Moore, Mar Vista, California ($5,000); Jerry Winkley, Rollins, Montana ($4,000); and Jack Pink, Grosse Point, Michigan ($3,000). Junior winners *(bottom row, left to right)*: Charles Winslow, Jr., Springfield, Massachusetts ($4,000); Michael Barricks, Chicago ($2,000); Charles Gibilterra, Los Angeles ($3,000); and Bryce Arden Miller, Detroit ($5,000). *General Motors Corporation.*

William A. Moore's finished model won the 1956 first national scholarship, senior division, $5,000 award. An accurate clay model was made to work out the design ideas before starting the wood model. This model was carved from a single piece of poplar and silver-soldered, chrome-plated brass trim parts were applied. *General Motors Corporation.*

life and provided me with a fine career start. Beyond that, it formed many friendships among young men like the lifelong brotherhood of Art Russell and me. It was a priceless experience.

[Author's note: Bill enjoys oil painting and has one or two shows a year. He is also recreating his '42 Chevy Custom with three other classic cars waiting in the wings. He says he has delusions of grandeur. You can look up the paintings of William A. Moore under www.MAMMA.com.]

E. Arthur Russell

1956 Styling Scholarship and 1957 First-Place National Scholarship, Senior Division, $5,000 Award

by Art Russell, September 2002

When I was a boy living in Los Angeles, California, my father and I made model airplanes, cars and boats, mostly U-control airplanes we would fly on Sunday mornings. This was in the late 1940s and early 1950s. As a modeler I would read the model airplane magazines like *Air Trails* from cover to cover. In one of the issues of this magazine I found an ad for the Fisher Body Craftsman's Guild and it sounded like something I would like to do.

After receiving the packet of information I started drawing cars and working on my first Guild entry for 1951 made from balsa wood just like those model airplanes and boats. This model received a Third-Place California state award. My participation in the 1952 Guild competition was interrupted by another GM scholarship competition, the All-American Soap Box Derby, sponsored by Chevrolet. Each year after that, up to and including 1957, I designed and built a new Guild entry and as my age and experience progressed my models got better.

This is the completed scale clay model made by Art Russell for his 1956 Guild entry. After making many sketches and drawings, Guildsmen were encouraged to study their new design ideas three-dimensionally using clay. Cardboard temples, or lateral cross sections, traced from the clay model were used to ensure symmetry in the wood model. *E. Arthur Russell.*

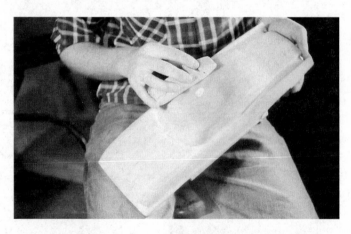

The carving of Art Russell's 1956 design from poplar is shown nearing completion. Block sanding was used to remove high spots and occasionally "Plastic Wood" was used to fill low spots. Guildsmen's wood carving tools included a flat wood saw, a hacksaw, various chisels, an X-Acto tool kit, wood files and all grits of sandpaper. *E. Arthur Russell.*

In my junior year at Venice High School I met William A. (Bill) Moore, who was also interested in the Craftsman's Guild. We started to work together designing and working on our models in my father's workshop. My dad was a tool and die maker by trade. At this time, General Motors had a show that traveled around the country called Motorama, and when it came to the Los Angeles Pan Pacific Auditorium, Bill and I spent as much time as we could studying the futuristic show cars and the Craftsman's Guild models on display. At one of the Motorama shows we met Norman E. May, Guild technical representative, and he took an interest and talked to us about the program and our futures. In return, Bill took a series of how-to photos for Mr. May showing the step-by-step progress on both of our 1956 model designs. A step-by-step, how-to story about my 1956 styling scholarship award winner was published in the *Guildsman* (vol. 4, no. 3, 1956) and distributed to hundreds of thousands of Guildsmen across America. My buddy and lifetime friend Bill won the 1956 first-place national scholarship, senior division, $5,000 award. He had built the best model in the land, won first-place state California and I had won second-place state California and a styling scholarship.

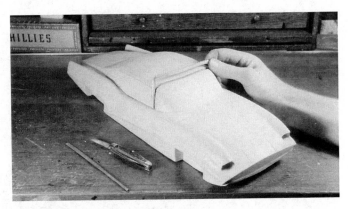

A U-shaped windshield metal trim piece is fitted to a groove on Art Russell's 1956 model. After final painting, the chrome-plated brass trim piece, or highly polished aluminum piece, was fitted flush with the surface of the model. The use of metallic brightwork was essential to building a winning model entry. *E. Arthur Russell.*

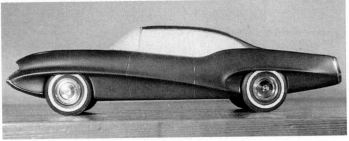

This Guild model won E. Arthur Russell (age 18) of Los Angeles a 1956 styling scholarship, $1,000 award. The clay model and final product looked identical. *E. Arthur Russell.*

In 1955 Bill won second-place state California and I had won third-place state California awards, and at this point we decided that the best way to win the top Guild awards was to go to Detroit and study the model entries first hand. After much talk and planning, my parents let me (age 17) and Bill (age 19) drive to Detroit in my

Art Russell shown spray painting a color coat of automotive lacquer on his 1956 Guild model entry using compressor-type paint equipment where lacquer and thinner are mixed. Most Guildsmen used auto touch-up spray cans purchased at a local auto parts store. After 10 or 20 coats, the final coat of lacquer was usually finished to a mirror-like luster with rubbing compound and wax. *E. Arthur Russell.*

1946 Chevrolet, which I had customized and painted myself. This was my first trip away from home and I have often wondered about the courage, fear and trepidation my parents must have felt that summer with two teenagers driving cross-country.

This was a real adventure for both of us, visiting relatives along the way. We removed the rear seat and partition from the Chevy, leaving enough room for a pair of lawn swing mattresses so we could sleep in the car. We drove Route 66, the fabled main drag from Los Angeles to Chicago. We made a sign for the car that said "Fisher Body Craftsman's Guild Expidition, July 27, 1955." The word expedition had been spelled wrong, but the Guild people we met loved it. While examining some of the model entries from the 1954–55 competition, Norman E. May arranged for us to meet a GM stylist who thoughtfully reviewed and critiqued our 1955 entries. The stylist told us to keep our future Guild model designs crisp and clean. The trip to Detroit helped, as Bill won the first-place national scholarship award the next year with a beautiful titian red and white sports car, and I won a styling scholarship with a metallic green sedan.

Bill and I applied to attend the Art Center School in Los Angeles. The only thing that got me into the Art Center's industrial design program was my Fisher Body Craftsman's Guild model-making experience, as I had never taken art classes in high school. Most of my time had been spent in the machine shop and drafting classes. I remember in geometry class we had to do a final project. Everyone else did math formulas, but I did a side view drawing of one of my Fisher Body models and illustrated the various geometric shapes involved in its construction. The teacher liked my project and I passed.

For the 1956–57 Guild competition, I took a semester off from my studies at the Art Center to concentrate on building my last Guild model. It won the 1957 first-place national scholarship, senior division, $5,000 award (age 19). After the scholarship winners were announced at Guild convention banquet, the first-place national junior winner, Daniel C. Greene (age 15), and I were spirited away in a GM corporate plane bound for New York City for interviews on the *Today Show* with Hugh Downs. Arriving at 3 A.M., groggy,

This sports car model won E. Arthur Russell (age 19) of Los Angeles a 1957 first national scholarship, $5,000 award. Art took a semester off from his Art Center School studies to complete his Guild entry. Some construction details are as follows: Body — poplar wood; trim — chrome-plated brass, silver-soldered brass parts; windshield and taillights — acrylic plastic; paint — nitrocellulose lacquer. The interior shows the level of interior details required. Note the speedometer numbers, pleated seat covers, gas tank cap and stick shift. *E. Arthur Russell.*

The 1957 Guild scholarship winners and the models they made. The senior division winners for 1957 were *(top row, left to right)*: Richard Sylvester, Lynnville, Iowa ($3,000); William Marks, Twin Falls, Idaho ($4,000); E. Arthur Russell, Los Angeles ($5,000); and David Koto, Birmingham, Michigan ($2,000). The junior division winners in 1957 were *(bottom row, left to right)*: Barry Herr, St. Louis, Missouri ($4,000); Chris Pappas, Youngstown, Ohio ($2,000); Daniel Greene, Medina, Washington ($5,000); Malvin Meador, Denver, Colorado ($3,000); and John Di Ilio, State College, Pennsylvania ($3,000). *General Motors Corporation.*

sleepless and excited, we were up again at 5 A.M. preparing for two broadcasts: one for the East and Midwest and the other for the West Coast. When we got back to Detroit, by commercial airline, Dan and I met a famous GM executive and automotive icon — Charles F. (Boss Kett) Kettering, director of the GM Research Laboratories and inventor of the electric starter, among other things.

The Guild experience was one of the most influential in my life and I have worked in the model-making and design field ever since. While working at Revell (the hobby model kit manufacturer), I helped make a model (1/2 scale) of the miniature model Napoleonic Coach made by teenagers during the 1930s, but this kit idea was never mass produced. I did most of the concept models for Craig Breedlove's Spirit of America land speed record jet engine powered car. I have been a vendor to Mattel Toy's Hot Wheels cars since 1970, doing designs and patterns for many of their new Hot Wheels products over the years

While working with Craig, I met a very talented young man named Bob Davids (who turned out to be another Venice High School alumnus like Bill and I) and since he was much younger, we got him interested in entering the Craftsman's Guild competition. I let him work in my workshop and in 1963 he won the first-place national scholarship, senior division, $5,000 award.

Looking back at the Guild after 40-odd years as a professional designer and model maker, I am still in awe of [the] high level of craftsmanship displayed in the top tier of models, especially considering that they were designed by boys and young men that had no training in design or model-making and had little or no access to professional tools. When Bill and I were working in my father's shop we had only a few basic power tools, and if we needed parts made on a lathe, we had to find a friend of a friend to loan us lathe time over at their place. The brass parts we made had to be silver soldered together before being chrome plated, and we used a very crude plumber's gasoline-fueled blowtorch to do the job. Thinking back, it would be very hard for me to duplicate any of those models today even with access to the most modern materials and tools.

But most important of all, Bill Moore has remained a lifelong friend and we both still love to talk about cars.

[Author's note: Art has retired, but occasionally creates master model patterns when the project interests him. He enjoys racing his GTV with the Alfa Romeo Club and is restoring a classic Giulietta Spyder from the ground up.]

Charles A. Gibilterra

1956 Third-Place National Scholarship, Junior Division, $3,000 Award, Age 15

by Charles A. Gibilterra, November 2002 (revised 8/2004)

Charles A. Gibilterra, designer, Carmel, California. Gibilterra's career has included commercial and residential interior design, commercial and residential furniture design and office product design. *Charles A. Gibilterra.*

Growing up in 1950s Los Angeles as a young teen was a special time, although at the time I didn't know it. Everything was happening, expectations were high, sci-fi movies and Westerns were big, as was interest in UFO sightings.

The '50s for me was a time of immersing myself in a host of creative projects, most of which were building model kits of sports cars, boats and airplanes all of wood and silk. Harry's Hobby House at Florence and Western was my second home.

It was around this time that I became aware of, and keenly interested in, the GM Motorama, an auto show, which arrived annually at the old Pan Pacific Auditorium, an art deco showplace perfectly suited to such an extravaganza. The Motorama was a spectacle of the most fantastic designs of the future, incredibly dazzling cars on turning platforms, spotlighted to accentuate their every detail. These cars had phenomenal painted surfaces that were deep and glassy. Beautiful young models used sweeping motions to point out all the automobiles' marvelous features that we could anticipate in tomorrow's transportation. I can still vividly recall the 1951 Buick Le Sabre created by Harley Earl as it turned with its form transfixing my attention. Unknown to me, Harley Earl was the driving force at GM at the time. His sense of sculptural form was pure wizardry. It hypnotized. Here was this magical auto show that engraved me with an excitement and wonderment about detail, form, presentation, and of course, a lifelong love for the automobile. It was at one of these Motoramas that I discovered the Fisher Body Craftsman's Guild competition.

The realization that I could design and build a scale model car of the future and enter it in this competition was my opportunity to enter the Motorama world of dream machines. Southern California was, and still is, a culture of automobiles. Sun, beach, babes and hot rods.

My 1955 design was a glass domed two-door with a low slung form of soft curves combined with defining edges. When finished, my dad built a shipping container for me and we notified the Guild that the family would be camping at Yosemite National Park during the scheduled winner notification period. I made my way to the Western Union office at Camp Curry, Yosemite, each day to get word if I was a winner in the competition. Then one day, in the second week, a yellow telegram arrived: "Congratulations STOP You are the State and Regional winner in Junior Division STOP Please forward your coat size and ring size STOP Will send further details STOP." I was elated beyond belief and overwhelmed with joy. I floated back to my campsite to share the news with my parents and brother.

Upon arrival in Detroit, we were received with major hospitality. There were banquets, a tour of General Motors and the new automotive design tech center. We were treated like celebrities. Entering the studios at the center, we viewed unbelievable auto designs rendered full-size in airbrush side profiles, and front and perspective presentations. There were the scale clay models as well as full-size clay mockups of future automobile designs. It was exhilarating! One day we were taken to see the rows upon rows of models made by other boys who entered the competition. Then came the big banquet. The moment was electric as the orchestra played background while the final scholarship winners were announced in a national radio broadcast. My name was not among them, but I already felt a winner and was ready for the next year's contest.

Important information was available from those in the know. It was made clear that any innovative design could become a grand prize winner, and also clear that an open sports car design had a greater chance of capturing the attention of the judges. So now I had a design brief from which to plan.

It was at this time that Bill Moore and Art Russell entered the scene by paying their own way to Detroit to participate in these festivities.[35] It was their effort to gain insight into what made for a winning model. They were older by enough at the time to make them seem to me much more mature. I looked up to them and listened to their questions of the officials. They were savvy guys on a mission of discovery. They were determined to win the top prize.

The next year (1956) my assignment to myself became to design an open roadster sports car. And again, I went at it with passion. Drawing after drawing, idea after idea, I had to get it right, then build it. That year I was the first-place state California and regional award winner, junior division, and rode the train from Los Angeles to Detroit with Bill Moore for the Guild convention. There was the expectant tension at the banquet table as I waited for the names of the top winners to be called. This time I won third place among the top national winners, junior division.

This win set the course of my life. I would be a designer. I truly now believed anything was possible, if you put yourself into it. I was 15 years old. So after high school I decided to study architecture and industrial design at the University of Southern California. It was an education that addressed problem solving, and in looking back, I made a good choice. I married my high school sweetheart, Alice, and after 42 years of marriage, three children and four grandchildren, it has been and continues to be a wonderful ride. We now live in Carmel, California, where we are completing building a new home and design studio. Though automobile design was not to be the road of travel for me professionally, it helped set the course and train my eye to recognize good design and hopefully produce it myself during my career.

Richard R. Sylvester

1956 Styling Scholarship, $1,000 Award, and 1957 Third-Place National Scholarship, Senior Division, $3,000 Award

Richard R. Sylvester was born in Newton, Iowa, on January 10, 1938. He built model cars for the Fisher Body Craftsman's Guild for five years, finally winning a styling scholarship in 1956, and a third-place national award in 1957. He attended Art Center School (now Art Center College of Design) during the spring of 1957 and worked for General Motors Styling during the summer of 1958. Since then, his education and professional focus has shifted from art and design to mathematical economics.

Now, with an MBA from the University of Southern California, a JD in law from Loyola University, a Ph.D. from UCLA in management and economics, and postdoctoral studies in electronics, he specializes in the application of mathematical models to exec-

This beautifully executed design made by Richard R. Sylvester won a 1956 styling scholarship, $1,000 award. Because of their boxy, utilitarian nature, station wagons were difficult to style, and relatively few were entered in the Craftsman's Guild Competition. William Hope (1960 styling scholarship) and Jerome Grunstad (1962 styling scholarship) were among the very few other Guildsmen to win a scholarship with a practical new station wagon design. *General Motors Corporation.*

utive decisions. As a staff advisor specializing in strategic planning, he has served major corporations such as General Dynamics, Lockheed, Hughes Aircraft, TRW and Northrup for the past three decades. He has made presentations to the science advisor for the President of the United States, the Congressional Budget Office, the Council of Economic Advisors and the Defense Science Board. For two decades he has been listed in Marquis' *Who's Who in the World* and *Who's Who in Business and Industry*, and he has been a featured lecturer at several national symposia, including a shared rostrum with former President Ford. He was the primary speaker for the Emmy nominated ABC documentary on defense industry economics.

He has been selected by major law firms, judges, and the boards of directors of many firms as an independent expert on issues involving strategic planning, acquisitions, turnarounds, initial public offerings and valuations. He has testified as an expert witness in economics and finance in Federal District Court, U.S. Court of Federal Claims and California Superior Court. Under contract from the U.S. Treasury Department he has analyzed transfer pricing and corporate valuation issues. His university teaching experience includes UCLA, USC, Loyola University, University of Redlands, Pepperdine University and California State University. His competitive academic awards include grants from the Ford Foundation, General Motors and the federal government. He has authored 14 books on mathematics, economics, law and management. His most recent book, *Calculus for Executive Decisions*, second edition, 2002, is distributed by Amazon.com.

William F. Marks
1957 Second-Place National Scholarship, Senior Division, $4,000 Award
by William F. Marks, August 2003

Winning second place for $4,000 in the 1957 Fisher Body Craftsman's Guild competition enabled me to return to Purdue University (after a year's absence) as a sophomore in mechanical engineering. After receiving my BSME, I became a first lieutenant in the marines and was stationed in Japan and near Los Angeles. During this time of active duty I was able to visit Art Center, which many of the Guild winners attended. In 1964, *Motor Trend* magazine sponsored a car design contest with four full-tuition scholarships to the Art Center School as the top prizes. I was one of the eight top winners in that competition. I used my limited military pay savings to start at Art Center and I majored in product design as well as transportation (car design). Thanks to my family, the GI bill, and being awarded a full-tuition Chrysler scholarship (my last year) I graduated with a BSID — an upgrade from the usual certificate — even though I had not enrolled in the school's BS program. The "Big Three" sent me to interview in Detroit but it turned out to be for engineering positions only. My mechanical engineering–industrial design education didn't fit in any box they had — and they weren't thinking outside of it. But, through the *Los Angeles Times*, I already had an offer from Douglas Aircraft. Aerospace experience appealed and transportation was more than just cars to me. I worked in the new DC-10 interiors engineering and industrial design departments.

The Art Center School recommended two-year stints on your first jobs to gain experience. I began my career, spending about that long at McDonnell Douglas, Long Beach, California; Westinghouse Major Appliances, Columbus, Ohio; Westinghouse Elevator, Gettysburg, Pennsylvania; and Amtrak, Washington, D.C. (where I met my wife, Christine, working in the design department). Plastics, as taught at Art Center by Cord designer Gordon M. Buehrig, was the material of the future and I sought to gain more plastics design experience by consulting full time in the Baltimore and D.C. area for the next six years. Answering an ad in the IDSA newsletter, I was hired from over 300 candidates by the engineering plastics division of DuPont. Experience in aerospace, stress analysis and plastics with my clients, such as Black & Decker, helped. For the next 15 years I worked on the design of new plastic products from Rollerblades to car bodies. Each year I averaged 50 projects and as many visits to firms in the USA, Japan and Europe. A million pounds of plastic sales was generated each year from my involvement in the development of new plastic applications. DuPont offered me early retirement in 1997, exactly 40 years after my Guild win. I'd done it all: from marker pens and the drafting board to the keyboard of the Cray supercomputer. My old transportation instructor at Art Center, Mr. Strother MacMinn (who had approved my entrance portfolio), told me not only did I have a great design career, but I had topped it off by becoming a materials expert too.

I live in Wilmington, Delaware, the home of DuPont, and occasionally visit the old lab to keep up on the new materials and applications. Together, my wife and I will travel the world even more when she also retires soon. She has 31 years at Amtrak, having held a variety of management positions. She earned two degrees, going to night school at the University of Maryland and Johns Hopkins. I attend the program called Life Long Learning at the University of Delaware, taking Japanese, financial analysis, and French horn. The Guild award helped me to start in design, and I continue to pursue my interests along this never-boring path.

Allen T. Weideman

1957 and 1958 First-Place State Award, Utah and
Regional Winner (Region 17—Colorado, Utah, Kansas

by Allen T. Weideman, June 2003

My first interest in art began as a child during World War II. I was fascinated with military aircraft and I enjoyed sketching pictures of fighter planes. My mother was my biggest supporter and would always encourage me. After the end of the war, my interest was drawn to cars that I saw on the road. One summer my father took me to a traveling General Motors Motorama, one of Harley J. Earl's show car extravaganzas. This show provided opportunities to see all their current and future models. While there I saw two GM stylists designing new cars and was mesmerized by their illustrations and drawing techniques. They drew very quickly and were able to create very exciting and futuristic ideas. I knew I wanted to make my career in design and I wanted to be just like those stylists.

I continued sketching cars in my free time. I first heard about the Fisher Body Craftsman's Guild contest at a West Lake High School assembly in Salt Lake City where I was a sophomore. I decided to enter the contest. In the coming months I designed and constructed my first model entry, which won the first-place Utah state award in 1955 and 1956. I went on to win regional awards in 1957 and 1958.

I traveled to Detroit the years I won regional awards to attend the annual Craftsman's Guild convention. I had never been out of state before and I was wide-eyed with excitement. While there I met many individuals in the design industry and was captivated by student work presented in a catalogue from the Art Center School in Los Angeles,

This is the convertible sports car model made by Allen T. Weideman (age 18) which won the 1957 first Utah and regional award. Guildsmen loved convertible sports car designs. *Allen T. Weideman.*

California. From that moment on I focused my dreams on attending that prestigious institution. I knew that design would be my life's work.

A call to the U.S. Army interrupted my plans briefly, but after discharge I applied and was accepted at the Art Center School. I was a struggling student working part-time jobs at night and going to school during the day. I was fortunate enough to receive a full scholarship that began the second year and I remain grateful to this day for that helping hand. What a boost when the scholarship came to my aid.

Art Center was a challenging and enjoyable experience. I met many well known designers and talented students who would ultimately influence my professional career. Industrial design was my major and I graduated in 1966. I felt lucky, indeed, for I had numerous intriguing job offers including ones from General Motors, Philco-Ford, Sylvania, IBM and Raymond Loewy International. It was a difficult choice, but I felt IBM offered the greatest opportunity. I relocated in northern California (the Bay Area) and worked on the IBM 360 System and related programs.

I left IBM to start my own design service and shifted my focus to product packaging design. My projects have presented me with unique experiences and opportunities and my product packaging designs have received many awards from design industry professionals.

I owe much of my success to the valuable lessons I learned from my experiences in the Fisher Body Craftsman's Guild competitions. I learned early the importance of planning and completing a task within a given time frame. I received encouragement from many friends, teachers and associates in the design industry which helped shape my career aspirations. I have great memories of those Fisher Body Craftsman's Guild model car competitions.

I enjoy the P-38 National Association. My lifelong buddy and friend from the Craftsman's Guild and my Salt Lake City high school days is Dr. Gilbert McArdle of Gettysburg, Pennsylvania, who was the 1955 first-place Utah state and regional winner (Region 17 — Colorado, Utah, Kansas).

Terry R. Henline

1957 Styling Scholarship and 1958 Second-Place National Scholarship, Senior Division, $4,000 Award

by Terry R. Henline, September 2002

I was the 1958 second-place national scholarship, senior division, $4,000 award winner. Prior to that time I had built four other models, which had won state and regional awards as well as a 1957 styling scholarship ($1,000 award) from the state of Nebraska (Lincoln), where I lived. I attended the Art Center College of Design in Pasadena, California, graduating with honors and a degree in industrial and transportation design in the spring of 1961.

Upon graduation, I was employed by General Motors Styling (which became General Motors Design) and over the years I held the

Allen T. Weideman (age 16) with his 1955 first Utah award winning Guild model outside in Salt Lake City, Utah. One of Allen Weideman's Guild heroes was Gilbert McArdle, also of Salt Lake City and a 1955 regional winner. Allen Weideman is a product packaging and merchandising expert. *Allen T. Weideman.*

position of chief designer in various studios including Buick, Chevrolet and Pontiac. As a point of interest, the first car created under my total design direction was the very first Chevrolet Monte Carlo for 1970. I was the chief designer in one of the Pontiac studios for 17 years, during which time we created the 1988 Pontiac Grand Prix, *Motor Trend*'s "Car of the Year," among many other designs. I worked on many of the Grand Am models as well during this period.

I was made the director of design for the General Motors Advanced Concept Center in southern California in 1990, where we created a wide variety of concept vehicles. After three years, I returned to Detroit to become the brand design director of all Pontiac design and the director of General Motors truck design activities. I continued in the latter capacity until the late '90s. During my final two years at GM Design, prior to retiring, I was director of Hummer design, a newly acquired brand for GM. The production Hummer H-2 was created under my direction using almost totally math-derived computer aided

Terry R. Henline (age 17) shown at his basement workbench in Lincoln, Nebraska, working on his 1958 scholarship award winning design. Every Guildsman needed an inviolate place to work and dream about winning the competition. Note the Craftsman's Guild bag under the workbench from the previous Guild convention, where Henline won a 1957 styling scholarship. *Terry R. Henline.*

Terry R. Henline of Lincoln, Nebraska, won a 1958 second national scholarship, senior division, $4,000 award with this model. It was carved from a solid piece of poplar wood, with over 80 separate pieces of polished aluminum used for details, and painted a metallic blue. According to Mr. Henline, the model is still in "very good" condition as of November 2002. *Terry R. Henline.*

design techniques. I retired from GM Design in the summer of 2001 after completing a career in automotive design spanning 40 years.

During the eighth grade in Nebraska, I created and built my first Fisher Body Craftsman's Guild model car. Little did I expect I would become an actual automobile designer in the "big city" far away. But we all have visions of what the future may bring and from that point on being a designer was, in fact, my dream. Through five years of experience and model-building with the Guild, I discovered the value of creativity and found a drive within myself to achieve my very best. It was an invaluable lesson and it has served me well over the years.

John B. Di Ilio

1957 Third-Place National Scholarship, Junior Division, $3,000 Award

by John B. Di Ilio

As a teenager I was, of course, a car nut who, entertaining ideas of becoming an automobile designer, graduated from drawing cars in class to designing and executing a Craftsman's Guild car model. But I eventually became an architect, for a series of reasons both comical and ironic.

When I won the junior division regional first-place award, the trip to Detroit and the experience of meeting and talking to real live car designers—and winning a national award—strengthened my conviction that this was the career for me. But on that same fantastic trip I also began to have second thoughts about it.

When we visited the dramatic new GM Tech Center in the summer of 1957 I saw for the first time, in person, real High Architecture. While the complex was built for my favorite subject—cars—I realized I was very interested in those sleek buildings as well. But then there were those cars, and their designers—why, we actually got to meet Chuck Jordan, and saw Motorama show cars just like we had seen in the car magazines, so I was more fascinated than ever by car design. However, some of the practical aspects of the profession began to give me pause.

Stylists accompanying us on our tour bus told of late hours to complete designs on time, the need to take into account many different opinions—of superiors as well as customers—as a design evolved, and finally, the desirability of an engineering education to understand whether design ideas were feasible. But my father was an engineer (he taught mechanical engineering at Penn State, and so his interest in cars was focused under the hood, not on it). But with the naivete of youth I was sure that engineering training would just dilute my design ideas with "practical" concerns. I had also seen articles in car magazines that suggested stylists weren't paid all that well.

But as I looked around State College, I saw architects apparently having fun in their creative work and living well enough to be able to afford nice cars (obviously an important goal!). So I decided to become an architect because—I thought—I could still have fun designing, but make more money, and be my own boss. Neither of these last two goals quite panned out.

Fortunately, other aspects of the architecture profession have proven to be very satisfying, though time pressures and the need to deal with many opinions turned out to be—surprise!—also true in architecture. Building design and construction is a much more customized process than designing and manufacturing a production automobile, though, and consequently using existing building technology is usually necessary to meet budgets and schedules.

From my experience in auto and building design, I would say that car design is the more difficult and constraining of the two. Packaging people comfortably, together with their cargo and the mechanicals to move them rapidly and efficiently, and enclosing it all in an attractive, affordable shape that will sell — and then designing it all over again in a few years — has to be a daunting (if exciting) task. Architecture is fun, but I still get a big kick out of checking out the massing, stance, proportions, surface development, details, et al. of both new and older cars on the street in Philadelphia, where my wife and I take the train to work, saving our car for weekend fun. (Our current car is our second Honda — sorry, GM — although we previously owned a 1973 Opel Manta, a great Chuck Jordan design, for many years.)

For me the Guild experience was a turning point in my life. I had never completed such a complex, self-imposed project before. My parents — and my friends — were surprised that I pulled it off — and on time — but they didn't fully understand how fascinating and exciting it was to me. My father rashly promised me during the car's construction that if I won a major prize he would buy me a car. He made good on his promise: a '52 Chevy convertible, my first GM car.

But the most valuable reward from the competition was self-confidence and self-discipline. For an entire year I conscientiously went straight home after school and worked on my car instead of hanging out with my buddies. (Having blown my first entry attempt, I registered early for the '56–'57 competition and developed my clay study model over the summer before that.) This focus on goals, and the fascination with the process of design (whether cars or buildings), have been lifelong benefits of my experience with the Guild.

Paul Tatseos

1957 Styling Scholarship and 1958 Third-Place National Scholarship, Senior Division

by Paul Tatseos

As was the case with many Fisher Body Craftsman's Guild participants, my first exposure to the competition was a school presentation that explained the model-making process, awards and General Motors' participation. Prior to that I had no idea of what Fisher Body was or that it was a part of GM. Having been born and raised in Boston, which was not a hotbed of the car culture at the time, the idea of Detroit, GM, and the fact that cars were actually designed by someone called a "stylist" who worked for one of the "Big Three" had not entered my mind.

I remember always being fascinated by airplanes, cars and the way they looked. The 1953 Studebaker coupe designed by Raymond Loewy, the 1953 Corvette and 1954 Buick Skylark are strong memories of exciting cars that appealed to me on a emotional basis.

The Guild school presentation opened my eyes to the automobile design process and at the same time to the whole industrial design profession. I suddenly became aware of the fact that most of the products, packaging and architecture I admired were actually designed by people and did not occur spontaneously.

I had some model-making experience at the time, having made plastic and rubber band airplane models, but nothing to prepare me for the skills involved in producing a

Craftsman's Guild level model. My first two attempts were extremely crude, the first being a solid plaster model that probably weighed in at 20 pounds. The second was slightly better, but still far from a "good try."

The event that changed the quality of my models was a visit by one of GM's traveling exhibits that included several Craftsman's Guild winning models. Now I had some idea of the level of finish that was required to win an award and the amount of time and effort it would take. I immediately began to plan my next model.

I dropped the idea of a plaster model because the clay modeling, making of molds, casting of plaster and the inherent problem of achieving fine detail, were beyond my ability. I had no experience with fiberglass and so did not attempt that process. I found a solid clear plank of poplar large enough to make three or four models and started to carve the wood directly from drawings, eliminating the clay modeling process entirely. This was something the *Guildsman* newsletter did not recommend but which I felt would allow me to spend more time on fine detailing. Fortunately my

Paul Tatseos became a GM interior designer and interior studio design chief. Now retired from GM, he is a design consultant. *Paul Tatseos.*

ability to transfer the ideas from a two-dimensional drawing to a three-dimensional hard model was sufficient to produce a state award winning car. This, I believe, was an inherited trait; I had no idea how difficult that process was for most people. I seemed to be able to do it naturally and I give myself little credit for an ability, I'm sure, passed on by one of my ancestors.

My 1956 state award included a trip to Detroit and a visit to GM Styling (now GM Design) and the fabulous GM Technical Center, an architectural masterpiece of the era, which had just opened in 1955. After the traditional environment of Boston, the Technical Center was like stepping 50 years into the future. The visit convinced me that this was where I wanted to be, and that designing cars was what I wanted to do.

Talking to the designers who judged the models, and who also happened to be the people who designed the real cars, was an eye opening experience. Plus, I saw the national award winning models and got an even better idea of what I had to do to achieve that level. Speaking to the GM designers who judged the models also exposed me to the existence of the design schools that I would need to attend if I wished to work for one of the automobile companies. I planned to visit Pratt Institute in Brooklyn and contact Art Center School in Los Angeles and apply to both.

Unfortunately, I did not win a national award in 1956. I did go back home with an even stronger desire to win a national award. Having won a state award exposed my name to some of the other competitors in the Boston area and several of them contacted me and we arranged to meet and discuss the competition. A few of us became friends and one of them won the state competition the following year in 1957.

Since I did not win a 1957 state award, I listened to the radio broadcast of the Guild awards banquet. While my friend did not win a national award, I was surprised to hear my name mentioned as a 1957 styling scholarship award winner. This encouraged me to make another attempt in 1958. I won a 1958 state award and another trip to Detroit.

My visit to Detroit in 1958 was my next to last chance to win a national award. I had applied and had been accepted at Art Center School and had planned to build my next model there if I did not win an award in 1958. Had I known how difficult and home-work-intensive the work at Art Center would be, the thought would never have crossed my mind. The only comparison in difficulty to my first semester at Art Center was my army basic training, although I think I got more sleep in basic. Fortunately I won the 1958 senior third-place national award and could go to Art Center with a clean slate.

Art Center was both an inspiration and a rude awakening. While I thought I was a pretty fair designer at the time, Art Center immediately made me aware of another higher level of skill and ability. Art Center at the time was probably the top school in the country for automotive design; students in my first group of classes included a nuclear physicist who wanted to design cars, plus several Japanese men including a gentleman who was the chief designer for a Japanese company that was planning to sell their cars in the U.S. If I remember correctly, the company's name was Toyota. To a 19-year-old from Boston the mix of young students, older men who were changing careers, foreign students from exotic places and a group of instructors who actually were professional working designers was heady stuff indeed.

Fortunately after graduation I received an offer to work at GM and completed the round trip back to the Technical Center to begin my career.

I still see many friends whom I met at Art Center. Most of them ended up in the automobile industry in one way or another. Others went into other fields, but wherever they are, we were all changed by the time we spent there.

Without the Guild experience I doubt if I could have made it through Art Center or GM. The skills, both physical and mental, that I learned in those Guild years prepared me for the effort required to complete my degree and a 35-year career at GM Design.

In all these years the Guild experience was a solid foundation upon which I could build additional skills and knowledge as I progressed through school and a career, always understanding that perseverance and dedication to a goal will eventually bring success and a feeling of pride in its achievement.

Harrell C. Lucky

1955 Second-Place Arkansas State and 1956, 1957,
and 1958 First-Place State and Regional Winner
(Region 15—Louisiana, Arkansas, Oklahoma; revised 8/2004)

I brought from those four years of competition very important attitudes and world-views that became a core part of my life's values: (1) Never give up; (2) One should always trust the imagination; (3) Doing something well, holding to a high standard, and refusing to accept inferior work are rewards in themselves; and (4) Life exists at its fullest in the balance between art and logic.

During my senior year in Little Rock Senior High School, because of the activities within my local church, I decided to go into church music. That led me to Southern Nazarene University and an undergraduate degree in music education. Having decided on music education, I went ahead for my masters and doctorate in Music from Southwest Baptist Theological Seminary School of Church Music. I then accepted a position in the music department of Eastfield College, in Dallas, Texas, where I am presently working.

I have been director of music at Lakeview Park Church of the Nazarene, the First Presbyterian Church (Dallas) and Preston Hollow Presbyterian Church (Dallas). I was also artistic director and conductor of the Irving Chorale, a large community chorus in the Dallas-Fort Worth area.

I married my college sweetheart in 1962 and we just celebrated our fortieth anniversary. She is a writer and creator of educational curricula for young children, and I have been her musical director and producer, having written and produced 35 albums for children for national publishing houses. We have three children. My love for automobiles has continued. I have owned a 1934 Ford five-window, a 1950 Ford Coupe, three 1960 Austin Healey BT7Ls, a 1963 MGB, several Porshes, a race-prepared 1973 Corvette coupe, and am now happy with my 1992 Corvette coupe. I am a licensed pilot and fly a beautiful Mooney M20J, which my wife and I enjoy greatly.

Kenneth James Dowd
1957–1959 Third-Place State Award and Honorable Mention, Colorado

I devoured every *Motor Trend*, *Hot Rod*, *Car Craft* and *Custom Cars* magazine I could afford to quench my thirst for things automotive. The experience of turning paper sketches into real three-dimensional Craftsman's Guild models was something few others understood, but many admired. There was something very special about designing, carving, sanding and solving shape and form problems and selecting trim and color. I decided at an early age to become an automobile designer.

After a short stay at Colorado State University, I quit to work and save for the Art Center College of Design. It was during this

Kenneth James Dowd was a Guildsman from the Denver, Colorado, area who entered the competition twice, in 1957 and 1959. One model car he made was a third place winner and the other was an honorable mention. Ken J. Dowd became vice president of Teague Aviation Studios, Everett, Washington. Teague Aviation Studios designs Boeing aircraft interiors and occupant packaging. *Kenneth J. Dowd.*

period that I put those Guild talents to work on real cars as I was able to get a job in a body and paint shop. I soon started my own business custom painting cars and when I left to attend the Art Center I had a pretty good business going.

When I started at Art Center, I knew I wanted to become an automobile designer. In the process, I came to realize that I had to become an artist. This was not a title all my peers were comfortable with, but I loved it. I was resolved to spend my life as both an artist and designer. The Art Center experience was just what I needed, as it was an opportunity to devote 100 percent of my time and energy to art and design. However, as all Art Center alumni know, it was also the beginning of a humbling experience.

My chief source of income during school was derived from drawing and painting race cars. I would go to drag races and special events on weekends and go around car-to-car selling my illustration work. I would sell on Saturday, work all night, and deliver on Sunday. Going without sleep was not unusual for an Art Center student. I was soon discovered by some magazines and was able to do a number of front covers, posters and brochures.

I was eventually awarded a Chrysler sponsored scholarship for which I am eternally grateful. I had job offers from the "Big Three," a master's degree opportunity with Chrysler, but being a Ford man to the core, I accepted the Ford offer.

I spent seven years at Ford rising to the position of senior designer. Along the way I had the good fortune to work for Larry Shinoda in the Special Projects Studio.[36] I worked on show cars, race cars and special production cars such as the Boss Mustang and Cougar Eliminator. I was able to develop something of a personal relationship with two of my heros: Bill Stroppe and Mickey Thompson. The highlight of my Ford years was the opportunity to work in Australia for a year. One of the projects I worked on was the Ford Fiera, a simply tooled vehicle for underdeveloped countries that is still being built today in the Philippines some 30 years later.

It's amazing how events shape our lives, or maybe, how our lives shape events. The interest in building and architecture I had as a kid hammering nails on the neighbors' garage, the Craftsman's Guild, the auto magazines, the Art Center College of Design, and finally a job at Ford which would lead to my wife of 32 years, Janette, and two now grown children, Vanessa and James.

The oil crisis and the generally poor economy sent me across country to Seattle to a new job to design VIP aircraft at Walter Dorwin Teague Associates (now called Teague). This opportunity led to the design of two Bicentennial Anniversary Edition Kenworth trucks. These were the first bi-level aerodynamic sleepers in the industry, and I am proud to say that the aero-roof designs are still in production and the original Bicentennial Editions have become something of a collector's item. I am currently vice president of the Teague Aviation Studio, one of the largest industrial design studios in the world, working for one of our oldest design clients, namely the Boeing Company.

William R. Molzon

1959 Second-Place National Scholarship, Senior Division, $4,000 Award

by Bill Molzon, August 2003

I built my first Guild model in 1953, which I think won a third-place Ohio state, $75 cash award. I then won second-place Ohio state awards, $100 cash, in 1954 and 1955.

This William R. Molzon model won a 1959 second national scholarship, senior division, $4,000 award. Molzon pursued dual degrees in engineering and industrial design and started his own automotive consulting firm. *William R. Molzon.*

I started to attend General Motors Institute (GMI) in Flint, Michigan, in 1956 so I took a few years off from the Craftsman's Guild competition. In 1958 I won a first-place Ohio state, $150 award, and then a 1959 second-place national scholarship, senior division, $4,000 award.

After a trip to Detroit and a chance to see a display of the winning models at the GM building, I finally got an idea of the level of workmanship that it took to win. At that time, if you won the Ohio-Michigan region, you were virtually assured of winning a national award. That region, which I had to compete in, was very tough!

I co-opped with Fisher Body Central Engineering in Warren, Michigan, from 1956 to 1960 when I went to GMI and was in the product engineering area. I remember I had a very enjoyable conveyor belt research project, which lasted several months, in the old process development lab. This resulted in an offer to do a fifth year at GMI to implement the results of the research, but by then, the Guild scholarship had made it possible for me to head out to Los Angeles and attend the Art Center School and study transportation design. This, after being exposed to the field of industrial design through the Guild, was what I decided to go into as a career.

After I graduated from the Art Center School, I worked at General Motors from 1963 to 1969 as an exterior designer. I met Paul Tatseos (one of the book's participants) originally at the Art Center School where he was a year or so ahead of me. At GM he was in interiors and I was in exteriors, which were separate design studios. I did see him around the building occasionally and always had a high regard for his design ability and for him as a person.

Without the experience of the Guild, I'm sure I would never have gone into design. The Guild experience gave me the means to pursue a design education at the Art Center School in Los Angeles, and more importantly, I had the opportunity to learn about pursuing a career in the field of automotive design.

My career has been primarily that of an industrial designer, but, particularly in recent years since I started my own design consulting business, I've been able to combine aesthetics with product engineering as part of the services I provide my clients. I have also had the opportunity to work with an engineering consulting firm (in a purely engineering function) in the design of body structures and suspension systems, so I consider myself both an industrial designer and a product engineer. I enjoy both equally.

I have always thought that the Craftsman's Guild was one of the most outstanding educational activities GM ever sponsored (along with GMI of course) and always felt it had an immense payoff for the corporation for developing youth's interest in cars and the design process. I know that, having lived in a small farm town like Huntsburg, Ohio, if it hadn't been for the Guild I would never have found out about the design field and would probably have ended up in engineering in some other field. I recall that when I was at GM from 1963 to 1969, they did a survey of the designers as to whether they had participated in the Craftsman's Guild. Well over 50 percent had participated.

Like the Craftsman's Guild, General Motors Institute (GMI) was another great GM idea. GMI graduates, because of the co-op arrangement I think, tended to be more hands-on engineers and quite a few have been very successful in activities like racing as well as research and development. Also, I think a lot of kids (like myself) were there because the co-op arrangement gave them the means to be able to go to college, so they tended to be highly motivated and serious about their studies.

The Simone Brothers

Gerald, Eugene *and* Anthony,
1958 Styling Scholarship, Junior Division;
Eugene, *1960 Fourth-Place National Scholarship,*
Junior Division; and* Tony, *1961 First-Place
National Scholarship, Junior Division

Gerald "Jerry" A. Simone (Eldest): During my first year at Hope High School in Providence, Rhode Island, General Motors made a presentation about futuristic cars and gave out information about participation in the Fisher Body Craftsman's Guild. Of course, I was always interested in cars, so I thought it would be a great idea and came home that day to tell my dad I was going to build a model car for the Guild. I already had a great deal of skill in building model car and plane kits.

That first model won a state award. The next year my submission to the Guild was a junior regional winner that gave me a trip to the national convention and ultimately a styling scholarship award worth $1,000. I submitted several other designs with each one judged good enough for a regional award, but not a national scholarship award. My last entry in 1962 was a cross between a sports car and a sedan (sports sedan as we know it today) and both the interior and exterior were modeled in great detail, with a simulated convertible top, authentic wire wheels and drop-away interior dash. This design was a senior regional award winner.

Upon my graduation from Bryant College in 1964, Ford Motor Company offered me a job in their styling and engineering Center in Dearborn, Michigan, as their color and design coordinator. I worked there several years, and began taking evening classes in engineering, but in 1967 decided to attend the University of Michigan College of Pharmacy and graduated in 1972.

Since graduation, I have returned to Rhode Island and have worked in various pharmacy departments in both retail and hospital settings. I married my wife Carol (Toppa) in 1970 and we have lived in several Rhode Island communities. My present home is in

This "fast-back" 1960 design by Eugene Simone of Providence, Rhode Island, featured a clear plexiglass canopy and was affectionately named "Vulcan." It won a fourth national scholarship, junior division, $2,000 award. *General Motors Corporation.*

Portsmouth, Rhode Island, and I work at the Eleanor Slater Hospital in Cranston, Rhode Island, as a staff pharmacist. My interest in cars has continued to this day and I have owned several Corvettes, including a 1964 coupe and a 1999 convertible.

Eugene "Gino" Simone (Middle): During my eighth grade year at my local junior high school, Fisher Body had a touring show that made a presentation about the Guild. My brother Gerald had already built his first model car and was on his second, which eventually won him a styling scholarship. I decided to join the competition and after winning a state award in 1958 and 1959, I entered my third and national award winning model car in 1960.

The 1960 design was structured to complement the human body. The driver's area allowed 360 degree visibility around the car, the shoulder area had high head and neck protection not seen in any cars of that era and our attempts to make a clear plastic top were under way. This was a family goal.

In addition, the 1960 model car, named Vulcan, did not have a steering wheel, but instead had two hand controls. It was extremely futuristic for its day, featuring a fastback design and a rear bumper design to absorb collisions. The term "fastback" was first used to describe my model. After a whole new era of production cars came out with that body style, I could only hope I helped influence that design revolution.

Upon graduation from high school, I received a degree from Bryant College in 1964 and Rhode Island College in 1967. I attended officer candidate school in 1966 and retired from the Rhode Island National Guard as a lieutenant colonel after 30 years of service. I had a brief career as a teacher before beginning my current profession as a financial consultant. I have worked for 35 years with Merrill Lynch Financial Group and during that time I was also president of the Rhode Island Association of Investment Firms. I currently live in North Smithfield, Rhode Island, with my wife Debra (a Spanish teacher), and my two children, Francesca (17) and E. Justin (16).

I will always remember the experience with the Guild and how it influenced my life. I still get excited when I see new vehicles and also see how some Guild design ideas I remember from 40 years ago show up in current production automobiles.

Anthony V. Simone of Providence, Rhode Island, won a 1961 first national scholarship, junior division, $5,000 award with this model. It had a clear bubble canopy as well as machined and chrome-plated bevel gears for hubcaps. Using a drill press with male and female molds, Simone made many clear plastic canopies, heating them in the oven, before the perfect part emerged. The temperature and timing had to be perfect for the part to be worthy of a national award. *General Motors Corporation.*

Anthony "Tony" V. Simone (Youngest): I am the youngest of the three Simone brothers from Providence, Rhode Island, and the son of two second-generation Italians who knew nothing but hard work. They wanted more for their sons.

Early in years, I had little or no aptitude for paper and pencil design, but found I enjoyed creating things from clay and wood. I was what you would call educationally handicapped, as reading and speaking were a real challenge for me. School was not easy, but the Guild gave me a creative outlet and the chance to earn a college education. I used the opportunity to compensate for my personal handicaps and graduated with a BA from Providence College in 1967. Next to the 1961 Guild scholarship, that was one of my personal victories. Always on the verge of failing out, I learned from the Guild the value of follow-through, perseverance and determination.

I became a certified elementary school teacher with a passion for helping the low functioning student. I knew all too well the feelings and frustrations of these individuals. Success as a teacher led me to get a master's in school administration. I found myself an assistant principal and then principal. I have been credited with bringing some low functioning schools up to high performance levels. In the late 1990s I earned an advanced degree in school administration and was nominated twice for "Principal of the Year" in New Hampshire.

The three Simone brothers of Providence, Rhode Island, were *(left to right)* Gerald, Anthony and Eugene, seen circa early 1960s. Together they made over 15 model "dream car" designs for the Guild competition and won approximately $10,000 in scholarships and cash. Each of them won a GM college scholarship. Other than Gerald's brief design career at Ford Motor Company, the Simone brothers did not pursue the auto design field. Gerald, Eugene and Anthony became a pharmacist, a financial manager and an international educator, respectively. (Note Chevrolet Impala circa 1959–60 in the background.) *Meghan Simone with permission of Gerald, Eugene and Anthony Simone.*

As an advocate for at-risk students, I developed and piloted alternative methods of education based on the principles of the Craftsman's Guild. You can learn many things using your hands and education comes in different ways to different people.

I had a bimonthly newspaper column on educational issues and was selected by New Hampshire Public Television to host a live interactive program on educational topics twice a month, which was broadcast in four New England states.

I am currently pursuing another passion with my wife, namely international education. I have lived and worked in Cairo, Egypt, and Jakarta, Indonesia, and have studied the various educational systems in these locations. I have been married to Jennifer Patten Swisher for 28 years, who shares my passion for teaching abroad, and we have two daughters, Meghan and Mia.

Two guiding principles are important to me, the first coming from my mother, "Always do your best and the best will come to you," and the second coming from the Craftsman's Guild, which instilled in all of us the ability to dream, to work hard and to be persistent to see a job well done.

Ronald C. Pellman

1960 Second-Place National Scholarship,
Senior Division, $4,000 Award

by Ronald C. Pellman, December 2002

When a Guild representative gave a presentation to my high school assembly in the fall of 1955 the car bug had already bitten me. Having started on my first hot rod, his presentation sold me. I also had experience designing, building and competing with gas powered model airplanes, so I had some relevant modeling skills that I could exploit to advantage in constructing a car model. My first Guild entry was a station wagon molded from fiberglass.

I was working on my hot rod when the call came in July of '56 that I had won a trip to Detroit for first place in New York and Connecticut in the Guild's junior division. I had high hopes for a national award, but they were not fulfilled. At the convention I saw the outstanding levels of design and craftsmanship required for a top award.

For the '57 competition I designed a convertible sports car. Because I had experience with fiberglass, I stayed with that material. Again, I won a trip to the convention, and again, I went no further.

The '58 competition overlapped with my busy senior year in high school so I had to implement time saving measures. I sketched a design I could build using the cockpit section of my '57 model, thus saving some construction time. Starting construction of my '58 entry by sawing the front and rear thirds off of my '57 model was definitely the most gut-wrenching moment in my Guild experience.

The model turned out well and I was awarded another trip to Detroit. My craftsmanship was awarded 198 out of a possible 200 points, but again, a national award eluded me.

In the fall of 1958, I started mechanical engineering studies at Carnegie Tech, so I

Front view of the model made by Ronald C. Pellman (age 16) from Snyder, New York, that won the 1957 first state New York and regional award. *Ronald C. Pellman.*

did not build a car for the '59 competition. The 1960 competition was my last year of Guild eligibility and I wanted one last try. I carved a sports car design from wood in my dorm room.

This model received the 1960 second-place national scholarship, senior division, $4,000 award, and earned just one point short of a perfect score for craftsmanship.

While I was at Carnegie Tech, a Ford Motor Company executive visiting my department dean's office noticed the trophy that Fisher Body had awarded to Tech in recognition of my 1960 award, and asked to meet me. That chance occurrence eventually led to my accepting a position in Ford's chassis engineering organization following my graduation in the spring of 1963.

Soon I was assigned the production design responsibility for all of the steering columns and shift linkages in U.S. and Canadian Ford and Mercury cars. Eventually I was promoted to principal engineer of

Ronald C. Pellman became a Carnegie Mellon University graduate, engineer, entrepreneur, inventor, executive consultant, president/CEO, SCCA race car designer/driver, and author. *Ronald C. Pellman.*

Rear view of the 1957 Guild model made by Ronald C. Pellman. *Ronald C. Pellman.*

advanced vehicle concepts, where my Fisher Body experience helped in my work with the advanced styling studios. While in advanced concepts, I formed the somewhat visionary notion that someday electronics would play a key role in many vehicle systems. To prepare myself, I studied electronics in night school. That led to a position in electronics R&D for a manufacturer of machine tool controls. Although I resigned from Ford, I continued to work with my former Ford group as a consultant. In fact, my consulting relationship with Ford continued for the next 30 years.

Cars have been the central theme of my professional and avocational life. For 25 years I raced cars with SCCA, driving in Formula Ford, and later in Formula Continental and Class C Sports Racing. I designed and fabricated most of the cars myself. I won seven Northeast Regional Championships and finished in the top ten in the 1995 CSR National Championship before retiring from competition in 1996.

In my consulting career I have served as the president of four companies, two of which I founded. I have worked on over 300 new product, new business development, and technology planning projects for leading companies in the US and Europe, many of them in the automotive industry. I have directed numerous seminars on creative problem solving, new product development, and innovation management. I have a broad range of patents and am coauthor, with a former business partner, Gifford Pinchot, of the book *Intrapreneuring in Action: A Handbook for Business Innovation,* published in late 1999 by Berrett-Koehler.

The lessons I learned as a young man competing in the Fisher Body Craftsman's Guild and the creative spirit instilled in me by that experience have been major factors in shaping my whole career.

Stuart Shuster

1960 Second-Place State Award, Kentucky
"Most Earnest" Guildsman, Entering Nine Times, 1952–1960

by Stuart Shuster, August 2003

Stuart Shuster worked at Peter Muller-Munk Industrial Designers in Pittsburgh, Pennsylvania, before taking a position at General Motors Styling. At GM, Mr. Shuster has worked in a variety of capacities including the Corporate Identity Group, the Industrial Design Department, Commercial Vehicle Interiors, the Truck Brand Character Studio and the Cadillac Brand Character Studio.

He has also been involved in the educational relations program at the University of Cincinnati Design School, his alma mater, and he works with industrial design students in an advanced automotive design program. Mr. Shuster is a member of the Alumni Board of Governors at the Design School and in 1998 he received their Distinguished Service award.

Stuart B. Shuster, former GM designer, currently a creative resources consultant and recruiter of innovative design talent for General Motors Corporation. *Stuart B. Shuster.*

Stuart Shuster Guild Entries by Year, Score Sheet Number, Age, Model Type and Award

Year	Score Sheet No.	Age	Model Descriptors	Award (State)
1952	—	12	Balsa wood	— (PA)
1953	—	13	Family sedan	— (PA)
1954	#4916	14	Station wagon	Third State (KY)
1955	#1601	15	—	Second State (KY)
1956	# 701	16	—	Honorable Mention (KY)
1957	# 614	17	Sports car	Second State (KY)
1958	# 994	18	Sports car	Third State (KY)
1959	#4186	19	Sports car	Second State (KY)
1960	—	20	Corvair influenced design	Second State (KY)

[Stuart Shuster must also be an archivist, as he has one of the finest collections of Craftsman's Guild score sheets available. Note the high score sheet numbers #4916 and #4186 for 1954 and 1959, respectively. The score sheet number comes from the consecutive number initially marked on the bottom of each incoming model entry, with a tag or magic marker, at shipping and receiving in Warren, Michigan. Given these score sheet numbers, in 1954 there may have been 5,000 or more models and in 1959 well over 4,000 model entries.]

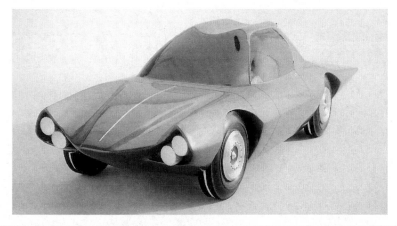

Front view *(top)* and rear view of the Guild model made by Stuart B. Shuster which won the 1960 second state Kentucky, senior division, award worth $100. *Stuart B. Shuster.*

During his early days at GM Styling in Warren, Michigan, Bill Mitchell (V.P. GM Styling) requested design proposals for a series of awards and trophies for a newly planned International Craftsman's Guild. Stuart designed a bronze medallion and a large trophy with sculpted automotive speed shape.

Terry R. Henline, GM stylist, organized an event in November 1980 in which the GM Styling Guildsmen were photographed with Chuck Jordan. This is really an important, momentous "proof of the pudding" photograph *(see page 146)*. Seventeen of Chuck Jordan's brightest and most talented young stylists and designers were present for the photograph: Paul Tatseos, John Folden, Stan Parker, George S. Prentice, Robert Menking, Charlie Stewart, George Gadda, George Anderson, Stuart Shuster, Roy Tiesler, John Wozena, Tom Semple, Kirk Jones, Gordon Brown, Elia Russinoff, Chuck Torner, and Dennis Little. Some of the GM Styling Guildsmen were not present for this photograph.

The classic vintage photograph was recorded in winter 1980–81 at about the same time as interview(s) for a *Special Interest Autos* (February 1981) article about Guildsmen working at GM Styling.[37] The faces in the published article match those in the subject photograph very well. The suit lapels did not necessarily match. Stuart Shuster confirmed that November 1980 was the photograph's date.

Ronald James Will

1961 First-Place National Scholarship, Senior Division, $5,000 Award

by Ronald J. Will, September 2003

I saw my first Fisher Body model in a neighbor's 1955 *Guildsman* issue. I couldn't believe kids created these cars, certainly I couldn't.

But boys back then in Michigan City, Indiana, raced in the Soap Box Derby. I met Derby experts who taught me racing tips. By 1958 I won my local race and headed to the nationals in Akron, Ohio. We were allowed to repaint our racers. So, in the Chevy body shop, at age 15, I mastered the techniques to produce a spectacular, hand-rubbed, black lacquer paint job. In Akron I placed tenth and loved winning. What to do next?

In 1958 we moved to Hobart where GM gave a presentation on the Guild. Now I felt ready for the Guild. I expected to win my first year in 1959, but only won $25. An upper classmate, Brian Skogler (later of Ford Design), was already a regional winner who knew Indiana competition was tough. I had to find Guild experts. So, I wrote to previous Guild winners. I received several detailed letters back. Years later I worked with some of these guys, such as Bill Scott (GM Design) and Bill Molzon.

After completing my 1960 car, my dad took us to the judging in Warren. This is where I learned how to win. In the auditorium I saw a sea of models covering hundreds of tables. Judges at the tables were quietly picking the winners and determining the possible careers of teenage boys. The generous Guildsmen's letters paid off. I won a regional award that year. I didn't win any national awards, but I could sense it.

I picked the brains of design judges Ron Hill, Jerry Brochstein and Emil Zowada. Basically, they said, "Look at the points." The highest points were for creative designs with that "wow" appeal. I had great scores for craftsmanship; I just needed that "wow" car. The answer came at the 1960 Chicago Auto Show. Virgil Exner displayed the futuristic, asymmetrical Plymouth XNR. That was my inspiration to start drawing. I remember

Tom Covert (now of GM Design) and myself at football games drawing cars, ignoring the game.

This car had to be it. In college, I would have no time for hours of filing brass bumpers or molding plexiglass windshields in my mother's oven. The paint job had to be unique. My father's new 1961 Olds had a Twilight Mist option. It was perfect, a silvery color with a hint of purple. I knew I had something, but school finals were eating time. I made a plea to my principal, who allowed me to finish after the model was done. My prom date was not as understanding. I left the dance to put on another coat of Twilight Mist. She never forgave me.

But it worked out. I won regional and traveled to Detroit again. When the picture of my car came up on the giant screen at the Fisher Body (FB) Auditorium as the first-place senior winner, I couldn't believe it. That couldn't be my car up there, that little model I built in my basement in Hobart, Indiana.

Ronald J. Will, Manager of Product Planning and Design, Subaru, contributed to the Outback and Forester designs for the U.S. market. *Ronald J. Will.*

Our school group eventually ended up taking three national awards, a styling award and later several design jobs. I later met my Indiana competition, Geza Loczi (of GM & Volvo Design) and Al Flowers (of GM and Nissan Design). They played a big part in the success of their companies. I ended up at GM and worked in the Corvette, Camaro studio—a dream job. I worked on cars from the late 1960s and 1970s including the Aerovette, the 1978 twenty-fifth Anniversary Corvette, and others.

I still had this itch to design my own car and left GM in 1976. I changed my life, married Pat, who is unbelievably forgiving about car projects, and moved to California. I wanted to build a drivable car with that "wow" factor. The Turbo Phantom ended up being a Honda powered three-wheel design. After our daughter Jessica's birth, I needed to get a temporary "real" job. The temporary job with Subaru has lasted 23 years. I helped create both the Outback and Forester. What's next, another "wow" car?

James W. Green

1961 Third-Place National Scholarship, Junior Division, $3,000 Award, Age 15

by James W. Green, October 2002

It was an advertisement in a 1957 *Boys' Life* magazine that first piqued my interest in the Fisher Body Craftsman's Guild. The great picture of a futuristic model that had won the previous year made me want to try making a design of my own. Four years and four models later, I had won a national scholarship.

Similar to the Thomas H. Semple model, this model by James W. Green, age 15 (1961 third national scholarship, junior division, $3,000 award), is a highly complex design with an amber colored acrylic canopy and hollowed-out, finished interior. The construction details are as follows: Body — balsa wood covered with fiberglass; canopy — amber colored acrylic; trim — chrome plate and aluminum; paint — enamel; and interior — miscellaneous fabrics. Green became vice president of an architectural engineering firm. *James W. Green.*

My first model was a painted combination of balsa wood blocks that generally resembled (not too surprisingly) a '57 Chevy; it won absolutely nothing. My second model was more creative with a large, streamlined, tear-shaped block of poplar wood that today would be considered a minivan. It won an honorable mention in the state of Ohio, which seemed like a real improvement.

After studying other models and construction techniques in the Guild publications, my third Guild entry was a major leap forward in style and materials. Using fiberglass and plexiglass I won a first-place Ohio state award. Unfortunately, Ohio happened to be in the same region with Michigan (Region 10) and those guys from Detroit were hard to beat. Fortunately, Ohio had enough entries that the following year (1961, the year I won a national scholarship) it was made into a separate region (No. 9). This was good because I had fewer competitors, got to go to Detroit for the convention and tour the GM production and styling facilities. But the highlight for me was the awards banquet and seeing a huge photograph of my model flashed on the screen at the end of the hall as a national scholarship winner.

In those days, the scholarship almost paid for my engineering degree at Purdue University. High school physics, the space program and space travel had captured my imagination, so I went into aeronautical and astronautical engineering. But I maintained my ties with the auto industry with a summer job at AC Spark Plug in Flint, Michigan, designing and developing a new type of speedometer.

With both a bachelor's and master's degree in aero/astro, the lure of the space industry led me to a job with McDonnell Douglas in St. Louis developing fighter aircraft control systems and simulators as well as on-board computer software for the space shuttle. I was part of a small group of eight professionals who developed a rudimentary, pilot-in-the-loop, air combat simulator. This achievement was given credit for being critical to winning a multibillion dollar F-15 contract from the U.S. Air Force. The group of eight became an office of 250 in a few years. After the flight simulator projects I became head of an R&D group pursuing computer systems, visual generation and display systems, avionic systems, voice recognition techniques, touch-screen cockpit displays and computer image generation techniques and systems (now known as video games).

After 15 years with McDonnell, my father-in-law finally enticed me to change careers, move to Houston and join his small engineering firm named JKH Mobility Services, Inc., which specialized in automated people movers for airports. I became president of JKH and held that position for ten years until the company was sold. Then I joined a larger architect/engineering firm, Daniel, Mann, Johnson and Mendenhall, which did airport planning and design projects, as Vice President.

The highlight of my life is my family: my wife Ette and our three sons, Brian, Adam and Eric. My sons are all Baylor Bears; Brian graduated as an electrical engineer in 2000 and the twins are juniors with Adam majoring in accounting and Eric majoring in electrical engineering, computer science and pre-law.

Harry E. Schoepf
1961 National Styling Scholarship, $1,000 Award
by Harry E. Schoepf

The winning model was a 1/12 scale, light yellow enamel, two-door convertible. The body of the car was carved from laminated basswood and the bumpers, grille, and tail-light trim were fabricated from aluminum stock. Aluminum tubing was used for the exhaust pipes. The separate windshields (one for the driver and one for the passenger) were hand-formed from 1/16" thick acrylic and bonded in place. The wheel covers were fabricated from large flat washers, large lock washers and steel thumb tacks soldered together and then chrome plated. The seats were made from 1/16" aluminum, cut to shape and bent, then covered with lightweight corduroy fabric. The interior carpeting was a dark fabric cut to fit and installed with contact cement. The steering wheel was heavy gauge copper wire formed and painted. Mr. Schoepf generously donated his model to the National Museum of American History, Smithsonian Institution, Washington, D.C., in 1987 for their permanent collection.

Harry E. Schoepf enjoyed model-making as a youth in Manchester, New Hampshire, and entered the Fisher Body Craftsman's Guild Model Car Competition six times (1957–1962), winning at the state and regional levels. In 1961, at the age of 19, he won a styling scholarship award for excellence in design and a $1,000 university trust fund to the college of his choice.

Mr. Schoepf used his Guild university trust fund to attend the Art Center College of Design in the industrial design program, majoring in transportation design. After his junior year at ACCD, he applied for and won a summer job at Caterpillar tractor company working with professional designers. This led to his first job, after graduation, working in design research and product development at Caterpillar. After military service, he continued to work in the industrial design field at the Royston Company, Hasbro toy company, Raytheon Corporation in Saudi Arabia (which included a special design project for Prince Khalid Bin Sultan of the Saudi royal family), and served as a faculty member at the University of Bridgeport, Connecticut, in the college of engineering.

Mr. Schoepf's hobby has been antique cars since 1966, starting with a 1926 Ford

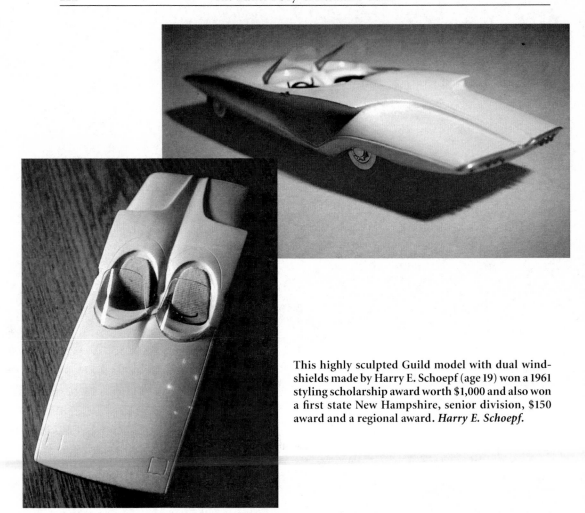

This highly sculpted Guild model with dual wind-shields made by Harry E. Schoepf (age 19) won a 1961 styling scholarship award worth $1,000 and also won a first state New Hampshire, senior division, $150 award and a regional award. *Harry E. Schoepf.*

Touring car given to him by his uncle, then a 1923 TT C cab, a 1921 roadster and a 1913 Ford chassis. These cars formed the nucleus of his hobby of restoring Model T Fords. In 1990 he began seriously to write a book about the 1926 Ford Touring car, but this idea was transformed into writing a how-to book about a ¼ scale model of a 1913 Model T chassis after having acquired the parts from various sources with intentions of restoring it as a companion car to his '26 Touring.

As an industrial designer with engineering-oriented skills, plus illustration, "quick-sketch" and model-making capabilities, the concept of a scale model how-to book combining both his professional and antique car hobby abilities had great appeal. The how-to book he began writing in 1992, about a ¼ scale model of a 1913 Model T chassis, will be complete with three-view drawings, exploded views, photographs, parts lists using original Ford part numbers, assembly instructions and full color illustrations. The idea is to create a scale version of a very historic automobile that is absolutely accurate in every conceivable detail right down to the smallest individual nut and bolt. The ultimate objective is to produce a technical how-to book oriented toward the model-building fraternity so that others can participate in a project that is both challenging and tremendously rewarding.

Harry E. Schoepf, industrial designer, 1913 Model T Ford expert and master craftsman. *Harry E. Schoepf.*

Research for the project, which has been on going for the last ten years, has required the acquisition of authentic 1913 Model T parts from a variety of sources around the country as well as consultations with numerous Model T reference books and the New Hampshire Model T Club. Measurements taken from the full-scale parts are transferred to a computer aided design program (CAD) which is used to create drawings with dimensions in ¼ scale.

Using his hobby machine shop, Mr. Schoepf cuts the parts from scrap brass except for such parts as the steel rear axles, drive shaft, driver shaft roller bearings, bearing sleeves and races, and front wheel bearings. The brass frame parts are fastened with aluminum rivets. The differential housing is fabricated from 18 individual parts and silver-soldered together. Mr. Schoepf breaks the full-scale Ford parts down to their basic geometric shapes on a computer, then creates the separate pieces with his machine shop equipment, and assembles them mostly with silver solder. Hickory spokes for the scale model were made from the hickory spokes of an unserviceable, authentic Model T wheel. Tires were molded out of polyurethane using plaster molds formed from scale wood patterns of the tires.

Mr. Schoepf has a complete hobby-oriented machine shop built over the years from flea market purchases. For example, he has a Waltham watchmaker's lathe, a machinist's toolbox (with micrometers, gauge blocks, and machine cutting tools), a Delta drill press, a Sherline milling machine, as well as grinders and tumblers, to name a few things. Hand filing, silver soldering and other manual operations are often needed.

As of today, the frame, axles, working differential, suspension and wheels, an operable transmission (about the size of the palm of your hand), and radiator (complete with brass tube core construction) has been completed. Work is also progressing on the engine block and all its internal components.

Mr. Schoepf's partially completed, ¼ scale model of a 1913 Model T chassis was the highlight of the New Hampshire National Tour several years ago (1996). Several articles praising his work have appeared in *The Vintage Ford* magazine (vol. 32, no. 4; vol. 32, no. 6; vol. 34, no. 4; and vol. 38, no. 1). Because of this incredible combination of profession and hobby, he has traveled to Dearborn, Michigan, to show his work to Ford engineers. This is all very reminiscent of his traveling to Warren, Michigan, in 1961 to attend the Guild convention and banquet to show his work to William L. Mitchell, Chuck Jordan and GM stylists and designers.

Mr. Schoepf still envisions many more years of work including the building of a body and engine to go with the chassis (and a second book on the fabrication of two or three body styles). No doubt, this is going to be a magnificent model when it is completed.

Patrick B. Saturday

1961 Styling Scholarship, $1,000 Award

by Patrick B. Saturday

Having won a styling scholarship award on my first attempt in the 1961 FBCG competition, I wish I had participated earlier, as my initial entry became my last due to age limitations. That experience, however, is one I shall always remember.

Many times during the almost one-year project, giving up to pursue other fun things was always an option. But as my parents always told me, finish every project you start and you will always gain knowledge from it! They were right. Not only was there the satisfaction of the finished model, there was an award and recognition of my efforts by professional designers and judges.

The night before my model was due in Warren, Michigan, I was still finishing some details, and I worked through the night until 7 A.M. the next day. At that point my parents personally drove me and my entry to Warren, Michigan. We arrived with one hour to spare before the deadline. I slept in the back seat of the car with my model on my lap.

This convertible sports car model made by Patrick B. Saturday won a 1961 styling scholarship award worth $1,000. The construction of this convertible requiring 560 hours was as follows: Roof — clear acrylic dome that was vacuum formed over a plaster model the contestant had made; body — 1" thick laminated, poplar hand-carved with cardboard templates and sealed with three coats of fiberglass resin; paint — 10 coats of lacquer primer and 11 coats of color lacquer (with hand compounded final coat); metal trim — parts made from brass were nickel plated and then chrome plated; wheel covers — made of brass turned on a lathe; taillights — red and clear plastic cut, glued together and buffed to fit; interior floors — felt paper; and dashboard graphics — photographic negative scaled to fit. *Patrick B. Saturday.*

After the service in the navy during the Cuban Missile Crisis, I attended the American Academy of Art in Chicago where I pursued my design talents. I then began my career in graphic design and printing, which has continued for almost 40 years.

I have been fortunate to have won many design competitions, even some national awards, that have taken me to places like Washington, D.C., and Hawaii. Living near and working out of South Bend, Indiana, I was lucky to have been involved in some of the advertising and promotion for the Avanti automobile that was produced there at that time.

I have always been a car nut. Some of the fun cars I've owned include a 1940 Ford, 1957 Thunderbird, 1966 Corvette Roadster and a 1966 Mustang.

The styling scholarship was a personal achievement, but my two children Kelly and Kary are my greatest accomplishments. They, along with our grandchildren, continue to make Barbara and me very proud. In my den are the scholarship certificate, the trophy, and my model car to remind me of the once-in-a-lifetime experience of the Fisher Body Craftsman's Guild competition.

Michael R. "Bobby" D'Mura

1962 National Styling Scholarship, $1,000 Award

by Michael R. D'Mura, September 2002

I had built a number of wooden models by my twelfth birthday when the plans for the 1957 Guild competition arrived in the mail. I began my first car immediately. The first three models were not very good; however, my big break came with the third one in 1959 when I won the junior regional award. It was at the Guild convention that I was able to see what it took to be competitive. Metal moldings and bumpers, cloth or vinyl interiors, and especially a spray paint job were absolute musts.

I won five more regional awards. To me, the trips to Detroit were more valuable than anything else. Being able to see that giant industry where a single plant employed

Rear profile view of the model made by Michael R. (Bobby) D'Mura of Flagstaff, Arizona, which won a 1962 styling scholarship award worth $1,000. This model also won the 1962 first state Arizona and regional senior division awards. Note the partially completed interior (e.g., driver's side interior is completed in detail with a windshield, but passenger-side compartment's outline is indicated by scored lines). D'Mura became a prosthodontist. *Dr. Michael R. (Bobby) D'Mura.*

twice as many people as lived in my town, the design studios, assembly lines, and proving grounds were invaluable life experiences and memories I'll keep.

My final year of the competition was my junior year of college and by then I had decided to pursue a career in dentistry. I also had joined the army reserves and spent my first nine years in dentistry in the active army. I was moved around a lot and even got to visit Vietnam. While in the army dental corps I trained in the dental specialty of prosthodontics. This branch of dentistry involved the replacement of missing teeth and facial structures and is the best place in dentistry to utilize the skills developed in model-making.

In 1978 my wife and I left the active army and moved to Phoenix, where I continued to practice dentistry and also remained in the reserves. At that time I also became involved in my family's land and cattle business. I retired from the army in 1993, but I still practice dentistry and help with the cow business.

As for model-making, I have never stopped. There are over 400 models sitting on shelves in my workshop. They vary from spaceships to submarines. Most are plastic kits, some wood and some scratch built. At present I'm building a desktop wooden model of a Lockheed Constellation (1/96 scale) for a gift and have several other projects pending.

I believe the most valuable attributes a person gained from the Guild competition are perseverance and patience. It has been almost 40 years since I finished my last model car for the competition, but I will never forget the wonderful time it was for me and I'll never forget the generosity shown by General Motors and Fisher Body for giving me the opportunity of a lifetime.

John M. D'Mura

1964 Second-Place National Scholarship, Junior Division, $4,000 Award, Age 13

by John. M. D'Mura, September 2002

Currently I am a professor of science at New Mexico State University at Carlsbad. The fall of 2002 marks the beginning of my twenty-fourth year at NMSU-Carlsbad. I teach physics and physical science. The skills I learned in my three years of the Guild competition and the appreciation of aesthetic design has added greatly to my vocation to teach at the undergraduate level. Over the years I have designed and built hands-on versions of my physics demonstrations.

John L. Jacobus
1961 First-Place State, Maryland, Junior Division, and 1962, 1964, 1965, and 1966 First-Place Maryland State, Senior Division, $150 Awards

The Guild saved my life twice. Before age 11, I was a problem child and very mixed up. There had been calls from the elementary school principal. My mother was on a first name basis with my teachers. The 22-caliber bullets I'd taken in for Ms. Barkley's afternoon Show and Tell had created quite a stir. Because my father worked in the field of vocational-technical education, he brought home the famous *Designing and Building a Model Automobile* manual and introduced me to the Fisher Body Craftsman's Guild. He had me fill out the enrollment card for him to mail the next day. After that I was constructively engaged in life and consumed in understanding what this model building was all about. There was no more time for trouble, bullets or Show and Tell.

My father, Dwight, loved the Guild, and what it represented, as he too had a craftsman's background. At age 32, he had started the Essex Bronze Guild in Essex Fells, New Jersey, and using the vitreous enamel process, made beautifully engraved bronze architectural pieces. I have a picture of him working at a gas kiln with his white lab jacket and I have a price sheet from 1932. He was a 31-year-old entrepreneur during the height of the Depression.

The model made by the author, John L. Jacobus (age 16), of Baltimore, Maryland, which won the 1962 first state Maryland, senior division, award worth $150. The score sheet shows that this model (No. 2566) received 342 points out of 450, or 76 percent. Maryland was part of Region 6, with Delaware, West Virginia, Virginia and the District of Columbia. There were about 10–15 Guild entries from Maryland that year. It is estimated that 4,000 or more models were entered in the Fisher Body Craftsman's Guild competition in 1962. After working at Fisher Body Division in Warren as a design engineer, Jacobus became an auto safety engineer for more than 30 years. *General Motors Corporation.*

The author, John L. Jacobus, automotive safety engineer, technical writer and Guild historian. *Author's collection.*

By age 11, I had shaped one car model from clay, cast one from plaster and carved one out of a solid block of balsa wood that looked like the Coopers' (our neighbors') 1957 Plymouth Fury. (I loved the fins on that Exner designed Fury. They were magnificent!) My father praised these crude attempts including the one I baked in my dear mother's oven; even when the Pittsburgh Green enamel over-spray partially coated the hardwood flooring in my grandmother's bedroom. Over-spray was better than bullets any day of the week.

The second time the Guild saved me came during the Vietnam War. In the patriot division, my family had done its part, with my father's brother Malcolm serving in France during World War I and his sister's sons, Art and Bobby, serving on battleships in the navy during World War II. One of their sons (a cousin) had been a Vietnam helicopter pilot. The New Jersey clan was red, white and blue.

I won the draft lottery in my community under President Nixon and would have been on my way to Southeast Asia, except that I was a Fisher Body employee working at a 12' lofting table at the GM Tech Center in Warren, Michigan. I was working on components for the 1974 and 1975 models. The Fisher Body Division personnel office applied for, and obtained for me, an Occupational Deferment (Classification II-A) and I remained safely at General Motors during the remainder of the Southeast Asia conflict. It wasn't until I studied the Guild in recent years that I came to understand Fisher Body's World War II legacy. You name it, they made it. Fisher Body Division managed 17 wartime plants and made B-25 and B-29 components and subassemblies, light tanks, antiaircraft guns, Sperry and Bendix designed aircraft navigational instrumentation and shells.

I really got involved in the Guild program as a teenager and participated from 1961 to 1966, right into the middle of college. I never won an award above the first-place state level, maybe a few hundred dollars, but have always believed the Fisher Body Craftsman's Guild was a valuable experience.

This author's father, Dwight P. Jacobus, at work in the mid–1950s. As a professional in the vocational-technical education field, he loved the Fisher Body Craftsman's Guild. *Author's collection.*

The real hook for me was my father driving me to Warren, Michigan, to see the 1962 winning models on display in the lobby at Fisher Body Division headquarters. This was an eye opening experience as the models appeared to be made by professionals, not amateurs like myself. The level of perfection and craftsmanship displayed exceeded my experience by tenfold. My observations, at the time, were as follows: (1) painted surfaces were compounded and waxed to a mirror-like finish; (2) every detail was scaled and proportioned exactly — rear view mirrors, instrument panels, stick shift, radio antennas, white walls and hubcaps; (3) symmetry was perfect and the execution was flawless; and (4) metal trim was polished or chrome plated and fitted to the body, inlaid like a piece of Chippendale furniture. The winning models were, without a doubt, works of art suitable for the finest museum New York had to offer.

One model caught my eye. Roy Dickey's 1962 first-place national scholarship, senior division, award winner had "Dunlop 85" in raised lettering to perfect scale, in an arc, on the side wall of the tire. This was hair raising to see.

On the same trip I had been invited to tour the GM Styling studios because I had scored a promising number of points, although shy of the 85 percent needed to be a regional winner. A GM personnel representative sat down and told me about working at General Motors and what I needed to do to qualify. For a 16-year-old this was an exciting experience, but it was a long ride back to Baltimore.

While attending engineering school at the University of Maryland I spent the summer semester (1965) at the Art Center College of Design in Pasadena, California, and studied industrial design. I know my parents made a sacrifice for me to fly out to Los Angeles and spend the summer in southern California drawing cars. But they believed in the Guild too and its promise for a future.

The 1967–1971 design engineering experience carried me into auto safety engineering at the U.S. Department of Transportation (DOT) at the newly formed safety regulatory agency, where I enjoyed a 30+ year career and recently retired.

In auto safety we talked about car and truck safety products and ideas every day. I enjoyed a productive career there and contributed to dynamic side impact protection regulations for cars and light trucks, school bus safety regulations, upgraded rear impact guards for "under ride" protection on tractor-trailers, upgraded upper interior head protection on passenger cars, the reformulation of frontal air bag regulations, and heavy truck antilock effectiveness studies. I especially enjoyed working with industry as the recent new technologies for side and head air bags emerged. I believe front, side and head air bags have tremendous life saving potential. I've always felt that my 30+ years of public service with DOT, saving lives with auto safety public policy, more than made up for my lack of military service.

Robert E. Davids

1963 First-Place National Scholarship, Senior Division, $5,000 Award

by Robert E. Davids

I became very interested in model airplanes at age eight and model cars at age ten. At age 12, living in Venice, California, I fell in love with the pinstriping on cars so much so that I asked my dad to buy me a kit from a car magazine. I practiced on the flat freezer every night for a year, then started painting bikes, helmets, cars, or anything for free just to look at the stripes. This led me to spray painting helmets candy apple, and cars at age 14. I also started making foam and fiberglass surfboards that year. This combination led to drag racing as my next-door neighbor was John Peters, owner and builder of the now-famous Freight Train. All this led me to a job with Craig Breedlove and his Spirit of America, where I met Bill Moore and Art Russell. Both Venice High grads had won first place in the Fisher Body competition in 1956 and 1957, respectively. I was a 1961 Venice high school graduate.

They both told me I was a natural and should enter the Guild competition. I did a little research and decided to enter. They encouraged me to write to as many former winners as possible to get their input on how to win. I got overconfident and declared to my mother that I was going to win. It took me 11 months to complete the model car and I gave up everything except my music (I played trombone in a symphony). No dates, parties; nothing except the model. I had false starts. I knew I was capable of building a winning model, but I underestimated the importance of design. Bill and Art gave me input and a lot of encouragement. I actually built most of the car in Art's shop in his garage. Their input and critiques were most helpful, but they insisted that I had to do the work myself. I sent the model to GM on June 3, 1963, and then went to Bonneville Salt Flats, as I was part of the Craig Breedlove land speed record team.

I received a telegram from the Guild (July 16, 1963) stating I was a first-place state

On his first attempt at the competition, Robert E. Davids (age 19) of Mar Vista, California, won the 1963 first national scholarship, senior division, award worth $5,000. Some construction details are as follows: Body — yellow poplar; trim — chrome-plated brass; greenhouse — vacuum formed plexiglass; interior — completely detailed and finished; and paint — original color called platinum pearl green. This model required 1,000 labor hours over 9 months to complete with 4–5 months spent in the clay design stage. The magnificent chrome wheels, with 12 fins each, were assembled as brass parts in a machined aluminum fixture and silver-soldered to a brass hub and rim. The hub was an allenhead crew and the outer rims were turned on a lathe. The complete chrome-plate job cost $4.50. *General Motors Corporation.*

California and regional winner (former winners said that I would be a scholarship winner if I was notified by telegram). Because of the land speed record attempt, I was not going to attend the Fisher ceremony in Detroit, or so I thought. GM called me and insisted that I attend. GM sent me detailed instructions on getting to Detroit, and an airline ticket.

The second day of the Guild convention, I was taken aside and asked to take a private ride to GM Technical Center. There, I met William L. Mitchell and began a long friendship. We called Breedlove to see how each day went. (On August 5, 1963, Craig Breedlove and the Spirit of America set the land speed record at 407.45 mph.) To my amazement I actually won the top national senior division prize in the Guild competition, worth $5,000. I had thought at times I would have to eat crow after what I said to my mother. I returned to the salt flats and we set a new record that year.

I returned to Venice and with the help of Art Russell I landed a job at Revell as a master modeler. I wrote a magazine article for *Model Car Science*, February 1964, about my success and was invited by the GM Management Club to be a speaker at three different meetings. What a blast to tell my story in large crowds.

In December 1963, I received a call from Bill Mitchell saying he wanted to have lunch at the Irisher Restaurant on Third Street in Los Angeles. We met along with "Tink" Adams, owner and founder of Art Center School, Jorge Jergensen, and Strother MacMinn. Mitchell wanted me to start at the Art Center School studying automobile design the following week. Tink said, "No way," as "we have entry rules." Mitchell won. I started at the Art Center School in January 1964.

The following three years were the toughest of my life, but I graduated with honors in September 1967. Tink doubled my workload to prove to Mitchell that he had made a mistake. I nearly died from lack of sleep, but finished tops in the transportation industrial design curriculum (called the "Trans" department).

GM had been in touch with me all through Art Center (the school changed its name during my sixth semester in 1966 to Art Center College of Design). Although car companies were not hiring that year, GM hired me, and I met great people including Harley Earl. I was promoted to be the designer in Studio X, Mitchell's private playground. Bill Mitchell put me through management training school at night.

I was working on the XP893 when I received a call from Bill Moore, who now was with Bill Lear in Reno, Nevada. He asked me to join Lear Motors. (The Lear Jet, Lear Steam Car and eight-track stereo were some of Bill Lear's accomplishments among many innovative ideas.) I joined Lear in January 1969. In 1970 I started my own design company, DISC, Inc., and worked for many companies including a small toy slot machine company.

I stayed with Lear until the middle of 1972 then went on my own. I struggled, but the company grew and in 1978 I sold out and went with a start-up company that is now the largest gaming company in the world—International Game Technology. I got to name the company and design the logo and many other products. IGT paid my way through Cal Tech's Management/Leadership Masters extension program. I was an apprentice to a great man named Sy Redd and I met the great management book writer, Bob Townsend. Bob's book *Up the Organization* changed my life. I was going to be a leader. I left IGT in 1984 and I took a year off. I was married with two daughters. October was my first trip to Hong Kong as a design expert.

I became a partner to a casino in September 1984 and continued to work for the small toy slot company. I left the casino at the end of 1987 and went to Hong Kong to help the small slot company (I had designed all of their products). They were in trouble and asked me to consult for six weeks while they went to Europe to make sales. I became general manager and an equal partner in 1988 and I ran the company. While with IGT, I noticed how people were drawn to the electronic poker games we made for TV screens.

I invented a small version that would fit in your hand and would be a portable adult entertainment toy. Our small company started to grow, from 8 people to 7,200. We took Radica Games public in 1994. I was now a chief executive officer. We had ups and downs. During one down period many other toy and game companies were copying us. I invented a small hand-held game that would revolutionize hand-held electronics: Bass Fishin'. You could cast, troll and fight a fish. This game became the highest profit-making electronic game in Wal-Mart history, and Radica Games did well also.

After 12 years living in Asia, I resigned my CEO position to be vice chairman and start a new business that was my passion. I started a vineyard in 1998 and a winery in 2001 that grows and produces world class Pinot Noir wine. I named the company after the marine layer of fog that covers the vineyard at night — Sea Smoke. I am now semi-retired and live six months a year in Bahamas, fishing and boating. I also consult for companies.

I can truly say that winning the Fisher Body Craftsman's Guild was the turning point in my life, and I am sorry that it is not with us today. While at Art Center I influenced two Guild winners: Bruce E. Claypool (1967 styling scholarship winner at age 18) and David C. Goelz (1967 first-place national scholarship, senior division, $5,000 award winner at age 20). In more recent years, David C. Goelz played "Gonzo" on the Muppets.

My 1963 winning car resides with me in my home in Reno, Nevada. Venice High was a magic place in the 1950s and 1960s, the movie *Grease* was filmed there; that about explains it all!

The Pietruska Brothers

**Richard — *1963 First-Place National Scholarship, Junior Division;*
Ronald — *1964 Styling Scholarship and
1967 Fourth-Place National Scholarship, Senior Division;*
Michael — *1965 Second-Place National Scholarship, Junior Division;*
and Robert — *1966 Regional, Junior Division***

Albert and Vera Pietruska of Stamford, Connecticut, were the parents of nine children: five boys and four girls. They owned an upholstery shop and all of the children grew up working there from an early age. Many say they grew up with hammers in their hands. They all learned craftsmanship, quality and how to use the tools of the furniture trade.

Richard, Ronald, Michael and Robert were the last of the nine kids. They were introduced to the Fisher Body Craftsman's Guild contest by their older sister Ellie and her husband Hank Haga, who was a GM designer.[38]

In their first year of the competition, Richard and Ronald were both state award winners. The second year saw Richard winning a regional award and going on to win the 1963 first-place national scholarship, junior division, $5,000 award. In 1964 Ronald won a regional award and went on to win a styling scholarship, $1,000 award. This was also the year that Michael was eligible to enter and he won a state award. In 1965 Ronald moved into the senior division and won a regional award. Michael also won a regional award that year and went on to win the 1965 second-place national scholarship, junior division, $4,000 award.

Ronald continued to enter the contest for the next few years, culminating in a 1967 fourth-place national scholarship, senior division, $4,000 award. The youngest brother, Robert, was a regional winner on his first try in 1966 at age 11, but unfortunately, the contest was discontinued soon after.

Growing up in the family business was a great help to their model-making skills and having each other for advice and

Ronald E. Pietruska (age 18) of Stamford, Connecticut, won the 1967 fourth national scholarship, senior division, award worth $2,000 with his Open Competition design. Construction: fiberglass, lacquer finish, aluminum wheels and bumpers. Ronald studied at Pratt Institute and went into the museum and exhibit design field. *Michael A. Pietruska.*

Michael A. Pietruska (age 12) on the left places his award winning model in the Fisher Body display case at the General Motors Futurama Exhibit at the 1965 New York World's Fair. On the right, his brother Ronald E. Pietruska (age 16) was a senior regional winner that year. Michael was awarded a 1965 second national scholarship, junior division, $4,000 award. *Michael A. Pietruska with permission of General Motors Corporation.*

guidance was also very important. Each child in the Pietruska family has benefited from this upbringing. In their own right, each has attained success in varied creative lives. Quality craftsmanship is something each family member is known for in their respective fields, just as their parents were in their upholstery business.

Richard used his scholarship trust fund to attend the Art Center College of Design to study industrial design. He branched out in his studies, earning a master's degree in fine arts from the ACCD. He became an instructor at ACCD and is so today. He has also become a recognized fine art automotive sculptor and illustrator. Ronald received his degree in industrial design from Pratt Institute and has worked extensively in the museum and exhibit industry on many major projects in his career.

Michael attended ACCD, receiving a degree in environmental design. He has worked in the office furniture industry, as an exhibit designer and as a toy and game designer for Milton Bradley. Robert decided to continue in the upholstery business and has been very successful at it.

Chances are you or someone you know has seen and enjoyed one of Richard's sculptures or illustrations, has been to one of Ronald's museum exhibits, has enjoyed one of the games Michael has done, or is sitting in a finely crafted piece of upholstered furniture done by Robert.

In each of their careers, the model-making experience with the Fisher Body Craftsman's Guild has greatly influenced the Pietruska brothers and really helped shape who they have become. Each continues to build models as part of their design experience, to effectively help convey any idea they need to get across. They are very proud of their accomplishments with the Guild as individuals, but mostly as a family. It was really a thrill to be that successful in such a competitive contest. It was a great contest and a turning point in their lives.

Richard Ray

1962 Honorable Mention, 1963 Regional Winner, and 1964 Styling Scholarship, $1,000 Award

by Richard Ray

Growing up in the Detroit area, I was always interested in cars. Most family and friends worked either directly or indirectly for one of the "Big Three." I was continually building and customizing plastic 1/24 scale model cars. I was vaguely aware of the Fisher Body Craftsman's Guild, but became instantly interested when a Guild representative came to my high school and made a presentation on the program.

Although my father was strict about the rule that I had to build the car myself, he helped through every step of the process using his mechanical skills. He was probably somewhat skeptical about how serious I was about completing an FBGC model, since the first model was made from a scrap piece of 2 × 6 found behind the garage. After rough shaping, the wood was covered with fiberglass resin for the final surface. The model was painted with acrylic lacquer (paint quality became the highest scoring area of all my cars). The first car took a 1962 honorable mention in the state of Michigan and I was thrilled.

Since I lived only a few miles from the GM Technical Center, I was able to visit the judging site to see the quality of the competition first hand. I still believe this was a huge advantage in subsequent models.

Richard Ray, director of commercial vehicle marketing and planning, DaimlerChrysler Corporation (retired). *Richard Ray.*

The second car was initially sculpted in clay and a plaster female cast was made from the clay pattern. Fiberglass resin was used in the mold to form the body. Since I chose an open roadster design, I faced the challenge of forming a full interior as well as clear windshield (a piece of broken boat windshield provided the raw acrylic plastic). Trim was formed from aluminum and polished to a bright finish. The result was a 1963 regional winner for Michigan and a trip to the annual Guild convention.

Since I lived in the Detroit area, I was deprived of an airplane ride to the convention. However, being picked up in a chauffeur driven Cadillac did impress the neighbors. The convention was a dream for a 16-year-old car freak. The visit to GM Styling and a talk by Chuck Jordan was the highlight. This was complemented by talks with other GM designers who accompanied us on various parts of the trip. The enthusiasm generated by the week resulted in me being wide awake at 2 A.M. sketching ideas for the next Guild car. The comradeship of a large group of young men with similar interests was great.

My third car was built using techniques similar to the second, although I used Bondo for the base material since it more easily accommodated subsequent patching. It was a closed coupe to avoid the time and labor associated with fabricating a clear windshield and an interior occupant space. Although I had moved up to the senior division, I was still disappointed when I won a second-place Michigan state award and did not get to return to the convention. However, the model car design did win a 1964 styling scholarship, $1,000 award, for excellence in design.

A fourth car was started but not finished due to school activities.

As a result of winning a styling scholarship with my third car, I received a letter from GM Styling inviting me to visit. I grabbed this opportunity and told them that I wanted to attend GMI and be sponsored by GM Styling. The application process was lengthy, but my FBCG experience was critical in successfully obtaining the needed GM Styling support. They understood that the techniques I had used to build my models were the same ones they used to build full-size cars in their studios.

My career since then has remained in the automotive product development area with General Motors, American Motors and now DaimlerChrysler AG. After stints in product planning on projects such as the Jeep Grand Cherokee and Dodge Ram, Dakota

This model made by Richard Ray of Detroit won a 1964 styling scholarship worth $1,000. Richard attended General Motors Institute, contributed to marketing studies for the new 1990 AMC Jeep and became director of commercial vehicle marketing and product planning for DaimlerChrysler AG. He is now retired. *Theodore A. Becker.*

and Durango trucks, I am now director of commercial vehicle marketing and product planning. This involves defining future products that customers will want to buy and is the kind of job I visualized during my FBCG days. Also, I am interested in old cars and have a 1964 Pontiac GTO and a 1930 Packard Touring.

David P. Onopa
1963 Honorable Mention, Junior Division;
1964 Regional Junior Winner;
1965 Third-Place State Senior Division; and
1966 Senior Regional Winner from the State of Pennsylvania

Born in Reading, Pennsylvania, I had a fascination with motor vehicles almost as far back as I can remember. In 1963 at the age of 15, I entered the Fisher Body Craftsman's Guild annual design competition for the first time. After winning an honorable mention, I was encouraged to pursue this interest further. The following year, I was a Regional winner of the annual design contest in the junior division, and then again in 1966 in the senior division. Although I never quite managed to win one of the top national awards, it was through my exposure to the GM Styling design studios during the national conventions in Detroit that I became aware of industrial design as a profession, and specifically of the Art Center College of Design as a educational alternative.

I was enrolled at Penn State University studying mechanical engineering with the idea that this would be a good foundation for an eventual career in design, but after a year and a half, it became clear that I was simply forestalling the inevitable, so I transferred to Art Center, where I had the great fortune to study under the likes of Strother MacMinn and Gordon M. Buehrig; I was awarded full scholarships from Ford and General Motors, and finally graduated with honors in early 1970.

My first experience in the professional world came at Porsche AG in Stuttgart, Germany, where chief designer Tony Lapine hired me to join the exterior design studio. This proved to be an invaluable experience both professionally and personally for the next two years, during which time we worked on concepts for the 928 and 924 models. The true value of having gained international experience at such an early age was something I didn't fully appreciate until years later.

In 1972, I moved back to the States to work for Chrysler Design in Highland Park, where I was assigned to the "B" body exterior studio. We worked on a variety of Chrysler, Dodge and Plymouth models including the first Chrysler Cordoba. However, the very difficult times resulting from the 1973–1974 oil embargo led to massive layoffs in the auto industry and particularly at Chrysler, which eventually affected me; this is how I found my way back to Pennsylvania and Mack Trucks in early 1975.

The Mack Trucks situation proved to be a very good fit for my design orientation in that the vehicles were very functionally based. In a number of ways, it was similar to the experience I had in Germany at Porsche; very much an engineering-oriented atmosphere.

When Mack Trucks was acquired by Renault SA in the early nineties, I once again found myself part of a European design organization. This one was led by Patrick LeQuement, V.P. of design at Renault DDI in Paris. This influence was very healthy and invigorating for our group in the U.S., as it gave us the energy of another viewpoint and exposed us to the latest techniques and technologies of one of the most vibrant design organizations in the auto industry.

Most recently, in early 2001, Volvo AB completed the purchase of Renault's RVI Truck unit including Mack, which has resulted in our current organization. We are now a four-studio product design group: Volvo Trucks (Gothenburg), Renault Trucks (DDI Paris), Volvo Trucks NA (Greensboro, N.C.), and Mack Trucks (Allentown). This new company now is the world's second largest truck manufacturer.

For the past 27 years, I have been involved in the design of virtually all Mack products in some way or another. Working for an American institution like Mack has been an infectious experience; it has presented me with many challenges and rewards along the way. But the prospects today, with the new opportunities we see, make this as exciting a time as I've had in my career. The Fisher Body Craftsman's Guild design competitions, and the experiences that it provided for me, became a critically important influence on my choice of a career in design.

Rowland Kanner
1964 Styling Scholarship, $1,000 Award
by Rowland Kanner

During the period of 1960 to 1961 my older brother had obtained literature from the Fisher Body Craftsman's Guild, but his true interest at the time was aircraft and not

This model designed by Rowland W. Kanner (age 17) won a 1964 styling scholarship, $1,000 award. Some construction details are: poplar wood body, aluminum bumpers, plastic lights, silvered brass trim and metallic GM lacquer paint called "Lagoon Blue." Window trim was made from HO guage railroad track plated with silver using a silver nitrate rubbing formula. Vacuum-formed wheelcovers wore silver metallic paint. The model required 400 hours of labor. Kanner became vice president of technology at Atrion Medical. ***General Motors Corporation.***

automobiles, so the information accumulated on a workbench in our basement. At that time, I was fascinated by anything having wheels and a motor, and could identify the year, make and model of almost every car on the road.

For my parents this fascination with cars was both a blessing and a curse. When I wasn't out on my bike or over at the farm next door, they knew they could find me working in the shop. Actually, they often didn't need to see or hear me to know I was working on a model since the noxious spray paints I used, which gave such a superior finish over brush paints, smelled up the whole house.

Upon entering high school, my interest in cars and the magazines dedicated to them started to shift away from the vehicles in *Hot Rod* magazine toward those in *Sports Car Graphic*, where total performance was combined with flowing body forms. I was inexplicably drawn to the beautifully styled foreign sports racing cars from companies named Ferrari, Porsche, Jaguar, Lotus, Alfa Romeo, Maserati and the numerous specialty makers that produced those slick aerodynamic, knee high sports cars.

That was about the time I spotted the Craftsman's Guild literature my brother had left lying on the workbench. The literature showed a broad range of contestants' cars and some of them were remarkable in their freedom from contemporary conventions. As I unfolded the Guild's rules sheets and dimensioned outlines showing wheel sizes, wheel placements and passenger placements, I realized that here was a chance to combine my budding design and styling skills along with my model-building talents to compete against others for something really significant — a chance at a college scholarship.

Work on my first entry in the Guild was started in 1962 for the 1963 competition. Numerous sketches were prepared showing a variety of design possibilities. From these sketches a coherent design began to emerge and in time, the car I wanted to build started to take shape on paper. From this I sketched and refined views of the side, front, rear, top and bottom in 1/12 scale. A material to make the model then needed to be chosen. After reading all the handy how-to tips available in the Guild literature and reviewing material choices of rigid polyurethane foam, wood or plaster, I started my first model in plaster since wood sounded hard to work, I knew nothing of rigid polyurethane foam and I'd already had some experience with plaster. Plaster was cheap and I already had some on hand. I created a block of plaster, transferred key points, axle locations and prominent style lines to the block and began cutting, carving, sanding and filing to make the various views meld together. After the passage of several weeks and the creation of an enormous amount of white dust that settled upon everything in the basement, my first design became a three-dimensional form.

After several months the model received its final lacquer finish by spray can, wheels and hubcaps were affixed, bumpers were mounted and the taillights were finally installed. Having worked so long on this model, I knew every defect and each detail I would have liked to improve upon, but my time was up and although I felt reluctant to do so, I knew I had to send it in. A stout shipping case was built from ¾" plywood, into which the model was packed and then taken to the railway station to be shipped to General Motors by Railway Express. I figured I had about 250 hours invested in this project. It was a long summer, waiting to hear whether all this work would be rewarded.

My second design was less inhibited by conventional thinking and thus much "further out" than the first one. Wood actually proved easier to work in many respects. It was easier on the tools and far less gritty and dusty. New bumpers and taillights were again formed of the same materials as the first model, but they were much better formed. Since I wanted a thin "chrome" strip to delineate the roof edge, I shaped pieces of HO gauge track rail to fit into the window edge groove and then plated the part with silver using a silver nitrate rubbing formula found in a chemistry book. Hubcaps this time were vacuum formed using a borrowed toy vacuum former and a pattern I'd made. These caps were then painted with metallic silver paint. I remember selecting a metallic GM color for this car, Lagoon Blue, which seemed to enhance the visual impact of its shape. In the end I had put over 400 hours into this one and I felt very good about the result. Perhaps due to all the effort I'd put into this model and my intense concentration upon getting it right, I can still remember the morning my grandfather drove me to the Railway Express office to ship it off. There was relief in having completed the job well, excitement about the prospects offered by a new contest and some sadness in having to let go of my creation. This summer seemed to last longer than the previous one.

In time, I received a letter from the Guild informing me that my efforts were to be rewarded with a $1,000 styling scholarship. I was pleased with the outcome but wished I had done better. Another design was already in progress at that point and although I was not too old to compete again, I was scheduled to begin college that fall and simply would not be able to devote the necessary time to complete another model. Efforts put into sketches of this new design were not entirely wasted, however, since I kept them posted at my desk for inspiration throughout my freshman year.

The college scholarship I received through participation in the Craftsman's Guild assured a strong financial start to my formal education. What might not have been as obvious at the outset are the benefits of the discovery and self-education that accrued during participation in the Guild program itself. These informal lessons have often proved to be quite valuable in my pursuit of various personal and professional endeavors. Ultimately, the manual skills learned, the sensitivity to line, form and proportion that was gained, the discipline of solving problems in three dimensions and learning to dedicate myself to completing an extensive intense project, turned out to be just as beneficial as the scholarship award itself.

[Author' note: Mr. Kanner donated his 1964 styling scholarship model to the National Museum of American History's permanent collection.]

Theodore A. Becker

1964 Third-Place State Award, Illinois, Senior Division, $50, and
1965 Second-Place State Award, Illinois, Senior Division, $100

As a teen on a visit to the University of Illinois with my father I saw a display of industrial design students' models. It is easy to say this was the biggest influence for me wanting to be in the industrial design profession.

My father's influence promoted my participation in the FBCG. The first year I did not get my car completed in time. The next year my car placed third in Illinois. The next year was my last year of eligibility and one of two cars I entered won the second place Illinois state award.

Following high school I started university at the local community college and eventually transferring to Northern Illinois University. Uncle Sam then wanted me to serve the country, so I enlisted in the navy (1968–1972).

At the end of my navy tour, I returned to Illinois and entered the University of Illinois at Urbana/Champaign. In 1974, continuing to use my veteran's benefits, I started graduate studies at the Rhode Island School of Design, then transferred to North Carolina State University where I finished my master's degree in product design.

I then entered the design profession, working for a mix of consultant design studios and corporate design offices, working on a variety of products ranging from popcorn makers to electronic medical equipment (none in the transportation design field).

I have been working the past 16 years for a major appliance manufacturer, and as a designer and design manager the last six years in east Tennessee. Some of the products I have designed have won design awards. Fifteen utility and design patents have been issued with my name on them, and several others are pending.

I have been active in the Industrial Designers Society of America (IDSA) since I was an undergraduate student, and have held multiple offices including the chair of the Florida and the Tennessee Valley chapters. I am currently the treasurer for the Tennessee Valley Chapter and, concurrently, the treasurer for the multiple chapter Southern District.

"Exploring the world around us" is the way I describe non-work activities. I am a certified open water SCUBA diver and have a private pilot's certificate. Land travel is where I do most exploring, even though this may include standing in water, fly casting, or looking for a small white ball in a variety of locations.

John M. Mellberg

1966 Second-Place National Scholarship, Senior Division, $4,000 Award

by John M. Mellberg, September 2002

My first introduction to the Fisher Body Craftsman's Guild model car competition was through an ad in *Boys' Life* magazine when I was in the third grade. My first Guild entry, which earned a second-place Illinois state award ($100), was in 1961 when I was a sophomore in high school. Prior to 1961 I had built many static and flying model aircraft, as well as plastic car models, which was helpful experience prior to designing and building my first Guild model entry. Also, during this time I drew cars and was constantly competing with a friend for best design and illustration. From 1962 to 1966, I was the first-place Illinois state winner, and Midwest regional winner, and had the good fortune of winning the 1966 second-place national scholarship, senior division, $4,000 award.[39]

John M. Mellberg, creative vehicle stylist, Thomas Built Buses. *John M. Mellberg.*

My first 1961 entry was shipped to Detroit by Railway Express and arrived damaged. With each entry that followed, my dad, grandfather and I would drive from Chicago to Detroit to safely hand-deliver what I had created. At Fisher Body Division headquarters in Warren, Michigan, we were welcomed by C.W. McClellan, the Guild administrator, or Rolf Amundson, who took receipt of the Mellberg designed models, and we were given a brief tour of the Fisher Body engineering facilities. The tours were wonderful and eye opening experiences and both my dad and grandfather, who had auto industry roots, were very impressed.

With each year that I entered and won a regional award and the associated trip to Detroit, I gained insight and learned a lot by meeting the other regional award winners and seeing their fine models. When the national scholarship winners were announced at the banquet dinner, the best of the models were recognized, and being there to see those models, their standard of design and their exquisite level of craftsmanship, was truly inspirational. Winning the top honors was elusive for me. It took five years of hard work and determination to win a national scholarship award, but it was worth all the effort.

During my senior year in college I was recruited by GM Styling's Roger Martin and Lee Knight, and was offered a job at the Tech Center upon my graduation in May 1968. After four years, I took a position at J.I. Case Corporation as styling supervisor for agricultural tractors and construction vehicles. After 13 years there, and then seven years designing automotive aftermarket truck accessories, I joined Emergency One, Inc. and led the team that designed and developed the first composite bodied fire rescue truck, an innovative vehicle called the E-One Daytona. I'm presently employed by Daimler Chrysler's Freightliner TBB Bus Group, designing new bus vehicles.

Throughout my career I've used the styling disciplines, modeling skills and tools I first learned during my participation in the Fisher Body Craftsman's Guild. I have been

This Guild model constructed by John M. Mellberg of Park Ridge, Illinois, won the 1965 first state Illinois and regional awards. This outstanding model featured a transparent, wrap-around, plexiglass windshield; a complete detailed and finished interior; a louvered backlight or rear window; a leather covered roof; redwall tires (instead of whitewall) and red pinstriping to accent body lines. *General Motors Corporation.*

creating, designing, developing and building vehicles all my life and the thrill and excitement of this is always with me.

The Guild's original purpose and intent remains valid today, despite today's generation not having the interest, patience, nor design or craft skills needed to hand-build a scale model automobile from scratch. I am grateful that my generation was able to realize and benefit from GM's Fisher Body Craftsman's Guild.

Carlyle W. "Mac" McClellan
Former Guild Administrator (1957–1968)
by Ms. Ruth C. McClellan, August 2003

My husband Mac joined the Fisher Body Division of General Motors Corporation, as a field representative in January 1946 after having served in the South Pacific during World War II. Mac's first boss was William S. McLean, who had been the Guild secretary at the time of the first model car competition in 1937. We were both natives of Hamilton, Ohio, and both graduates of Miami University in Oxford, Ohio.

After working in the public relations and advertising department in 1946 as a field representative, Mac was appointed administrator for the Fisher Body Craftsman's Guild in 1957. He served in that capacity until 1968 when the Guild was discontinued. At that time, Mac joined the personnel department of Fisher Body Division.

As Guild administrator, he hired and trained the Guild field representatives, almost all to my knowledge, right after their graduation from college. These people visited hundreds of high schools in the fall each year promoting the Guild. Many of them stayed with General Motors Corporation and others went on to jobs in other corporations and

A 1976 family photograph of Carlyle W. "Mac" McClellan with his wife Ruth Carol Ganter McClellan and their three sons (left to right) Daniel (deceased), William and David. "Mac" was the Guild administrator from 1957 to 1968 and was fondly remembered by Guildsmen as their friend at the Guild conventions. According to the *Petoskey News-Review* (Tuesday, May 6, 1997), "his friends refer to him as *Mr. Republican*, but perhaps a better moniker for Carlyle W. 'Mac' McClellan would be *Mr. Community*." Mac McClellan passed away May 4, 1997, at age 83. *Mrs. Ruth Ganter McClellan.*

advertising agencies, successful in their various capacities. Some of the Guild field representatives at the time were Rand Shackleton, Walter Overhart, Chester A. "Chet" Francke, Victor Olesen and Harry Kelly.

Mac planned every Guild convention and always did so with enthusiasm. He felt that discontinuing the Guild was a big mistake. What better way to develop talent, interest and plans for the future. G. Rolf Amundson, a Guild general supervisor, was my husband's right-hand man. Mac's years after the Guild were in GM personnel matters.

At the yearly Guild convention in Detroit, school superintendents and their wives participated in feting the winning Guildsmen coming from Dallas, Los Angeles, San Francisco, Miami, Chicago, New York, Memphis and Cincinnati, to name a few of the school systems that endorsed the Craftsman's Guild. I still keep in touch with Faye Hall, whose husband Dr. Joseph Hall (deceased) was the superintendent of the Miami school system. Another attendee at Guild conventions was Mr. Robert W. Henderson (deceased), a 1934 Guildsman and Napoleonic Coach national scholarship winner, by the way, who was executive vice president of the weapons program at Sandia Corporation in Albuquerque, New Mexico. I still keep in touch with his wife, Berchie Henderson, after all these years.

Other directors of public relations and advertising in the Fisher Body Division, responsible for the Guild, included William S. McLean, James P. Wines, Joe Hainline and Norman E. May. Joe Hainline was Mac's last boss. Norman E. May was hired by Mac as a Guild staff person and never became the Guild administrator. He later became director of public relations and advertising. The Fisher Body public relations and advertising staff, at the time, included John J. Jendza, Rolf, and Florence "Flossie" Stolman among others.

At one point, Rolf served as the *Guildsman* newsletter editor and the assistant editor, and Johnnie Jendza served with Rolf as the *Guildsman*'s art director.

Flossie is the one who took care of the million and one details in order to make the Craftsman's Guild flow smoothly. She retired from GM with 48 years of service. At age 81, Flossie is still a fully functional Secretary and likes to organize Fisher Body personnel gatherings for retirees. She is secretary of the much larger Fisher Body Engineering Retirees Club.

Mac retired at the age of 62 and we built a retirement home where I still live in Harbor Springs, Michigan. An article in the *Petoskey News-Review* ("Friends Recall 'Mac'") gives an idea of how he spent his retirement. I doubt any man found his retirement more gratifying and how fortunate we were to share those 21 years!

We both loved to travel and once took our two younger sons to Europe for five weeks. Later, after retirement, he and I enjoyed a memorable trip to New Zealand and Honolulu.

Mac's chief interest in retirement was his involvement with the National Republican Party. Twice he was a delegate to the national convention.

We often called our house the "McClellan Motel" as the Lansing Republican contingent (the governor included) and state candidates often stayed here.

We were the parents of three fine sons. Sadly, our eldest died in October 1993 and preceded Mac in death by four years. The adage "time heals all wounds" is not accurate. Time lessens the pain, but the wound remains.

Many of the Guild leaders and field representatives remained friends with my husband and years later, and prior to Mac's death, while he was ill with cancer they visited him and they drove here for his memorial service.

Afterwards

From the participant's point of view, the Craftsman's Guild was a form of self-expression, entertainment and fun, whereas most ordinary folks would have called it pure work and torture. Who in their right mind would have ever spent 1,000 hours of their valuable time hand-crafting a miniature model Napoleonic Coach or 500 hours designing and building a model car? However, once a Guildsman got hooked on the praise, recognition and an occasional check from GM, it is easy to see how they kept working toward a top scholarship award.

The Craftsman's Guild must have been a fairly primal experience as their fond memories and recollections of the "days of yore" are still fresh and vivid for some participants as far back as 1931 (Donald C. Burnham) and 1936 (Henry B. Larzelere). You could almost rank the Guild experience right up there with playing catch with dad at the park or at the church picnic. Although barely a blip on their lifetime of experiences, that Guild scholarship still stands out for many as a critical, pivotal, defining moment when their lives changes forever. For many, their Craftsman's Guild achievement is still on their resume as a significant accomplishment.

GM and Fisher Body Division knew what they were doing in promoting an industrial arts aptitude test, or what the author calls an industrial design prep test, that measured both creative ability, aesthetic design ability and intelligence. Social scientists have always wanted to have a test to measure creative ability and the right hemisphere of the brain. On aptitude tests administered today by smart corporations, if you do well, you have a chance of being hired. The literature makes clear that as far back as 1937, lacking automobile design schools and formal auto design training opportunities for young students, Harley J. Earl and the Fisher brothers collaborated with corporate executives to fill this fundamental void, and start their own school in the form of a design competition.

The participants' essays show that drawing automobiles, building a miniature model coach or a scale model dream car, combined with their early love of automobiles, piqued their interest in pursuing the creative design process. Regardless of their ultimate vocation, these innate creative skills and abilities were identified and nurtured early on by the Craftsman's Guild. Similar to successful persons in professional sports such as football, baseball, tennis or golf, their skills and abilities were usually developed from a very early age.

As shown by the essays, these skills and abilities have never evaporated, as many former Guildsmen still enjoy designing and making things with the principles of quality craftsmanship that they learned many, many years ago.

Good clean design is timeless, which explains why so many of the Craftsman's Guild designs shown in this book, although scratch-built 40–50 years ago by amateurs, look contemporary by today's design standards. The detail and scale are uncanny, and overall, the models are deceptively real-looking. If a contestant couldn't envision this, and wasn't working at this level, he was definitely not scholarship material.

Whatever the reasons Chairman Roche and the other GM executives had for ending the Guild, there is much reason to believe that GM management made a mistake in discontinuing the program in 1968. By 1968, the seeds had only been sown. Who can blame them for canceling an educational program the potential of which had yet to be realized?

Obviously, the former Guildsmen who participated in writing this book want the Craftsman's Guild legacy passed down to the next generation of America's creative young people. The following are ideas generated to achieve that end:

1. The hope for the book is that a portion of the proceeds from its sale can be used to build a Guildsman's Scholarship Fund at the Art Center College of Design to help support young creative men and women who desire to become auto designers or product designers. The majority of the book participants attended that college of design.

2. Guild reincarnates are an obvious way to carry on the legacy. The three *Automobile Quarterly* Car Styling Contests (1987 to 1991), the *Motor Trend* 2000-2003 International Design Contests, the *Truck Trends* 2003 Design Contest, and the *2003 AutoCar Young Designer of the Year* contests are examples of Guild reincarnates and the desire to expose students and adults to challenging auto design problems, the design process, and implementation of Harley J. Earl's philosophy that competition stimulates the best ideas in everyone.[40,41]

   A new Craftsman's Guild paradigm called the Chuck Jordan Automobile Designer's Competition, named after the Auto Hall of Famer to whom this book is dedicated, might be implemented with some aspects of the above programs that would be coeducational, international, multimedia, with student (with design major and non-design major subcategories) as well as adult (amateur) competition categories, and a $10,000 grand prize for the top student designer. An alternative to prize money would be a summer student position, all expenses paid, at a major Detroit-based auto manufacturer's design studio working with the professionals.

   Specific design problems posed by the contest and changed annually would be solved by the contestants either using two-dimensional drawings (e.g., rendering or "quick sketch" techniques) or three-dimensional modeling techniques (e.g., Chavant clay on polyurethane armature or liquitex polymer on rigid polyurethane foam), but the images of these solutions could be entered digitally at home and emailed to the judges. Students could use graphics software to enhance their design solutions.

   There would be an adult amateur category, but without computer aided design techniques. It is well known that there are some wonderfully talented, amateur, adult automobile designers like Henry F. Rom (1953 fourth-place national scholarship, senior division, $1,000 award winner), who still uses the Guild process to design and transform his automobile ideas into highly prized, scale realities for a hobby. Mr. Rom's passionate auto designs were featured in *Collectible Automobile* magazine in 1993 and 1994.[42] The creative mind is always in motion and age would not be a factor in the new Chuck Jordan Automobile Designer's Competition.

3. The FBCG Friends and Associates hope that educators reading this book will see the value of the Craftsman's Guild paradigm as a tool for identifying young, untapped design talent and as a way for kids to express themselves, build confidence and find a place for themselves in the world. Creative abilities need to be identified early on, encouraged and supported in our schools. Because of time constraints, or lack of funds, nurturing design creativity in youth is a low priority in our secondary schools. There are magnet schools in the author's community that nurture those talented in math, science, engineering and the creative arts. There might be opportunities in programs like these to expose selected groups of students to a six-week unit of the "Guild

process" as part of a mix of creative design activities. The students could be exposed to hands-on, scratch-building the Guild way, leading to a completed and finished 3-D model from either clay on a polyurethane foam armature or liquitex polymer on rigid polyurethane foam) which would be exhibited for the other students.

The Aussies found their own way to do it in 1968. The Australians in the GM Holden Craftsman's Guild liked to use a block of foam material called Daycell (G35 PVC), a block about 18" × 6" × 4" to begin the process, and coat the final, smooth shaped surfaces with cornice plaster mixed with 1/30 part dextrin, to create a hard shell over the foam core. According to them, "with DAYCELL Foam, dental plaster and a few basic tools, durable model cars can be built in a fraction of the time required of other materials" (*Guildsman*, vol. 3, no. 1, 1968, GMH Craftsman's Guild).

The hard shell is the exterior working surface. Lines can be scored in the hard shell to indicate door opening areas, folding or "hard" convertible top storage areas, deck and truck lid opening areas, concealed headlight openings, etc. This hard shell surface is sanded smooth with very fine sandpaper, primed and painted with lacquer. Any divots, dings and low spots can be filled quickly with the same cornice dental plaster and 1/30 ratio dextrin mixture. Of course, a drawing and clay model are still needed to make templates or you can always use the "rock of the eye" method. The tools they recommended for this method were a saw, file, sandpaper and chalk or magic marker.

Anthony V. Simone (the top '61 national scholarship junior division winner), a professional international educator, has taken up the charge and written an essay, presented in Appendix L, that discusses the meaning and value of the Guild process in an educational or institutional venue.

4. A series of Chuck Jordan young designer summer camps, held in the auto capital of the world and taught by professional auto designers and stylists, are needed to expose secondary school youth to the automobile design process. This would be equivalent to the Interlochen Arts Program, with students screened to determine their passion for automotive design, or the creative arts in general. Highly focused morning and afternoon sessions would include studying the classic automobile design processes and techniques; studying the antique and classic automobiles design cues and marquees in the Detroit metropolitan area auto museums; working with, and alongside, automobile design sculptors, stylists and designers; touring the design studios of GM Ford, DaimlerChrysler and VW; and finally, culminate in the completion and critique of a scale model automobile that would be displayed at one of the annual Detroit auto exhibitions—"Eyes on Design" or "Concours D'Elegance."

5. The Society of Automotive Engineers (SAE) Foundation promotes "Wheels in Motion," which is an educational program taught by volunteers to introduce engineering principles to primary school students. A similar program could be instituted for introducing the Guild process and the principles of automobile design to our young people, but promoted by the Industrial Designers Society of America (IDSA).

A student auto design kit needed to support a small, scale model car (consisting of Chavant modeling clay, a block of rigid polyurethane foam, sandpaper, scale wood wheels and two axles, a small can of spray paint, several grades of sandpaper, rubber cement, etc.) would be used as a teacher's aid to help teach the principles of automotive design. The fundamental teaching techniques to be used in this program would be consistent with an open classroom, or free-form-expression approach, where kids would learn by doing. Alternatively, the Cub Scout Pinewood Derby Kits which are sold at craft stores like Michaels or hobby shops like Hobby City could be substituted. A small polyurethane foam block 10" × 3" × 2" could be substituted for the wood.

Readers are invited to pass on their ideas about the above, or to request further details, by contacting the author at www.fisherguild.com.

Non Sequitur

> As a member of the Fisher Body Craftsman's Guild, *I pledge myself to build honestly with my own hands all work I may undertake in the Guild*— to strive to perfect myself as in craftsmanship — to conduct myself in all things with the industry, steadfastness, and fair dealing befitting a Master Craftsman.—1937 Guild Identification Card

One issue remains to be addressed, and that is how to reconcile the Guildsman's Official Guild Pledge Card declaration (I did my own work!) and the obvious evidence throughout this book clearly indicating that it would have been impossible, in some cases, to have done every ounce of work.

Many "armchair" Guildsmen have spent years trying to second-guess how some of these models were made and, in their own minds, reconcile the expertise represented in front of them with the ages of the contestants. The author has tried to explain this euphemistically with terms such as family "know-how," and the passing of model-making skills and knowledge down from generation to generation. Despite these words, there were definitely family secrets behind each success story that we will never know.

This is not to detract from those thousands of remarkable Guildsmen who worked alone, and did 100 percent of their own work, but there are obvious signs of outside support or technical assistance in some cases—for example, a seamstress or consultant on millinery matters; a tool and die set made by a local artisan to stamp out nettlesome, repetitive brass sheet parts; a machined aluminum jig and fixture to facilitate silver-soldering a complex number of brass parts together; intricate lathe work on rubber tires and wheel covers; and the plating of brass parts. Let's face it: most contestants did not have electrolytic vats in their basements for chrome plating, or a foundry in the back shed for casting aluminum bumper parts; nor did they have vacuum-forming equipment in their garages. (There were toy vacuum machines on the market at the time, but these were way too small for the clear canopy parts we are talking about.)

Guildsmen were told explicitly in the program literature that they could seek adult advice, guidance and suggestions, but that adults were not to do any of the work. There were Guild clubs with adult advisors sponsored by schools and some select GM divisions. James Barnett of Anderson, Indiana (a 1963 regional winner), stated, "Community and industrial support for the program in this city was substantial and it is only now in retrospect that I can fully appreciate the guidance Guildsmen received" (letter to the author, March 30, 1985). Someone even suggested that the small towns worked together on these Guild projects like they were community affairs.

In a phone conversation, the author asked Robert E. Davids about this phenomenon, specifically since three first-place national scholarship, senior division, award winning scale model designs had been produced in Art Russell's father's shop by the collaboration of two, then three, Venice High School buddies, namely Bill Moore (1956), Art Russell (1957) and Bob Davids (1963). Recognizing the fact that all three guys were budding design geniuses, I told him that this result was statistically impossible unless there were some unusual tools or techniques involved. Bob Davids replied, "Venice High School was a magical place in the 1950s and 1960s, the movie *Grease* was filmed there, and that about explains it all." The secret of their success is, and will remain, a part of Venice High School history.

Clearly, for some of the overly competitive Guild folks, the model coach and dream car designs and their execution were family affairs. There was huge scholarship money as well as praise, recognition and prestige on the line. The competition was fierce, with the winning models were becoming more and more sophisticated each year. The "fight or flight" emotion took over and the family's survival reflex kicked in. The gloves came off. Two or three brothers could pool their know-how in an "us against them" race. A technically savvy adult could step in to pinch-hit ever so briefly. A win-at-all-costs mentality was at play.

Even the author had an ad hoc system dependent on his family. My father, Dwight, was my Macco lacquer and lacquer thinner purchasing agent, East side Baltimore chrome-plate and plexiglass contact man, engine lathe outsource and, above all else, shipping box carpenter. My grandmother, Mary K. Lindsey, who had lived with us for years, took control of all incoming French translation work from Mrs. Potter's French III class at Baltimore Polytechnic for the last weeks in May and into June as the Guild deadline swiftly approached. Her help created a scarce commodity called time, and this would be required as I tried to achieve, but never got even close to achieving, the Fisher Brothers' almighty, cherished level of craftsmanship.

As far as can be determined, GM and Fisher Body management countenanced these practices as top honors were still awarded to some despite these apparent refinements of the Guild rules. The judges were experienced and could spot the signs of professional interference. Legally, GM and Fisher Body had the means in the rule book to disqualify any person and his model entry. They set the rules and standards of behavior for the contestants. If everyone agreed to the unwritten rules of behavior then everything was fair regardless of the Official Guild Pledge Card.

This, then, was the essence of the Guild's family secret, but this was also the reality of the competition.

Recovery and Identification

The following are examples of recovery, identification and preservation and should be of interest to collectors. As noted earlier, Fisher Body Central Engineering was forced to clear out its basement storage room of Guild models in 1984. These theoretically were sold at auction, distributed to corporate or divisional personnel for safekeeping, or given to loving homes. Eventually, some of these models will return to the marketplace through estates sales and auctions.

Often times, the Guild models sold at auction, or flea markets, have been recovered for identification and preservation. The author has accomplished this several times, including the acquisition of the 1931 Napoleonic Coach made by Wallace Lench sold on eBay. One of the Internet "name search" engines was used to locate relatives of the builder and complete the identification and provenance process.[43] The three scale model dream

The 2004 Guild reunion and banquet was held June 26, 2004, at the GM Tech Center in Warren, Michigan, and included an exhibit of the Craftsman's Guild models for family and friends. Another public exhibit of the Guild models occurred June 27, 2004, at the Eyes on Design antique car event held at the Eleanor and Edsel Ford Estate in Grosse Pointe Shores, Michigan. Several hundred Guildsmen, including their guests, attended the 2004 Guild reunion. Shown visiting at the Eyes on Design even are three top scholarship winners: (left to right) William A. Moore (1956), Virgil M. Exner, Jr. (1946), and E. Arthur Russell (1957). *Photograph by author.*

car designs made by George W. Aschen III (Kirkwood, Missouri) for the Guild competition (1957, 1958 and 1960) were also recovered by the author from the Antique Automobile Club of America's flea market in Hershey, Pennsylvania. The scholarship winning scale model cars are probably worth thousands, if preserved in excellent condition, properly identified, and with the essential provenance elements (e.g., name of the contestant, their state/city, age of contestant, year entered, a Certificate of Design and Craftsmanship with the appropriate name and year, competition award level and any corroborating news paper or magazine articles).

A Fisher Guild model car that Ronald Konopka (aka Kaye) had purchased at a Toledo toy fair 15 to 20 years ago was recently identified as the 1953 third-place national scholarship, junior division, $2,000 award winner designed by Thomas A. McDonnell (one of the McDonnell brothers of Stockton, California). *Collectible Automobile* magazine, in April 1993, reported the recovery of James Mariol's 1947 first-place national scholarship, junior division, $4,000 award winner from a Midland, Michigan, flea market several years earlier. This model is now owned by Hampton C. Wayt of Aiken, South Carolina.

On the other side of the equation, there are also examples of Guild folks (e.g. Milton J. Antonick 1955, Gary Graham 1954 and Henry Huizenga 1957) who, for sentimental reasons, would like to recover the models they made for Craftsman's Guild and sold 40–50 years ago to Fisher Body Division for a few hundred dollars each. If the reader has any comments on this contact the author at www.fisherguild.com.

A 1932 miniature model Napoleonic Coach and many of the model cars made by Guildsmen (representing 1937 to 1968) were dusted off and exhibited as part of the festivities to honor the historic Fisher Body Craftsmans Guild at a reunion held June 26–27, 2004, in Detroit. This exhibit of models was held at the Eyes on Design event on June 27, 2004, at Grosse Point Shores, Michigan. Gary Graham ('54), on the right side with name tag, is examining Stewart D. Reed's 1968 national scholarship winner, with Elia "Russ" Russinoff (in baseball cap) standing behind to Gary's left. Also identifiable is Harvey E. Whitman ('48) photographing Jerome A. Grunstad's 1962 Styling winner. Some of the second row foreground models on the table *(left to right)* include those designed and crafted by Virgil M. Exner, Jr. ('46), Charles M. Jordan ('47), William A. Moore ('56) and Richard R. Sylvester ('57)—all national winners. Jordan had to borrow his model from the Henry Ford Museum and Greenfield Village collection in Dearborn, Michigan, for the two-day 2004 Guild Reunion weekend event. A lot of fun for all! *Photograph by author.*

Non-Guild Memorabilia

A beautiful and pristine miniature model Napoleonic Coach shows up at the AACA flea market at Hershey annually, made of sterling silver with 24 karat gold highlights.[44] This is a piece of Fisher Body Division or corporate memorabilia from 1973 and not Craftsman's Guild memorabilia.

Guild Reunions

For information about the 2004 Guild Reunion, please see the e-zine entitled *The Automotive Chronicles*, November 2004 (www.automotivechronicles.com), or see *Collectible Automobile*, December 2004. Please contact the author at www.fisherguild.com for information about future Guild Reunions.

Accredited Industrial Design Programs

See www.idsa.org.

Appendices

A. FISHER BROTHERS IN BRIEF

All the Fisher brothers apprenticed at their father Lawrence's Norwalk Horse and Carriage business before, as was customary, leaving home to seek their fortunes. With the financial help of their uncle Albert, Frederic and Charles established the Fisher Body Company, to make open and closed automobile bodies from a composite of wood and metal, on July 22, 1908. In 1916 several Fisher plants were incorporated to make the Fisher Body Corporation and by 1919 it had grown to be the biggest automobile body manufacturer in the world. In 1925 Fisher Body Corporation bought Fleetwood Metal Body Company, a custom body builder for Cadillac among many other marquees. Because GM wanted a steady supply of automobile bodies, they purchased a three-fifths interest in Fisher Body Corporation in 1919 and the remaining two-fifths in 1926 for a total of $234.7 million. In 1926, Fisher Body became a division of General Motors Corporation. All the brothers went into the automobile business, except Howard, and became GM executives.

FREDERIC J. FISHER (1878–1941)

Frederic studied at the Andrew F. Johnson Carriage and Automobile Body Drafting School in New York City. He started Fisher Body Company on July 22, 1908, with his brother Charles. He had two years of business school training in Sandusky, Ohio. He was elected to the GM board of directors in 1923 and retired from his GM management responsibilities in 1934.

CHARLES T. FISHER (1880–1963)

Charles started the Fisher Body Company on July 22, 1908, with his brother Frederic. He was elected to the GM board of directors in 1923. He retired from GM management in 1934 and in December 1934 secretly commissioned Roscoe C. "Rod" Hoffman to design a prototype advanced automobile design (four-door, rear-engine, streamlined) called the X-8 for possible production if the Fisher brothers' anticipated purchase of Hudson Motor Car Company became a reality. The Hudson deal was never consummated but prototype X-8's were built.

WILLIAM A. FISHER (1886–1969)

William gained a business school education around 1912 and joined the Fisher Body Company by 1915. He became president of the Fisher Body Division around 1925–26 and was president of the Fisher Body Craftsman's Guild in 1930. He retired from GM management in 1944.

LAWRENCE P. FISHER (1888–1961)

Larry Fisher is the only brother believed to have received a formal college education. He was flamboyant and extroverted and a natural-born salesman. He joined the Fisher Body Company in 1912 as the superintendent of paint and trim, and was elected to the GM board of directors in 1923. He brought Harley J. Earl from Hollywood to Detroit to design the 1927 Cadillac LaSalle with the support of Alfred P. Sloan, Jr., and was president of Cadillac from 1925 to 1934. He retired from GM management in 1944, but remained active on the board of directors.

EDWARD F. FISHER (1891–1972)

Edward studied at the Andrew F. Johnson Carriage and Automobile Body Drafting School in New York City. Joined the Fisher Body Company in 1913 after his graduation. He became vice president in charge of production at Fisher Body Division, GMC. He retired from GM in 1944 but remained active on the GM board of directors until 1969. The Fisher Body Craftsman's Guild was discontinued in 1968, possibly in anticipation of the last Fisher sibling (Edward F.) leaving General Motors.

ALFRED FISHER (1892–1963)

Alfred studied at the Andrew F. Johnson Carriage and Automobile Body Drafting School in New York City and joined the Fisher Body Company in 1913 after his graduation. He became vice president of engineering at Fisher Body Division, GMC, and retired from GM management in 1944.

HOWARD A. FISHER (1902–1942)

The youngest of the Fisher brothers, Howard was in charge of the Fisher family's real estate interests, particularly the art deco styled Fisher Building (across the street from the GM Building in Detroit) which was dedicated in 1927 and completed in 1928.[1]

B. SKIP GEEAR'S FBCG FOUNDATION AND MINI-MUSEUM

In 1996 and 1999, Guild reunions were held at the Fisher Body Craftsman's Guild Foundation and Mini-Museum in Eagle Point, Oregon, which overlooks the Cascade Range. The museum houses an original set of blueprints and scale plans drawn by Frank Riess for the Fisher brothers from which the two original master model Napoleonic Coaches were constructed by Walter C. Leuschner and the Fleetwood Metal Body Company. From these master blueprints, a scaled-down and less elaborate set of plans, three sheets initially, and then a large 24-page instruction book (12″ × 20″ unfolded and flat) were written for the Guild contestants.

The mini-museum has all of the above original Guild memorabilia as well as 24 Napoleonic Coach models in various forms, including, among others, one 1932 Canadian model with a first place in each scoring category (e.g., paint craft, trim craft, woodcraft, and metalcraft); one 1947 first-place Florida state and regional winner; one 1933 second-place Montana state winner; a complete 1932 coach kit in its original shipping boxes (labeled $9.75 for Wood, Metal, Trim and Paint Kit combined); several partially completed Napoleonic Coach kits; a partially completed Traveling Coach for the Apprentice Craftsman Class (with all hand-made pieces); a recently acquired 1934 national scholarship winning Napoleonic Coach; a mint condition 1935 Traveling Coach, junior division, State of Washington entry which was resubmitted as a senior division entry in 1936; and a complete coach kit once owned by the executive secretary to the president of GM in 1937.

The mini-museum houses seven model cars from the late 1930s through the early 1950s model car competition. One is a 1937 second-place Washington State, senior division winner; another is a 1948 third-place Florida state winner; and two others are 1950 and 1951 second-place Florida state winners, respectively. Also, as part of the collection, resides a 1947 Virginia state honorable mention winner.

Guild shirts and tams, and almost the complete collections of Albert W. Fischer (1931), Howard Jennings (1931), Raymond S. Doerr (1931), Donald C. Burnham (1931) and Richard H. Conibear (1947) are on hand. The focal point of the collection is a full-size Fisher Body Napoleonic Coach (the only one in the world) built by Mr. Francis Londo (a 1934 coach contestant). And, of course, Guild trophies, awards and a file of personal correspondence a foot thick. Mr. Skip Geear can be contacted at FBCG Foundation, 161 Rockingham Circle, Eagle Point, Oregon, 97524.

C. COACH-BUILDER'S BIOGRAPHIC SURVEY FORM, JUNE 1997

Dear Guild Friend,

Not a lot is known about the men who built the Napoleonic Coaches/Traveling Coaches for the Fisher Body Craftsman's Guild Competition 1930–1948. What is known and published is out of date. We would like to update the Foundation's files at the Museum and your responses to some or all of these questions would be highly appreciated. You should be aware that this information may be used in the future to write and publish article(s) about the Guild. If you run out of space, please write on the back or add a sheet.

Name: (First) _____ (Middle) _____ (Last) _____

1. State/City where I grew up: _____

2. Year(s) I participated in the FBCG: _____

3. State, Regional, National Award(s) received: _____

4. Age at the time of each entry: _____

5. If you built a Napoleonic Coach, how many hours of time were required? What was the most difficult part? What was the most ingenious thing you did?

6. The Traveling Coach was introduced in 1934. Did you build one? Number of hours required to build one?

7. How did you learn about the Napoleonic Coach or Traveling Coach competitions (manual arts instructor, GM dealership, Boy Scouts, radio coverage of the Guild convention, newspaper or magazine ads, etc.)?

8. Who was primarily responsible for encouraging/mentoring you through this difficult project?

9. Did your family, high school manual arts teacher or the Boy Scout leader help you on your project or were you essentially on your own?

10. Why did you enter the Guild competition?

11. Did members of your family, your manual arts teacher or your Scout master have skills that helped you complete the project? What were those skills?

12. Did you have a lot of shop tools/equipment in your home when you grew up? If so, what were the tools you used to make your coach?

13. If you did not have a lot of shop tools/equipment in your home, did you hand-craft your own tools or did you borrow them?

14. Was your coach model handmade or did you purchase a coach kit? If you purchased a coach kit, please check one of the following:

    a. Purchased the complete coach kit. _____

    b. Purchased the wood kit only. _____

    c. Purchased the metal trim kit only. _____

    d. Purchased the upholstery kit only. _____

15. If you did not use a complete coach kit, did you purchase your paint locally, and if so, what kind of paint did you use?

16. Considering the depth of the depression in 1932, did you feel your family was more or less fortunate than most people at the time?

17. If you won a FBCG coach scholarship, did you view this as the only way to advance your education or one of many options?

18. Did your winning the Napoleonic Coach competition allow you to further your education?

19. Did your participation in the FBCG lead to other outside avocational/vocational interests in life (e.g., worked for Fisher Body Division of General Motors or some other part of the automotive industry, became a product designer or engineer, enjoy model-making as a hobby, became an antique or classic car enthusiast, love woodworking, like to make violins or cellos). Please explain and be specific.

20. Did you serve in the military during World War II? What did you do?

21. What was your life's career path or vocation?

22. Do you still have your Napoleonic Coach or Traveling Coach model in your possession?

23. Is the coach model still in its original condition or has it been restored?

24. If you no longer have your coach model, where is it now? (Please list name and address for the Museum's records.)

25. Do you want the foundation to keep your answers confidential? YES _____ NO _____

26. Signature _____

(This form was distributed by Skip Geear, FBCG Foundation and Mini-Museum, Eagle Point, Oregon, around July 1, 1997, to Coach-Builder Reunion attendees.)

D. FISHER BODY DIVISION'S ROLE DURING WORLD WAR II

The Guild competition was discontinued during World War II (1940 to 1945). Apparently 1940 or thereabouts was the last year Guild awards were made before the war, and 1946 was the first year Guild awards were made after the war.

On February 10, 1942, about 65 days after Pearl Harbor, the U.S. government shut down civilian auto production. The U.S. auto industry as a whole produced 20 percent of U.S. war materiel for World War II. GM produced 50 percent of that amount, or $12 billion worth, of which $8 billion was foreign to GM's normal operations. Two-thirds of GM plants worked on planes, from sections of B-25 bombers to complete planes for the navy. Near the end of the war, GM was making complete bombers (*Ward's Quarterly*, summer 1966). This is consistent with their heritage. Fisher Body Company had played a role in World War I, making 2,005 airplane bodies between 1917 and 1918.

Fisher Body Division and its plants would play a major role in the World War II effort. Before the war (July 25, 1941) only one Fisher plant was awarded the navy "E" pennant for production efficiency — a flag with six stars.[2] During World War II, Fisher operated 17 plants, three of which were government owned. At the end of the war, every Fisher Body plant was awarded an army-navy "E" for production efficiency and 27 stars had been added to those flags by the time production ended (*Tomorrow's Look Today*). During the war years, the logo in Fisher Body print ads changed from "Body by Fisher" to "Armament by Fisher." One ad stated you could "bank on craftsmanship, better than a rabbit's foot." Others said the "Body by Fisher" emblems stood for "craftsmanship in war."[3,3A]

Fisher Body Division made tanks, critical bomber subassemblies, delicate aircraft instruments, and antiaircraft guns and assemblies. In cooperation with U.S. Army ordinance development engineers, Fisher made 18,500 fast tanks and tank destroyers including the General Sherman M-4 medium tank (75mm) and the M-26 "Tiger Tamer" tank (90 mm).[3,3A]

Fisher made B-25 subassemblies. In addition, Fisher Body made B-29 superfortress subassemblies including dorsal fins, horizontal stabilizers, rudders, elevators and ailerons, flaps, wing tips, outboard wings, turret parts and engine nacelles. Engine nacelles required hundreds of fixtures and the assembly of thousands of parts. Fisher Body Division was an assembler of aircraft parts, not an aircraft manufacturer.[3,3A]

Fisher assembled a Bendix Corporation–designed remote indicator compass (for accurate course control) and air position indicator (for latitude and longitude readings for the navigator at a glance). Also, Fisher assembled a Sperry-designed gyro-horizon indicator and directional gyro indicator. These instruments were used by bombardiers to indicate "true course" for night flying conditions, or blind flying conditions, and were necessary for precision targeting. Four hundred thousand of these delicate, sensitive instruments were made by Fisher Body plants.

And finally, Fisher assembled a 5" antiaircraft gun designed by the Navy and innovated an automatic loader/ram design for a gun-breech housing, called Strato-Flak.[3A]

In light of this proud and patriotic heritage, draftsmen, engineers and technicians less than 27 years old who were eligible for the draft and working at Fisher Body Division headquarters could receive, if requested, an Occupational Draft Deferment (II-A Classification) during the Vietnam War era.

E. MODEL CAR COMPETITION RULES AND REGULATIONS

There were rules that regulated the fairness of the competition.

Solo Work and Honor Code

Two boys could work together, but not on the same model. In the later years of the Guild, teens were encouraged to organize clubs, and Fisher Body published a booklet entitled "Organizing a Model Car Club." Contestants were permitted to seek advice, but not physical assistance, from another person. The Guildsman certified by signing the Official Guild Pledge Card that the model entry was his and his work alone.

Eligibility (Residence and Age)

Contestants were considered residents of the state where they had permanent residence on the date the model entry was shipped. The contestant's age, for purposes of eligibility and competition peer group, was determined as of September 1 of the new competition year. This determined whether they would be in the junior or senior division in July of the next year. To be eligible, the contestant had to adhere to and satisfy (1) the prescribed instructions in the how-to manual and (2) the prescribed specifications in Drawings A, B, and C of the sketch sheet. In other words, in order to be eligible for the judging process, the model had to meet the minimum and maximum specifications or it would be rejected as oversize or undersize.

The Guild's 1/12 scale precluded the entry of assembled plastic kits available at commercial hobby shops (which were usually 1/24, 1/25, 1/29, 1/32, 1/35, or 1/48 scale) and the submission of customized miniatures. The required 1/12 scale models reflected the thinking of American youth while illustrating their exceptional talent and ability.

States Organized into Regions

States were organized into 20 groups or regions. The single regional winner was selected from among the first-place state winners in a particular region (20 juniors and 20 seniors). The national scholarship winners were selected from these 40 regional winners (sometimes more, if GM sons were winners and duplicate awards were made). In 1960–61, because of the huge number of entries from urban centers, some states including New York, Pennsylvania, California, Ohio, Michigan, Indiana, and Illinois became their own regions.

Ineligibility

National award winners were retired to a loosely knit Guild alumni association and could no longer compete. Styling award winners were no longer eligible for another styling award, but were still eligible to compete for state, regional and national awards. Guild alumni were famous for returning to Detroit to attend the annual Guild convention banquet and joining the other industrialists, scientists and leading educators in honoring the new regional and national winners. One of the jobs of the Guild alumni president was to mobilize the past winners. The interesting thing was to learn what they were doing and, especially, which auto companies had hired them.

Because the Guild alumni had to be contacted for the banquets each year, mailing lists with addresses were generated and updated over the years. It was these mailing lists of national scholarship winners, squirreled away for posterity by pack rats, which were reconstructed by the author for the Smithsonian project (1985) and this book (2002 and 2003).

Judge's Authority

The judges were to be design experts (GM stylists and designers) and professional industrial arts teachers from the Detroit secondary school system. The model entries were judged anonymously. The working judges employed a score sheet with specific craftsmanship and design criteria (some objective but mostly subjective) and with available points in each category. The decisions of the working judges were approved by an honorary board of judges. There was no process or procedure in which a contestant could protest his score, or award, as Fisher Body headquarters did not publish and distribute the scores of all models for all the participants to review. In order to preclude any disputes, all of the judge's decisions were final and binding on all contestants. The only people who could have possibly visual comparisons of the final products were the 40 regional winners who met each other and saw each other's designs. In the October or November following the competition year, each contestant received the Report to Contestants or the original score sheet for his entry along with a letter of praise that urged consideration of the next year's competition.

Communicating with Judges

Unusual features, not obvious or self-explanatory to the judges, were to be listed, described and attached to the bottom of the model. Category C (Open Competition) models, in particular, had to be labeled on the bottom with (1) a description of the purpose of the vehicle, (2) a complete explanation of any unusual seating arrangements, and (3) an explanation of all original features that were not self-explanatory.

Shipping and Receiving

Clay models lacked durability and were not eligible for the Craftsman's Guild competition. Models were not required to have any moving or working parts. More than one model could be entered, but only the highest scoring model would be given an award. (George R. Chartier, Richard L. Beck, John M. Mellberg and the Simone brothers are examples of Guildsmen who entered two models in one year.) The model entry had to be accompanied by a signed Official Guild Pledge Card (both the contestant's and the parent's signatures were needed), permanent address and a birth certificate or similar documentation. The model entry had to be received by 12 midnight on the closing date of the competition (usually during the first week of June) by means of a Railway Express agency, U.S. Postal Service or hand delivery. The submitted model entries remained the property of the builder and were returned in September.

Awards

Separate trophies were awarded to the school in the case of national, regional, styling and first-place state winners. Certificates of Design and Craftsmanship were awarded to all entries. In the case of the son of a GM employee being a winner, a duplicate award was made to the next highest scoring model. Up until 1955 the top national scholarship awards were as follows: two $4,000 awards, two $3,000 awards, two $2,000 awards and two $1,000 awards (one junior and one senior each). Beginning with the 1956 competition, the top national scholarship awards were as follows: two $5,000 awards, two $4,000 awards, two $3,000 awards and two $2,000 awards (one junior and one senior each) plus ten national styling scholarship awards worth $1,000, awarded for excellence in design without regard to age, state, region or state award level.

Non-Confidentiality Agreement

The contestants were notified that no model car ideas would be accepted in confidence and that the corporation and its licenses were freely entitled to use any such designs or ideas.

Further, they stated, "It is possible that a submitted model may include a design or idea which General Motors Corporation may use at sometime." Also, GM and its licensees could freely use, for advertising purposes and publicity, reproductions of likenesses, statements, names and addresses of Guild members and models or reproductions of models submitted by them. At some point in the process, Guildsmen provided their personal photograph to Guild headquarters either with their Official Guild Pledge Card or upon request by telegram when the winners were known. In the 1950s GM purchased some of the top award winning designs, further asserting their ownership rights.

F. Popular Construction Techniques Used by Guildsmen

Clay and Symmetry

The Guildsmen were encouraged to sculpt their 1/12 scale models out of clay. A board with station lines drawn ½" to ¾" apart and perpendicular to the longitudinal center line of the model was set up to do this. An armature consisting of blocks of wood drilled with ¼" holes, was arranged to the approximate shape of the finished model car, to conserve the amount of clay required. The November 1948 issue of *Mechanix Illustrated* called this the "Swiss Cheese Method." The boys were instructed to transfer their two-dimensional ideas from the tracing paper to the three-dimensional clay model and explore other ideas using clay. Clay was purchased from a local hobby shop, or the Guild provided the name of a supplier who sold stylists clay at a modest cost.

As suggested by the Guild's how-to book, a clay model of the finished design was needed to work out the details of the three-dimensional design and to obtain cardboard template sections. Cardboard templates were needed in order to transfer the design symmetrically along the centerline of the wood model. Model symmetry was included in a scoring category called Workmanship and would be an important consideration during the judging process.

In 1951 the how-to manual told contestants how to make their own modeling clay, how to shape and carve their own clay modeling tools from common wooden utensils, and how to make clay model "styling tools" (e.g., baseboard with longitudinal section lines, a right angle block for holding templates perpendicular, a 360 degree guide rail around the perimeter of the clay mold, and use of the right angle block and marker gauge.)

The marker gauge was used to make perpendicular section lines in the clay. Cardboard templates were fitted into the clay at each section line every ½" or ¾" to the longitudinal center line of the clay model. The templates made on the left side were flipped over and the mirror image was used to create a symmetrical right side of the model. These techniques helped create a crude three-dimensional coordinate system so the symmetry of the model was perfect and the maximum Workmanship score could be received.

The *Guildsman* newsletter elaborated on how to create a symmetric clay model, without cardboard templates, by making a designer's bridge, a vertical block with horizontally adjustable sharpened dowel pins to locate points on a curved section of the clay model. With the pins adjusted horizontally, the stylist's gauge would be flipped around to the opposite side of the clay model and fitted to a longitudinal guide rail and template section line. A professional designer's bridge has a series of vertical and horizontal adjustable dowel pins (with numbered division marks), and the whole device moves longitudinally on a rail system. The *Guild News* showed Lew Jacobs (1953 scholarship winner) with a crude designer's bridge (without the pins), but from which vertical and horizontal measurements could have been taken and transferred from side to side to achieve symmetry.

No matter how it was done, the left-hand side of the model had to look like the right-hand side. Alternatively, Guildsman preferred to use the "rock of the eye" or "eyeball" method. This latter method was the true mark of a craftsman and Guildsman.

Rubber Mold Plaster Casting Method

A method recommended in 1948 was the rubber mold plaster casting method, in which a room temperature vulcanizing rubber (RTV) or liquid rubber was painted over the clay model pattern. The rubber molded surfaces could accommodate "negative draft" around bumpers, windows or concave surfaces below the belt line. Harvey E. Whitman used this technique for his 1948 first-place national scholarship winning design.

Vasoline or silicone were applied to the clay pattern as a parting compound. Layers of liquid rubber were applied over the clay model, intermixed with layers of surgical gauze for strength. A rectangular wooden box 5–6" high was built around the air-dried rubber coated clay model to act as a dam while a thick layer of casting plaster was applied for structural purposes. A piece of cardboard was placed down the longitudinal centerline so the plaster casting could be separated into two pieces. After setting, the two pieces of plaster were separated and the rubber and gauze mold was released from the clay pattern and flipped over. The whole structure was assembled upside down with a large cavity. The Guildsman poured a new batch of casting plaster into this cavity and that "male plug" became the model car for the competition. To promote drying of the plaster model without cracks, the center was scooped out, or hollowed out, to create an even wall thickness. Because the RTV was durable, multiple impressions could be taken until a perfect model shape was obtained.

Chip-Mold Plaster Casting Method

For the 1948 competition, the Guild also recommended the chip-mold plaster casting method. This method essentially destroyed the clay model pattern. The contestant covered the clay model pattern with a thick layer of plaster thus making a one-piece mold. The clay model was then extricated or removed in pieces from the one-piece plaster shell mold. The inner surfaces of the mold cavity were cleaned, sanded and shellaced. Using soap as a parting compound, a casting plaster mix was poured into this mold. This cast part, or male plug, became the model for the competition, but first the Guildsman had to chip away the outer mold with a hammer and chisel, thus destroying it.

Five-Piece Mold Plaster Casting Method

Depending on the number of undercuts below the belt line or to accommodate bumpers, the casting plaster mold might have to be made in several pieces, further complicating the process. For example, in 1948 and 1951 the Guild recommended the five-piece mold plaster casting method. This method was adopted throughout the remaining model car competition years in the Guild how-to manuals.

For this later method, the Guildsman built dams out of ribbons of clay and took separate impressions of the front, rear, left side, right side and then top of the clay pattern. Cheesecloth was added to the female mold parts to give bending strength and prevent breakage. This method allowed multiple molds to be made from a single clay pattern. It was often necessary to take multiple impressions to remove casting flaws (like a dentist taking multiple impressions for a new crown, especially to pick up the gum line).

The inside mold surfaces were sanded lightly and finished with shellac. Vasoline or a mold release agent like silicone was applied to the smooth shellaced surface to serve as a parting compound. The female mold of the model car was assembled upside down (cavity opening upward) and a "male plug" was poured using casting plaster.

Finishing a Plaster Model

The male plug, or 1/12 scale model car, was broken away from the female mold parts, cleaned and sanded to remove mold parting lines ("flash") or other imperfections. At this point aluminum or brass trim parts had to be cut, filed and fit to the plaster body. Brass HO gauge track from the local hobby shop could be fashioned into window moldings around the windshield or side windows or rear daylight opening (DLO). The brass parts would have to be chrome plated. The edge of a steel rule was used to score the door, truck and hood opening lines. The plaster model car surfaces would be smoothed with fine sandpaper and primed before painting with enamel or lacquer. The window areas would be painted black or gray (different from the body color) to indicate glass.

A plywood board would be glued or pegged over the hollowed-out bottom of the plaster model car so that wheels could be attached firmly to the plywood. From 1946 to 1953, the Guildsmen had to make their own wheels. With the start of the 1954 competition, rubber wheels were supplied free of charge by the Guild. The wheels (2⅞" outside diameter) were to be turned out of wood on a homemade lathe using an old washing machine motor, or the contestant was encouraged to mold wheels out of plaster of Paris.

Elia Russinoff (1949) had a 4-in-1 bench-top lathe he used to make wheels. Some participants used maple or apple crate wood. Alternatively, a standard guide and kit was available from the Craftsman's Guild vendor with ready-made wooden wheels and other parts.

A pair of holes drilled in the plywood board along the centerline would match pegs in the bottom of the shipping crate so the model stayed stationary and would not be damaged. The contestant was encouraged to attach a tag to the bottom of the model describing any special features the judges would not find obvious.

Other Construction Methods (Laminated Wood, Wood Block and Rigid Urethane Foam)

There were a number of model car construction techniques suggested and described in the Guild's how-to booklet. The new body style options introduced in 1954 required new approaches such as longitudinal laminated wood, lateral laminated wood, a solid block of balsa wood, a model airplane construction technique, and the polyurethane block method. These were the prescribed methods. There was also the fiberglass lay-up technique, not covered by the Guild, and there were variations of all the above such as fiberglass over wood, Bondo (polyester body putty) over wood or plaster, and others.

Since sets of blueprints, or surface developments with sections and section lines, were not part of the prescribed Guild methods, a clay model was often a necessity in order to try out ideas in three dimensions and derive the necessary templates. The templates guaranteed symmetry in the finished model. Perfect symmetry guaranteed a high score in the Workmanship category. There were bolder methods such as the "rock-of-the-eye," technique in which the Guildsman mentally kept track of the model's rectangular coordinate system by periodically measuring from the centerline or relying on innate talent and "seat-of-the-pants" ability to make both the right and left hand sides match. Don Held indicated that his 1960 award winning model was all built by "eyeball."

Longitudinal Laminated Wood Method

One method advocated by the Guild was to laminate ½" or ¾" thick pieces of wood (basswood, white pine, sugar pine or poplar) cut to the longitudinal outline of the model car design finalized from a scale drawing or a scale clay model. The pieces of wood were laminated together with white glue or two-part epoxy (resin and hardener). This provided a rough shape for the design.

Another variation on this theme was to laminate the body pieces below the belt line (the area and surfaces below the window sills) after precutting the wheel openings in the outermost laminates. The pieces above the belt line for the solid-top "greenhouse" or clear plastic canopy would be fabricated and finished separately. The canopy parts would be located with pins or pegs for final assembly.

Solid Block of Balsa Wood Method

The Guildsman could employ a solid block of balsa wood purchased at his local hobby shop to carve and sculpt the body of his model car. Top, side, front and rear views taken from a scale drawing were transferred to the top, sides, front and rear of the balsa wood block. The young craftsman would cut away the excess balsa wood with a saw and use inexpensive carving tools to shape the model. A can of "plastic wood" would normally be kept near by to fill and rebuild excessive dips and valleys. This was an extremely difficult method unless the Guildsman maintained some of the flat surfaces of the block for reference planes or had a set of templates from a clay model. The reference planes were needed to make measurements to ensure symmetry. To succeed, you had to have the eye of a Henry Moore (one of the great modern contemporary sculptors), a lot of luck, or a finished clay model nearby to make templates of each section of the model. Benjamin B. Taylor (1950 fourth-place national scholarship, junior division, $1,000 award) and Gale P. Morris (1949 third-place national scholarship, junior division, $2,000 award) made their top award winning models from balsa wood.

Lateral Laminated Wood Method

Another method advocated by the Guild was the "loaf of bread" method (circa 1948) in which ½" or ¾" thick pieces of wood (white pine, sugar pine, or poplar) were cut to the approximate cross section of the model car at ½" or ¾" intervals, stacked longitudinally together and glued with white glue or two-part epoxy. In order for this method to work, a high quality scale drawing with various views and sections cut every ½" to ¾" was needed. By preshaping the symmetric, cross-sectional area of each block of wood longitudinally along the centerline of the model, the need for templates or a stylist's bridge could be significantly reduced and very little work remained to be done with a wood chisel. This method was used by George Aschen III of Kirkwood, Missouri, for his 1960 model.

Model Airplane Construction Method

The model airplane construction method was another technique described by the Guild for contestants around 1950, but it faded shortly thereafter. Since boys liked to make flying balsa wood model airplanes, this method was supposed to appeal to them. First, a very accurate scale drawing of the model design with various views and cross sections was needed.

Bulkheads at various section lines were cut out with a band saw, or hand coping saw, and assembled every 1" or so longitudinally on a flat surface or board. Strips of thin veneer or "stringers" (balsa wood, basswood or mahogany) were applied longitudinally from the frontmost bulkhead section to the rearmost bulkhead section. The front and rear of the model would be solid contoured blocks of wood supporting a center longitudinal stringer.

To make this construction method work, the Guildsman would have needed a three-view surface development plan, or blueprint plans, from which sectional templates could be traced and cut; and a very fine toothed coping saw or jeweler's saw (preferable a power band saw) to cut out all the parts and pieces. Although simple in appearance, this method was very sophisticated. It's no wonder this idea disappeared quickly from the Guild literature.

The brilliance of the Guild print materials was in (1) providing clear, self-explanatory illustrations and (2) making complex things look simple. The Guild was a master at making things look easy, when in fact what was being prescribed were complex model making techniques. For example, the model airplane method advocated by the Guild would have required a power jigsaw to accomplish all the intricate cuts and to keep things square. The construction of the designer's bridge or stylist's bridge required sophisticated tools such as a power table sander and drill press, again in order to keep things square. Most contestants didn't have these tools. The Guild was also a master at explaining things with illustrations. And, of course, most kids didn't have mechanical drawing or drafting until high school. Surface development, a form of mechanical drawing, used for the cutting of section lines to make templates, would have been unknown to all Guildsmen except a very small percentage at design schools, as this was a college freshman pursuit.

Polyurethane Block Construction Method

Another method, promoted for the 1967–1968 competition (the last year of the Fisher Guild) as a fast model building technique, was to sculpt or carve a model from a block of rigid polyurethane foam. (Styrofoam plastic was not suitable.) The block of rigid polyurethane foam would be 20" × 8" × 5" (L × W × H) in volume. The material is soft and easily sanded using various grits of sand paper and carves "like butter with a sharp knife." The smooth finished foam surface was coated with a commercial polymer modeling paste called Liquitex. This surface was smoothed and painted. A clay model of the finished design would be needed to make the necessary templates in order for this method to work, or points on a completed left side could be transferred to the right side with cardboard templates.

Fiberglass and Polyester Resin Techniques

Fiberglass and polyester resin techniques were used by Guildsmen, but were not described in the Guild literature. Guildsmen generously employed fiberglass and polyester resin over wood. Pep Boys auto supply stores had fiberglass kits for auto body repair projects. Sears, Roebuck and Company sold fiberglass and polyester repair kits for boats. Guildsmen bought these kits for a few dollars as the quantity of material provided amply met the needs of the model being designed. Another popular material used was Bondo, a polyester based auto body putty. Using wood or plaster as an armature, the Bondo could be spread with a plastic applicator and sanded when dry to a very smooth plastic surface finish, ideal for a high luster paint job.

Wheel Attachment

There were several wheel attachment methods described in the Guild literature. There was the wood screw attachment method, for a wooden model. Centerlines of the front and rear wheel axles had to be located on the model within the wheel well openings. Holes were drilled in the hard rubber wheel at the center point for the shank of the screw. The problem was to accurately locate the center of the rubber wheels and precisely locate the front and rear axle centerlines. This was critical to a successful winning model. During the scoring process for Scale Fidelity the judges had a jig or fixture for assessing front and rear wheel alignment, or tracking, as well as wheelbase width and length. Tires had to be square to the longitudinal centerline of the model and perpendicular to the ground. All four tires had to touch the ground simultaneously; no rocking allowed. Open wheels could be mounted flush with the fender's edge.

This was no easy task unless planned early on in the design phase of the model project. The surfaces for mounting the tires had to be maintained perpendicular to the bottom of the model through the construction process. The centerlines of the axles had to be drawn square

Scale Wheel Design Changes

Year	*Wheel Dimensions and Design Changes by Year*
1937–1953	The 1937 specs called for a 2³⁄₁₆" wheel diameter and ⁹⁄₁₆" width. Wheels were homemade on a lathe or molded from casting plaster. 1946–1953 two- and four-door, six-passenger family sedan body styles with wheels. 2⁷⁄₁₆" O.D., ⅝" width and 1⁵⁄₁₆" hubcap I.D. by ⅛" deep.
1954–1957	1/12 scale hard rubber wheels were supplied free of charge on presentation of a coupon of proof signed by a parent. Sedan, convertible, two- and four-door hardtop and station wagon body styles added. 2⁷⁄₁₆" O.D., ⅝" width, and 1⁵⁄₁₆" hubcap I.D. by ⅛" deep.
1958–1962	Slightly smaller hard rubber wheels with smaller hub cap I.D. provided free of charge. Sedan, convertible, two- and four-door hardtop and station wagon body styles possible. 2¼" O.D., ⅝" width and 1¼" hubcap I.D. by ⅛" deep.
1963–1968	Category A: Regular size wheels provided free of charge. 2¼" O.D., ⅝" width and 1¼" hubcap I.D. by ⅛" deep.
1963–1968	Category B: Small car and sports car size wheels provided free of charge. 2¹⁄₁₆" O.D., ⅝" width and 1¹⁄₁₆" hubcap I.D. by ⅛" deep.
1963–1968	Open Category C (Open Competition) could use either 2¼" O.D. or 2¹⁄₁₆" O.D. wheels or combination with new wheelbase configurations possible.

O.D. = Outside diameter and I.D. = Inside diameter. All wheel size dimensions were compatible with Specification Drawing A up to and including 1953, Specification Drawings A and B from 1954 to 1962, and Specification Drawings A, B, and C in 1963 and after.

to the bottom centerline and transferred vertically into the wheel well. A wheel center point has to be punched or drilled as a permanent reference.

There was the half-wheel attachment method in which a screw was driven perpendicular to the tread of the wheel into the wheel well opening and the head of the screw countersunk. Because of fender skirts, or partially covered rear wheels, this was primarily a rear axle solution. In the late 1940s and early 1950s it was a popular design idea to have both front and rear wheels partially covered. The half-wheel method then became a front and rear axle solution. Partially covered wheels, front or rear or both, had to be offset from the fender edge according to exacting Guild dimensional specs. For front tires this allowed clearance for steering movement, suspension jounce and changing of tires in the real world. For the rear this allowed clearance for vertical wheel suspension jounce and changing of tires in the real world.

In addition, the Guild advocated the partial dowel pin method in which a ³⁄₁₆" hole was drilled in the center of each of the hard rubber tires and a ³⁄₁₆" hole was drilled into the body of the model. A wooden dowel pin was driven into the model and became an axle center point. The hard rubber tire was press fit onto the pin.

Another method was the complete dowel pin method in which a ³⁄₁₆" diameter hole was drilled out of each wheel and a groove cut across the bottom of the model at the front and rear axle centerline points. A wooden axle of ³⁄₁₆" diameter was inserted in the groove across the entire width of the model and attached to the bottom with finishing nails or glue.

Scale Wheel Design History

Initially for the competition, boys had to make their own 1/12 scale wheels on a lathe from maple or apple wood or mold them using casting plaster. These were 2³⁄₁₆" (1937) and then 2⅞" outside diameter starting in 1946. In 1954 a Fisher Body vendor manufactured a 2⅞" O.D. hard rubber wheel for the contestants which were distributed free of charge. This was a major advance and was calculated to increase the number of participants. In 1958, a slightly smaller diameter rubber wheel (2¼" O.D.) was introduced to reflect changes in real-world tire designs, and in 1963, an even smaller diameter scale rubber wheel design (2⅛" O.D.) was introduced to support Category B, Small Cars and Sports Cars. The latter two wheel sizes were designed to accommodate the 11 different body styles contestants could make 1963–1968.

Guildsmen were never happy with the hard rubber molded wheels Fisher Body supplied so they cut and polished them on lathes, added raised lettering to the sidewalls spelling out specific tire brands, painted thin yellow, red and white walls, and made completely new wheels of their own choosing, whatever enhanced their dream cars. The hubcaps or wheel covers were another exercise in ingenuity requiring hand-filing of round aluminum stock, vacuum forming of plastic vinyl sheet, chrome-plating of brass, polishing of aluminum or bronze, and of course, filing of chromed drawer-pulls from the kitchen cabinets or chromed gliders from the legs of dining room chairs. Everything in the home was fair game including Dad's chromed martini stirrer.

G. The Awards and Regional Awards System

1946, 1947 and 1948 Competitions

The post–World World II Guild scholarship awards system for 1946, 1947 and 1948 is very confusing. In 1946 and 1947 the miniature model Napoleonic Coach and model car competitions were conducted simultaneously. By 1948, the coach competition had been phased out per a recommendation of the International Guild Advisory Board. Nonetheless, coaches were still king of the hill in 1946 and 1947 with the highest prize money awarded for first and second place.

The dual competitions obviously strained the Craftsman's Guild budget (normally about $20,000 was earmarked for scholarships) so a plan was devised to award first- and second-place scholarships of $5,000 and $3,000, respectively, to the top two senior and top two junior miniature model coach builders. There were lots of other awards: 588 cash prizes starting at $100 and going downward and 18 all-expenses-paid Guild convention trips (*Popular Mechanics*, November 1946 and November 1947).

Similarly, for the model car competitions in 1946 and 1947, a plan was devised to award first- and second-place scholarships of $4,000 and $2,000, respectively, to the top two senior and top two junior model car makers. As in the coach competition, there were 588 cash prizes starting at $100 and going downward and 18 all-expenses-paid Guild convention trips. Thus, in 1946 and 1947 the total scholarships awarded equaled $28,000 and the total cash awards (including the university trust funds) were $85,000 and $65,000, respectively, in 1946 and 1947. In 1948 the cash prize total available was $65,000, similar to 1947.

A Craftsman's Guild advertisement in *Popular Mechanics*, November 1947, encouraged boys to get ready for the upcoming model car competition (with no mention of coaches) in 1948 with scholarship awards ranging from $1,000 to $4,000 in both the senior and junior divisions, for a total of $20,000 in scholarships and a grand total $65,000 in prizes. The actual scholarship awards were first place, $4,000; second place, $3,000; third place, $2,000; and fourth place, $1,000.

A *Mechanix Illustrated* article from November 1948, showing head Guild judge Victor L. Olesen, does not mention or show any coaches. The transition the Fisher brothers and Harley J. Earl had dreamed of was complete, and boys competing in the post–World War II Craftsman's Guild program would become automobile designers concerned with design, styling and aesthetics.

1953–1954 Model Car Competition

The winners in this competition received a total of $90,000 in scholarships and cash awards. The first-place state award-winning model cars competed against one another in the same region to determine the regional winner. There were 20 regions, or groups of states. The judges had to determine the individual junior and senior division winners of the regional awards, which included all-expense-paid trips to the Guild's four-day national convention, valued on the average at $750 to $890 each (with 40 awards in all, this was equal to $30,000 to $36,000 in aggregated value). The eight national scholarship winners (four junior and four senior division) were selected from the regional winners. First place, $4,000; second place, $3,000; third place, $2,000; and fourth place, $1,000. The state awards were first place, $150; second place, $100; third place, $50; and four honorable mention awards at $25 each. A certificate of design and craftsmanship was given to all entries.

The Guild regions by number in 1953–54 consisted of the following states:

Region 1. Maine, New Hampshire, Vermont
Region 2. Massachusetts, Rhode Island
Region 3. New York, Connecticut
Region 4. New Jersey, Delaware
Region 5. Pennsylvania, Maryland
Region 6. West Virginia, Virginia, District of Columbia
Region 7. North Carolina, South Carolina, Georgia
Region 8. Alabama, Florida, Mississippi
Region 9. Kentucky, Tennessee
Region 10. Michigan, Ohio
Region 11. Illinois, Indiana
Region 12. Wisconsin, Minnesota
Region 13. North Dakota, South Dakota, Nebraska
Region 14. Iowa, Missouri
Region 15. Louisiana, Arkansas, Oklahoma
Region 16. Texas, New Mexico, Arizona
Region 17. Colorado, Utah, Kansas
Region 18. Idaho, Wyoming, Montana
Region 19. Washington, Oregon (+ Alaska in 1959–60)
Region 20. California, Nevada (+ Hawaii in 1959–60)

In the 1955–56 model car competition year, the transition year for scholarship awards, the national scholarship awards for the top junior and senior division winners were increased by an increment of $1,000 as follows: First place, $5,000; second place, $4,000; third place, $3,000; and fourth place, $2,000. Ten styling awards were added consisting of $1,000 scholarship trust funds for a high score in the Design category of the score sheet. Styling scholarships were awarded to contestants with unusually high scores (usually 90 percent of points) in the Design category, but only average scores in the Craftsmanship category. They were awarded without regard to the contestant's age, regional residence, total score or state award level. For example, in 1967 Dennis A. Little of Lyndhurst, Ohio, a third-place state award winner ($50 cash award), won a $1,000 styling scholarship for excellence in design. He had been an honorable mention ($25 cash) winner in both 1965 and 1966. The styling awards were announced during the Guild convention. There were now a total of 18 national scholarship trust funds awarded.

By the 1960–61 competition year, the states had been reorganized into 20 new geographical regions. Only regions 1 and 14 stayed the same. Region 12 was renumbered 13. This occurred because Fisher Body monitored the quality and quantity of model entries and where they came from. Large population centers like Chicago or Los Angeles produced large numbers of models. Because they were so competitive, states like New York, Pennsylvania, Ohio, Michigan, Indiana, Illinois and California were broken out into separate regions. They could support their full complement of 16 available state awards.

After Hawaii and Alaska became states in 1959, regions 17 and 19 were modified accordingly. By the 1960–61 competition year, Alaska had been incorporated into Region 17 (MT, WY, ND, SD, and AK) and Hawaii had been incorporated into Region 19 (WA, OR, ID, NV and HI). The new Guild regions by number in 1960–61 consisted of the following states:

Region 1. Maine, New Hampshire, Vermont (stayed the same as 1953–54)
Region 2. New York
Region 3. Massachusetts, Rhode Island
Region 4. Connecticut, New Jersey
Region 5. Pennsylvania
Region 6. Maryland, Delaware, West Virginia, Virginia, and District of Columbia
Region 7. North Carolina, South Carolina, Kentucky, Tennessee
Region 8. Florida, Mississippi, Alabama, Georgia
Region 9. Ohio
Region 10. Michigan
Region 11. Indiana
Region 12. Illinois
Region 13. Wisconsin, Minnesota (stayed the same as 1953–54, but changed region number from 12 to 13)
Region 14. Iowa, Missouri (stayed the same as 1953–54)
Region 15. Nebraska, Kansas, Arkansas, Oklahoma
Region 16. Texas, Louisiana
Region 17. Montana, Wyoming, North Dakota, South Dakota, Alaska
Region 18. Utah, Colorado, Arizona, New Mexico
Region 19. Washington, Oregon, Idaho, Nevada, Hawaii
Region 20. California

H. Detroit Guild Convention Details for Selected Years

1950

In attendance at the Guild banquet, August 15, 1950, held at the Book-Cadillac Hotel, was Dr. George J. Fisher, national BSA commissioner and honorary FBCG president. The master of ceremonies was Bert Parks and the guest speaker was Charles F. Kettering, a GMC director.[4] There were Guild alumni (16 Napoleonic Coach scholarship winners and 12 model car scholarship winners) in attendance. Richard A. Teague, a young GM Stylist at the Tech Center (who would become AMC's VP of styling) was there along with Frank C. Riess, one of the original designers of the miniature Napoleonic Coach.[5] Two future GM presidents were there: Edward N. Cole (Cadillac Motor Division) and James M. Roche (Cadillac Motor Division). After the scholarship awards were made, the young Guildsmen "chatted-up" their model car designs and hobnobbed with Chuck Jordan and other judges in attendance.

By August 1950, 2,371,000 boys and young men had cumulatively enrolled in the Guild, $788,000 in scholarships and cash awards had been made, and 91 national scholarship awards had been won since 1930.

1951

The Guild convention was held August 14–17, 1951. Guildsmen swarmed the new Le Sabre show car and Harley J. Earl stood there giving them a first-hand introduction to his new "baby." J.J. Cronin, GM vice president and Guild president, acted as the banquet toast-master and screen star Robert Young was the radio emcee for the coast-to-coast Guild scholarship awards radio announcements and post-awards wrap-up interviews with the likes of Charles F. Kettering, a GM director; Charles E. Wilson, GM president and CEO; and the top Guild Scholarship winners.

1952

By 1952, there had been cumulatively $880,000 in scholarships and cash awards and 115 national scholarship awards had been made by the Craftsman's Guild. Since 1930, some 10,000 boys (cumulatively) had received a state or regional award (*Guide Light*, December 1952).

1953

There were cumulatively 3,235,000 boys and young men enrolled, $983,000 in scholarships and cash awards given, and 123 national scholarship winners. Since 1930, some 11,225 youths (cumulatively) had received cash awards (*Your Son's Future*).

1954

There were 131 boys who had won scholarships worth a total of $400,500.

1956

Three young men from Los Angeles were big winners in the model car competition: William A. Moore, first-place national scholarship, senior division, $5,000 award; E. Arthur Russell, styling scholarship, $1,000 award; and Charles A. Gibilterra, third-place national scholarship, junior division, $3,000 award. Paul Tatseos (Boston, Massachusetts) was a senior regional winner, and Ronald C. Pellman (Snyder, New York) and Harrell Lucky (Little Rock, Arkansas) were junior regional winners. Harley J. Earl and Charles F. Kettering were members of the honorary board of judges. Three Fisher brothers (Edward F. Fisher, Charles T. Fisher and William A. Fisher) were guests at the Guild awards banquet, where Charles M. Jordan, chief designer at the Special Studios, GM Styling, was the guest speaker. Another guest was Edward N. Cole, general manager of Chevrolet Motor Division and future GM president. Sammy Kaye and his orchestra provided the entertainment along with the Varsity Glee Club of Purdue University. James P. Wines was Guild administrator.

1957

The proposed itinerary for the 1957 convention, called the "Adventure of a Lifetime," would last from July 30 through August 2. Two days of the convention would be devoted to tours and sightseeing in and around Detroit, including the Detroit Zoological Gardens, a tour of GM's Technical Center and Styling section, an afternoon of swimming and sports at an island club at beautiful Lake St. Clair and luxury living every evening at Detroit's famous Book-Cadillac Hotel. The most exciting moment would be the announcement of the scholarship winners at 8:30 P.M., Tuesday, July 30, during a nationally broadcast awards dinner in the beautiful auditorium of the Fisher Body administrative building (*Guildsman*, vol. 4, no. 5, 1956).

By 1957, the number of Guild enrollees since 1930 had reached a total of 4.5 million, with 179 scholarship awards valued at $525,000 and more than $875,000 in cash and other awards shared by thousands of boys and young men winning state and regional honors. A total of $1,400,000 scholarships and cash had been cumulatively awarded by this time.

1958

There were cumulatively 5 million Guild enrollees or members, $1,500,000 in scholarships and cash awards, and 198 scholarship winners (*Fisher Body Craftsman's Guild*).

1961

At the 1961 Guild banquet, after Edwin C. Klotzburger, president of the Guild, presented the scholarship awards, the guest speaker was Dr. Lawrence R. Hafstad, VP of GM's research laboratories and member of the Guild's honorary board. Dr. Hafstad paid tribute to the 44 regional and scholarship winners by saying, "Creativity is a rare and valuable talent. It should become doubly so as the technology revolution in which we are living proceeds along its course. Everything we do opens new opportunities to do more. However fast we move, the terrain keeps opening wide before us and the horizon continues to recede."

By the 1961 Guild convention, a total of 258 Guild scholarships had been awarded and a cumulative total of $1,875,000 in scholarships and cash awards shared by thousands of young American designers and craftsmen (*Guildsman*, vol. 9, no. 1, September 1961).

In 1961 Ronald J. Will (age 18) of Hobart, Indiana, was the first-place national scholarship, senior division, award winner, with an asymmetric design and Anthony V. Simone (age 15) of Providence, Rhode Island, was the first-place national scholarship, junior division, award winner, with a clear bubble-top design.

Ron Will built an asymmetric, convertible sports car, which consisted of 54 miniature wood and metal parts that required 700 hours to complete. For this bold, new, innovative design, no two surfaces of the car were alike; a one-time trick, but legitimized by Virgil M. Exner, Sr.'s asymmetric show car called the XNR.

Anthony V. Simone's model was a silver-gray sports coupe utilizing a simple and clean design. A clear plastic bubble top was featured. The fully exposed exhaust system gave his model a sports car appearance. Hubcaps were constructed from bevel gears and chrome plated (*Guildsman*, vol. 9, no. 1, September 1961).

1962

In 1962 there were 46 regional winners, which included six duplicate awards given to the sons of GM employees. By the 1962 Guild convention year, a total of 279 scholarships had been awarded and a cumulative total of over $2 million worth of scholarships and cash awards had been distributed. Guildsmen still wore the blue blazer with the diamond shaped Guild insignia. (These were soon to be replaced by light blue Palm Beach sports coats with dark blue slacks in the remaining conventions through 1968.) Kaizo Oto (1962 third-place national scholarship winner) noted that most of these young people had never owned a sports jacket before coming to the Guild banquet.

At the 1962 convention banquet the 800 attendees were addressed by Dr. Lee A. DuBridge, president of the California Institute of Technology and member of the honorary board of judges. Dr. DuBridge stated, "The whole project, in short, was for these young men an adventure in learning — an adventure in understanding — an adventure in putting learning to work — and learning by doing. ... Everyone has proved he is a winner. ... And they will choose the college to which they go in the same spirit. ... They'll find the college which offers the greatest challenge and opportunity to develop their particular talents."

The special activities for the Guildsman included a visit to a Shakespearean museum, a golf-swing demo at the Bloomfield Hills Country Club, viewing full-size experimental Corvette styling designs, inspecting clay styling models, and visiting the GM Proving Grounds and GM Styling.

By 1962, there were cumulatively 7 million Guild members.

1964

At the 1964 Guild banquet, Lowell Thomas, world traveler and CBS commentator, was the master of ceremonies. The Four Lads, a popular singing group, provided the entertainment.

There were some important people in attendance that night: Edward N. Cole, now VP for GMC Car and Truck; Elliot "Pete" M. Estes, general manager of Pontiac Motor Division; Edward F. Fisher, GM director (one of the original seven Fisher brothers); Robert W. Henderson, VP Sandia Corporation (1934 Napoleonic Coach national scholarship winner); William L. Mitchell, VP GM, in charge of styling staff; Carlyle W. McClellan, FBCG administrator; Edwin C. Klotzburger, VP GM, Body and Assembly Group (and 1961 Guild president); and Semon E. Knudsen, general manager, Chevrolet Motor Division.[6]

One of the principal sponsors of the Guild was the late Charles F. Kettering, a General Motors vice president, who for more than 25 years directed the activities of the GM Research Laboratories. At one Guild banquet, "Boss Kett" said, "It doesn't make any difference whether a boy wins one of the top awards or not. All of them — winners and those who didn't win — receive an award that goes with them through life. They have learned to do a job well. That simple technique of excellence of accomplishment and exactness to detail will be useful always. There is so much to do in the world. The world needs men such as these boys will turn out to be" (*American Youth*, September–October 1960).

1968

32,800 models had been carved, sanded and painted by Guildsmen, 10 million boys and young men had enrolled cumulatively and 387 individuals had won university trust funds valued at $2,400,000.

I. ANALYSIS OF SOME ASPECTS OF THE 1963 AND 1966 MODEL CAR COMPETITIONS

Fisher Body allocated 874 cash awards (state, regional and national awards combined) in 1963 and 1966, or about 16 (874/51) per state. This is the rough benchmark that will be used to see how the various states and regions performed in the model car competition. The number and types of awards received in 1963 and 1966 came from the announcements mailed

PERCENT OF MODELS RECEIVING AWARDS AND PERCENT OF AWARDS DISTRIBUTED AT THE STATE LEVEL IN 1963 AND 1966

Year	Actual Awards	Number of Entries	Percentage of Models Rewarded	Number of State Awards	Percentage of Awards Distributed
1963	571	4,137*	13%	874	65.3%
1966	407	2,949	13%	874	46.6%

*Estimated from table at top of opposite page.

annually to participants in the fall.[7] This document contained the name, city, state, school name and award level of each contestant who received a scholarship or cash award.

Overall Distribution of Awards for 1963 and 1966

As shown in the first table above, only 13 percent of the model entries received awards in both 1963 and 1966 and only 65.3 percent and 46.6 percent of the available awards were given away in 1963 and 1966, respectively. This suggests that GM was faced with model quality problems. It appears that either many states had an insufficient number of entries in order to produce 16 award-worthy models, or many states had an insufficient number of high-quality models, or there may have been a minimally acceptable GM score below which no state cash awards were considered.

The low overall award rate (13 percent) can be rationalized. It was previously suggested that the truly amateurish, oversize and undersize models were probably dropped before being scored because they failed to meet the basic Scale Fidelity requirements. A model entry had to pass what is called the laugh test. It was also previously discussed that a contestant's model had to receive 50 to 60 percent of available points to be in the running for a state level cash award. Interest in model-making as a hobby among teenage youth in America had waned, and competition with other extracurricular time demands crowded out the FBCG. "Excellence in craftsmanship" was no longer a family priority. The competition was very stiff to begin with, but General Motors and Fisher Body had very high standards and expectations. Finally, the working judges were not obligated to make awards just because GM and Fisher Body allocated 16 cash awards per state. There was room for subjective judgment and discretion.

The obvious assumption the author made, when initially looking at the Guild awards, was that each state's cash awards were completely consumed in any given year. In fact, GM felt no obligation to give away cash awards unless they were earned by achieving some minimum threshold score or some minimum level of integrity. (In an article about the Guild in *Automotive History Review* no. 34, spring 1999, the author misinterpreted the number of awards received as being equal to the number of model entries.)

Awards by State

The states with the most award winning models in 1963 and 1966 were California, 16/16; Connecticut, 16/15; Florida, 14/16; Illinois, 17/15; Indiana, 21/22; Massachusetts, 16/14; Michigan, 24/24; Minnesota, 14/16; New Jersey, 17/17; New York, 16/16; Ohio, 23/18; Pennsylvania, 17/16; and Wisconsin, 20/16.

California, Illinois, Indiana, Michigan, New York, Ohio and Pennsylvania, designated as regions in their own right, held their own with a full complement of 16–17 state awards available. Some got more than their designated share; for example, Indiana, Michigan, and

ESTIMATE OF THE NUMBER OF ENTRIES FOR 1963

	1963 Competition Year	*1966 Competition Year*
No. of $ Awards Rec'd	571	407
No. of $ Awards Available	874	874
No. of Model Entries	4,137*	2,949

*Estimated using the proportions ratio $\frac{571}{x} = \frac{407}{2,949}$ where x = the number of 1963 model entries.

DISTRIBUTION OF ACTUAL AWARDS BY REGION IN 1963 AND 1966 (ALL AWARD LEVELS)

Region Number	*1963 Actual Number of Awards*	*1966 Actual Number of Awards*
1. ME, NH, VT	13	5
2. NY	16	16
3. MA, RI	28	28
4. CT, NJ	33	32
5. PA	17	16
6. MD, DE, WV, VA, DC	43	30
7. NC, SC, KY, TN	44	24
8. FL, MS, AL, GA	31	26
9. OH	23	18
10. MI	24	24
11. IN	21	22
12. IL	17	15
13. WI, MN	34	32
14. IA, MO	30	11
15. NE, KS, AR, OK	45	21
16. TX, LA	35	13
17. MT, WY, ND, SD, AK	25	11
18. UT, CO, AZ, NM	42	20
19. WA, OR, ID, NV, HW	34	27
20. CA	16	16
Totals	**571**	**407**

Ohio, because of duplicate awards to the sons of GM employees. These states had a high number of Fisher Body plants and other GM plants.

The *Guildsman* newsletter stated, "For 1960–61, in many Regions, several duplicate state awards were given. In Michigan, for example, all but 2 awards offered in the competition were duplicated. Indiana, Michigan, and Ohio were awarded the highest number of awards because they had a large number of duplicate awards, reflecting the presence of a number of GM and Fisher Plants and a high number of employee sons participating" (*Guildsman*, 1960–61).

States with the least number of awards in 1963 and 1966 included Alaska, Delaware,

Montana, North Dakota, Vermont, Maine, Idaho, and Hawaii. The following Guild policy explains why some states had so few awards: "Some cash awards in the regional judging occasionally go unclaimed. ... If, for instance, only a small number of model cars are entered from a small or sparsely-populated state, the judges feel that they are not obligated to grant all the awards in that state merely because there are as many model cars submitted as there are awards available" ("Decisions Made by Judges Final").

At least one award was made in each of the 50 states including the District of Columbia during 1963 and 1966.

Awards by Region

Between 1963 and 1966, there was a 28.7 percent overall drop in the number of qualified models, but there were reductions of 50 percent or more in the number of qualified models from regions 14, 15, 16, 17, 18 and 19. These reductions in awards involved 43 percent of the states.

1963 and 1966 Competition Demographics
(Age, Education) for Award Winners Only

The following table shows that in 1963 and 1966, 81 percent of the Guild award winners were in the senior division (ages 16–20) and attended high school or college. Sixty-five percent were enrolled in high school and 16 percent were enrolled in colleges or universities. Ninety-two unique colleges and 66 universities were represented by college-age Guildsmen in the 1963 and 1966 competition years, respectively. Only a few vocational-technical trade schools were represented. The top national winners tended to be young people 19 or 20 years old who had built multiple Guild models.

Only 17 percent of the award winners in 1963 and 1966 came from the junior division (ages 11–15). This group could have had a large number of entries, but few may have been award-worthy due to the contestants' lack of experience. But, despite their inexperience as model-makers, some national scholarship awards were made to 12 and 13 year olds. For example, in 1964 John D'Mura was a 13-year-old national scholarship winner and in 1965 Michael A. Pietruska was a 12-year-old national scholarship winner. Normally, the top junior division national scholarship winners were age 15, or at the top of the bracket, having worked their way up.

EDUCATION (AGE) DISTRIBUTION OF AWARD WINNERS
FOR 1963 AND 1966 COMPETITIONS

School Type	Age Interval	1963*	1966*
Elementary	11 years old	0.97%	2.21%
Junior High	12–15 years old	17.51%	16.57%
Senior High	16–18 years old	65.76%	64.63%
College/University	19–20 years old	15.76%	16.57%
Total		100.00%	99.98%

*Unknowns were redistributed where school type was not indicated.
Source: "The Fisher Body Craftsman's Guild Announces."

Beginning in the early 1960s, Fisher Body expanded the age intervals for the junior and senior divisions. The junior division was expanded from 12–15 to 11–15 years old and the senior division was expanded from 16–19 to 16–20 years old. Despite the fact that Fisher Body expanded the age range of the junior division to accommodate 11 year olds, or 20–25 percent more in that age bracket, only 1–2 percent of the award winners came from this part of the population.

Duplicate Awards and Favorite (GM) Sons

A duplicate award was made to the next highest scoring model in the case of a tie with the son of a GM employee. For example, in 1961 there were national scholarship duplicate awards at both the senior and junior third-place national scholarship award level. In 1962 there were three national scholarship duplicate awards made, namely the third-place national scholarship, junior division, the fourth-place national scholarship, junior division, and the fourth-place national scholarship, senior division. Again in 1963, there was one duplicate award at the third-place national scholarship award level, junior division. In 1966 there was one duplicate award at the fourth-place national scholarship level, junior division.

REGIONAL AWARDS AND STATE REPRESENTATION

Year	Regional Awards	Duplicate Regional	Duplicate National	States Represented
1957	42	2	Unknown	29
1963	50	10	1*	31
1966	45	5	1**	27

*$3,000 junior division duplicate, GM son.
**$2,000 junior division duplicate, GM son.

The above table shows that, as indicated in the rules, duplicate awards were made at the regional level and at the national scholarship level to eliminate the perception that sons of GM employees had an advantage. Also, it shows that over 60 percent of the states (and Washington, D.C.) were represented by an award winner.

Furthermore, of the 874 cash awards available (without double or triple counting), 65.3 percent were awarded in 1963 and 46.6 percent were awarded in 1966. Both conditions reflect a decrease in the number of quality models and the imposition of a minimum threshold score. But the quantity of model submissions did not reflect a lack of interest on the part of teenagers to build model dream cars, as thousands continued to flood the Fisher Body Auditorium.

One can hardly call a 25 percent decline in model entries, from 4,000 models to 3,000 models, a significant loss in interest among teenagers in model-building. Although there was a numerical decrease, an executive or CEO intent on discontinuing the Craftsman's Guild would be hard pressed to explain how 3,000 model entries reflected a lack of interest. Clearly, 3,000 entries was more than in many prior years. In 1966, there was strong interest in scratch model-making and the Guild competition, but quality was definitely dropping as teens no longer had the time to devote to this extracurricular project.

In 1963 the majority of the awards (99.9 percent) went to the average high school and college age population, whereas only five awards went to vocational-technical high schools. In 1966 the majority of the awards (99.9 percent) went to the average high school and college age population, whereas one award went to a vocational-technical high school student. The Fisher Body Craftsman's Guild appealed to college-bound kids. We can compare this to the Ford Industrial Arts Awards Program, a Guild paradigm of the 1950s, 100 percent of their awards went to vocational-technical school students who may not have been college-bound or as university oriented. The Guild appealed to a broad, academically inclined, college-preparatory-school population of teenagers.

Although only representing 15.6 percent of the aggregate of Guildsman receiving awards, students from a plethora of colleges and universities participated in the 1963 (n = 92) and 1966 (n = 66) Guild competitions. One of the theories about the demise of the Guild in 1968 was that high school students had too many extracurricular demands, SAT performance was stressed over excellence in craftsmanship, and many preferred social activities to solitary pursuits like making models. Although the participation of college-age youth in the Guild may challenge this notion, this can easily be explained. Many of the national scholarship winners were 19- or 20-year-old college age youths who were fully engaged in the competition after many years of work. They couldn't just throw the experience away. They were hooked, so they continued making models in college.

The fact that students from the Art Center College of Design dominated the Guild winner's circle, year after year, testifies to the excellent training in surface development (mechanical drawing), clay modeling (clay tool-making, cams, drags, etc.), and fiberglass model-making that freshman industrial design students received from people like Joe Thompson and Joe Ferrer. Some key schools with automotive engineering and transportation industrial design programs were not even represented in the 1963 or 1966 Guild competitions.

1963 AND 1966 AWARD RECIPIENTS FROM INSTITUTIONS WITH AUTOMOTIVE ENGINEERING OR TRANSPORTATION INDUSTRIAL DESIGN PROGRAMS

School Name or Type	Number of Awards in 1963	Number of Awards in 1966
General Motors Institute	2	0
Art Center College of Design	3*	5**
Pratt Institute	3	0
Illinois Institute of Technology	0	0
Rhode Island School of Design	0	0

*In 1963, ACCD awards consisted of Jim Bieck, national styling scholarship, $1,000 award; Geza Loczi, third-place state Arizona, $50 award; and Robert Aikins, fourth-place national scholarship, $2,000 award.
**In 1966, ACCD awards included honorable mention, second-place state awards, styling scholarship (Fred Duddles) and first-place national scholarship, senior division, $5,000 award (Ovid O. Ward).

The Art Center College of Design, Pratt Institute, Illinois Institute of Technology, and the Rhode Island School of Design had the most popular transportation industrial design programs in the country at the time. These are still the top programs with the addition of the Academy of Art University (San Francisco, California) and the College for Creative Studies (Detroit, Michigan) among many others. The latter two programs did not exist during the Guild era. The Industrial Designers Society of America (IDSA) has a list of accredited schools with industrial design programs (see <www.idsa.org>).

J. OVERSEAS CRAFTSMAN'S GUILDS

Background

GM Suisse adopted the U.S. model car competition on their own volition and translated all the Fisher Body Guild materials into German and French. They announced their competition in October 1964 and by January 15, 1965, had 500 model entries in hand.

GM headquarters seized on this opportunity to build and improve international relations. Bill Mitchell was the prime mover who sold General Motors Overseas Operations (GMOO) on establishing Craftsman's Guild programs, initially as clubs for employees' sons, at Vauxhall Motors Ltd. in England and Adam-Opel AG in West Germany. The thrust of his sales pitch was to have the top 1965 overseas Guild winners compete with the top 1965 U.S. Fisher Guild winners for the same scholarships. The sticking point, however, was whether the overseas Guild winners should compete for the same pot of Fisher university trust funds as the U.S. Fisher Guild winners. Instead of sharing the funds, Fisher Body Division, GM Styling and GMOO eventually agreed to have an International Craftsman's Guild Award, with gold, silver and bronze medallions as awards, for the top three senior division winners from Vauxhall, Opel, Suisse, Holden and U.S. Fisher Guild. Bill Mitchell and the Styling staff would vote for the top three winners by secret ballot.[8]

Because of an austerity program, Vauxhall dropped their VCG in 1968 and GM Holden didn't get started until 1967. These events threw a monkey wrench into Bill Mitchell's International Craftsman's Guild Competition plans. The gold, silver and bronze medallions never got minted and the big International Craftsman's Guild gala proposed for New York City never materialized.[9]

The bottom line was that from 1965 to 1969 the top overseas Guild winners won up to the equivalent of $1,500 in cash from their sponsoring plants, came to America in the summer for a ten-day tour, participated in the Detroit Guild conventions, and took home two styling scholarships worth $1,000 each in both 1967 and 1968.

Beginning in 1965, Craftsman's Guilds were organized in the United Kingdom (Vauxhall Craftsman's Guild), Switzerland (Modelauto Wettbewerb), West Germany (Adam Opel Modellbauer Gilde), and Australia (Holden Craftsman's Guild) and sponsored by the General Motors Overseas Division. Except for the Opel Modellbauer Gilde, which lasted from 1965 to 1979, it is believed the other programs existed only a few years (1965–1969).

Vauxhall Craftsman's Guild

The Vauxhall Craftsman's Guild was headquartered at Vauxhall Motors Ltd., Luton, Bedfordshire. Mr. Ron How organized the Vauxhall program in 1965 for 16 to 20 year olds as a four-month pilot program, which lasted from March 31, 1965, to June 5, 1965. Designed to discover and encourage young men with design and creative abilities, there was £500 total in prizes and cash: first prize, £100; second prize, £75; third prize, £50; and fourth prize, £25. The first-place winner joined the Guild convention in Detroit. The competition was open to Vauxhall employees' sons from Luton, Dunstable and Ellesmere Point as well as full- and part-time students from Luton College of Technology.

In 1965 the winners were Terence Kirk, a Vauxhall apprentice (£100); Lutz Schelisch, a Vauxhall apprentice (£75); Emlyn Thomas of Bedford (£50); and Peter Savage of Dunstable (£25). The pilot program was a success and the Craftsman's Guild was officially launched for all British residents August 24, 1965, with a £500 top prize (£750 total value in prizes). The three classes of models that could be made were Class A: saloon, convertibles and estate cars; Class B: small cars and sports cars; and Class C: open category (unconventional, "space age" concept vehicles, etc.). For the 14- to 15-year-old age group there were two £25 prizes.[10]

In 1966 there were 32 finalists. The top winners were Christopher Field (age 21) of Kingsteignton, Devon, who received £250 and a ten-day trip to the USA; Gordon Bedingfield (age 20) a Vauxhall apprentice, who received £150; Martin Elliot of Draycote, Warwickshire, who received £75; Philip Guillot, a Scheffield grammar school student, who received £40; and the top girl contestant was Ms. Gillian Bailey (age 19) of Beccles, Suffolk, who won a black leather traveling case. The other winners were awarded model-making tool kits.

The Vauxhall Guild had its own publication called *Guildsman News*. There were two divisions, which separated schoolboys from young men. The model styling and design judges came from the Vauxhall Styling Department and the craftsmanship judges came from Vauxhall's Apprentice and Training School. Guild field representatives visited schools and showed a short color film about the program.[11]

In 1966–67 the competition incentives expanded to £2000 in prizes, a £50 junior division (age 11–15) award with a trip to the European continent, and a £500 senior division (age 16–20) award with a trip to the USA.

It is believed that the Vauxhall Craftsman's Guild was terminated in 1968 at the same time as the Fisher Body Craftsman's Guild due to a plant austerity program.[12]

GM Suisse Model Auto Competition (Modelauto Wettbewerb), 1965–1968

Opel Suisse responded to the author's summer 2002 request for information, but regrettably they were not able to provide any records of the Modelauto Wettbewerb from their archives. From GM interorganizational letters, it is known they announced their Guild program in October 1964 and had 500 model entries in hand by January 15, 1965. It is also known that Bill Mitchell was pushing the timing of the overseas Guilds so their top winners could join the Fisher Guild convention and banquet in Detroit in late July.

Adam-Opel Modellbauer Gilde (Model-Builder's Guild), 1965–1979

In 1970, the sixth model car competition was about to begin. Prior competitions had seen cumulatively over 5,030 model car entries and 510 prize winning individuals. The prizes were as follows: senior division (ages 17–21) prizes: first place, DM 7,000 and a trip to America; second place, DM 5,000; third place, DM 3,000; fourth place, DM 2,000; and fifth place, DM 1,000; with 45 other items for contestants. Junior division (ages 12–16) prizes: first place, DM 2,500; second place, DM 2,000; third place, DM 1,500; fourth place, DM 1,000; and 66 other items for participants. The program was coeducational.

Art teachers from the secondary schools in Ruesselsheim and Frankfort, in conjunction with designers and builders from the Opel Ruesselsheim plant, winnowed out the best designs from among the submissions using a point system that had proven its value for years. The deadline in 1970 was April 15. Unlike the U.S. with a full school year, it is presumed they had only a few months to design, build and finish a model car.

In 1970, 87 percent of the model entries came from the junior division and only 13 percent came from the senior division. The Opel Model Builder's Guild participation rate in 1970 was 5.8 percent (1,759/30,227) compared to the overall Overseas Craftsman's Guild participation rate of 1.79 percent (2,510/139,702) and a U.S. rate of 0.50 percent to 0.66 percent. (These numbers are not directly comparable because the years are not identical.) The numbers suggest a great deal of enthusiasm at Opel over the idea of scratch-building, model-making, auto styling and auto design.

Mr. H. Barth was the head of the Model Builder's Guild program at Opel. The scoring criteria were similar to the U.S. Guild: originality, craftsmanship, possibility of realization in the future, and exportability were on the agenda. Modellbauer Guildsmen had their own newsletter called the *Gilde-Informationer*, and the *Opel-Post* newsletter carried the contest news for all Opel employees. During its peak years of 1976–1977 and 1979, there were 2,687 and 2,773 Opel model entries, respectively, compared to 4,137 in 1963, a peak year for the U.S. Fisher Guild. Opel had a cumulative total of 23,764 model entries between 1965 and 1979. Of that number, 62 percent of the Opel model entries were judged as "individuals" (junior and senior divisions), whereas 38 percent of the model entries were judged by "school."

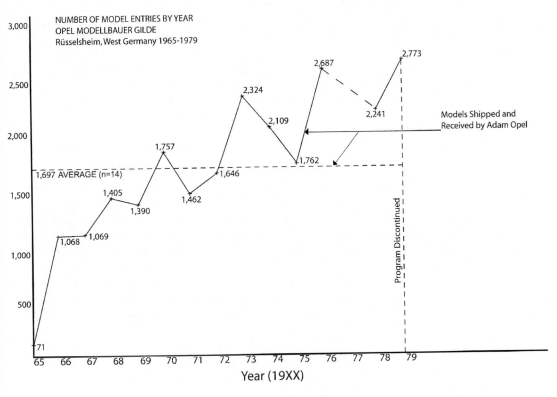

NUMBER OF MODEL ENTRIES BY YEAR
OPEL MODELLBAUER GILDE
Rüsselsheim, West Germany 1965-1979

Year (19XX)

Source: *Opel-Post* 1979 newsletter, Adam Opel AG Ruesselsheim, West Germany.

Cash prizes were awarded to schools with the best scoring collective efforts of 15 or more models submitted and between 1969 and 1970, "school" participation had increased by 50 percent.[13] Some of the winning schools received prizes worth several thousand DM. The models from a particular school presumably were judged and scored as a whole. According to the *Opel-Post*, "The outcome of the competition among the 'schools' showed how important it is that teachers foster the notion of competition within the context of industrial arts education."

The values and virtues of the Opel Model Builder's Guild were the same as the Fisher Body Craftsman's Guild: "...the teaching of individual tenacity, industry, perseverance; the strength to overcome set-backs; and the courage to deny oneself one thing or another because concentrated work on ones model is needed for days and weeks if something worth while is to be accomplished" (*Opel-Post*, June/July 1970).

By 1972, the eighth year of the program, over 163,000 participants had sent in applications and nearly 10,000 model entries had been received cumulatively. After the applications were received, the young model builders received plans, building instructions, and tips. Over 35,000 placards had been distributed to schools, youth groups, juvenile centers, branches of the Office of Young People's Affairs and franchise dealerships in support of the 1972–73 competition. An experimental school assembly program called "View of the Future" was seen by some 110,000 youths during the 1971–1972 school year.[14]

The above graph shows the number of model entries by year (1965–1979) for the Opel Model Builder's Guild.

GM-Holden Craftsman's Guild (General Motors–Holden Ltd.)[15]

A Craftsman's Guild similar to the U.S. Fisher Guild was operated in Australia for three competition years from 1965 to 1969 (1966–67, 1967–68 and 1968–69). The competition was open to high school boys aged 16 to 21 on March 1. A junior competition was suggested for 1967–68, but this idea was never carried out. There were no female contestants as in the Opel Modellbauer Gilde. It was open to the public on a nationwide basis and to GM-Holden apprentices. There were no age brackets or age divisions; however, there were three model design categories, namely family saloon class, sports and small car class, and open class.

As in the USA, the models were 1/12 scale and a free specification sheet and booklet concerning construction methods was supplied. Hard rubber wheels (2" O.D.) were supplied free upon request. The models were to be designed on paper and then converted to three dimensions using clay and wood. In the third competition, Daycell (a lightweight, rigid foam material) was introduced to help ease the construction of the models.

The awards and incentives consisted of $1,000 (Australian dollars) for educational purposes for first place as well as a three-day visit to Melbourne to attend a winner's banquet and a ten-day trip to the USA for the Fisher Guild convention. The second-place ($800), third-place ($600), fourth-place ($400) and fifth-place ($200) winners were also sent for the three-day visit to Melbourne. Further awards consisted of 20 tool kits for commendable entries, and all who entered were awarded a Certificate of Design and Craftsmanship. Many boys submitted more than one model in a year, but only the highest scoring model was considered for an award.

In the first competition there were 7,274 enrollments, 96 models were received and there were 586 wheel requests. In the second competition there were 5,798 enrollments and 58 model entries submitted. In the third competition year there were 7,961 enrollments, 61 models were entered, and there were 562 wheel requests.

The winners in the Holden Craftsman's Guild were:

1966–67: First place, Ian Hall ($1,000); second place, Kerry Cross ($800); third place, Robert Beasley ($600); fourth place Keith Bailey ($400); and a joint fifth place, Josephus Bakker and David Parsons ($200 each).

1967–68: First place, Malcolm Webster ($1,000), Noble Park, AS; second place, Robert Beasley ($800), North Balwyn, AS; third place, Noel Woolley ($600); fourth place, David Parsons ($400); and fifth place, David Henderson ($200), New South Wales, AS. In 1967–68, the Aussies distinguished themselves, as three of the top five Australians also won Fisher Guild styling scholarships ($1,000 each)—namely Webster, Beasley and Henderson.*

1968–69: First place, Robert Beasley ($1,000); second place, Anthony Poschinger ($800); third place, Noel Woolley ($600); fourth place, Ronald Bray ($400); and fifth place, Christopher Green ($200). The top 25 contestants were given awards totaling $6,000.

GM-H Craftsman's Guild, Melbourne, Australia

	1966–67	1967–68	1968–69
Enrollees	7,274	5,798	7,961
Model Entries	96	58	61
Wheel Requests	586	N/A	562

What Might Have Been

The Vauxhall Craftsman's Guild and Opel Modellbauer Gilde were co-educational, open to high school youth, and publications from these organizations highlighted the accomplishments of young women, some of them being among the top 40 winners. Unfortunately the Vauxhall, GM Holden and GM Suisse Guilds did not survive past 1968, whereas the co-ed Opel Modellbauer Gilde in West Germany was the most successful and operated from 1965 to 1979.

*Guild styling scholarships worth $1,000 each were awarded to Franco Del Bon of Zofingen, Switzerland, and to Norbert Orthey of West Germany in 1968.

GM Overseas Operations Craftsman's Guilds[16]

Program	City	1965 Enrollees	1966 Enrollees	1966 Entries	1967 Enrollees	1967 Entries
Vauxhall Ltd.	Luton, England	854	48,000	435	103,000	1,117
GM Suisse	Biel, Switzerland	5,500	8,800	303	9,154	202
Adam-Opel	Ruesselshiem, W. Germany	1,161	18,480	1,068	20,274	1,095
GM Holden	Melbourne, Australia				7,274	96
Total		7,515	75,280	1,806*	139,702	2,510

*The Fisher Body Craftsman's Guild in 1966 had 2,949 model entries. Italy, Norway and France were considering Craftsman's Guild programs (*General Motors World*, September 1966).

If Bill Mitchell's dream of an International Craftsman's Guild Award with a big New York City gala had come to pass, here's who the top contenders would have been in '65, '66, '67 and '68:

Top Senior Division Contenders for Bill Mitchell's Proposed International Craftsman's Guild Competition Award for 1965, 1966, 1967 and 1968

Year	Name	Country
1965	Heinrich L. Jakob	West Germany
	Terence John Kirk	England
	Jean-Claude Guggisberg	Switzerland
	Geza Loczi	United States
1966	Klaus Brod	West Germany
	Fritz-Ulrich Brinkmann	West Germany
	Christopher Howard Field	England
	Willi Max Frei	Switzerland
	Ovid O. Ward	United States
1967	Jacques Nordmann	Switzerland
	Gerhard Kistner	West Germany
	Ian Hall	Australia
	Phillip Guillot	England
	David C. Goelz	United States
1968	Robert Kohler*	Switzerland
	Otto Schaumberger	West Germany
	Malcolm Webster	Australia
	Grant Onnie	United States
	----	England (austerity program claimed Vauxhall Craftsman's Guild)

*Robert Kohler from Geneva, Switzerland, and Ian F. Hall from Geelong, Victoria, Australia, won $1,000 styling scholarships for "Excellence in Design" in the Fisher Body Craftsman's Guild competition in 1967.

K. U.S. Guildsmen by Name, Year(s), University and Vocational Interest

Summary of Coach Builders by Name, Highest Award Year(s), Education and Vocational Interests

Name	Highest Award Year(s)†	Education and Vocational Interests*
Donald C. Burnham	1931	Purdue University; GM engineer 17 years; Westinghouse 25 years, CEO and chairman of board.
Raymond S. Doerr	1931	University of Michigan, GM engineer, violin maker.
Albert W. Fischer	1931	GM research, development engineer, electromechanical instrumentation, violin maker.
Wallace Lench	1931	Chevrolet Flint Plant, 40 years as journeyman die maker.
Gordon L. Drummond	1931, 1932	University of Michigan, engineer, Fisher Body employee, Guild tech staff.
Emmett E. Day	1931, 1932	MIT engineer, teacher for 38 years, professor of engineering, University of Washington.
Charles W. Gadd	1931, 1932, 1933	MIT engineer, GM research 39 years, auto structures and biomechanics research.
Henry B. Larzelere	1932, 1936	Medicine, thoracic surgeon.
Stanley Knochel	1933	Craftsman, engineer, designer, draftsman, inventor, and entrepreneur.
Myron Webb	1933	No information available.
Michael D'Mura	1932, 1933	No information available.
Robert W. Henderson	1934	University of California, engineer, Manhattan Project, Trinity Site, Los Alamos, New Mexico, VP Sandia Corporation.
Robert W. Russell	1933, 1934, 1937	Chemist and paint formulator, Dutch Boy company.
Monroe P. Bean	1931	Shop teacher and rural mail carrier.
Wilfred McClain	1931, 1932, 1933	Industrial engineer, Alcoa, 1932–1976.
Walter H. Preston	1932, 1933	University of Nevada, structural civil engineer.
Karl Moldenhauer	1932, 1933	Aircraft industry 45 years.
Robert L. Dingle	1933	Civilian, Dept. of Defense, USAF.
Leo C. Peiffer	1946	Leo C. Peiffer Architects, P.C., celebrating their their 51st year (2003) in Cedar Rapids, Iowa.

*See list of abbreviations at the end of Appendix K.

†The exact years of FBCG participation of each of these Guildsmen is not necessarily known. The year or years of their highest award(s) in the Guild competition are shown if supported by documentation. They are in ascending order by year, not alphabetically ordered. In some cases only the highest award

Summary of U.S. Model Car Makers by Name, Highest Award Year(s), Education and Vocational Interests

Name	Highest Award Year(s)	Education and Vocational Interests*
Theodore M. Mandel	1937	Wayne State University, Fisher Body Division, Guild tech staff.
Richard Arbib	1937	Pratt Institute, product designer, auto futurist.
Virgil M. Exner, Jr.	1946	Cranbrook, Notre Dame, fine arts, automobile designer, design consultant, retired.
Charles M. Jordan	1947	MIT engineer, auto designer and executive, VP of GM Design, retired.
Galen Wickersham	1948, 1949, 1950, 1952	GWU, ACCD (1959–62), automobile designer, 41-year GM Design Center career with 39 years in interior design studios. Retired from GM.
Harvey E. Whitman	1948	GMI, Oldsmobile engineer, 40-year GM career.
Stanley C. Waechter	1949	University of Cincinnati Design School, industrial designer, GM Creative Services, retired.
Gale P. Morris	1949	ACCD, industrial designer, Tektronix, Inc.
Elia Russinoff	1949	Pratt Institute, auto designer, GM Design staff, 40 years, retired.
Ronald C. Hill	1950	ACCD student, GM designer, chairman of industrial design department at ACCD, retired.
Robert A. Cadaret	1950	ACCD, GM designer and illustrator (deceased).
Edward F. Taylor	1951	ACCD, asst. exec. designer, GM Design, retired.
George R. Chartier	1953, 1954	Designer/Modeler at Ford Motor Company with a 37-year career (retired). Originally from Wisconsin.
Gary Graham	1954	University of Washington, engineer, Boeing, president, Contemporary Design Company.
Charles W. Pelly	1954	ACCD, founded Designworks/USA), entrepreneur, auto designer, product designer.
James Lee Garner	1954, 1955	SE Missouri State College, artist, engineer, designer, and craftsman.
Gilbert McArdle	1955	Univ. of Penn., medicine, surgeon, Gettysburg.
Robert F. McDonnell	1955	ACCD, designer and architect, Disneyland, Euro Disney and luxury custom homes.
William A. Moore	1955, 1956	ACCD, industrial designer and artist/illustrator. Painter of ancient cultures, wildlife and nature.
Charles A. Gibilterra	1955, 1956	University of Southern California, industrial design degree, designer, interior architectural designer, home and office furniture designer, consumer product designer.

year(s) is shown or their "best" year(s). Art Russell entered six times, but only 1956 and 1957 are shown — both scholarship award years. In other cases, the complete range of years of participation are shown, if available. See Chapter III, "Secrets of Success," "Multiple Models" (pages 75–78) for further exact entry years for some of the model car builders.

Name	Highest Award Year(s)	Education and Vocational Interests*
Allen Weideman	1955–1958	ACCD, IBM product designer, owner of International Packaging Group, Inc. Retail packaging design and graphics expert.
E. Arthur Russell	1956, 1957	ACCD, product design and development. Develops and designs prototypes, models and patterns. Retired.
Richard R. Sylvester	1956, 1957	University of Southern California for MBA, Loyola for JD in Federal Law and UCLA for Ph.D., mathematical economist. Academician.
William F. Marks	1957	Dual Purdue mechanical engineering and ACCD industrial design degrees, Dupont plastics product designer.
Terry R. Henline	1957, 1958	ACCD, designer, chief designer, director of design, GM Design staff, 40-year career. Retired.
Paul Tatseos	1957, 1958	ACCD, chief interior designer, GM Design staff, 35-year career. Design consultant.
Harrell C. Lucky	1955–1958	Professor of music, Eastfield College, Dallas, Texas.
Kenneth J. Dowd	1957–1959	ACCD, VP Teague Aviation Studios (formerly Walter Dorwin Teague Associates).
John B. Di Ilio	1957	Penn State, Columbia University, Architecture.
Gerald Simone	1958	Bryant College, five years at the Ford Design Center, University of Michigan, pharmacist.
William R. Molzon	1953–1959	GMI Engineering ('60), ACCD industrial design ('63), GM exterior designer ('63–'69), design consultant
Eugene Simone	1960	Bryant College, Rhode Island College, investment executive and financial consultant.
Stuart Shuster	1952–1960	University of Cincinnati Design School, GM stylist, consultant to GM Creative Resources and Educational Relations.
Ronald C. Pellman	1956, 1957, 1958, 1960	Carnegie Mellon football player, mechanical engineer, inventor, business consultant, executive, coauthor.
Anthony V. Simone	1961	Providence College, junior high school principal, and principal of an international school in Jakarta, Indonesia.
Ronald J. Will	1961	GM stylist and designer, moved to Subaru and has contributed to the highly successful Forester and Outback designs, as Manager of Product Planning and Design at Subaru N.A.
James W. Green	1961	Purdue University, aeronautical and astronautical engineer, VP architectural engineering firm.
Harry E. Schoepf	1961	ACCD, industrial designer, 1913 Model T Ford expert, aspiring author.

Name	Highest Award Year(s)	Education and Vocational Interests*
Patrick B. Saturday	1961	American Academy of Art, 40-year graphic design and printing career.
Michael R. D'Mura	1957–1964	Medicine, dentistry, prosthodontics. Hobby model maker.
John L. Jacobus	1961–1966	University of Maryland, BSME, Catholic University MME, Fisher Body design engineer, auto safety engineer for 30+ years, retired. Writer.
Robert E. Davids	1963	ACCD, GM designer, product designer, entrepreneur, CEO and executive, vintner.
John M. D'Mura	1964	Professor of physics and the physical sciences at New Mexico State University.
Thomas H. Semple	1964	President, Nissan Design America.
Richard Ray	1964	GMI, director of commercial vehicle marketing and planning, DaimlerChrysler AG (Retired).
Rowland Kanner	1964	VP of technology, Atrion Medical Products, Inc.
Richard Pietruska	1963	ACCD, instructor at ACCD.
Michael A. Pietruska	1965	ACCD, environmental design, Milton Bradley toy and game designer, furniture and exhibit designer.
Ronald E. Pietruska	1967	Pratt Institute, industrial design, museum and exhibits industry.
Robert Pietruska	1966	Runs family upholstery business with the eldest of five brothers.
Theodore A. Becker	1964, 1965	RISD, North Carolina State, studied product design, Maytag designer and design manager. Retired from Maytag, active in IDSA.
Geza A. Loczi	1965	ACCD, director of design, Volvo Monitoring and Concept Center.
David P. Onopa	1963–1966	Penn State, ACCD, director of design, Mack Trucks, Inc.
John M. Mellberg	1961–1966	Art Institute of Chicago, University of Chicago, creative vehicle stylist, design development specialist.
Dale A. Gnage	1966	University of Rochester, engineer, Delphi Automotive Systems, retired.
Stewart D. Reed	1964, 1968	VP design, Prince Corporation, and started Stewart Reed Automotive Design. Designed the Cunningham C7 show car for Bob Lutz.

List of Abbreviations

MIT Massachusetts Institute of Technology
USAF United States Air Force
ACCD Art Center College of Design
USC University of Southern California
RISD Rhode Island School of Design
UNC University of North Carolina

IDSA Industrial Designers Society of America, Inc., Dulles, Virginia
GWU George Washington University, Washington, D.C.
GMI General Motors Institute (now Kettering University

L. The Fisher Body Craftsman's Guild: A Model for Educational Reform

by Anthony V. Simone[*]

The world of public and private education is constantly in change. For most parents and many students these changes are not visible. This is mostly due to the fact that the system changes ever so slowly. As we pass through the educational process ourselves this becomes our benchmark as to how we would like to see our children educated. Some adults obviously feel the system failed them and thus might take a different view and welcome reform.

The American educational system was never designed to do what it is presently doing — educating everyone, whether they want it or not. This has been a noble and costly crusade and one that is protected in our country's original charters. It is the state's responsibility to educate its citizens. The history of education is well understood by most people as the cornerstone of our democracy and we hold to the idea that an educated society is one that will endure and for us develop a better America. Having laid this basic foundation, why would the Fisher Body Craftsman's Guild be a model for educational reform? Aren't we doing the best we can already? Why would we go back to the old European models of trade guilds? What is the "Guild process" and how can it improve or even change the way we educate our youth?

The Guild was founded on core values built around a process that leads a person from a design format to the actual completion of a product. In this case, the product was a scale model of a futuristic car. The Fisher Body Craftsman's Guild mobilized the male youth of this country to help them become a larger enterprise than they were already. Whether General Motors intentionally exploited the creative talents of those generations of young boys is up for debate. At the least, it made future car buyers — General Motors clients. What it did do and did well was instill in the pool of talent the design process which includes creativity, the acquired knowledge of trial and error, the theories of methods and means and the greatest of all gifts, the ability to work with one's hands. Side benefits that were also important to these young individuals were praise and recognition, which the Guild did very well in its trans– America school presentations. Not to be forgotten was the enormous public display the handcrafted scale models cars received both in this country and internationally.

What does all this have to do with education? What the Guild managers probably did not recognize, when first developing the program, was the great value our society would eventually place on the principles of creativity, self-esteem, perseverance, and one that educators call "stick-to-it-izm." These were values discussed but never really incorporated in the curriculum of schools as they are today. Many of the remaining, living Guild members were educated in a time when rote memorization was the rule of the day. Those who could not, or would not, play this game did not succeed or move on to the next stage of education — college. Those who had talents with their hands were looked upon as second-class citizens, ones who would occupy other lesser jobs, possibly our future tradespeople. All of this changed in the 1960s and '70s with massive federal programs dealing with special-needs students. It was recognized that not all students learn the same way. Not all students have the natural ability to memorize and analyze volumes of facts. Unfortunately, at the same time, the Guild was being phased out of existence. It was a sad time since education would have embraced the basic core values of the Fisher Body Craftsman's Guild.

*1961 first-place national scholarship, junior division winner, and principal of the Pattimura Campus, Jakarta International School. This appendix was submitted August 31, 2003.

The Guild never enjoyed these new trends in education, which celebrated differences and diversities, and which today are, or are becoming, the hallmark of our educational system. Research studies have shown that students who are recognized for some special talent early in their lives will go on to be successful individuals. This is not to say that if you don't win at something you will be a failure; it just shows that being recognized for a talent and getting praise and recognition will breed motivated individuals. Few countries can or will attempt to educate all their populations to the extent that is presently being done in America. So, the changes that have been made since the '50s have created a society of youth able to go on to college with, or without, financial aid. This was the big draw of the Guild competition — university trust funds and scholarship money. Added to this is the computer explosion, which has reserved working with your hands, today, mostly for hobbyists. Those who do make a living working with their hands, or as a tradesperson, are doing so in what are becoming nontraditional occupations. Who would have imagined this?

So, what can we learn from the Craftsman's Guild era, a time of unlimited creativity among the male youth? We can learn that students need to use the knowledge they are acquiring in a way that promotes creativity and self-expression. Years ago, the Outward Bound experience that was offered countrywide, and eventually worldwide, was adapted to physical education programs in many U.S. schools. It became a huge success and is now viewed as a cornerstone of modern physical education programs. It helps develop confidence and show what teamwork is all about. The Guild process could be that same model. It can offer a framework for students to learn how to use their knowledge and skills in a way that they can use them in the real world. Every student will at some point in his or her life need to hang a picture, paint a wall, figure the square area of a rug or build something. The Guild process will teach and encourage the vital talents needed to create a project and see it through completion.

The proposed program would appeal first to students who have an aptitude for designing and building a futuristic car of their creation. It would graduate into offerings to students interested in building model homes, landscaping designs or things as radical as a theme park. The object would be to meet the interest of the students in an independent way and to teach them the skills common to completing any project. Starting with an idea and going though the Guild process, a student would learn valuable skills while earning credits of independent work in a school setting. The number of credits or the value of a grade or mark would be determined by the different school's administration.

The Guild process is a systemic approach to develop a creative concept and to proceed through a series of tasks that will eventually see an individual's project to completion. The process is the same that is done in the world of auto design, home construction and commercial architecture, or any creative endeavor.

The project would require research and study, creating sketches, building a clay model if applicable, and finally building the final product. It would allow a student to use skills already acquired in math, language arts and science classes. It would require the use and application of materials and techniques such as the priming and spray painting of clay; fiberglass lay-up and new epoxy resins; the polishing of brass, bronze, and aluminum; the cutting, gluing and polishing of Plexiglas; the sanding and oiling or staining of mahogany; the shaping of plastics like REN board (a plastic composite wood) or rigid polyurethane foam; applying the West System low viscosity epoxy resins, and the use of adhesives such as our loyal friends Super Glue and Gorilla Glue. Many other materials used in industrial and commercial projects will be part of the experiences, such as Masonite, Foam Core board, acetate, vinyl and Styrofoam. Painting, sanding, scale drawings, and a variety of other finishing skills will be added to the process as needed. The length of the project and the value to grade or amount of credit would be part of the contract that the student signs with his or her supervisor. These projects would be done on an individual basis with each one different from the other. All of this is consistent with independent study, which is embraced by most Western schools.

Towards the end of the educational process a presentation assembly would be scheduled so that the students can share what they have learned with their family, friends and the community. A formal presentation would be made to add the final touch to the process, which is that of public speaking, a basic skill needed to be successful in the future, and a real world experience. Giving recognition to the students would be a large part of the organizers' responsibility to the students and the school system being worked with.

It would be the responsibility of the organizers to provide the process, printed material and instructors trained in the Guild process. This process has been designed by individuals who have lived the lives of auto designers, engineers, and artists and tradespeople of all kinds. With the use of this system the educational process becomes more relevant and rewarding. It would bring theory to reality and the classroom to life. These are not new theories we are talking about, just a new way to deliver real-world experiences in a formal educational setting. The Guild process, built on the legacy of the Fisher Body Craftsman's Guild auto design competition, needs to be considered as a model for educational reform in some school systems. It can be a stand-alone program or integrated into the curriculum. In either case, students win and our country rekindles the energy of a past generation. To do less would not be in the spirit of our great nation.

M. Persons Officially Assigned by GM Styling to Be Design Judges[17]

1954	1957	1960	1963	1966
R. Phillips	J. Kojima	C. Stewart	L. Casillo	R. Lonberger
	K. Genest	J. Ewen	T. Henline	J. Bisignano
	C. Pohlman	T. Daniels	D. Swanson	R. Orr
		J. Stockham		
1955	**1958**	**1961**	**1964**	**1967**
R. Veryzer	K. Carlson	E. Zowada	G. Hirshberg	G. Bell
B. Bollinger	R. Carr	J. Brochstein	R. Hubbach	R. McCrea
	P. Deseen	R. Bolt	R. Luyckx	D. McIntosh
	R. Dustan			
1956	**1959**	**1962**	**1965**	**1968**
H. Bretzner	P. Furey	W. Kady	D. Wood	D. Clark
G. Pyshe	J. Hulbert	L. Johnson	C. Mason	R. Wittine
D. Hronek	P. Jacobsen	D. McElfish	K. Moravek	L. Johnson
	J. Nelson			

The people from GM Styling that were responsible for judging the "Design" part of the score sheet were teamed with industrial arts teachers from the Detroit public school system who were responsible for the judging the "Craftsmanship" part of the score sheet. The names of the industrial arts teachers who participated as part of these teams are unknown except for one, Mr. Claude W. Reagan, who was remembered fondly by Mrs. Ruth Ganter McClellan. There were some big hearted, giving and caring gentleman who worked the Guild program, like Mr. Victor L. Olesen, head judge in 1948, who had been with the Guild since 1937.

Abbreviations, Acronyms and Terms

AACA Antique Automobile Club of America.

AAU Academy of Art University, San Francisco, California.

ACCD Art Center College of Design, Pasadena, California (post–1966).

ACS Art Center School, Los Angeles, California (pre–1966).

Armature Wood or polyurethane superstructure for a clay model used to save the volume of required clay material and to provide rigidity.

Beltline An imaginary line on an automobile body at the bottom-edge of the window glass.

Bondo A polyester-based auto body filler sold at auto parts stores and used by Guildsmen to construct model car parts or whole model cars.

Brother Earned greeting and salutation of one Guildsman to another Guildsman.

BSA Boy Scouts of America.

BSME Bachelor of Science Mechanical Engineering.

BSID Bachelor of Science Industrial Design.

Bubble Top Clear canopy with 360 degree view, compound surfaces made with acrylic or acetate plastic, heated and vacuum formed or heated and formed between a wooden male mold and a plaster female mold.

Cams Stationary templates used with a "drag" to form a compound clay surface.

CCS College for Creative Studies (formerly Center for Creative Studies) Detroit, Michigan.

CCCA Classic Car Club of America.

Certificate of Design and Craftsmanship Each contestant received a certificate for entering the Craftsman's Guild competition regardless of the award received.

Chavant The brand name of a professional automotive styling clay softened with dry heat.

Clay Buck Same as a clay model or clay pattern used to work out design ideas three-dimensionally and used for making cardboard templates. Since clay designs could not be entered in the competition, templates were used to transfer the finished and per-fected clay design to a more durable material like wood. Alternatively, the clay buck could be cast in plaster.

Clay Model *see* Clay buck

Clear Canopy Bubble top of a model car made from clear acrylic or acetate plastic.

Compound Surface An automotive body surface curved both laterally and longitudinally.

Craftsman An artist, designer, engineer, and perfectionist working with mind and hands.

Daycell The Australian's brand name for rigid polyurethane foam used to make model cars.

DC District of Columbia or Washington, DC, the nation's Capitol.

Design Categories A, B and C Consisted of 11 body styles that contestants could make for the Craftsman's Guild competition.

DLO Daylight Opening or windows in an automobile.

Drag A moving template used to shape a compound clay surface.

Drawings A, B and C Illustrations of the maximum and minimum Guild design specifications for a particular body style of model car and directly corresponded to Categories A, B and C.

DuPont E.I. duPont de Nemours and Company, Incorporated.

English Wheel A hand operated machine used by craftsmen to stretch and form one-of-a-kind curved and complex sheet metal parts for one-off show cars, custom cars and hot rods.

Family Dynasty Name given when each son or brother in a Guild family won a university trust fund in the Fisher Body Craftsman's Guild.

FBCG Fisher Body Craftsman's Guild, 30001 Van Dyke Road, Warren, Michigan.

Female Mold Generally a plaster mold with a concavity or concave surface.

Fiberglass Lay-up Fine mesh or fine weave fiberglass cloth is laid-up in a female plaster mold on top of a thin resin gel coat. The cloth is saturated with polyester resin. The female plaster mold was first prepared by sanding and then sealed with lacquer and coated with a silicone mold release agent.

Fisher Body Company Original name of what later became Fisher Body Corporation and then Fisher Body Division of GMC.

Fisher Body Public Relations and Advertising Managed the FBCG program from 1953 through 1968 at the Fisher Body Central Engineering Offices, 30001 Van Dyke Road, Warren, Michigan.

Fleetwood Metal Body Company Also called Fleetwood Auto Bodies; became Fleetwood Corporation. This operation was purchased by the Fisher Brothers in 1925 to guarantee a steady supply of high quality auto bodies.

Futurama General Motors exhibit at the 1938 New York Auto Show featuring the first show car, Harley J. Earl's Buick Y-Job, and the name used for one of GM's 1939 World's Fair Exhibits.

Futurliner A modified GM motor coach carrying technology exhibits from city to city and state fair to state fair during the 1953 to 1956 period.

GM General Motors.

GMAD General Motors Assembly Division.

GMC General Motors Corporation.

GMMA General Motors Media Archives.

GMOO General Motors Overseas Division.

Gratiot Auto Supply Retailer where local Detroit Guildsmen got their auto lacquer and thinner, Bondo, chrome tape and other model-making supplies.

Greenhouse The glass area on an automobile body above the beltline.

Guildsman Name earned only by those entering a model coach or model "dream car" in the Fisher Body Craftsman's Guild Competition.

GWU George Washington University, Washington, D.C.

Hall of Progress Name of GM's main 1933 and 1934 World's Fair exhibit.

"Hardtop" Describes a model car made with a clear bubble top for side windows, rear DLO and windshield, but with the roof area finished with a material like vinyl or leather or an opaque paint color.

Hardtop Body Style Greenhouse with missing vertical roof support structure (called B-pillars) between the front A-pillars and rear C-pillars or sail panels.

HCG Holden Craftsman's Guild.

Holy Grail The Guild's "Designing and Building a Model Car" booklet.

Hydrocal Brand of professional casting plaster for making male and female molds.

ID Industrial Design.

I.D. Inside diameter in inches.

IDSA Industrial Designers Society of America.

IIT Illinois Institute of Technology.

L × W × H L = length (inches), W = width (inches) and H = height (inches).

Loaf of Bread Method A model construction technique where lateral cross sectional pieces of wood were laminated to create the model car as opposed to laminating pieces of wood longitudinally and parallel to the centerline of the model.

Male Mold Wooden or plaster mold with convex or protruding surface to make a part or parts.

Marker Gauge A vertical block of wood and a sliding metallic blade used to "mark" a vertical section in the clay model at specific station lines. The cardboard templates had to be cut, by trail and error, to fit this cross section as closely as possible.

ME Mechanical Engineering.

MIT Massachusetts Institute of Technology.

Modelauto Wettbewerb Model Auto Competition, sponsored by GM Suisse.

Modellbauer Gilde Model Builder's Guild, sponsored by Adam Opel AG.

Motorama Harley J. Earl's famous 1950s show car extravaganzas that got kids interested in the Fisher Body Craftsman's Guild.

NAASP North American Association of School Principals.

Naugahyde Simulated leather made of plastic popular in the 1950's.

Negative Draft Refers to undercuts in a plug, clay pattern or clay buck that would interfere with the removal of the outer, multi-piece plaster mold parts.

Nitrocellulose Lacquer Paint Available in brush and spray formulations, marketed under the Duco brand name (made by DuPont) and used by Guildsmen.

O.D. Outside diameter in inches.

Parade of Progress A group of 12 Futurliners, or mobile exhibits, used by GM to sell their technologically advanced automotive ideas.

Pattern Three-dimensional wood shapes used to form windshields from heated flat clear acrylic or acetate plastic. A sculpted clay model car was a pattern used for making plaster molds.

Plastic Wood Popular cellulose fiber wood filler with an anti-shrink formula. Used by Guildsmen to construct model car parts or whole model cars.

Plexiglass An acrylic plastic.

Plug The cast part, or model car itself, removed from a multi-piece female mold.

Pumice Powder Used with water between coats of paint to sand the surface to a very fine finish.

Red Bank Brand name of a professional automobile styling clay softened with the application of dry heat.

REN Board Synthetic wood formulated with mahogany saw dust.

Rigid Polyurethane Foam A closed cell rigid foam recommended by the Guild as a faster and quicker method of making a model car.

RISD Rhode Island School of Design.

Rock-of-the-Eye Method The symmetry of the model car and/or parts was established solely by the "naked eye" and a ruler.

RTV Room temperature vulcanizing rubber used by Guildsmen to make rubber molds from a clay model and from which the model car was cast in plaster.

SAE Society of Automotive Engineers.

Saloon Car British term for a family sedan.

SAT Scholastic Aptitude Test.

Scale Fidelity or **Fidelity to Scale** Adherence to maximum and minimum Guild specifications in Drawings A., B. and C.

Scholarship Trust Fund Agreement Signed by the Guildsman who won college scholarship and a Trustee of the Bank of Detroit.

Shellac Common, ordinary household wood sealer or wood primer used by Guildsmen.

Silicone Mold Release A parting compound, or inert lubricant, used between clay and plaster, or used between the fiberglass gel coat and plaster, to prevent the materials from bonding and locking together permanently.

Solid Top A model car with solid greenhouse or solid canopy with window glass areas indicated using white, gray or black paint.

Station Lines A grid of lateral lines ¾" to 1" a part running perpendicular to the model's centerline, running from one end of the clay model to the other, and used for locating vertical section "marks" and section templates.

Stylist's Bridge A professional tool used by designers, in place of templates, to transfer section points from the left side to the right side of a full-size clay automobile design. Guildmen were encouraged to make their own Stylist's or Designer's Bridge from scratch.

Surface Development A mechanical drawing technique (using plan, side, front and rear views of an object) to define cross-sections at each predetermined station line.

Suisse French for Swiss referring to GM Switzerland, a subsidiary of GMC.

Swiss Cheese Method Drilling of holes in the clay buck armature to give the clay points of adhesion.

Templates Cut from cardboard to trace the lateral cross-sectional outline, to the centerline, at a particular station line on a clay model. Used to transfer points from the left side of the model to the right side or vice versa.

Tolerances This term is implicitly used as the figures +/- ¹⁄₁₆" and +/- 0.007" appear in the text. These are expressions of accuracy or precision. Professional model-makers working in wood can keep within ¹⁄₁₆" of a nominal dimension, and Henry Larzelere noted that he reproduced the wheel spokes of his coach within +/- 0.007 or ⁷⁄₁₀₀₀ of an inch which means high precision.

"Trans" Major Industrial Design student with a Transportation Major.

UCLA University of California at Los Angeles.

UNC University of North Carolina.

University Scholarship Trust Funds College scholarships won by Guildsmen for excellence in both "design" and "craftsmanship."

USAF United States Air Force.

USC University of Southern California.

VCCA Vintage Chevrolet Club of America.

VCG Vauxhall Craftsman's Guild.

"Woods Metal" Metal compound with a low melting temperature used in the coach competitions.

Acknowledgments

This is the end of a long road for me that began in August 1984, doing volunteer work, at home, for transportation curators Roger B. White and William L. Withuhn of the National Museum of American History, Smithsonian Institution. The original "call to arms" to the author written by Mr. Withuhn August 21, 1984, which started this whole project, was as follows: "I agree that these models and their genesis reveal a great deal about the American attitude toward the automobile from the 1940's through the 1960's."

Because Guild information exists as disparate pieces, and former participants are not organized in any formal way, it's easy to understand why a book was never written before. With the arrival of Internet technology, search engines, digital images, and email communications, the barriers to writing a book about such an esoteric subject were overcome.

One of the continuing hurdles for me was marketing. I had tried to market the idea of a Craftsman's Guild "coffee table" book over the years and I have a stack of rejection letters to prove it. The coffee table book would have employed many of the wonderful color photographs obtained in duplicate from the NMAH Guild exhibit participants, which the author had preserved and presented in this book. Through the Society of Automotive Historians, Inc., the people who have always encouraged me to work on this project, a publisher was found. The book would have to cover everything about the Guild. This required further research and more personal contacts.

It took over one hundred personal contacts (phone calls, letters, and emails) with knowledgeable people, in addition to what I already had in hand, to write this book. About 50 percent of the text for the book (the essay section) was written by the Guild folks. I discovered that phone interviews didn't work because of the potential for misinterpretation, but that the essay approach worked very well. I wrote the remaining 50 percent of the book.

The Napoleonic Coach chapter would have been a major stumbling block to any book, except that I had a Guild technical consultant, expert and friend in Oregon named Skip Geear who taught me about preserving Guild memorabilia and who taught the oral history of the Napoleonic Coaches, the Craftsman's Guild and Fisher Body, in general. I did, however, have to hit the books on my own, obtaining my first set of Napoleonic Coach plans, and color photographs, from Richard H. Conibear (1947 regional Napoleonic Coach winner from Lakeland, Florida) many years earlier (1984). I had to fight long and hard to get the coach story.

I want to thank all of you who called and contributed your Guild knowledge, shared those old anecdotal "war" stories, sent names and addresses, and expressed your support and enthusiasm. Everyone had something to contribute that was useful and that made the job easier for me. You have all been wonderful friends to do this for me. It has always been one of my dreams to write a Guild book and I thank you for sharing my dream and making it possible. Thank you to the reader for taking the time to read this technical story. If you were familiar with the Guild, or participated, I hope this answered some of those nagging questions you've held onto since 1952. You are now free to move on with your lives! It was a long arduous journey, but a very worthwhile, satisfying and rewarding ride.

Guild Technical Consultants

The author wishes to express his appreciation and gratitude to Mr. Skip Geear, Vintage Chevrolet Club of America (VCCA) member, 1930 and 1932 technical advisor, for his hundreds of emails and untiring contributions to this book.[1] He helped me write and assemble what eventually became Chapter II in the fall of 1997 for the Second Biennial Automotive History Conference, sponsored by the Society of Automotive Historians, Inc., which was held in Dearborn, Michigan, in September 1998. A debt of gratitude is owed to Skip and Charlotte Geear for their generosity in letting me review their fabulous collection of Fisher Body Craftsman's Guild memorabilia in Eagle Point, Oregon, at the June 1996 reunion and on the occasion of a second visit in December 1999. Thank you for sharing your knowledge, your file cabinets full of data and your expertise about the history of the Craftsman's Guild. Without the Geear family's support and assistance this book would have been impossible to even consider.

As a Guild expert and Guild friend ('61–'66), Mr. John M. Mellberg was instrumental in helping get the new Guild book, specifically Chapter III, to the publisher on schedule. His contacts with industrial designers at GM and throughout the auto industry were invaluable during the writing and editing of the book. In addition, John is a leader, a diplomat, a good PR man and an excellent salesman. He is truly a jack of all trades.

John M. Mellberg, my right-hand man, salesman, public relations guru, auto historian, and design consultant, was essential to writing this book. To be helpful on a project like this you had to have a photographic memory not only of Guild facts and trivia, and the files to back it up, but of history trivia in general, like the names of the stars in the 1958 Academy Award winner *Gigi*. He loved to talk to Guild folks and successfully ferreted them out of hiding so I could speak to them. No one escaped his scrutiny, including John J. Jendza, Mrs. Ruth Ganter McClellan, Rolf Amundson (the Swedish spelling form), Richard Herdegen, and Florence Stolman, the Guild secretary for many years. He has given of his time generously on two occasions for full-length manuscript reviews. John devoted hundreds of hours, not to mention the dozens of necessary emails, to getting this book off the ground and to the market place.

Individual Contributors

The following individuals contributed recent (2002–2003) phone calls, letters, emails, autobiographic and biographic essays, signed copyright permission forms, donated Guild memorabilia and/or their personal stocks of vintage photographs. The author is indebted to them all. Guild participation dates are denoted for some by parentheses ( ).

Donald C. Burnham (1931), Charles Drummond, Dr. Henry B. Larzelere (1936), Frederick D. Roe (1936), Peter Wozena (1937), Virgil M. Exner, Jr. (1946), Leo C. Peiffer (1946), Charles M. Jordan (1947), Harvey E. Whitman (1948), Elia Russinoff (1947, 1948, 1949), Stanley Carl Waechter (1949), Gale P. Morris (1949), John Martin Smith (1949–1950), Ronald C. Hill (1950), Michelle Cadaret-Schulz, Edward F. Taylor (1951), Galen Wickersham (1948, 1949, 1950, 1952), George R. Chartier (1953, 1954), Gary Graham (1954), Charles W. Pelly (1954), Joan Gregor, Dr. Gilbert McArdle (1955), James Lee Garner (1954, 1955), William A. Moore (1955, 1956), Charles A. Gibilterra (1955, 1956), Dr. Harrell Clinton Lucky (1954–1958), Robert F. McDonnell (1955), Mrs. Bobbie Purdy, John B. Di Ilio (1957), William F. Marks (1957), Richard R. Sylvester (1956, 1957), E. Arthur Russell (1956, 1957), Terry R. Henline (1957, 1958), Paul Tatseos (1956, 1957, 1958), Dave Antonick, Allen T. Weideman (1955, 1956, 1957, 1958), William R. Molzon (1959), Gerald Simone (1958, 1962), Kenneth James Dowd (1957–1959), Robert C. McLellan (1959, 1960), Stuart Shuster (1952–1960), Eugene Simone

(1960), Ronald C. Pellman (1956–1960), James W. Green (1961), Anthony V. Simone (1961), Meghan Simone, Ronald J. Will (1961), Patrick B. Saturday (1961), Harry E. Schoepf (1961), Alan Lee Flowers (1962), Robert E. Davids (1963), Rowland Kanner (1964), Thomas H. Semple (1964), Dr. Michael R. D'Mura (1957–1964), John D'Mura (1964), Richard Ray (1962, 1963, 1964), Theodore A. Becker (1964, 1965), Michael A. Pietruska (1965), John Hambrock (1957, 1958, 1959, 1961, 1964, 1965), Geza Loczi (1965), Dale A. Gnage (1966), John M. Mellberg (1961–1966), David P. Onopa (1963, 1964, 1965, 1966), Ms. Ruth Ganter McClellan, Richard A. Herdegen, Rand Shackleton, Rolf Amundson, Ms. Florence Stolman, William L. Porter, Richard Earl (Harley J. Earl's grandson)), Skip Geear, Jerry Turner, Ron Konopka, and Steve L. Wolken.

Individuals Donating Guild Models to the 1984–1991 Fisher Body Craftsman's Guild Exhibit Project and Permanent Collection at the National Museum of American History, Behring Center, Smithsonian Institution, Washington, D.C.

Donald C. Burnham, 1931 Napoleonic Coach scholarship, junior division, $5,000 award winner.
Harvey E. Whitman, 1948 first-place national scholarship, senior division, $4,000 award winner.
Gale P. Morris, 1949 third-place national scholarship, junior division, $2,000 award winner.
Edward F. Taylor, 1951 third-place national scholarship, senior division, $2,000 award winner.
Gilbert McArdle, 1955 regional award winner, Region 17.
E. Arthur Russell, 1957 first-place national scholarship, senior division, $5,000 award winner.
Harry E. Schoepf, 1961 styling scholarship, $1,000 award winner.
James W. Green, 1961 third-place national scholarship, junior division, $3,000 award winner.
Richard J. Johnson, 1962 styling scholarship, $1,000 award winner.
Rowland Kanner, 1964 styling scholarship, $1,000 award winner.
Dale A. Gnage, 1966 first-place national scholarship, junior division, $5,000 award winner.

Former Guildsmen, Model Makers and Contributors to the Guild Exhibit and Book Projects

MINIATURE MODEL NAPOLEONIC COACH
BUILDERS BY HIGHEST AWARD YEAR

Donald C. Burnham, 1931 Napoleonic Coach scholarship, junior division, $5,000 award winner.
Howard F. Jennings, 1931 Napoleonic Coach scholarship, junior division, $5,000 award winner.
Albert W. Fischer, 1931 Napoleonic Coach scholarship, senior division, $5,000 award winner.
Raymond S. Doerr, 1931 Napoleonic Coach scholarship, senior division, $5,000 award winner.
Myron O. Webb, 1933 Napoleonic Coach scholarship, junior division, $5,000 award winner.
Stanley Knochel, 1933 Napoleonic Coach scholarship, junior division, $5,000 award winner.
Victor V. DeCenzo, 1934 Napoleonic Coach, fourth-place national scholarship, junior division, award winner.
Norman L. Larzalere, 1934 Napoleonic Coach scholarship, $1,000 award winner.
Henry B. Larzalere, 1936 Napoleonic Coach scholarship, senior division, $5,000 award winner.
Leo C. Peiffer, 1946 Napoleonic Coach scholarship, senior division, $5,000 award winner.

Eugene F. Schweitz, 1946 Napoleonic Coach, second-place national scholarship, junior division, $3,000 award winner.[2]

Donald F. Schonholtz, 1947 Napoleonic Coach $5,000 scholarship, senior division.[3]

Richard H. Conibear, 1947 Napoleonic Coach regional award winner and model car maker 1948–1951.

Franz O. Ibisch, 1932 Napoleonic Coach $5,000 scholarship award winner, senior division.

John Rempel, Jr., Napoleonic Coach builder (circa 1985–86).

MODEL "DREAM CAR" MAKERS BY HIGHEST AWARD YEAR

J.M. Sorensen, 1937 second-place state Minnesota, junior division.

Peter Wozena, 1937 state winner from Detroit, Michigan.

Virgil M. Exner, Jr., 1946 first-place national scholarship, junior division, $4,000 award.

Charles M. Jordan, 1947 first-place national scholarship, senior division, $4,000 award.

Rev. Philip J. Rauth, 1947 second-place national scholarship, junior division, $2,000 award.[4]

Harold L. Simon, 1948 regional and scholarship winner.

Gale P. Morris, 1949 third-place national scholarship, junior division, $2,000 award.

Lew W. Jacobs III, 1949 fourth-place national scholarship, senior division, $1,000 award.

Roger D. Teter, 1949 third-place national scholarship, junior division, $2,000 award.

Robert A. Cadaret, 1950 first-place national scholarship, senior division, $4,000 award.

Benjamin B. Taylor, 1950 fourth-place national scholarship, junior division, $1,000 award.

Webster Benner, 1951 second-place national scholarship, senior division, $3,000 award.

Edward Frasier Taylor, 1951 third-place national scholarship, senior division, $2,000 award.

Anthony S. Hendrick, 1951 second-place national scholarship, junior division, $3,000 award.

Paul H. Richardson, 1951 first-place national scholarship, senior division, $4,000 award.

William A. Keyser, 1952 second-place national scholarship, junior division, $3,000 award.

Noland Vogt, 1948, 1949, 1950, 1951, and 1952 from Nebraska. Won four first-place state and two regional awards.

Galen Wickersham, 1948 and 1949 state and regional awards; 1950 and 1952 state awards, Washington, D.C.

Robert C. Relyea, 1952 fourth-place national scholarship, junior division, $1,000 award.

Henry F. Rom, 1953 fourth-place national scholarship, senior division, $1,000 award.

Robert H. Leger, 1953 fourth-place national scholarship, junior division, $1,000 award.

George R. Chartier, 1953 first-place state and 1954 second-place state Wisconsin awards, Sr. Div.

James Lee Garner, 1954 and 1955 senior regional winner from Bloomington, Missouri.

Gary Graham, 1954 first-place national scholarship, senior division, $4,000 award.

Aime S. DeReggi, 1954 third-place national scholarship, senior division, $2,000 award.

Charles W. Pelly, 1954 second-place national scholarship, junior division, $3,000 award.

Adrian A. Bruno, 1955 second-place national scholarship, senior division, $3,000 award.

Thomas F. Greene, 1955 first-place national scholarship, junior division, $4,000 award.

Milton Antonick, 1955 first-place national scholarship, senior division, $4,000 award.

Anthony Mauldin, 1955 regional winner.

Dr. Gilbert McArdle, 1955 senior regional winner from Salt Lake City, Utah.

Carl K. Utz, 1955 junior regional winner.

Murray A. Milne, 1955 first-place state Michigan; 1956 second-place national scholarship, $4,000 award.

William A. Moore, 1956 first-place national scholarship, senior division, $5,000 award.

E. Arthur Russell, 1956 styling scholarship, $1,000 award and 1957 first-place national scholarship, senior division, $5,000 award.

Patrick O. McKittrick, 1956 first-place state Indiana and 1957 styling scholarship.

William F. Marks, 1957 second-place national scholarship, senior division, $4,000 award.

John B. Di Ilio, 1957 third-place national scholarship, junior division, $3,000 award.

Anthony "Tony" Joy, 1957 styling scholarship, $1,000 award.

David C. Byram, 1958 styling scholarship, $1,000 award.

Dr. Harrell C. Lucky, 1954–1958, three-time regional winner.

Gary W. Law, 1958 second-place national scholarship, junior division, $4,000 award.

Karl H. Kaiser (father of Kenneth Kaiser, deceased Guildsman who won the 1958 fourth-place national scholarship, senior division, $2,000 award).

John T. Williams, regional winner in 1956, 1957 and 1958.

Allen Weideman, 1955 and 1956 state awards, and 1957 and 1958 regional awards, Salt Lake City, Utah.

Ken Saylor, 1958 third-place national scholarship, junior division, $3,000 award.

James T. Sampson, 1957 styling scholarship, 1958 first-place national scholarship, senior division, $5,000 award.

Joseph Ferraioli, 1958 fourth-place national scholarship, junior division, $2,000 award.

Randal Wiginton, 1958 regional winner.

William R. Molzon, 1959 second-place national scholarship, senior division, $4,000.

Ronald C. Pellman, 1958 regional award and 1960 second-place national scholarship, senior division, $4,000 award.

Stuart Shuster, state winner from Pennsylvania (1952 and 1953) and Kentucky (1954 to 1960).

Newell Bringhurst, 1958, 1959, and 1960 regional award winner and styling scholarship winner.

Eugene Simone, 1960 fourth-place national scholarship, junior division, $2,000 award.

Billy R. Miller, builder of three Guild models during the 1957 to 1960 period.

Donald F. Held, 1960 second-place national scholarship, junior division, $4,000 award.

Ronald J. Will, 1961 first-place national scholarship, senior division, $5,000 award.

Anthony V. Simone, 1961 first-place national scholarship, junior division, $5,000 award.

Patrick B. Saturday, 1961 styling scholarship, $1,000 award.

Joseph B. Arnold, 1961 styling scholarship, $1,000 award.

Harry E. Schoepf, 1961 styling scholarship, $1,000 award.

James W. Green, 1961 third-place national scholarship, junior division, $3,000 award.

Michael Anton Bruckdorfer, 1962 styling scholarship, $1,000 award.

Raymond C. Canarra, 1962 second-place national scholarship, junior division, $4,000 award.

Philip Bonine, 1962 styling scholarship, $1,000 award.

Alan Lee Flowers, 1962 fourth-place national scholarship, senior division, $4,000 award.

Jerome A. Grunstad, 1962 styling scholarship, $1,000 award, from Ortonville, Minnesota.

Richard J. Johnson, 1962 styling scholarship, $1,000 award.

Wade H. Barrineau, 1962 styling scholarship, $1,000 award.

Kernie D. Erickson, 1962 first-place national scholarship, junior division, $5,000 award.

Dr. Michael R. D'Mura, winner of six regional awards (1957–1964) and a 1962 styling scholarship, $1,000 award.

Mary Lou Collyer (mother of Donald Collyer, deceased Guildsman, 1962 fourth-place national scholarship, junior division, $2,000 award).

Tristram Walker Metcalfe, 1963 regional award winner. Won two regional awards.

Robert Aikins, 1963 fourth-place national scholarship, senior division, $2,000 award.

James Bieck, 1963 styling scholarship, $1,000 award.

Kaizo Oto, 1961 styling scholarship, $1,000 award, and 1962 third-place national scholarship, senior division, $3,000 award.

Wolfgang Rueckner, 1963 regional winner.

James Barnett, 1963 regional winner from Anderson, Indiana.

Robert G. Sirna, 1963 regional winner from Michigan.

Richard John, 1963 regional winner, 1964 junior regional winner, and 1964 first-place national scholarship, junior division, $5,000 award.

Michael B. Antonick, 1964 second-place national scholarship, senior division, $4,000 award.
Lance Prom, 1964 junior regional winner and 1966 styling scholarship, $1,000 award.
Joseph W. Catalano, 1964 styling scholarship, $1,000 award.
Rowland Kanner, 1964 styling scholarship, $1,000 award.
Walter Peeler, 1964 fourth-place national scholarship, junior division, $2,000 award.
Richard Ray, 1962, 1963 regional winner, 1964 styling scholarship, $1,000 award.
Theodore A. Becker, 1964 and 1965 Illinois state awards.
James E. Cotter, 1965 second-place national scholarship, senior division, $3,000 award.
Michael A. Pietruska, 1965 second-place national scholarship, junior division, $4,000 award.
Ronald Steinhilber, 1961–1965 regional awards, five in a row.
Tom Hibschman, 1962–1965 Indiana state winner.
Terence J. Kirk, 1965 first-place winner, Vauxhall Craftsman's Guild (VCG), Luton, England.
John Hambrock, 1965 styling scholarship, $1,000 award.
David P. Onopa, 1963 honorable mention, 1964 junior regional, 1965 third-place state and 1966 senior regional.
Carl A. La Roche, 1965 regional winner and 1966 fourth-place national scholarship, junior division, $2,000 award.
David Constance, whose brother Leonard Constance won a 1966 fourth-place national scholarship, $2,000 award.
Larry Hagen, 1966 third-place national scholarship, junior division, $3,000 award.
LaMont Kucker, 1964–1966, regional winner in 1966.
Dr. Charles R. Costello, 1963 junior regional winner and 1966 state winner from Greensburg, Pennsylvania.
Richard B. Lee, 1966 regional winner.
Don Patty, 1966 regional winner from Bradford, Ohio.
John M. Mellberg, 1966 second-place national scholarship, senior Division, $4,000 award.
Albert W. Brown, 1966 first-place state Missouri and regional winner.
Dale A. Gnage, 1966 first-place national scholarship, junior division, $5,000 award.
David G. Catalano, 1967 fourth-place national scholarship, junior division, $2,000 award.
Stephen M. Paulson, 1967 second-place national scholarship, senior division, $4,000 award.
Thelma Virginia M. Eby (mother of Larry K. Eby, deceased Guildsman who won a 1967 styling scholarship, $1,000 award, and 1968 national scholarship award).
Spencer L. Mackay, 1968 styling scholarship, $1,000 award.
Stewart D. Reed, 1964 first-place state Michigan and regional award and 1968 fourth-place national scholarship, senior division, $2,000 award.
Bradford J. Roark, 1965 and 1968 regional winner from Spearfish, South Dakota.

Key Supporters and Resources for Both the Guild Exhibit and Guild Book Projects

These individuals did not necessarily participate in the Guild themselves, but believed in the importance of documenting the Craftsman's Guild history.

Jennifer Knightstep Lesniak, GM Media Archives, General Motors Corporation, Detroit.
Hampton C. Wayt and collection, Aiken, South Carolina.
Sam Fiorni, editor, *SAH Journal*, Society of Automotive Historians, Inc.
Zachary Taylor Vinson, editor, *Automotive History Review*, Society of Automotive Historians, Inc.
Lawrence P. Fisher II, a Fisher grandson named after his great uncle Lawrence P. Fisher (fourth eldest of the seven Fisher brothers), former president of Cadillac. His father is Charles T. Fisher III, GM board of directors (retired).

Mr. Bill Holleran, archivist, Richard P. Scharchburg Collection of Industrial History, Kettering University, Flint, Michigan.

Mr. Nicholas Berberat, manager of public relations, Opel Suisse, Biel, Switzerland.

Mr. Ernst Peter-Berresheim, archivist, Adam-Opel AG, Ruesselsheim, Germany.

Mr. Bryan Millin, internal communications manager, Vauxhall Motors Ltd., Luton, England.

Ms. Samantha Cooper, GM Holden archivist, the State Library of South Australia.

Mr. Richard Fisher, Alexandria Translation Services, Alexandria, Virginia.

Ms. Renee L. Fairrer, national director of marketing and communications, Boy Scouts of America (BSA).

Mr. James W. Sponseller, editor of "Fisher Body OnLine" Web site, and former public relations administrator for Fisher Body Division, GMC.

John F. Smith, chairman of the board, West Grand Boulevard, General Motors Corporation, Detroit, Michigan.

William L. Withuhn, curator of transportation, Transportation Collections, National Museum of American History, Behring Center, Smithsonian Institution.

Roger B. White, road transportation specialist, Transportation Collections, National Museum of American History, Behring Center, Smithsonian Institution.

Grace and Richard Brigham, and Charles L. Betts, Society of Automotive Historians, Inc.

Brian J. Wynne, executive director of Industrial Designers Society of America (IDSA).

James J. Bradley, head of the National Automotive History Collection, Detroit Public Library, Detroit, Michigan (deceased).

Library of Congress, Washington, D.C.

Kristina Goodrich, executive director of the Industrial Designers Society of America (IDSA), Dulles, Virginia.

Nancy Cunningham, educational relations, GM Design, GM Tech Center, Warren, Michigan.

Cindy Boron, educational relations, GM Design, GM Tech Center, Warren, Michigan.

Stuart Shuster, educational relations, GM Design Center, GM Tech Center, Warren, Michigan.

New York City Public Library, New York.

Lowell Paddock, editor, *Automobile Quarterly*, Newport Beach, California.

Julie M. Fenster, contributing editor, *Automobile Quarterly*, Newport Beach, California.

Dennis Adler, editor, *Road and Track*, Challenge Publications, Los Angeles, California.

John A. Gunnell, editor, *Old Cars Weekly and Marketplace*, Iola, Wisconsin.

Strother MacMinn, former GM designer, instructor at Art Center College of Design, Pasadena California (deceased).

Dr. David L. Lewis, professor of business history, University of Michigan.

Ms. Margaret Brucato, director of alumni relations, Art Center College of Design, Pasadena, California.

Ms. Leora W. Newton, assistant director of alumni resources, Pratt Institute, Brooklyn, New York.

Unsung Heroes and Heroines[5]*: Fisher Body Division Folks and Their Suppliers and Contractors Who Managed the Day-to-Day Craftsman's Guild Operations*

DIRECTORS OF PUBLIC RELATIONS AND ADVERTISING

William S. McLean
James P. Wines
Joseph R. Hainline

Norman E. May
Florence "Flossie" Stolman, secretary

Fisher Body Craftsman's Guild Executive Management

William S. McLean, Guild secretary
James P. Wines, Guild administrator
Carlyle W. "Mac" McClellan, Guild administrator (1957–1968)
G. Rolf Amundson, general supervisor
Walter Maeder, first administrator, GM Suisse, Modelauto Wettbewerb, Biel, Switzerland
Richard A. "Dick" Herdegen, GM Overseas Operations Division, Guild representative in the
    United Kingdom (Vauxhall Craftsman's Guild) and Australia (Holden Craftsman's Guild)

Craftsman's Guild Supervisors and Representatives

Richard A. "Dick" Herdegen, *Guildsman* editor and assistant editor
V.B. "Irv" Irving, *Guildsman* editor and writer
Nick Popely, *Guildsman* editor and writer
John J. Jendza, *Guildsman* art director, Fisher Body public relations and advertising
Bill Quigley, *Guildsman* writer and contributor
Varnum Bowers, *Guildsman* writer and contributor
Rand Shackleton, field supervisor, western regions

Fred Pettyjohn	Art Cope	Roy C. Boyer
Don Langley	Steve Vandenbrook	Albert E. Smith
George Morrison	Paul Cusick	John D. Hoddick
Don Brown	Gary Gerteen	E. H. Mitchell
Bob Chernick	J.C. Mills	Dale E. Artz
Ken Koller	Andy Miller	Milton Leander
Claude McCammon	Chester "Chet" Francke	William L. Brown
John Rolls	Jim Facilis	Edward T. Kason
Gary Horton	George Owen	Frank C. Riess
Dave Garrard	Joel Higgins	James R. Umphrey
Don Campbell	Walter Overhardt	Norman E. May
Harry F. Kelly, Jr.	Hap Dunne	Bruce McCristal
Victor L. "Ole" Olesen	Bob Fell	

Mail Department

Jim Hands, department head
Marie Wilson, secretary
John Karsnick

Steve Oros
Charlie Gerringer

Printing Department

John Karsnick

Director of Building Security, Fisher Body
Central Engineering, Warren, Michigan

Ed Aldridge

FBCG Staff Photographer

John J. Jendza, Jr.

PUBLICITY STAFF

John Carr   Edna Miller
James W. Fuson   John Nanovic

GM STYLING STAFF

(See Appendix M for specific Styling personnel assigned by year to be a FBCG judge.)

Other Suppliers and Contractors

George D. Wanner Company, Dayton, Ohio: made Napoleonic Coach parts kits (early 1930s).
Lewis Model Kit Company: made Napoleonic Coach parts kits (circa 1938).
H.B. Stubbs, Detroit, Michigan: made Napoleonic Coach parts kits (post–World War II); made the rhomboid shaped, glass traveling exhibit cases with rotating platforms for the model cars; made soft aluminum trim kits (I, II and II) for model car makers.
L.G. Balfour Jewelers: made engraved silver loving cups for state, regional and national coach winners (1930s); made sterling silver signet rings for regional winners (late 1940s and early 1950s); made trophies for state, regional and national model car winners (1950s and 1960s).

FISHER BODY ADVERTISING AGENCIES

John and Adams   Darcy and McManus
Darcy   Kudner
McManus   Kudner, McManus, John and Adams

AUTO STYLING CLAY MANUFACTURERS

Chavant Clay Models, Inc., Jersey City, New Jersey
Red Bank Clay, Red Bank, New Jersey

Chapter Notes

Preface

1. Museum patrons could read this brief description in a minute or less at the exhibit case. These lines are quoted, with some modifications, from the placard which used to accompany the Fisher Body Craftsman's Guild Exhibit at the National Museum of American History, Behring Center, Smithsonian Institution, Washington, D.C. (October 1991 to spring 2001). In the third paragraph, the word "Several" was changed by the author to "Many" and in the fourth paragraph, the word "several" was changed to "many." These changes are shown in brackets. Mr. Roger B. White and William L. Withuhn, Curator of Transportation, are to be credited with precipitating much of the basic research behind this book. Roger White fielded dozens of phone calls (1984–1991) from Guild folks and shared his insight about the meaning of the Craftsman's Guild program with the author.

2. As chief designer at the Pontiac Studio at GM in the late 1960s and early 1970s, Porter led the design team that created the Firebirds, GTOs, Catalinas, Bonnevilles, etc., of that era. The 1970 F-Body (Pontiac Firebird and Chevy Camaro) was in production for 10 years. Later, from 1980 until his retirement in 1996, he was chief designer of Buick #1 Studio, where the Park Avenues, Le Sabres and Rivieras were designed. Source: personal correspondence between William L. (Bill) Porter and John L. Jacobus, dated June 2, 2003. Also see *Art of the American Automobile: The Greatest Stylists and Their Work*, Nick Georgano, Smithmark Publishers (page 256).

Chapter I. Introduction

1. From the personal papers and Guild memorabilia loaned by Virgil M. Exner, Jr., to the author on August 26, 2002.

2. "Wheels for a Waiting World: The Story of General Motors," Christy Borth, *Wards Quarterly*, summer 1966, Powers and Company, Inc., 550 West Fort Street, Detroit, Michigan, 48226.

3. *General Motors and the Fisher Body Craftsman's Guild*, a 4-color brochure. Copyright 1957.

4. Charles M. Jordan's personal selected Guild memorabilia and files. There were six scholarship winners (average age 26) like T.R. Henline, R.C. Hill, C.M. Jordan, A.L. Joslin, E.F. Taylor and E. Russinoff, 20 state award winners (average age 30.5) like Henry Haga, Dave Holls, Don Logerquist, Stanley Parker, George Gadda, George Anderson, Charlie Stewart, Peter Wozena and Byron Voight, and 21 other Guild participants (average

age 28.5) on the payroll. William L. Mitchell affectionately called them his Young Turks.

5. AIA: American Institute of Architects.

6. Raymond Loewy opened shop in 1929 and is credited with being a product designer and automobile designer. In the product arena, he designed the Coca Cola dispenser for drugstore fountains, the Exxon and U.S. Postal Service logos, the famous Lucky Strike cigarette package, Eversharp pens, Schick razors, and the Skylab's interior, among many other things. On the automotive front, he and his associates streamlined train locomotives and tractors; created the Greyhound Bus Scenic Cruiser, the Hupmobile, the postwar "Studie," and numerous one-off show cars; and contributed to the design of the early 1970s safety cars being designed by the automakers for the U.S. safety agency.

7. The Stewart-Warner ad makes clear this was an auto safety device with phrases like "a life preserved … smites on coming drivers square in the eyes," and "a new safety factor for the sweet moving four wheel–brake age."

8. There were 900 awards advertised, valued at $50,000, including 4 college scholarships.

9. There were five congressional acts and one executive order (EO) that effectively made up the New Deal. The five congressional acts were the Federal Securities Act, the Civilian Conservation Corps, the Federal Emergency Relief Administration, the Public Works Administration and the Home Owners' Refinancing Act. The EO set up the National Labor Relations Board.

10. A group of 12 modified GM motor coaches traveled together in a caravan or what was called a "Parade of Progress," from state fair to state fair, in the 1953 to 1956 time frame, touting the virtues of GM technology and automotive advances. The exterior side-wall panels of the buses opened vertically like garage doors, and one would contain the winning Fisher Body Craftsman's Guild models. One of these coaches is being restored today in a project sponsored by the National Automotive and Truck Museum of the United States, Auburn, Indiana, in what is called the GM Futurliner Restoration Project. See <http://www.futurliner.com/rom/html>. Also, see *The Kettering Perspective*, volume 40, no. 3 and the winter 2000 issues, Kettering University Alumni Association, 1700 W. Third Avenue, Flint, Michigan, for further details.

11. Reprint of "Fisher in the News," August 4, 1984, in the *Tribune Courier* (Ontario, Ohio) on the occasion of the 75th anniversary of the Fisher Body Division, General Motors Corporation.

12. The author has tried several times to do the math, but to no avail. Insufficient data is available.

13. A 1966 Fisher Body press release stated that about

600 model coaches were entered in the first competition year, but the *Detroit Times*, dated August 31, 1931, stated that 1,350 model coaches were received. The latter figure is considered more reliable. The *Detroit Times*, dated August 24, 1931, stated there were 148,000 Guild enrollees that year, whereas other Guild print materials indicated there were 145,000 members in 1931.

14. Although female students attended the assembly programs across the USA, only boys or young men were eligible to compete in the U.S. Fisher Body Craftsman's Guild competitions.

15. Notes from Charles M. Jordan's personal Guild memorabilia files, received September 12, 2002.

16. Mr. James M. Roche was the chief executive officer at the time.

17. Approximate dates.

18. Approximate dates.

19. Possibly the advertising agency Batten, Barton, Durstine and Osborn.

20. The school superintendents that constituted the Guild's advisory board recommended that the Napoleonic Coach competition be discontinued after the 1947–1948 competition year. *Guide Light* magazine, November 25, 1947, vol. 14, no. 1, Guide Lamp Division, GMC, Anderson, Indiana.

21. If Fisher Body Division had remained intact its 100th anniversary would be celebrated July 22, 2008. General Motors' 100th anniversary will be celebrated September 16, 2008.

Chapter II. Napoleonic Coach Competition (1930–1948)

1. The Fisher Building was awarded a bronze medal by the Detroit Chapter, American Institute of Architects (AIA), for the beautiful marble tower. This building remains a monument to art deco architecture.

2. "Body by Fisher," Michael Lamm, editor, *Special Interest Autos*, issue #45, May–June 1978.

3. The author wishes to thank Lawrence P. Fisher II, named after his great uncle Lawrence P. Fisher, the former president of Cadillac, and son of Charles T. Fisher III, for sharing the William A. Fisher Scrapbooks #1 and #2 on a CD-ROM created by the Fisher family to preserve their history. The author has relied heavily on this CD-ROM to better understand the Fisher family's life and times.

4. "Wheels for a Waiting World: The Story of General Motors," Christy Borth, *Ward's Quarterly*, summer 1966.

5. See Appendix A for a short biography of each brother.

6. It is speculated that McClellan Barkley, the famous artist and illustrator, could have been that artist, as his color rendering appeared in Fisher Body print ads and were famous for female fashion and style throughout the 1920s. The Fisher brothers wanted to leave the reader with an impression of feminine style, elegance and haute couture from their closed automobile body advertisements.

7. In 1925 Fisher Body Corporation owned the Fleetwood Metal Body Company, so W.C. Leuschner could have been a Fisher Body Corp. employee subject to direction by the Fisher brothers.

8. Napoleon Bonaparte divorced his first wife, Josephine, because she couldn't bear him an heir. Marie-Louise, however, did provide a son and heir to the Emperor Napoleon.

9. The medieval guilds the Fishers' ad agency playfully mimicked would become symbolic of the powerful trade unions that eventually would dominate the auto industry landscape, and of the paternalism these organizations represented.

10. This story was contained in the Napoleonic Coach plans and instructions printed by Fisher Body Division some 65–70 years ago. This same story is on the Internet today. Search under the key words "Fisher Body Craftsman's Guild" or "Fisher Body OnLine." Look for the Skip Geear's Fisher Body Craftsman's Guild Foundation and Mini-Museum.

11. The author did find a possible connection between Walter Leuschner of Berlin and the folks at Fleetwood, Pennsylvania, albeit a long shot. One of the Fleetwood founding fathers was Ernest Schebera, considered one of the best automobile body designers in the country at the time, who had received his technical education after Austrian normal school in Berlin and later sold carriages in Berlin before coming to America around 1913. Although this is pure speculation on the part of the author, Ernest Schebera probably knew the Leuschner family as a competitor in the Berlin carriage trade.

12. See Appendix B for further details.

13. "General Motors' Fisher Body Emblem Has Royal Background," from *Fisher on the News* (internal newsletter) reprinted in the Ontario, Ohio, *Tribune-Courier*, August 4, 1983, in honor of the Fisher Body Division's 75th anniversary.

14. "Auto Bodies by Fleetwood," K.H. Stauffer, *Antique Automobiles*, July–August 1977.

15. "Fleetwood, The Royal Coachman," Parts I and II, Truman S. Fuller, Jr., *The Classic Car Magazine*, vol. XV, no. 3, fall 1967, published by the Classic Car Club of America.

16. The paint kit offered for sale by H.B. Stubbs Company, 4484 Cass Avenue, Detroit, Michigan, included white primer, light blue or Lilac Blue Duco (brush), blue-black or dark blue Duco (brush), a vermillion Duco (brush), white Duco (brush), brush lacquer thinner, bronzing liquid or banana oil and gold bronze powder. The Lilac Blue dominates what the eye sees when looking at a coach such as the 1931 Napoleonic Coach made by Wallace Lench (age 15) of Flint, Michigan, which is preserved by the author in a Plexiglas case. As the story goes, Wallace Lench, at age 20, took his three-dimensional resume to the Flint Chevrolet plant. He was a member of the second graduating Apprentice Class of 1936 and worked as a journeyman die maker for 40 years. There are other stories like the one from Judy Quesenberry about her Uncle Bill (William Shaffer) who used his unpainted 1936 or 1937 coach as a resume to get a job, thus saving the family farm from foreclosure. This family story is still being told today.

17. *Detroit Times* (probably summer 1930) article entitled "Today Is the Last Chance to View Model Coach," Detroit Times Chapter of the Fisher Body Craftsman's Guild, Times Building, 1370 Cass Avenue, Detroit, Michigan.

18. "Fisher Body OnLine" Web site and the section "Building the Napoleonic Coach," <http://www.geo-cities.com/sponcom26/CoachMuseumCottonCoach.html>. Cotton is a misspelling. This refers to the 1934 National Scholarship award winning coach made by Truman Cottom.

19. Noteworthy lyrics were "…The honors gained by

patient toil / The goals that skill has won / Are stepping stones to greater things / A worthy work begun...."

20. "Michigan Youth Wins Fisher Coach Award: Scholarships Presented to Four at Dinner Climaxing Napoleonic Body Contest," *Detroit Times*, August 24, 1931. There were 145,000 to 148,000 enrollees in 1931 with 1,350 miniature model coach entries, of which 104 state winners were brought to Detroit by train for the convention banquet and given 50 bucks each for spending money. The 1,350 models represents a less than 1 percent participation rate.

21. "Raymond S. Doerr and Arthur Brisbane Meet," *Detroit Times*, August 26, 1931.

22. The 104 attendees in 1931 means that eight duplicate awards were made due to sons of GM employees also being winners. By 1932 and 1934 Canadian winners were also in attendance.

23. "GM's 34 Year Talent Search: The Fisher Body Craftsman's Guild," Wicke Humble, *Special Interest Autos*, issue #61, February 1981.

24. Herbert Lozier, who worked as a model maker for Raymond Loewy, reported 600+ coach models being made in 1931. See Chapter 13, "A Golden Opportunity for Model Makers," where Fisher Body Division News Release information is quoted, as contained in the book *Model Making*, Herbert Lozier, Chilton Book Company, Radnor, PA, copyright 1967. The *Detroit Times*, August 31, 1931, reported 1,350 miniature model coaches being made.

25. The "reach" was a structural member or beam that connected the rear axle with stabilizers to the fifth wheel and front axle. The front axle pivoted on the fifth wheel.

26. The contestant had to work with a plethora of interior trim materials including velvet, ivory silk, gold braid, rabbit's fur carpet, embroidery floss, black patent leather, white leather, gold beads and gold cord. Tassels, French knots, fringes, and embroidery were required to complete the coach body design inside and out. Such textile technologies as needlepoint, crochet and weaving were employed in order to complete the task.

27. A copy of the Coach-Builder's Biographic Survey Form, June 1997, can be found in Appendix C.

28. The gilding process or application of gold leaf isn't as complicated as it sounds. Gold foil booklets are available today for a low cost ($30) containing sheets 0.0001 mm thick and varying from white gold to bright canary yellow gold. A gilder's glue or "gilder's milk" is applied to the smoothly sanded and sealed wood substrate. A static-electricity-charged squirrel's tail is used to move the ash-like pieces of gold foil to the substrate. An ox or sable hair brush is used to gently burnish or rub the malleable gold foil around the substrate object. A much stiffer, agate-tipped burnisher can be used to rub tight spots and rub out the final finish. The leftover pieces of gold are called "skewings." Source: *Gilding and Goldleafing Seminar*, April 27, 1997, held at the "G" Street Fabrics in Rockville Maryland. This art was taught to the author by a professional gilder named Marva E. Gordon, of Glenelg, Maryland.

29. Brigadier General C.H. Mitchell was the dean of faculty of applied science and engineering, University of Toronto, and on the Guild's international board of judges. Source: *The Guildsman*, May 1934, vol. 1, no. 2.

30. General Curtiss LeMay would lead the incendiary bombing of Tokyo, Japan, at the end of World War II. Bob Considine wrote the book *30 Seconds Over Tokyo* after the war.

31. The same age intervals or age brackets applied as for the Napoleonic Coach competition — junior division (ages 12–15) and senior division (ages 16–19) The Canadians did not compete in the Traveling Coach competition.

32. *Guide Light*, vol. 14, no. 1, November 25, 1947.

Chapter III. Model Car Competition (1937–1968)

1. *Special Interest Autos*, February 1981, #61. Interviews probably around November 1980 with Chuck Jordan and many GM designers who participated in the Fisher Body Craftsman's Guild.

2. *A Century of Automotive Style: 100 Years of American Car Design*, Michael Lamm and Dave Holls, Lamm-Morada Publishing Company, Inc., P.O. Box 7607, Stockton, California 95267.

3. Harley J. Earl pioneered the use of clay as a styling medium, set up separate styling studios, gave each motor division unique styling cues, held styling competitions among his designers, and founded a school for young auto designers in the late 1930s. He is remembered for his 1951 Le Sabre show car with its wraparound windshield, the 1953 Corvette (America's first sports car) and GM's Motorama (1953–1961) Exhibits containing futuristic automotive ideas which fascinated 10.5 million Americans. The wraparound windshield from the 1951 Le Sabre was quickly adopted by the industry as a whole in the mid–1950s. His correspondence course for young auto designers was called the Detroit Institute of Automobile Styling (DIAS). He also managed the Harley Earl Corporation, an industrial design firm.

4. The Hoffman Motor Development Corporation had a $168,000 contract and purchased the prototype bodies from Budd Company. "Body by Fisher," Michael Lamm, editor, *Special Interest Autos*, issue #45, May–June 1978.

5. *A Manual for Guildsmen in the 1937 Model Car Design Competition: Details and Instructions for Designing and Making a Model Automobile, Influence of Designing and Your Opportunity of Expression*, Copyright 1937 Fisher Body Craftsman's Guild. A work booklet (size 11 × 18 unfolded and flat) with graph paper for sketching to scale, B&W lithograph, and consisting of 12 pages of instructions and the awards system. A 1/12 scale model would be made of wood and/or other materials (balsa wood, white pine, California redwood, cypress or bass wood were suggested). The contestants made their own wheels out of cardboard and wood rings (2¾" diameter). The Fisher brothers used the same regional awards system to organize the states as they did for the Traveling Coach competition (see Chapter II). The back cover of the 12 page booklet announced the awards: $47, 350 in awards with two $5,000 four-year university scholarships (one junior and one senior), 686 state cash awards (first place $100, second place $75 and third place $50 with four runners-up awards of $25 each per state and per age division), and 18 regional award winners (nine junior and nine senior) with free trips to Detroit. The 1937 model car manual makes it clear that the Guild was still an educational foundation, "devoted to the development of handiwork and craftsmanship among boys of the North American continent."

6. With the 18 model car regional winners, the "Party by Fisher" could have grown to include 140 youths in 1938 and 1939, including six duplicate awards for good

measure. There were 98 Napoleonic Coach first state winners, 18 Traveling Coach regional winners and 18 model car regional winners. The scale model car competition and the Traveling Coach competition both used the same nine regions to organize the states and have a manageable and fair way of making awards.

7. The exact competition year for Richard Arbib was 1937, when he won a first-place New York senior division, $100 award. This was confirmed by an article (1938) provided by Frederic A Sharf (Boston, Massachusetts), a collector of original Richard Arbib automotive renderings. This was also confirmed by another Arbib collector and expert, Hampton Wayt (Aiken, South Carolina). There are both Guild and Arbib collectors, members of a very small fraternity.

8. See Appendix D.

9. Follow-up letter from William L. Mitchell, director of GM Styling, to the top 20 Senior Guild winners of 1955, dated March 6, 1956, offering automobile styling career advice and counsel, a list of colleges with industrial design programs, and opportunities for portfolio evaluations by the Styling staff.

10. *Designing, Modeling, Building a Model Automobile*, Fisher Body Craftsman's Guild, Fisher Body Division, General Motors Corporation, Detroit 2, Michigan, copyright 1951.

11. *Designing and Building a Model Car*, Fisher Body Craftsman's Guild, Fisher Body Division, General Motors Corporation, Detroit 2, Michigan, copyright 1962.

12. Inter-organizational letter from J.W. Griswold, director of public relations, GM Overseas Operations in New York City, to N.J. Stork of Adam-Opel AG and W. Swallow of Vauxhall Motors Ltd., dated November 27, 1964, about starting Craftsman's Guild programs.

13. Former Guild employees and Guild managers such as Richard A. "Dick" Herdegen, Rolf Amundson, Rand Shackleton, and Ruth C. McClellan (the widow of Mac McClellan) provided primary and supplemental background information necessary to the creation of the generalized organization chart.

14. *American Youth*, volume 1, number 5, September–October 1960, Ceco Publishing Company, Dept. AY, 3-135, General Motors Building, Detroit 2, Michigan, John H. Warner, editor.

15. Inter-organizational letter from W.E. Fish, general sales manager, Chevrolet Motor Division, Chevrolet Central Office, to all Chevrolet dealers, dated November 27, 1951.

16. Inter-organizational letter from C.W. McClellan, Guild administrator, to Charles M. Jordan, GM Styling, dated December 4, 1962. During the 1960s, Chuck Jordan had a number of titles in the Guild literature: Executive-in-Charge of Exterior Design, Executive-in-Charge of Exterior Automotive Styling, and Executive-in-Charge. The succession of GM Styling and Design Executives was Harley J. Earl, V.P. GM Styling (1940–1958); William L. (Bill) Mitchell, V.P. GM Styling (1958–1977); Irvin Rybicki, V.P. GM Design (1977–1986); Charles M. Jordan, V.P. GM Design (1986–1992), Wayne K. Cherry, V.P. GM and Ed Welburn, V.P. GM Design (current) North American Design Center.

17. Harlow H. Curtice was *Time* magazine's Man of the Year, January 2, 1956.

18. "600,000 Youth Work on Autos of Tomorrow," *New York Times*, April 2, 1967, p. A3. The writer Edward Hudson, was referring to the 600,000 enrollees or members of the Guild, of which only ½ to 1 percent actually submitted a model entry and could wear the mantle of "Guildsman" or "Brother."

19. The Overseas Craftsman's Guilds at Vauxhall Motors Ltd. in Luton, England, and Adam-Opel Modellbauer Gilde in Russelsheim, West Germany, were coeducational with a few teenage girls finishing among the top 40 model makers in their respective countries. A recent contender for GM's top design chief job, to replace Wayne Cherry, was Ms. Anne Asensio, executive director of design, responsible for interiors, quality and brand character.

20. In Fisher Body Division sales literature for the Craftsman's Guild and the discussion of success stories, the statistic refers to the university scholarships trust fund winners; 90 percent had either completed or were pursuing undergraduate degrees at an accredited college or university.

21. 23,253 Scouts completed the optional scratch-building merit badge called "Model Design and Building" in 1977; 7,066 in 1981; 1,665 in 1996; and 2,270 in 2000. Cumulatively, 137,472 Scouts had completed this scratch-building merit badge in 1981; 175,472 in 1996; and 183,624 in 2000. 2.5 million annually participate in the Cub Scout's Pinewood Derby a scratch-building design contest. Letter from Ms. Renee L. Fairrer, associate national director, marketing and communications, BSA Headquarters, Irving, Texas, to J. Jacobus, dated April 18, 2002.

22. Phone conversation October 2, 2003, with Mr. Rand Shackleton, of Cross Village, Michigan, former Midwestern supervisor, FBCG, retired PR and advertising executive and, currently, an independent filmmaker. Rand Shackleton is a friend of Ruth Carol Ganter McClellan, the wife of the former Guild administrator C.W. McClellan (deceased), who helped the author on numerous occasions with this project.

23. Letter from Terry R. Henline to author, dated September 21, 2002.

24. Inter-organizational letter, Fisher Body Division, subject: "Re-organization of the Craftsman's Guild Competition," from V.B. Irvine to C.M. Jordan, dated June 22, 1962.

25. The reader is referred to Appendix E for further details. The Guild's 1/12 scale precluded the use of customized, plastic model car kits purchased at hobby shops, as these were usually 1/24 or 1/25 scale. They were too small to be adapted.

26. "GM Worker's Son Wins Top Model Car Award," *Detroit Free Press*, August 25, 1949, and "Detroit Youth Wins $4,000 Model Auto Design Award" (from either the *Detroit Free Press* or the *Detroit News*, August 1949).

27. Rhodium, a rare white lustrous metallic element used to electroplate instruments, was used by one contestant to plate brass parts and dazzle the judges. However, chrome-plated brass parts were standard fare for Guild competitors as the program and competitors matured. Source: Letter from Norman E. May, Guild technical supervisor, to Allen T. Weideman, Salt Lake City, Utah, dated March 24, 1954. Allen was working on his first model then at age 15.

28. H.B. Stubbs and Company of Detroit also supplied coach kits to Guildsmen and fabricated exhibit cases used to promote the Guild in cities across the country.

29. See Appendix F for a detailed explanation of model construction techniques.

30. Phone conversations with Mr. Elia Russinoff (retired GM designer), August 28, 2002, September 28, 2002, and October 3, 2002. Also, "GM Worker's Son Wins Top Model Car Award," *Detroit Free Press*, August 25, 1949.

31. Correspondence from William F. Marks to the author, dated August 24, 2003.

32. Based on the actual score sheets, model numbers #1483 and # 2566 for Allen T. Weideman and John L. Jacobus, respectively.

33. Based on the actual score sheets, model numbers #1889 and #1925 for Allen T. Weideman and Ronald C. Pellman, respectively.

34. "Stanley F. Parker, 70, was a Chief Designer at GM and Guildsman," *Detroit News* obituary, dated April 30, 2001.

35. The reader should keep in mind that these ideas were popular during the time of the Guild competition and may not reflect current design practice or philosophy.

36. Patrick O. McKittrick, letter to the author, October 10, 1985. Gordon M. Buehrig was chief body designer at the Auburn, Cord, Duesenberg Motor Company and is associated with executing the following designs: Model "J" Berlin Duesenberg, 1935 Auburn Boattail Speedster, 1936 Cord "810" Sedan, 1937 Cord "812" Phaeton, Model SJ Tourster Duesenberg and the Model SJ Torpedo Duesenberg. Fifty percent of his Duesenberg designs were produced in sheet metal. "SAE to Hear Famed Designers," *Automotive News*, date unknown (probably 1989 or 1990). Also, "Living Legends, The Buehrig Collection," an advertisement from *Automobile Quarterly*, vol. 28, no. 4, 1991.

37. *The Guildsman*, volume 1, number 1, 1953 Convention Issue.

38. "$117,000 in prizes for modelers in: Fisher Body Craftsman's Guild," *Model Car Science* magazine May, 1965 and "600,000 Youths Work on Autos of Tomorrow," *New York Times*, April 2, 1967.

39. See Appendix M. for a list of judges.

40. Albert Drake, "Entering the Fisher Body Craftman's Guild Competition," *Old Cars Weekly*, June 29, 2000.

41. Dennis A. Little's 1965 design included two high risk features, namely canted front wheels and an asymmetric body design. Both had to be executed flawlessly to earn points. Dennis A. Little became a GM designer, as shown in a November 1980 photograph of GM Stylists who had been Guildsmen (provided by Stuart Shuster).

42. Email from Ronald J. Will to the author, dated September 1, 2003. Slight alterations have been made for clarity.

43. Letters in the collection of Mr. Charles M. Jordan, former V.P. GM Design, General Motors Corporation.

44. See Appendix H.

45. 1960 U.S. Census Data, Characteristics of the Population, University of Maryland Government Document Center, McKeldin Library, 4th Floor, College Park, Maryland. There were about 11,358,088 males eligible for the Craftsman's Guild program in 1960. If the Guild field reps, advertising, and other PR components of the program managed to sign up 600,000 youths annually during the 1960s, that would have been 5.3 percent of the eligible population.

46. For further details about the grouping of states into regions, please see Appendix G.

47. The reason the number of scholarship winners is a surrogate measure for regional market popularity is that the number of national scholarship winners is directly proportional to overall interest and participation at the grassroots level. The earlier discussion of the multiple models needed to win on an individual basis suggests hundreds of models were made by teenagers on a state and regional level, over the course of many years, in order to produce a half-dozen national scholarship winners.

48. In 1965–66 there was $117,000 in scholarships and cash announced. With $38,000 in scholarships and $43,350 in state awards, the remainder of $35,650 was allocated for the 40 regional winner trips or $891.25 per trip.

49. See Appendix H for further information on specific Guild conventions.

50. Letter from Roger D. Teter to author, dated April 24, 1985.

51. The author examined the scholarship trust fund agreement of Robert Eugene Davids, signed and sealed August 3, 1963. Bob Davids was the 1963 first-place national scholarship, senior division, $5,000 award winner.

52. The 1966 Craftsman's Guild budget was $700,000 as described in a GM press release transcribed in the book *Model-Making* by Herbert Lozier, Chilton Book Company, Radnor, Penn., Copyright 1966.

53. The last competition for the Fisher Body Craftsman's Guild was 1967–68. The top 1968 first-place national scholarship, senior division, $5,000 award winner was Grant Onnie from Highland Park, Michigan.

54. "In 1966, 565,000 boys between the ages of 11 and 20 enrolled in the competition." Since 1930, 10 million have enrolled." "For Immediate Release: News" from the public relations director, Fisher Body Division, July 1967. Other sources have indicated 8.4 million enrollees total. Ten million enrollees and 32,800 coach and car models were reported in *Fisher-in-the-News*, 75th anniversary, August 4, 1983, reprint in the Ontario, Ohio, *Tribune-Courier*. A model participation rate of 0.328 percent (32,800 / 10,000,000) using these figures is consistent with other calculations in the book showing less than ½ percent or less than 0.50 percent participation.

55. Ronald Johnson (age 15) of Portland, Oregon, labored 1,000 hours making a cast aluminum model for the 1947–1948 competition, and won a first-place national scholarship, junior division, $4,000 award. Contestants were supposed to use simple hardware store casting plaster, not foundry quality cast aluminum. A wooden pattern would still have been required to make an aluminum casting. *Mechanix Illustrated*, November 1948.

56. *Car Craft*, June 1962, and *Special Interest Autos* no. 61 (February 1981).

57. Internal memo dated April 21, 1967, from C.W. McClellan, Guild administrator, to C.M. Jordan, Styling, and another internal memo dated June 13, 1968, from C.M. MacKichan to William L. Mitchell. From the personal Guild memorabilia of Charles M. Jordan.

58. "Proposal for a Fisher Body Design Competition," July 3, 1973. Collection of Charles M. Jordan.

59. Letter from Norman E. May, general director, Fisher Body Division public relations, to the author, dated February 22, 1974.

60. Letter from James W. Sponseller, Fisher Body Division public relations administrator, to the author, dated August 16, 1984.

61. Model Construction Rate = Number of Model Entries/No. of Enrollees. U.S. Guild: 3,000/600,000 × 100 percent = 0.50 percent and 4,000/600,000 × 100 percent = 0.66 percent. Overseas guilds (1967): 2,510/139,702 = 1.79 percent.

62. Some details of the Vauxhall, Adam Opel, Holden and GM Suisse craftsman's guilds are discussed in Appendix J.

63. Inter-organizational letter, Fisher Body Craftsman's Guild, from C.W. McClellan, Guild administrator, to Charles M. Jordan, executive-in-charge, GM Styling staff, dated March 30, 1964.

64. Inter-organizational letter, Fisher Body Craftsman's Guild, from C.W. McClellan, Guild Administrator, to C.M. Jordan, executive-in-charge, GM Styling staff, dated October 7, 1965.

65. Inter-organizational note from James R. Hainline, Fisher Body public relations, to Charles M. Jordan, May 18, 1966, about an internal review of the success of the FBCG program in Europe, held May 12, 1966.

66. Internal memo dated April 21, 1967, from C.W. McClellan, Guild administrator, to C.M. Jordan, Styling, and another internal memo dated June 13, 1968, from C.M. MacKichan, GM Styling, to William L. Mitchell, GM Styling. Collection of Charles M. Jordan.

67. "Thoughts on Future Fisher Body Craftsman's Guild Competitions," Charles M. Jordan, July 3, 1973.

68. Internal memo dated January 30, 1967, from C.W. McClellan to Charles M. Jordan.

69. Internal memo, "Proposal for a Fisher Body Design Competition," dated July 3, 1973.

Chapter IV. The Search for Guildsmen

1. Letter from Raymond S. Doerr, 1931 grand national winner, to author, April 4, 1985.

2. See Appendix B for information about the FBCG Foundation.

3. See Appendix K for a summary of information about these and other Guildsmen.

4. "Scholarship Winners in Coach Model Contest; Albert Fischer, Donald Burnham, Howard Jennings and Raymond Doerr," *The Detroit Times*, August 24, 1931; "Party by Fisher," *The Detroit Times*, August 31, 1931; phone conversation between the author and Donald C. Burnham, March 25, 1992.

5. Quoted with permission from Chapter 4, "Napoleonic Coach Model Competition," from a draft of Mr. Burnham's memoirs, *Memories for My Family*, dated September 2003.

6. Quoted with permission from Don Burnham's memoirs, *Memories for My Family*, dated September 2003 (draft), with some very minor modifications for clarity.

7. Chapter 4, "Napoleonic Coach Model Competition," *Memories for My Family* (draft), by Donald Clemens Burnham.

8. *Your Son's Future, A Greeting to You, the Parent of a Member of the Fisher Body Craftsman's Guild*, Fisher Body Division, General Motors, General Motor's Building, Detroit, 2, Michigan.

9. "Designers of Your Far-out Car of 1970," Ralph Stein, *The Washington Sunday Star, This Week* magazine, September 15, 1963.

10. As a matter of reference, the official Guild photograph of the 1931 Donald C. Burnham Napoleonic Coach is GM Photographic Section image and Negative Number 20931-126.

11. Raymond S. Doerr Scrapbook 1931–35, #476,

National Museum of American History Archives, Smithsonian Institution, Washington, D.C.

12. Letter from Raymond S. Doerr to author, dated April 4, 1985.

13. *Violin Maker's Handbook: A Manual for Advancement of Violin Technology*, Raymond S. Doerr Woodcraft Specialties, 48 North 21st Street, Battle Creek, Michigan 49015, 1985.

14. "Once and Future Craftsmen: A Fisher Guild Scrapbook (1930–1968)," John L. Jacobus, *Automobile Quarterly*, volume 25, number 2, 1987.

15. Conversation with Stanley Knochel April 18, 1985, and interview on June 16, 1985; *Guild News*, vol. 5, no. 2, February 1950; scholarship awards dinner brochure, dated August 15, 1950; and phone conversation with Charles Drummond (son of Gordon L. Drummond) July 09, 2002.

16. *The Washington Post*, October 19, 1997, the "Wheels of Time" section, "The Fin-de-Siecle Ford: 1940 Deluxe Convertible Coupe."

17. See Bob Considine's column, "On the Line," probably *Detroit Free Press*, International News Service, August 21, 1947.

18. "Charles Gadd Retires: Thanks to His Research Your Car Is Safer Today," *GM Today*, vol.2, no. 5, June 1976.

19. There were 2 junior and two senior division national winners in 1933; Stanley Knochel won the other junior division first-place award.

20. When all the sons of a family won Guild scholarships, they were referred to affectionately as a family dynasty. Some of the other famous Guild family dynasties were the McDonnell brothers, Pietruska brothers (4 out of 5), Ferraioli brothers, Hagan brothers, the Law brothers and cousin, Whitman brothers, Greene brothers, Antonick brothers, and Catalano brothers, to mention a few.

21. The atomic bombs that were dropped on Hiroshima, Japan, on August 6, 1945, and on Nagasaki, Japan, on August 9, 1945, followed the July 16, 1945, Trinity Site test by just a few weeks.

22. Several sources were pieced together in order to write this biographic sketch: (1) Dr. William G. Henderson, Bob's son, generously contributed two typed Guild speeches (one was 1 minute and 20 second and another one was 1 minute and 35 seconds in length — presumably based on Bob Henderson's deliver cadence), both undated, which Robert Henderson probably had prepared to give at a Guild convention; (2) "The Craftsman's Guild Hall of Fame," *Guild News*, April 1949, vol. 4, no. 3; (3) an International News Service article written by Bob Considine for his syndicated column "On the Line" reporting on the 1949 Guild convention results; and (4) Robert W. Henderson's obituary reported in the *Sandia Labs News*, June 28, 2002, titled "Bob Henderson, Atomic Pioneer, Head of 'Z' Division in Albuquerque, Longtime Sandia VP, dies at age 87."

23. See Appendix K for more information about many of the model car makers who were contacted for this book.

24. "Nissan offers AAC Sneek Peek at new 'Z'," *Perspective* newsletter, January 2003, Academy of Art College, 79 New Montgomery Street, San Francisco, California; *Automobile Quarterly*, vol. 25, no. 2, 1987.

25. "Nissan's Hirshberg Lays Down His Pen," *Automotive News*, March 20, 2000; *Automobile Quarterly*, vol. 25, no. 2, 1987.

26. This list of GM personnel was compiled from

correspondence from John M. Mellberg (1985) and Ms. Nancy Cunningham, Educational Relations, GM Design (1985) as well as the Fisher Guild articles in *Special Interest Auto* (SIA #61), February 1981 and *Automobile Quarterly*, vol. 25, no. 2, 1987, and magazine articles about modern automobile designers and stylists in *Motor Trend* and *Cars and Parts* magazines. The author's correspondence files were also employed.

27. Information about Ford personnel provided by George R. Chartier, a professional modeler from Ford Motor Company. Letters to author, July 30, 2003.

28. A fourth architect, or architectural designer, in the book is Leo C. Peiffer from Cedar Rapids, Iowa. See his biography earlier in this chapter under "Coach Builders' Biographic Profiles."

29. George L. Hamlin, "Richard Arbib: Specialty Designer," *Collectible Automobile*, October 1992, pp. 41–45.

30. Hamlin, *Richard Arbib: Specialty Designer*; Blauer, "The Blue Sky Guy"; Bird, "Future Shock"; Keeps, "Auto Exoticism"; Lamm and Holls, *A Century of Automotive Styling*.

31. Letter from David Lewis, Professor of Business, University of Michigan to author (1988) and phone conversation between author and Virgil M. Exner, Jr., in 1985 and 2002.

32. *Ward's Quarterly*, summer 1966.

33. Allen, "Teen-Age Triumphs"; "Once and Future Craftsmen, A Fisher Guild Scrapbook (1930–1968)," John L. Jacobus, *Automobile Quarterly*, vol. 25, no 1. 1987; *Ward's Quarterly*, summer 1966 issue; *The Beaulieu Encyclopedia of Automobiles*, Volumes I and II, Nick Georgano, editor-in-chief, Fitzroy-Dearborn Publishers, 919 North Michigan Avenue, Chicago, Illinois; *Time*, April 8, 1957; *Business Week*, May 14, 1955; and *The Saturday Evening Post*, February 4, 1956.

34. The English Wheel consists of a large C-shaped arch that supports a 9-inch diameter, 3-inch wide, steel wheel. Positioned beneath this wheel is a smaller 3-inch barrel-shaped anvil wheel. Flat sheet metal is pushed and pulled back and forth, or stretched, between the wheels. The wheel is still used today for one-off prototypes, concept and custom cars, aircraft fuselage and wing panels.

35. The celebrated Los Angelenos who were top scholarship winners from the Craftsman's Guild and who pursued automotive and product design careers included Ronald C. Hill (1950), Robert A. Cadaret (1950), Charles W. Pelly (1954), Bill Moore (1956), Charles Gibilterra (1956), Art Russell (1956, 1957) and Robert E. Davids (1963).

36. Larry Shinoda was one of the principal designers of the split-window Chevrolet Corvette Sting Ray and the revolutionary 1968 Corvette Mako Shark model. He is also remembered for the 1970 Boss 302 Ford Mustang design. Larry Shinoda passed away November 13, 1997. "Trends—Detroit Report," *Motor Trend*, December 1992; "Noted Vette Designer Dies," *Automotive News*, November 17, 1997.

37. "GM's 34 Year Talent Search: The Fisher Body Craftsman's Guild," by Wicke Humble, *Special Interest Autos* #61, Bennington, Vermont.

38. Henry Haga was chief designer of the Chevrolet 2 Studio from 1963 to 1974, which developed Corvettes and Cameros. *A Century of American Style: 100 Years of American Car Design*, Michael Lamm and Dave Holls, Lamm-Morada Publishing Company, Inc., P.O. Box 7607, Stockton, California 95267.

39. I had the good fortune to be one of a handful of repeat regional award winners, in my case five times, which is what it took for me to finally achieve success in the competition. C.W. McClellan, Guild administrator, noted to me that there were less than ten five-time regional winners over the long history of the Guild. Letter from J.M. Mellberg to J.L. Jacobus, September 16, 2002.

40. The *Automobile Quarterly* Car Design Contests were judged by various auto designers, design educators and design executives from the auto industry such as Chuck Jordan (GM Design), Strother MacMinn (ACCD instructor), Gerald (Jerry) Hirshberg (Nissan Design), Richard A. Teague (retired AMC design executive), Robert Cumberford (design editor, *Automobile* magazine), John Herlitz (Chrysler exterior design executive), Fritz Mayhew (Ford's chief design executive), and Jerome Grove (president, College for Creative Studies, Detroit, Michigan).

41. The design theme for the 2003 *Motor Trend* International Design Contest was "Fast and Furious—2020 Personalized and Tuned for 2020." Held in conjunction with the California International Auto Show, the entry deadline was September 15, 2003. The judging deadline was October 28–29, 2003. What will personal "Tuner Cars" look like in 2020?

42. Mr. Henry F. Rom ran a small family business in Burnsville, Minnesota, but as a hobby, he has apparently maintained a strong passion and desire for designing unbelievably sexy, beautiful, scale model automobiles, using the Guild process. These designs were featured in the Letters to the Editor column, *Collectible Automobile*, February 1993 (page 4), June 1993 (page 5), and February 1994 (page 4). In one of the designs he tackled the age-old dilemma of how to make a four-door sedan look innovatively stylish and exciting. He really succeeds with one particular very contemporary-looking, elongated and low-center-of-gravity beauty that looks easily like a 2008 or 2009 Ford LTD or Crown Vic. A letter and photo from Mr. Rom also appears in the GM Futurliner Restoration Project's web page <http://www.futurliner.com/rom.htm>.

43. If the reader is interested in collecting either Fisher Body Craftsman's Guild or GMC Fisher Body Division memorabilia, www.ebay .com auctions offers a rich array of items daily.

44. The metallic Golden Anniversary Fisher Body Coach 1973, adorned in sterling silver and highlighted in 24 karat gold, which retailed for $2,000 to GM dealers, and were made in a limited edition of 1,000 copies by the goldsmiths and silversmiths at Silver Creations, Ltd., 428 Old Hook Road, Emerson, New Jersey 07630, are also seen at auctions and flea markets. A non-dealer might have paid as much as $5,000 originally to own one. Approximately 8" high and 16" long , these are not Fisher Body Craftsman's Guild memorabilia, but are Fisher Body Division, GMC, memorabilia and are highly valuable.

Appendices

1. "Body by Fisher," Michael Lamm. Also, see "Body by Fisher, The Closed Car Revolution," Roger B. White, *Automobile Quarterly*, vol. 29, no. 4, August 1991.

2. Ordinarily given only to service members, this award during World War II was also given to companies for production excellence, superior service, loyalty and devotion to duty.

3. "Fisher Body Corporation," Roger B. White, Smithsonian Institution, for the *Encyclopedia of America, Business History and Biography: The Automobile 1896–1920.*

3A. Various Fisher Body Division magazine print ads (full-page color ads) 1942–1945 describing and naming the products they contribute to the war efforts were utilized by the author.

4. Charles F. Kettering was an automotive pioneer who founded Dayton Engineering Laboratories which eventually became Delco, a successful GM Division, and is best remembered for developing the electric starter for the 1912 Cadillac. He was also involved in developing diesel locomotives, artificial hearts, ethyl gasoline (for anti-knock) and headed the GM Research Laboratories as well as became a GM Director.

5. In the 1950s, Richard A. Teague was a contemporary of Chuck Jordan's at GM Styling. He also briefly worked for Packard Motor Car Co. and was chief stylist (Chrysler Studio) at the Chrysler Corporation (circa 1956). He became VP of styling at American Motors Corporation (AMC) in 1964 and served in that position for 22 out of his 25 years with AMC. His name is associated with such designs as the AMC Pacer, Javelin, Hornet and Gremlin (*Automotive News*, May 13, 1991, p. 22).

6. William L. Mitchell took over from Harley J. Earl as VP of GM Styling in December 1958 and served in that position until 1977. Mitchell styled the 1938 Cadillac 60 Special and, as a 24-year-old chief designer and head of the Cadillac Studios, was responsible for the 1941 Cadillac line. He is best remembered for the 1960 Corvair, 1963 Buick Riviera, 1963 split-window Corvette "Sting Ray," 1966 Oldsmobile Toronado (FWD), 1968 Corvette "Mako Shark" model and the 1971 Buick Riviera. Bill Mitchell coined the phrase, "You've got to have gasoline in your veins to be a real car designer."

7. "The Fisher Body Craftsman's Guild Announces the State, Regional, and National Winners for the 1963 [1966] Model Car Competition." This was an internal publication sent to each Guild competition participant in September, prepared by FBCG Technical Staff, Fisher Body Public Relations and Advertising Department, Fisher Body Division, GMC, Warren, Michigan.

8. Inter-organizational letter from J.W. Griswold, director of public relations, GM Overseas Operations in New York City to N.J. Stork of Adam-Opel A.G. and W. Swallow of Vauxhall Motors Ltd., dated November 27, 1964, about starting Craftsman's Guild programs.

9. Letter from Earl C. Daum, GM vice president, to Harold G. Warner, GM vice president, dated August 10, 1966, urging that the European Guild winners at least share in the U.S. styling scholarship awards and offering financial support; inter-organizational letter, Fisher Body Division, from C.W. McClellan, Guild administrator, to C.M. Jordan, executive-in-charge, GM Styling staff, dated March 27, 1967; inter-organizational letter, Fisher Body Division, entitled "International Guild Competition," from C.W. McClellan, Guild administrator, to Charles M. Jordan, GM Styling, dated March 27, 1967.

10. *Vauxhall Mirror*, August 1965.

11. *Vauxhall Mirror*, February 1966 and July 1966.

12. Email from Terence J. Kirk to J. Jacobus, dated December 18, 2002.

13. Archives at Opel Engineering and Design headquarters in Ruesselsheim, Germany; selected old issues of the *Opel-Post* newsletter were translated by Alexandria Translations, Alexandria, Virginia.

14. Selected articles from *Opel-Post*, May 1970; June/July 1970; May 1971; June 1972; August 1973; and 1978 (month unknown).

15. The GM-Holden Craftsman's Guild information was provided by Ms. Samantha Cooper, Holden Archivist, the State Library of South Australia, P.O. Box 419, Adelaide, South Australia 5001 in a letter to J.L. Jacobus dated September 5, 2002. The archivist noted that at the present time, the general name is just Holden and the company name is Holden Ltd., but at the time of the Craftsman's Guild the company was known as GM-H (General Motors–Holden Ltd.). It is still colloquially referred to with variants of these names.

16. *General Motors World*, September/October 1965, September 1966, October/November 1967, and September/October 1968.

17. Information from Guild memorabilia in the personal collection of Charles M. Jordan.

Acknowledgments

1. Mr. Geear got interested in the Fisher Body Craftsman's Guild because Guild literature was invariably stuffed, one way or the other, in the 1932 Chevrolet literature he wanted to buy. He had two collections going simultaneously. One day he found a 1932 dealer poster announcing the Guild competition and he was off and running with one of the premier Guild collections in the USA.

2. In 1946 and 1947 the model car competition and the Napoleonic Coach competition shared limited resources. Due to funding constraints, first- and second-place model car winners received $4,000 and $2,000, respectively, whereas the first- and second-place coach builders won $5,000 and $3,000, respectively.

3. See note 2.

4. See note 2.

5. Sources include Richard A. "Dick" Herdegen, former Guild supervisor, who contributed substantially to compiling this data and information. Ms. Ruth McClellan, Mr. Randy Shackelton and Mr. Skip Geear also contributed generously to compiling this information. In addition, the author relied on his files of Guild memorabilia (*Guildsman* newsletters, etc.) to root out many specific but obscure details.

Bibliography

BOOKS, ARTICLES AND OTHER PUBLISHED WORKS

American Youth (CeCo Publishing Company, John H. Warner, ed.), September–October 1960, March–April 1963, January–February 1965.

"Awards to 26 GM Sons: 26 Boys from GM Families win $9,653 in Awards and Recognition in the 1949 Fisher Body Craftsman's Guild Competition." *GM Folks* 12:10 (October 1949).

Bayley, Stephen. *Harley Earl and the Dream Machine.* New York: Knopf, 1983.

Bieswinger, George. "The Glory That Was Fleetwood." *Today* magazine, in *The Philadelphia Enquirer*, June 29, 1975.

"Biggest Model Car Contest of Them All: The Fisher Body Craftsman's Guild Prepares to Award $117,000 in Cash and Scholarships to Model Builders." *Model Car Science* 1:2 (June 1963).

Bird, Charlotte. "Future Shock—In Design Richard Arbib Has Always Been Light Years Ahead: Here He Comes Again!" *Decor*, October/November 1992.

Blauer, Ettagale. "The Blue Sky Guy." *Art and Antiques*, April 1991.

Borth, Christy. "Wheels for a Waiting World: The Story of General Motors." *Ward's Quarterly*, Summer 1966.

Brierley, Brooks T. "The Return of the V-16—Seventy Years Ago It Was Cutting Edge Technology. Now It's Back." *America Heritage of Invention and Technology* 19:1 (Summer 2003).

Brigham, Grace. "Remembering the Fisher Body Craftsman's Guild." *Automotive History Review* No. 19 (November 1985).

Bruening, Jeff. "Back to the Future: Book Details the Bold Lines of the Fisher Body Craftsman's Guild." *designperspectives*, February 2004.

Cars of Tomorrow by Boys of Today (magazine), 1947–1948.

Considine, Bob. "On the Line," syndicated column, unknown publication, August 21, 1947.

Cumberford, Robert. "The Last Wild Man: There Will Never Be Another Bill Mitchell." *Automobile*, May 2002.

Davids, Robert E. "I Won the Fisher Body Contest ... So Can You!" *Model Car Science*, February 1964.

DeKruif, Paul. "Boss Kettering—The Man Who Failed Forward." *The Kettering Perspective*, Fall 1998.

Drake, Albert. "Entering the Fisher Body Craftsman's Guild Competition." *Old Cars Weekly*, June 29, 2000, pp. 18, 28.

"Dreamers Can Win, Too! These Nine Won $21,000 in Scholarships." *Young Men: Hobbies, Aviation, Careers*," February 1956.

Dube, B.P.B. "The Constant Czech." *Automobile Quarterly* 7:3 (Winter 1969).

"$85,000 in Awards for Boys, 1,220 Awards—University Scholarships, $2,000 to $5,000 Each—Cash Awards, Trips—in the Fisher Body Craftsman's Guild 1947 Model-Building Competitions." *Popular Mechanics*, November 1946.

Fisher Body Craftsman's Guild. Detroit: General Motors, ca. 1958–1959.

Fisher Body Craftsman's Guild Sketch Sheets. Detroit: General Motors, 1948, 1954.

Fisher Body Craftsman's Guild. *Craft Guilds: Their History and Influence.* Detroit: Fisher Body Corporation, 1930.

Fisher Body Craftsman's Guild. *Instructor's Guide: Designing and Building a Model Car,* Detroit: General Motors, 1966.

Fisher Body Craftsman's Guild, Fisher Body Division. *Body by Fisher.* Detroit: General Motors, 1956.

Fisher Body Craftsman's Guild, Fisher Body Division. *Designing and Building a Model Automobile.* Detroit: General Motors, 1948.

Fisher Body Craftsman's Guild, Fisher Body Division. *Designing and Building a Model Car.* Detroit: General Motors, 1962, 1964, 1965, 1966.

Fisher Body Craftsman's Guild, Fisher Body Division. *Designing — Modeling — Building a Model Automobile.* Detroit: General Motors, 1951, 1958.

Fisher Body Craftsman's Guild, Fisher Body Division. *An Expressway to a Career.* Detroit: General Motors, 1962.

Fisher Body Craftsman's Guild, Fisher Body Division. "The Fisher Body Craftsman's Guild Is Pleased to Announce the State, Regional and National Award Winners in Its 1963 Model Car Competition." Warren, MI: General Motors, 1963.

Fisher Body Craftsman's Guild, Fisher Body Division. "The Fisher Body Craftsman's Guild Is Pleased to Announce the State, Regional and National Award Winners in Its 1966 Model Car Competition." Warren, MI: General Motors, 1966.

Fisher Body Craftsman's Guild, Fisher Body Division. *A Manual for Guildsmen in the 1937 Model Car Design Competition, Details and Instructions for Designing and Making a Model Automobile.* Detroit: General Motors Corporation, 1937.

Fisher Body Craftsman's Guild, Fisher Body Division. *Plans and Instructions for Building a Miniature Model Napoleonic Coach.* Detroit: General Motors, 1932.

Fisher Body Craftsman's Guild, Fisher Body Division. *Plans and Instructions for Building a Miniature Model Traveling Coach: 1934–1935 Competition.* Detroit: General Motors, 1934.

Fisher Body Craftsman's Guild, Fisher Body Division. *Scholarship Award Banquet Brochure.* General Motors Corporation, General Offices Auditorium, Warren, Michigan: August 15, 1950; July 31, 1962; July 30, 1963; July 27, 1964; July 25, 1966; July 31, 1967; July 22, 1968.

"Fleetwood: Roots in Berks." *Reading-Berks Automobile Club (R-B-A-C)* magazine 55:5 (July 1977).

Fuller, Truman S., Jr. "Fleetwood, the Royal Coachman." *The Classic Car* Vol. XV:2, (Summer 1967), Vol. XV:3 (Fall 1967).

Georgano, Nick, Editor-in-Chief. *The Beaulieu Encyclopedia of the Automobile*, Vols. 1 and 2. Chicago: Fitzroy-Dearborn, 2000.

"GM Sons Share Scholarship Awards of the Fisher Body Craftsman's Guild." *GM Folks* 12:10 (October 1949).

General Motors and the Fisher Body Craftsman's Guild. Detroit: General Motors, 1957.

General Motors World, September–October 1965, September 1966 (45:5), October–November 1967, September–October 1968.

Georgano, Nick, with photography by Nicky Wright. *Art of the American Automobile: The Greatest Stylists and Their Work.* New York: Smithmark Publishers, 1995.

Guide Light (General Motors, Guide Lamp Division), 14:11 (November 25, 1947), 15:12 (October 29, 1948), 16:1 (January 28, 1949), 17:6 (July 28, 1950), 17:9 (November 17, 1950), 18:8 (November 23, 1951), 18:9 (December 21, 1951), 19:4 (June 6, 1952), 19:5 (July 7, 1952), 19:10 (December 19, 1952), 21:6 (September 1954), 21:7 (October 1954), 24:3 (March 1957).

Guild Experience Aided Their Careers. Detroit: General Motors, 1956.

Guild News, Official Bulletin of the Fisher Body Craftsman's Guild, 4:1 (1948 Convention Issue), 4:2 (March 1949), 4:3 (April 1949), 4:4 (May 1949), 5:1 (1949 Convention Issue), 5:2 (1950), 5:3 (March 1950), 5:5 (May 1950), 6:2 (January 1951), 7:1 (1951), 7:2 (January 1952), 7:3 (February 1952), 7:4 (March–April 1952), 8:4 (March 1953).

Guildsman (Australia), 3:1 (1968).

Guildsman, Official Publication of the Fisher Body Craftsman's Guild, 1:1 (1953 Convention Issue, Fall 1953), 2:1 (September 1954), 2:2 (February 1954), 3:3 (1955), 4:2 (1956), 4:3 (1956), 4:5 (Fall 1956), 5:2 (November–December 1957), 6:1 (August–September 1958), 6:2 (November–December 1958), 6:3 (1958), 7:1 (1959), 8:1 (1960), 9:1 (Fall 1961), 10:1 (Fall 1962), 10:2, 10:3, 11:1, 11:2, 11:3, 12:1, 12:2, 13:1, 14:1.

The Guildsman, Official Magazine of the Fisher Body Craftsman's Guild, 1:1 (April 1934), 1:2 (May 1934), 1:3 (June 1934), 1:4 (July 1934), 2:1 (January/February 1935), 2:2 (March/April 1935), 2:3 (May/June 1935), 2:4 (July/August 1935).

Gunnell, John. "Dream Cars Investigated." *Old Cars Weekly* 15:36 (September 1986).

Hamlin, George L. "Richard Arbib: Specialty Designer." *Collectible Automobile*, October 1992.

Humble, Wicke. "The Fisher Body Craftsman's Guild: General Motors' 34 Year Talent Search." *Special Interest Autos* #61 (February 1981).

"In the Fisher Body Auto Car Contest ... Dream Cars Win Too!" *Young Men: Hobbies, Aviation, Careers*, February 1956.

Jacobus, John L. "The Fisher Body Craftsman's Guild: An Illustrated History," adapted for *The Auto-*

motive Chronicles (e-zine), October 2003. issue, http://www.automotivechronicles.com/concept-sandrumors/oct03.php.

Jacobus, John L. Letter to the editor. *Smithsonian*, July 1999, p. 20.

Jacobus, John L., researcher. "Young Model Makers Took Trip." In Gunnell, John A., ed., *A Collector's Guide to Automobilia*. Iola, WI: Krause Publications, 1994.

Janicki, Edward. *Cars Detroit Never Built: 50 Years of American Experimental Cars*. New York: Sterling Publishing Company, 1990 and revised edition 1995.

Katz, John F., with photography by Roy D. Query. "Unfinished Symphony: The 1934 Bendix SWC." *Automobile Quarterly* 25:2 (November 1987).

Keeps, David A. "Auto Exoticism: The Art World Is Getting a High Octane Kick Out of the 1950's Dream-Car Drawings of Richard Arbib." *Details*, February 2000.

Koppen, von Thomas. "Coach-Building and Rationalization at the Turn of the Century: The Berlin-based Carriage Factories Kuhlstein, Neuss and Ruhe." *Technikgeschichte* 58:1 (1991). (Translated from German to English by Alexandria Translation Services, Alexandria, VA, January–March 2000.)

Lamm, Michael. "Body by Fisher." *Special Interest Autos* #45 (June 1978).

Lamm, Michael, and Holls, Dave. *A Century of Automobile Style: 100 Years of American Automobile Design*. Stockton, CA: Lamm-Morada Publishing Company, Inc.

Lewandowski, Jurgen. *Opel: The Company, the Cars, the People*. Munich: Sudwest Verlag GmBH and Company, 1995.

Loewy, Raymond. *Industrial Design*. Woodstock, N.Y.: Overlook Press, 1979.

Lozier, Herbert. *Model-Making*. Radnor, PA: Chilton, 1967.

MacMinn, Strother. "A Shark Is Not a Grouper: A Personal Profile of Bill Mitchell." *Automobile Quarterly* 26:2 (1988).

The Making of a Motor Car: Souvenir Guide Book. Chevrolet–Fisher Manufacturing Exhibit, GM Building, A Century of Progress, International Exposition, Chicago, Illinois, 1933.

McLellan, Robert C. "Fisher Body Craftsman's Guild Reunion." *The Automotive Chronicles* (e-zine), November 2004. http://www.automotivechronicles.com/articles/2004/nov/03/print-index.html.

Mellberg, John M. "Fisher Body Craftsman's Guild Reunion at the Eyes on Design 2004," June 15, 2004. http://www.cardesignnews.com/news/2004/040614fisher-body/index.html.

"Model Design and Building," Merit Badge No. 3280, Boy Scouts of America. Revised 1964; 1985 Printing. Irving, TX: Boy Scouts of America.

Oldenziel, Dr. Ruth. "Boys and Their Toys: The Fisher Body Craftsman's Guild, 1930–1968, and the Making of a Male Technical Domain." *Journal of Technology and Culture* 38:1 (January 1997).

"$117,000 in Prizes for Models in Fisher Body Craftsman's Guild." *Model Car Science* 3:5 (May 1965).

Pieler, Frank, and Poole, Chris. "A Pre-Retirement Chat with GM Chief Designer Chuck Jordan." *Collectible Automobile*, December 1992.

Purdy, Steve. "Recaptured Youth: A Reunion of the Fisher Body Craftsman's Guild." *Collectible Automobile*, December 2004, pp. 65-73.

"Richard P. Scharchburg Archives Dedicated." *The Kettering Perspective* 40:3 (2000).

"Robert A. Cadaret, Noted GM Designer." Obituary, *The Detroit News*, October 17, 2000.

Scharchburg, Richard P. "Charles Franklin Kettering." *The Kettering Perspective*, April/May 1998.

Scharchburg, Richard P. "The Kettering/GMI Alumni Foundation Collection of Industrial History Celebrates Their 25th Anniversary." *The Kettering Perspective*, Summer 1999.

Schild, James J. *Fleetwood: The Company & the Coachcraft*. Columbia, IL: The Auto Review, 2001.

Shuldiner, Herbert. "Model Dream Cars Build Dream Careers." *Popular Science*, October 1965, pp. 170, 171, 172, 211.

"$65,000 in Awards for Boys, 1,220 Awards—University Scholarships, $1,000 to $4,000 Each—Cash Awards, Trips—in the Fisher Body Craftsman's Guild 1948 Model-Building Competitions." *Popular Mechanics*, November 1947

"$65,000 for Model Cars: Cash and College Scholarships Await the Talented Youngsters Who Design and Build Winners in the 1950 Fisher Body Craftsman's Guild Competition." *Mechanix Illustrated*, November 1949.

Spatz, Don. "Days of Fleetwood Cars Recalled." *Reading* [PA] *Eagle*, date unknown.

"Stanley F. Parker, 70, Was Chief Designer at General Motors." Obituary, *The Detroit News*, April 30, 2002.

Stauffer, K .H. "Auto Bodies by Fleetwood," *Antique Automobile*" 41:4 (July–August 1977), p. 30.

"They Tried Again ... and Won." Author and magazine unknown, ca. 1953–1954.

"Tomorrow's Car: Prize Winning Model Designed and Built by Charles Jordan '49." *The Tech Engineering News* (Massachusetts Institute of Technology alumni magazine), December 1947.

Tomorrow's Look Today: Fisher Body at the Motorama. Detroit: General Motors, Fisher Body Division, 1953–1954.

Urette, Stephen D. "Dream Car Modelers Complete Competition: Winners Named in America's Biggest Model Car Contest." *Model Car Science* October 1964.

Vauxhall Craftsman's Guild (VCG). *Designing and Building a Model Car.* Bedfordshire, UK: Vauxhall Motors, 1965 .

Walsh-Sarnecki, Peggy. "GMI Is Kettering University: Institute for Engineers, Managers Weans Itself from GM." *Detroit Free Press,* January 29, 1998.

Wells, Stewart. "Not on the Way to Anywhere: Fleetwood, the Early Years." *Automobile Quarterly* 23:3 (November 1994).

"Winners Named in Giant Contest: Here Are the Winning Cars You've Been Waiting to See." *Model Car and Science* 5:10 (October 1967).

"Young American of the Month: Robert Eugene Davids." *American Youth* 5:1 (January–February 1964).

"Young Woodmere Man Designs 'ULTRA' Automobile of the Future," unknown publication, 1938.

Your Son's Future: A Greeting to You, the Parents of a Member of the Fisher Body Craftsman's Guild. Detroit: General Motors, 1953.

CORRESPONDENCE: LETTERS

Antonick, Michael B., of Galena, Ohio, to the author, April 3, 1985.

Arnold, Joseph B., of McMinnville, Oregon, to the author, February 27, 1985, and June 5, 1985.

Barnett, James, of Anderson, Indiana, to the author, March 30, 1985.

Barrineau, Wade H., of Conyers, Georgia, to the author, January 29, 1985.

Becker, Theodore A., of Coral Springs, Florida, to the author, August 5, 1985, June 23, 1985, and January 31,1986.

Benner, Webster, Jr., of Lakeland, Florida, to the author, April 8, 1985.

Brown, Albert W., Jr. of San Jose, California, to the author, February 1, 1985.

Bringhurst, Newell, of Visalia, California, to the author April 24, 1985.

Bruckdorfer, Michael Anton, of Augusta, Missouri, to the author, May 6, 1987.

Bruno, Adrian A., of Rolling Meadows, Illinois, to the author, April 8, 1985.

Burnham, Donald C., of Pittsburgh, Pennsylvania, to the author, April 19, 1985, September 26, 2003.

Byram, David C., of River Falls, Wisconsin, to the author, May 2, 1985, and July 24, 1985.

Canarra, Raymond C., of Madison Heights, Michigan, to the author, 1985.

Catalano, Joseph W., of Buffalo, New York, to the author, January 24, 1985.

Chartier, George R., of Northville, Michigan, to the author, August 7, 2003; August 29, 2003; September 4, 2003, and October 16, 2003.

Collyer, Mary Lou, of Menlo Park, California, to the author, March 19, 1985.

Conibear, Richard H., of Lakeland, Florida, to the author, October 23, 1985, October 29, 1985, and December 27, 1985.

Constance, David, of Charleston, Illinois, to the author, January 29, 1985.

Cook, Robert F., of Westport, Connecticut, to the author, 1985.

Costello, Dr. Charles R. Jr., of Greensburg, Pennsylvania, to the author, November 13, 1984.

Cotter, James E., of Akron, Ohio, to the author, April 10, 1985.

De Cenzo, Victor V., of Richmond, Virginia, to the author, March 30, 1985.

Di Ilio, John B., of Philadelphia, Pennsylvania, to the author, January 31, 1985, and May 21, 1985.

D'Mura, Betty Babbitt, of Flagstaff, Arizona, to the author, July 8, 2002.

D'Mura, Michael R. (Bobby), of Phoenix, Arizona, to the author, November 18, 1984.

Doerr, Raymond S., of Battle Creek, Michigan, to the author, April 6, 1985.

Dowd, Kenneth James, of Seattle, Washington, to the author, November 3, 2002.

Durdin, James D., of Baton Rouge, Louisiana, to the author, March 29, 1999, and May 5, 1999.

Eby, Thelma (Virginia) M., of Yacolt, Washington, to the author, April 15, 1985.

Erickson, Kernie D., of Mission Viejo, California, to the author, July 11, 1985.

Fischer, Albert W., from La Jolla, California, to the author, April 10, 1985.

Flowers, Alan Lee, of San Diego, California, to the author, March 1, 1985.

Garner, James Lee, of Bloomfield, Missouri, to the author, February 23, 1985; March 27, 1985; July 18, 1985; July 25, 1985; September 21, 2002 and October 2, 2002.

Gnage, Dale A., of Scottsville, New York, to the author, January 22, 1985.

Green, James W., of Houston, Texas, to the author, February 8, 1985, and June 28, 1985.

Greene, Thomas F., of Bellevue, Washington, to the author, April 2, 1985.
Grunstad, Jerome A., of Inver Grove Heights, Minnesota, to the author, January 27, 1985.
Henderson, William G., of Albuquerque, New Mexico, to the author, September 28, 2003.
Hendrick, Anthony S., of Rockville Center, New York, to the author, March 13, 1985, and July 17, 1985.
Ibisch, Franz O., of Saratoga, California, to the author, April 7, 1985.
Jacobs, Lew W., of Fayette, Missouri, to the author, April 2, 1985.
Jeffery, Christine L., GM Public Relations, Detroit, Michigan, to the author, August 27, 1984.
Jennings, Howard F., from Denver, Colorado, to the author, April 21, 1985.
Johnson, Richard J., of Brookline, Massachusetts, to the author, January 21, 1985.
Joy, Anthony "Tony," of Chautauqua, New York, to the author, February 12, 1985.
Kaiser, Karl H., of Tacoma, Washington, to the author, April 29, 1985, and January 6, 1987.
Kanner, Rowland, of Guntersville, Alabama, to the author, June 13, 1985.
Kaplan, Alan, of Boca Raton, Florida, to the author, June 29, 2003.
Keyser, William A., of Honeoye Falls, New York, to the author, June 11, 1985.
Knochel, Stanley, of Baltimore, Maryland, to the author, April 13, 1987.
Kucker, La Mont, of Worthington, Minnesota, to the author, March 10, 1985.
Kutza, James, of Chicago, Illinois, to the author, August 6, 1991.
Larzelere, Dr. Henry B., of Lynchburg, Virginia, to the author, September 3, 2003.
Larzelare, Norman L., of Anna Maria, Florida, to the author, April 10, 1985.
Law, Gary W., of Kennesaw, Georgia, to the author, July 8, 1985.
Lee, Richard B., of Longview, Texas, to the author, January 21, 1985.
Leger, Robert H., of Sulphur, Louisiana, to the author, February 27, 1985.
Lench, Raymond D., of Metamora, Michigan, to the author, August 13, 2000.
Lewis, Professor David, University of Michigan, to the author, January 10, 1986.
Lucky, Dr. Harrell C., of Dallas, Texas, to the author, March 26, 2001, and January 24, 2002.
Mackay, Spencer L., of North Hollywood, California, to the author, January 23, 1985.
MacMinn, Strother, of Pasadena, California, to the author, April 22, 1988.
Mauldin, Anthony, of Lewisville, Texas, to the author, February 2, 1985, and June 4, 1985.
Marks, William F., of Wilmington, Delaware, to the author, December 4, 1984.
May, Norman E., Fisher Body Division, Public Relations and Advertising, Warren, Michigan, to the author, February 24, 1974; to Lillian S. Walter, August 18, 1978.
McArdle, Dr. Gilbert, of Gettysburg, Pennsylvania, to the author, March 20, 1985.
McClellan, Ruth C., of Harbor Springs, Michigan, to the author, August 15, 2003; August 23, 2003; September 8, 2003; September 14, 2003; September 28, 2003, and October 5, 2003.
McKittrick, Patrick O., of Anchorage, Alaska, to the author, October 10, 1985.
McLellan, Robert C., of Houston, Texas, to the author, March 21, 1999, and July 1, 1999.
Mellberg, John M., of Racine, Wisconsin, to the author, November 11, 1985.
Metcalfe, Tristram Walker, of Plainfield, Massachusetts, to the author, November 25, 1984.
Miller, Billy R., of Pineville, Louisiana, to the author, May 7, 1985.
Milne, Murray, of Los Angeles, California, to the author, February 1, 1985, and July 16, 1985.
Moore, William A., of Reno, Nevada, to the author, December 10, 2002.
Morris, Gale P., of Portland, Oregon, to the author, February 18, 1985.
Onopa, David P., of Allentown, Pennsylvania, to the author, February 26, 1985.
Oto, Kaizo, of New York, New York, to the author, 1985.
Patty, Don, of Bradford, Ohio, to the author, January 26, 1985.
Paulson, Stephen M., of Thompson, Connecticut, to the author, 1985.
Peeler, Walter, from Seattle, Washington, to the author, July 24, 1985.
Peiffer, Leo C., of Cedar Rapids, Iowa, to the author, April 9, 1985, September 25, 2003.
Pellman, Ronald C., of Trumbull, Connecticut, to the author, March 14, 1985, August 19, 1985, and September 6, 1985.
Pelly, Charles W., of Agoura Hills, California, to the author, December 3, 1984, and March 27, 2000.
Pesanelli, David, of Washington, DC, to the author, December 7, 1984.
Pietruska, Michael A., of Pound Ridge, New York, to the author, November 26, 1984, and March 4, 1985.
Prom, Lance, of Westminster, California, to the author, February 8, 1985.
Quesenberry, Carl and Judy, of Macedonia, Ohio, to the author, September 1, 2000.
Rauth, Rev. Philip J., of Nebraska City, Nebraska, to the author, April 29, 1985.
Ray, Richard, of Brighton, Michigan, to the author, November 8 1984.
Relyea, Robert C., of Slingerlands, New York, to the author, March 16, 1985.
Rempel, John, Jr., of Kissimmee, Florida, to the author, January 20, 1986, and September 17, 2003.

Richardson, Paul H., of Bloomington, Minnesota, to the author, March 29, 1985.

Roark, Bradford J., of Spearfish, South Dakota, to the author, February 3, 1985.

Roe, Frederick B., of Holliston, Massachusetts, to the author, March 15, 1999.

Rom, Henry F., of Burnsville, Minnesota, to the author, March 20, 1985, March 23, 1985, June 6, 1985 and February 18, 1986.

Rueckner, Wolfgang, of Roxbury, Massachusetts, to the author, August 16, 1985.

Russell, E. Arthur, of Los Angeles, California, to the author, 1985 and July 11, 2002.

Sampson, James T., of Terra Haute, Indiana, to the author, January 30, 1985.

Saturday, Patrick B., of Michigan City, Indiana, to the author, February 27, 1985, and September 9, 1985.

Schoepf, Harry E., of Hartwell, Georgia, to the author, April 7, 1985.

Schonholtz, Donald F., of San Diego, California, to the author, April 6, 1985.

Schwietz, Eugene F., from North St. Paul, Minnesota, to the author, June 3, 1985.

Shuster, Stuart, of Birmingham, Michigan, to the author, August 11, 2003.

Simon, Harold L., of San Antonio, Texas, to the author, April 16, 1985.

Simone, Anthony V., of North Conway, New Hampshire, to the author, May 30, 1985, and July 22, 2002.

Sirna, Robert G., of Troy, Michigan, to the author, January 31, 1986.

Smith, John F., Chairman, General Motors Corporation, to the author, September 16, 1996.

Smith, John Martin, of Auburn, Indiana, to the author, October 16, 2003.

Smith, Robert D., to the author, November 18, 1984.

Sorensen, J.M., of Richfield, Minnesota, to the author, April 4, 1987, and February 8, 1988.

Sponseller, James W., Fisher Body Division, Public Relations, Warren, Michigan, to the author, August 16, 1984.

Steinhilber, Ronald, of New York, New York, to the author, November 14, 1984.

Taylor, Benjamin B., of Envirotek, Inc., Raleigh, North Carolina, to the author, July 29, 1985.

Taylor, Edward Frasier, of Farmington Hills, Michigan, to the author, March 25, 1985.

Teter, Roger D., of Sunnyvale, California, to the author, April 24, 1985.

Turner, Jerry, of Veradale, Washington, to the author, August 23, 1996, September 20, 2001, and October 26, 2001.

Utz, Susan G., of Southfield, Michigan, to the author, February 25, 1985.

Vogt, Noland, of San Francisco, California, to the author, March 19, 1985.

Waechter, Stanley Carl, of Elk Grove, California, to the author, February 2002.

Walter, Lillian S., of Wyomissing, Pennsylvania, to the author, July 21, 1999, August 3, 1999, November 12, 1999, December 6, 1999, and March 2000.

Wayt, Hampton C., of Aiken, South Carolina, to the author, August 8, 2001, and August 13, 2002.

Webb, Myron O., of Arkansas City, Kansas, to the author, June 16, 1985.

Weideman, Allen T., of Foresthill, California, to the author, June 2, 2003.

Wickersham, Galen, of Birmingham, Michigan, to the author, June 2003.

Wiginton, Randal, of Abilene, Texas, to the author, 1985.

Williams, John T., of Wilmington, North Carolina, to the author, 1985.

CORRESPONDENCE: E-MAIL

Antonick, Dave, of Royal Oak, Michigan, to the author, August 31, 2000, and September 5, 2000.

Becker, Theodore A., Maytag Major Appliances, Cleveland, Tennessee, to the author, September 9, 2002, and September 3, 2003.

Bishop, Dave, of Mystic, Connecticut, to the author, April 4, 2001.

Chartier, George R., of Northville, Michigan, to the author, July 2003 through September 2003.

Davids, Robert E., of Reno, Nevada, to the author, August 23, 2002.

Di Ilio, John B., of Philadelphia, Pennsylvania, to the author, October 10, 2002, and January 27, 2003.

D'Mura, John M., of Carlsbad, New Mexico, to the author, October 7, 2002, and October 29, 2002.

Dowd, Kenneth James, of Seattle, Washington, to the author, November 3, 2002.

Fisher, Lawrence P. II (son of Charles T. Fisher III), to the author, January 16, 2001, September 23, 2002, April 17, 2003, August 21, 2003, August 28, 2003, and September 10, 2003.

Gantz, Carroll, Chairman, Design History Section, IDSA, to the author, August 21, 2003.

Geear, Skip, of Eagle Point, Oregon, to the author, November 2002 through September 2003.

Hambrock, John, of Grapevine, Texas, to the author, March 7, 2001, and May 21, 2003.

Herdegen, Richard A. "Dick," of Birmingham, Michigan, to the author, August 2003.

Hill, Ronald C., of Newport Beach, California, to the author, August 12, 2002, June 9, 2003, and June 18, 2003.

Kanner, Rowland, of Atrion Medical Products, Inc., Arab, Alabama, to the author, September 23, 2002.

Kirk, Terence (Terry) J. (first place winner in the 1965 Vauxhall Craftsman's Guild [VCG] Competition), to the author, December 18, 2002.

Marks, William F., of Wilmington, Delaware, to the author, August 21–26, 2003.

McLellan, Robert C., of Houston, Texas, to the author, August 20, 2003.

Mellberg, John M., of High Point, North Carolina, to the author, September 2002 through October 2003.

Moore, William A., of Reno, Nevada, to the author, August 8, 2002, August 13, 2002, August 18, 2002, October 3, 2002, October 8, 2002, October 24, 2002, March 30, 2003, and June 25, 2003.

Onopa, David P., Director of Product Design, Mack Trucks, Inc., Allentown, PA (Guildsmen 1963 – 66), to the author, January 10, 2003.

Pellman, Ronald C., of Trumbull, Connecticut, to the author, March 22, 2003, and August 26, 2003.

Porter, William L. (Bill), GM automobile designer/stylist, to the author, August 17, 2002, May 19, 2003, May 23, 2003, May 24, 2003, July 12, 2003, and July 13, 2003.

Purdy, Ms. Bobbie (daughter of Robert F. McDonnell, 1955 scholarship winner), of Faugus, California, March 19, 2003, May 12, 2003, and May 28, 2003.

Russell, E. Arthur, of Los Angeles, California, to the author, October 15, 2002, and March 23, 2003.

Schoepf, Harry E., of Goffstown, New Hampshire, to the author, July 28, 2002, August 8, 2002, and August 25, 2003.

Schulz, Pete and Michelle, of New Baltimore, Michigan, to the author, January 28, 2003.

Semple, Thomas H., President, Nissan Design America, to the author, September 24, 2002.

Shuster, Stuart, of Birmingham, Michigan, to the author, May and October 2003.

Simone, Anthony V. (Tony), of Jakarta, Indonesia, to the author, August 28, 2003.

Simone, Gerald A., of North Smithfield, Rhode Island, to the author, November 19, 2002, and December 2, 2002.

Smith, Kevin, Editor in Chief, *Motor Trend* magazine, to the author, September 5, 2002.

Sponseller, James W., of Rochester, Michigan (a former Fisher Body Division Public Relations Administrator), to the author, June 23, 2003, and June 24, 2003.

Tatseos, Paul, of Birmingham, Michigan, to the author, October 17, 2002, and May 21, 2003.

Turner, Jerry, of Veradale, Washington, to the author, July 18, 2003, and August 29, 2003.

Wayt, Hampton C., of Aiken, South Carolina, to the author, August 12, 2002, August 30, 2002, September 4, 2002, October 24, 2002, and August 7, 2003.

Weideman, Allen T., of Foresthill, California, to the author, September 3, 2003, and October 7, 2003.

Will, Ronald James, of Voorhees, New Jersey, to the author, August–September 2003.

Wolken, Steve L., Cadillac Building, GM Technical Center, Warren, Michigan, to the author, September 12, 2002, and August 22, 2003.

TELEPHONE CONVERSATIONS AND INTERVIEWS

Aikins, Robert, Manager, Ford Exterior Design (1963 national scholarship award winner), January 5, 1985.

Amundson, Rolf, of Royal Oak, Michigan, October 21, 2003.

Becker, Theodore A., of Cleveland, Tennessee, November 1, 2002.

Bieck, James, GM Styling Assistant, Studio #3 (1963 styling scholarship award winner), January 5, 1985.

Bonine, Philip (1962 styling scholarship award winner), April 15, 1985.

Brucato, Margaret, Director of Alumni Relations, Art Center College of Design, 1985.

Burnett, David, machine productivity analyst (1966 regional award winner), January 15, 1985.

Catalano, David, of Buffalo, New York (1968 regional award winner), March 11, 1985.

Conibear, Richard H. (1947 Napoleonic Coach, regional award winner), October 20, 1985.

Cunningham, Nancy, Educational Relations, GM Design, Warren, Michigan, February 14, 1985.

Davids, Robert E., of Reno, Nevada (1963 first-place national scholarship, senior division), August 22, 2002, August 23, 2002, and December 2, 2002.

DeReggi, Dr. Aime S., of Boyds, Maryland (National Institute for Science and Technology [NIST], Gaithersburg, Maryland; and 1954 third-place national scholarship, senior division), April 7, 1985.

Di Ilio, John B., of Philadelphia, Pennsylvania, October 8, 2002.

Drummond, Charles, of East China, Michigan, August 12, 2002.

Earl, Richard (grandson of Harley J. Earl), of Detroit, Michigan, August 21, 2003.

Exner, Virgil, Jr., Manager, Ford Design Staff (1946 first-place national scholarship award winner), January 15, 1985.

Ferraioli, Joseph (1958 fourth-place national scholarship award, junior division), 1985.

Fisher, Lawrence P. II, of Bethesda, Maryland, November 25, 2000.

Fitzpatrick, Byron, chairman of Industrial Design Department, College of Creative Studies, Detroit, Michigan, August 26, 2003.

Garner, James, of Bloomfield, Missouri (1954 and 1955, first-place state Missouri and regional Award winner), March 3, 1985, July 11, 2002, September 24, 2002, and December 30, 2002.

Gibilterra, Charles A., of Carmel, California, August 26, 2002, and November 8, 2002.

Gnage, Dale A., Rochester, New York (1966 first-place national scholarship, junior division), March 3, 1988.

Graham, Gary (1954 first-place national scholarship award, senior division), July 20, 1985, August 28, 2003.

Green, James W., of Houston, Texas (1961 national scholarship winner, junior division), August 28, 2002.

Hagen, Larry (1966 third-place national scholarship award winner), January 26, 1985.

Held, Don (1960 second-place national scholarship award winner), April 23, 1985.

John, Richard, of Arlington, Virginia (1966 first-place national scholarship award winner), January 28, 1985.

Jordan, Charles M., of Rancho Santa Fe, California, former Guildsman and VP of GM Design (retired), August 20, 2002, and September 16, 2002

Knochel, Stanley, of Baltimore, Maryland (1933 first-place national scholarship, junior division, award winner), June 16, 1985.

Konopka, Ron, professional automobile design sculptor, Detroit, Michigan, September 13, 2002.

Kutza, Jim, of Chicago, Illinois, November 7, 1985.

LaRoche, Carl A., of Springfield, Virginia (1966 fourth-place national scholarship award winner), January 26, 1985.

McDonnell, Robert F., from Valencia, California (1955 national scholarship winner), September 27, 2002.

McMinn, Strother, former GM Designer and teacher/instructor at Art Center College of Design, 1985.

Mellberg, John M., Thomas Built Buses, High Point, North Carolina (1966 second-place national scholarship, senior division. $4,000 award), 1985, September 17, 2002.

Moore, William A. (1956 first-place national scholarship award winner), June 13, 1985, and August 7, 2002.

Morris, Gale P., of Seattle, Washington, August 27, 2002.

Newell, David, Chevrobilia, September 30, 2002.

Oto, Kaizo, of New York City (1961 styling scholarship and 1962 third-place national scholarship award winner), January 31, 1985, and July 31, 1985.

Peiffer, Leo C., of Cedar Rapids, Iowa, September 22, 2003.

Pellman, Ronald C., of Trumbull, Connecticut, July 11, 2002.

Pietruska, Michael, of Southwick, Massachusetts, September 29, 2002.

Rom, Henry F., of Burnsville, Minnesota (1953 fourth-place national scholarship award winner), January 21, 1985, and March 18, 1985.

Russell, E. Arthur, of Los Angeles, California, August 7, 2002, and September 18, 2002.

Russinoff, Elia Russ (1949 first-place national scholarship, senior division; GM), August 28, 2002, September 28, 2002, October 4, 2002, and October 22, 2002.

Sampson, James T. (1957 styling scholarship and 1958 first-place national scholarship award winner), October 6, 1985 .

Saturday, Patrick B. (1961 styling scholarship award winner), September 9, 1985.

Saylor, Ken, Ford Light Truck Studio (1958 third-place national scholarship award, junior division), 1985.

Schoepf, Harry E., of Goffstown, New Hampshire (1961 styling scholarship award winner), February 23, 1985, and July 21, 2002.

Schulz, Pete, and Michelle Schulz (daughter of Robert A. Cadaret, GM designer and 1950 first-place national scholarship, senior division), of New Baltimore, Michigan, October 21, 2002, and January, 2003.

Shackleton, Rand, of Cross Village, Michigan, October 2, 2003.

Simone, Eugene (1960 scholarship award winner), April 9, 1985.

Taylor, Benjamin B., architect, of Raleigh, North Carolina (1950 fourth-place national scholarship award winner), January 20, 1985.

Wayt, Hampton C., collector of automobile designer illustrations, Aiken, South Carolina, August 4, 2002, and September 4, 2002.

Weideman, Allen T., of Foresthill, California, June 25, 2003, and September 22, 2003.

Wickersham, Galen (retired GM designer), of Birmingham, Michigan, June 2003.

Wolken, Steve L., Cadillac Motor Division, GM Technical Center, Warren, Michigan, August 19, 2002, and September 12, 2002.

Wozena, Peter, of Bayonet, Florida, former Guildsman and GM designer, state winner in the 1937 model car competition, August 16, 2002.

OTHER SOURCES

GM Media Archives, General Motors Corporation, 200 Renaissance Center, MRC 482-B35-B24, P.O. Box 200, Detroit, Michigan 48265-2000. Jennifer Knightstep Lesniak, Media Specialist.

Gordon, John F. "You Are Important." Scholarship Award Banquet Speech, July 28, 1959, General Motors Corporation General Offices Auditorium, Warren, Michigan.

Jordan, Charles M. Private Guild memorabilia collection. 1947 Guild scholarship winner and former V.P. of GM Design, GM Technical Center, Warren, Michigan.

Looking Back to the Future. Washington, D.C.: PBS Video.

Pratt Institute, Sept. 1936–June 1939, Industrial Design Program, transcript of Richard Arbib and transmittal letter dated April 11, 1944, from James C. Boudreau, Director, Pratt Institute, Brooklyn 5, New York, supporting the award of a certificate of the Institute.

"Report to Contestants" (score sheets) from Allen T. Weideman (1955, 1957), Robert E. Davids (1963), E. Arthur Russell (1957), William A. Moore (1955), Ronald C. Pellman (1958), and George R. Chartier (1953, 1954, 1954). Source: Fisher Body Craftsman's Guild, Technical Staff, Fisher Body Division, GMC, Warren, Michigan.

Index

Numbers in **bold** indicate pages with photographs.